A MYSTERIOUS SOMETHING IN THE LIGHT

A MYSTERIOUS SOMETHING IN THE LIGHT

THE LIFE OF
RAYMOND CHANDLER

TOM WILLIAMS

CHICAGO
REVIEW
PRESS

Copyright © 2012 Tom Williams
All rights reserved

First published in Great Britain in 2012 by
Aurum Press Ltd
74–77 White Lion Street
London N1 9PF England
www.aurumpress.co.uk

This edition published in the United States in 2013 by
Chicago Review Press, Incorporated
814 North Franklin Street
Chicago, Illinois 60610

ISBN 978-1-61374-840-4

The following images, all featured in the photo insert of this book, were supplied by the
Bodleian Library, University of Oxford, with assistance from the estate of Raymond
Chandler. All MS Department/Chandler 83/Folio: photo insert p.1: 1 and 2; p.2: 5, 6,
and 103; p.3: 38 and 108; p.4: 40, 111, and 46; p.5: 52; p.7: 56 and 66; p.8: 103 and 57.

Interior design: PerfecType, Nashville, TN
Printed in the United States of America
5 4 3 2 1

This book is dedicated to Signe and to the memory of Edward Eason, grandpa, with love: 1921–2010

CONTENTS

ACKNOWLEDGMENTS

The title page of a book tends to promote the lie that it is the work of an individual, masking the truth that it is, in fact, a collective endeavor. This book is no different. Though it is my name on the cover, I could not have written it without the support of a great many people.

First and foremost, thank you to Graham C. Greene and the Estate of Raymond Chandler for allowing me to quote extensively from Chandler's work and also, to the libraries that house Chandler's archives. In California the staff at the Charles E. Young Research Library Department of Special Collections were always welcoming and patient even to the extent that, during my last weeks in California, they drew my attention to a new cache of letters, recently arrived, that helped alter the tenor of this book. In Britain, Chandler's papers reside with the Special Collection Department of the Bodleian Library at Oxford University. Dr. Judith Priestman, who curates the archive, and Colin Harris, who manages the reading rooms, along with their staff, were exceptionally helpful throughout this process. My thanks also to Dr. Jan Piggott, who was Keeper of the Archives at Dulwich College when I first visited it, and also to his successor, Calista Lucy. Her pamphlet, *A College Boy: Raymond Chandler at Dulwich College 1900–1905*, though written for a very different audience, was crucial to my understanding of Chandler's early years. I am also grateful to the staff at the British Library in London, where parts of this book were written, and the Special Collections Department at the University of Bristol, which made the Penguin Archive available to me, in particular the letters of Hamish Hamilton.

Of course, I must also acknowledge my debts to Chandler's previous biographers: the late Frank MacShane, Tom Hiney, and Judith Freeman. Judith in particular was both friendly and helpful. Thanks to both Robert F. Moss and to Loren Latker, whose own researches into Raymond Chandler have been very helpful to me. While we may not always have agreed on everything, we share the view that Raymond Chandler is a subject of endless fascination.

Thank you to the late Natasha Spender, to Randall Lloyd and to Sybil Davis, who answered my questions patiently. Also to Richard Rayner, who introduced me to both Carey McWilliams and to Leslie T. White and helped shape some of my thinking about Chandler. His own book, *A Bright and Guilty Place*, was an invaluable source of period material. Richard, I certainly owe you a beer.

I spent three months doing research in Los Angeles, California. Having never visited the city before, I arrived knowing no one but left with several good friends. Thank you to Philip Collins, Kay Tornborg, Zach and Kristina Ayers, Manhattan Perry, Richard Hodkinson, Clara Perez, Louisa Gamon, and Rachel O'Brien. Thanks also to Oliver Guy Watkins and Nick Leader in London, who shared their West Coast connections with me.

The idea for this book was first discussed in a small Cypriot restaurant in Tufnell Park and was nurtured with the help of several people. Thank you to Professor Rene Weis, Robert McCrum, and Alex Clark, all of whom read early drafts of the proposal and helped make it better with their comments. Also thank you to Claire Phillips, whose support at the beginning made this book possible and who deserved better.

Thank you to the team at Aurum Press who have put up with a lot from this writer. Specifically thank you to Melissa Smith, who did the picture research, to Louise Tucker who has answered my naive questions with fortitude, to Ray Newman and Mark Handley who worked on the copyedit, and to Liz Somers, who has done amazing work promoting this book. Lastly, thank you to Sam Harrison, my editor. To say that he is patient is an understatement. His unwavering faith and support under an immense amount of pressure, both personal and professional, has been astonishing and I am unworthy of it. I hope that I will be able to repay you one day.

At Chicago Review Press I should like to thank Yuval Taylor for his careful suggestions and additions, Allison Felus for her help preparing the text for an American audience, and Caitlin Eck for her fantastic efforts with publicity.

It goes without saying that my friends and family have had to put up with a lot while this book was being written. I am sorry for the get-togethers I canceled at the last minute and the dinners and drinks I had to miss. I am very grateful to you all. Specific thanks go to Mark Price, who read and commented on the early chapters, and to Gareth Cadwallader, whose own artistic travails remain an inspiration.

Thanks also to my mother, Judith Parkin, and my father, Gareth Williams, who remained supportive throughout, despite some testing times. And thank you also to my grandparents, who did not doubt that this was possible. Sadly my grandfather died while this book was being written. He was always a quiet inspiration to me and showed the value of books and learning. For that reason he shares the dedication of this book. I hope that he would be proud of it.

Lastly, to Signe, who did not know what she took on when she met me. Through the months and years she gave me the strength to get this book written, even when the task seemed insurmountable. Raymond Chandler never felt that his books were good enough to dedicate to the woman he loved, and he missed his chance. I don't want to risk that. Though this book is unworthy of Signe, it is the best I was able to do. It won't, I hope, always be.

PREFACE

In 1913 there were two arrivals in Los Angeles that would have lasting consequences for the city. The first was water, which came via a 223-mile aqueduct from the Owens Valley to the San Fernando Valley, and allowed the city to grow beyond the limits of its natural resources. As this great and controversial feat of engineering was nearing completion, the second arrived. He wore a sharp suit, a straw boater circled with the colors of an English public school and carried a silver-tipped cane. His name was Raymond Chandler.

Ray was twenty-five in 1913 and he had spent the previous few months in San Francisco, working odd jobs, trying to make ends meet while supporting his mother, who had only recently joined him in America from England. He had been drawn to Los Angeles by a chance meeting on the ship that had ferried him from London to the United States, but the decision to venture there would be the making of him. Behind him, he had a difficult childhood, a complicated adolescence, and a failed career as a poet. In front of him, he had seven novels and a series of screenplays that would make him one of the most famous writers of the twentieth century. But, as Ray stepped for the first time into the bright, bleached light of L.A., he could not know how his future would unfold. In 1913 he was just a young man, freshly arrived, looking to start a new life.

This book examines how that shy man, born in Chicago, raised in London, and educated in an English public school steeped in Victorian tradition, came to define modern Los Angeles. Ray, in the end, is remembered as the author who proved that pulp fiction could aspire to more than the plotting of violence, but that was not what he set out to do. From the start Ray saw crime writing as a way to learn the mechanics of storytelling, and though he wanted to write a crime novel, he also hoped that he would eventually move beyond his most famous creation, Philip Marlowe, and one day be able to forget mystery stories altogether. Privately he found his failure to do so frustrating, but publically he gave short shrift to any suggestion that he should write a serious novel. By the end of his life, I believe, he had come to understand that his inability to overcome Philip Marlowe was also part of his success. With each apparently futile attempt to write something other than a crime novel he managed to expand the boundaries of what it was possible to achieve within the genre and, in so doing, turned it into art.

Unfortunately, this achievement also came at a great cost. Alcoholism cast a long shadow over Ray's life. His father was a violent drunk and, despite being all too aware of his father's weaknesses, Ray could not prevent himself succumbing to the same addiction. Drinking, loneliness, and a peculiarly British form of arrogance sometimes made him seem distant and aloof, even to his closest friends. Often in his letters he comes across as bitter and short-tempered and in person he could be even worse. At other times, however, he could be warm and generous. He was patient with new writers and had a seemingly endless appetite to debate the issues of the day, whether they were literary, cinematic, political, or even culinary.

As a biographer I have taken an unflinching look at every stage of Ray's life, and what I have seen has not always been pleasant. Since his death in 1959, Ray has been charged with racism and misogyny, while others have trawled his novels for signs of both repressed homosexuality and homophobia. In the pages that follow, readers may find ample material upon which to build a case for all of these. I have, however, decided to resist the temptation to interrogate such attitudes. Neither have I spent time on the excuse that they are merely the product of a particular era. Ultimately, I have chosen to leave Ray's readers to reach their own conclusions.

My first encounter with Raymond Chandler took place at my university, where *The Big Sleep* and *Farewell, My Lovely* were featured in a seminar on crime fiction. Little did I think then that I would end up writing a book about the author of those novels; from the very first page I read, though, I was fascinated, not just with Philip Marlowe but also with the world in which he existed and that inspired his creation. So, in this book, I have tried to set Ray's achievement into a wider cultural and historical context. It has taken six years, and my research has taken me to California, Canada, and Oxford. It has been hard, often overwhelming, and in the end, it is impossible to set down a life on paper without some excisions and some difficult choices. I take responsibility for all of these. Likewise any errors contained herein are my own.

Raymond Chandler once joked that the biographies of writers that appear on the back of their books make them "dog themselves out in a velveteen smoking jacket, a cap with a tassel, a pipe full of Craven Mixture, and lollygag around admiring themselves instead of putting out a little careful but uneven prose."[1] He was always unnerved by pretension and, I suspect, the thought of a book about him would smack of exactly that. However, despite the darkness in his life, the more I understand about it, the better I appreciate his literary work. I hope that the shade of Raymond Chandler, wherever he may be, will see that this book is about connecting the two, and showing the real, lasting vitality of his art.

London–Los Angeles
2006–2012

CHAPTER ONE

"MY FATHER WAS AN ALCOHOLIC"

Raymond Chandler was born on July 23, 1888, in an upper room of a small, red brick house on Langley Avenue in Chicago, Illinois. A doctor, by the name of Martin Walter, had been called to help but the birth was straightforward and, after a few hours, Chandler arrived in the world. Within his lifetime Ray, as he was known to family and friends, would become associated with another city, Los Angeles, in another state, California, by writing a series of crime novels that feature tough men and even tougher women. At first, though, there was only one tough guy in his life: Ray's father, Maurice Chandler.

Very little is known about Maurice. He appears infrequently in Ray's letters and, when he does, it is with disdain and even shame. He was born on August 15, 1858, somewhere in Chester County, Pennsylvania, into a family that could trace its heritage back to Quaker settlers who had left Ireland in the seventeenth and eighteenth centuries. His parents, Amy and John Chandler, were farmers, wealthy enough to send their son to study engineering at the Towne Scientific School at the University of Pennsylvania. It was a good school with a sound reputation and, when Maurice matriculated in 1880, his parents had high hopes for him. Quakers were generally diligent and hardworking; Maurice, though, was not, and his university career was marked by a singular lack of success. He left after only two years, without a degree. The reasons behind Maurice's departure from university are not clear, but we know from his later years that he was a man who shirked responsibility, gave up too quickly, and was easily distracted. No doubt the qualities that made him a bad student also made him a bad father and husband.

He did, however, leave university in 1882 with enough education to achieve a certificate of proficiency, sufficient to get him a job as an engineer working for a Midwestern railway company at the heart of what was, in the latter half of the nineteenth century, a rapidly expanding industry. The impact of the railways on the economic shape of America was, for the first time, to link the outlying regions directly to commercial centers like Chicago. In turn, these cities became great *entrepôts*, with goods being sent to the great cities in the East and then on to markets beyond. Journeys that had taken days now took hours; large amounts of corn, pork, and beef could be delivered quickly, without risk of spoilage; and it was profitable for both rural regions and cities. From the 1840s, corn grown on the plains of Nebraska (then the world's largest cultivated region) was being sold across the world. The American Midwest was so essential to the international diet that it was known as the world's breadbasket.[1] This was a trade only made viable by the railways.

When Maurice Chandler joined the industry, many of the major rail-building projects were complete. The first transcontinental railway had been officially finished thirteen years earlier, on May 10, 1869, when the joining of the Central Pacific and Union Pacific lines was commemorated by the striking of a golden spike. Nonetheless, in an environment that saw one in every thirty-two Americans employed in the rail industry by 1881, it did not take Maurice long to find work with the Union Pacific company.[2] There were still plenty of smaller branch lines to be built as Chicago continued its expansion and his engineering qualification saw him attached to one of the many teams that planned routes, laid track, and repaired old, worn-out lines. The work was tough and that meant long hours and extended periods away from home. It kept him moving through the Midwest for five years, following the lines that radiated out of Chicago through Illinois, Nebraska, and Wyoming, so that his twenties were essentially nomadic. He measured out his bachelor days in the boarding house rooms in small towns and temporary company tenements.

Things changed for Maurice in 1886. He was working first in Omaha—then famous as a center of debauchery and illicit activity—and later in

Laramie, Wyoming. It was a new town—so new in fact that the trees that lined the roads were still saplings—and, compared to the excitement to be found elsewhere in nineteenth-century Omaha,[3] it was a quiet one. There he met the woman who would later become his wife. Her name was Florence Dart Thornton. She had bright blue eyes set in a strong square face and a head of thick brown hair that she would braid and pin into a chignon for formal occasions. She had only been in America for a year but her good looks had already caught the attention of many Laramie men.

Florence was born in Ireland in 1861 to Isaac and Anna Thornton who, like Maurice's parents, were Quakers. They lived in Waterford, which coincidentally was the same Irish city from which Maurice Chandler's ancestors had emigrated two or three generations earlier. In the middle of the nineteenth century, Waterford was a busy port, built on the River Suir, with a reputation for producing much-sought-after crystal and cut glass. For much of its existence it was considered Ireland's second city, and, like the rest of the country, was dominated by an Anglo-Irish elite. The Thorntons, as nonconformist Quakers, were not quite part of this elite but were close enough to rub shoulders with the city's leading families, and ran a successful firm of solicitors with offices in Waterford, Dublin, and Cork. Isaac was head of the firm and oversaw a prosperous business, providing the family with enough capital to live in a large house outside the city and keep themselves in considerable Victorian comfort.

Isaac died suddenly in the late 1870s, leaving Anna to take over the household. She was a tyrant and a bully by all accounts and brought up her five daughters and only son, Ernest, in strict adherence to her moral and religious code. When Ernest reached university age, she forced him to study law, which he agreed to reluctantly. He had no wish to join the family firm, but when it came down to it, Ernest could not resist his mother's will.[4]

The Thorntons, and Anna in particular, were fiercely proud of their Quaker roots, which, she believed, located them squarely in the upper echelons of the British Empire. The flipside of this was that Anna had a great disliking for both Catholicism and for the Irish working class that formed the bulk of the congregation, and she brought her children up to share that prejudice.[5] Anna could often be heard boasting that her family had no Catholic connections, not even by marriage: the Thorntons were pure Anglo-Irish Quakers.

A crisis came upon the Thornton family in the first years of the 1880s, in the person of a boiler inspector called Ernest Fitt. He had fallen in love with Florence's sister, Grace, and the two wanted to marry. Anna Thornton was appalled. She approached the problem of marriage in the same way that she approached Ernest's reluctance to study law: she attempted to bully Grace into giving him up. This time, however, Anna's victim would not be broken down and, when it became clear that there was no hope of compromise, Grace and her lover decided the only course open to them was to emigrate to America.

Twelve months later, at the age of twenty-five, Florence followed. Her motivation for leaving is less clear. She was not involved in any forbidden relationships as far as we know and could probably have looked forward to marriage, children, and security in Waterford had she stayed. But in the wake of Grace's departure, life there steadily worsened. Without her sister, Florence bore the brunt of her mother's wrath and, eventually, it became intolerable. America must have seemed like the answer to her prayers, and in 1886, with all the impetuousness of youth, Florence packed her possessions and left, with hardly a penny to her name save for what she could borrow or had secretly saved at home.

The journey itself was tough. It was rare for young women to travel unaccompanied and rarer still for them to do so without the support of their parents. At Queenstown, she boarded a ship to New York and, like the majority of emigrants, she found her place in steerage. For the ten days or so that it took to cross the Atlantic, she lived in dark, cramped, and dirty conditions, sharing her living space with crowds of fellow passengers, some as filthy as her surroundings. It was a journey for which her sheltered upbringing in Waterford could not have prepared her.

At first, many passengers would have been sick, unused to the movement of the sea. The stench would have been awful and respite, in the form of a trip to the upper decks, was only occasional. At night, Florence slept in a caged bunk cot with other women above and below her; by day she was ejected, forced to mingle with her fellow passengers while the accommodation was cleaned. Was she shocked by some of the people she met? Stowaways and runaways were not uncommon on the Atlantic crossings and her beauty would have no doubt brought unwanted attention. In her old life, men, other than those in her immediate family, would have remained mysterious creatures. On board a ship, they would be very real and very close.

There was music, at least. Emigrants would have packed fiddles and other musical instruments to help while away the journey, and groups would have gathered to sing hymns and favorite songs late into the night. The food, though, was not good. Old meat and thin soup were the daily diet.

After nearly two weeks of this, Florence landed at New York's Castle Garden, where immigrants were received until 1890 when the more famous Ellis Island opened. This was not the end of her journey, however, and she faced a night in a cheap New York boarding house before taking a train the next morning, first to Chicago, and then onwards to Laramie.

Traveling by train was no more comfortable than by ship. For two days she sat on rough, wooden benches, crammed into a plain carriage with only a stove to warm it, and a single toilet,[6] as the train rocked its way steadily through its almost one thousand–mile journey to Chicago. There was not even a view to alleviate the boredom. Robert Louis Stevenson, who made an identical journey only a few years earlier, in 1879, described what he saw as he passed through the deserts of Wyoming:

> To cross such a plain is to grow home-sick for mountains. . . . Hour after hour it was the same unhomely and unkindly world about our onward path; tumbled boulders, cliffs that drearily imitate the shape of monuments and fortifications . . . not a tree, not a patch of sward, not one shapely or commanding mountain form; sage-brush, eternal sage-brush . . . and for sole sign of life, here and there a few fleeting antelopes . . . there was not one good circumstance in that God-forsaken land.[7]

Better things did await Florence in Laramie.[8] There, she found her sister happily married to the boiler inspector and preparing to have children. They had made a good life in the town and Florence fit in with them easily. She was glad to have turned her back on Waterford, and in Wyoming she grew into a confident, happy young woman. She spent her days helping Grace at home—doing housework, shopping, looking after baby Muriel once she was born—while Ernest was at work. For the first time in her adult life, she could relax without the mantles of class and religion that had been forced upon her. She lived like this for a year and was content.

In 1887, just as she was finding her feet, her world changed again. How did this pretty Irish girl come to be introduced to a gruff railway engineer like Maurice Chandler? One possible explanation is that they met through her brother-in-law, Ernest Fitt.

Fitt looked to better himself in America and at some point was employed as a draftsman and later as a civil engineer.[9] If he worked in these roles as early as 1887, he may well have come across Maurice Chandler profession-ally, inviting his new friend to meet his wife and recently arrived sister-in-law, perhaps hoping that the young bachelor might take Florence off his hands. However Maurice and Florence met, there seems to have been an immediate attraction and their relationship moved with surprising speed, hastened no doubt by the knowledge that Maurice's time in Wyoming was limited. When his job finished he would have to follow the work and as this moment drew closer, Florence was forced to make a choice. Would she stay with her sister and brother-in-law, or would she go away with Maurice? In the end, with the same impetuousness that brought her to America, Florence chose Maurice.

The young couple were married at St. Matthew's Episcopal Church. They had known each other less than a year. The ceremony was performed amidst ominous quiet by the Reverend George Cornell and witnessed by a pair of drifters, William and Nettie Comley.[10] The circumstances of the marriage—the hastiness with which it came about and the fact that Ernest and Grace did not attend—raise questions. The relationship may have been a passionate one but was it, in the eyes of Florence's sister and brother-in-law, also a bad one?

Maurice and Florence stayed in Laramie for a couple of months and it was there that Ray was conceived. Ray always thought things might have turned out better had the Chandlers remained in the area but circumstances were against them and Maurice's work took him towards Chicago. Maurice knew Chicago well. He almost certainly lived there early in his career and would have traveled through it often while working. Florence had also visited before, but only briefly, stopping over for a few hours while changing trains on her way to her sister's. It was all new to her and certainly very different from the kind of environment to which she was accustomed.

There were six rail termini in Chicago, with trains from Wyoming ending their journey at Union Station. It was there that Florence disembarked. The first thing she would have noticed would have been the smell: the stench of rubbish and manure, mingling with the foul odor of the out-of-town stockyards,* blown in on the prairie winds.

Trains also made Chicago noisy and dangerous. Around a thousand a day came into the city, traveling along tracks that carved through the city. Since 1857, Chicago's railway network had been the largest in the world, and city authorities had little or no control over its expansion. It was the product of pure, unbridled capitalism. Tracks crossed major roads and intersections, blocking traffic and pedestrians while the iron monsters, tugging behind them innumerable wagons, belched their way to the station. It is hardly surprising that the accident toll was high in this environment and, in the year of Raymond Chandler's birth, an average of two Chicagoans were killed every day by trains.[11]

Perhaps most shocking of all for Florence would have been the city's sheer size. She had never fully experienced a place like Chicago but, after all, cities like it had not existed for long. Chicago was built on a different scale, to a different template, and, unlike older settlements, it had expanded not just outward but upward.

When Florence arrived in Chicago, it was already home to some of the most famous and innovative tall buildings in the world. In the past, urban skylines had been dominated by the spires, crosses, and domes of churches, mosques, and synagogues, but Chicago's skyline was characterized by capitalist rather than spiritual devotion. Each new building had to be bigger and better and Chicago soon became a perpetual building site. Mark Twain wrote,

> Chicago [is] a city where they are always rubbing a lamp and fetching up a genii and contriving and achieving new possibilities. It is hopeless for the occasional visitor to try and keep up with Chicago—she outgrows her prophecies faster than she can make them. She is always

---

*Animal slaughter occurred in the stockyards on a massive scale. Something like seventy thousand animals were brought in every morning, then sold and slaughtered immediately so that the whole process could begin again the next day. It was a process that saw nine hundred million animals slaughtered every year. (See Miller, *City of the Century*.)

a novelty; for she is never the Chicago you saw when you passed through the last time.[12]

Buildings like the Montauk Block (Burnham and Root, 1882–1883) and the Rookery (Burnham and Root, 1888) changed the way that Chicago's inhabitants looked at the city, and not always in a good way. People began to fear that the buildings were getting too tall—so tall, in fact, that they risked blocking out the sun itself, creating canyon-like streets never touched by natural light. These fears were not realized,[13] but it goes to show quite how little these architectural developments were understood and how intimidating they could be.

How strange Chicago must have appeared to Florence, who was familiar with the three- and four-story buildings of Waterford's industrial area. Buildings with ten, eleven, and even more stories would have seemed quite awesome and daunting.

Maurice and Florence set up their first home on Langley Avenue, close to the lakefront in Chicago's southeastern suburbs. Meanwhile, Maurice's job had not changed very much. Despite his new wife and the imminent arrival of his first child, he was still working out of and around the Midwest, and Florence often found herself alone. This made life very difficult for the expectant mother. She had no family in the immediate vicinity, and whatever support she needed had to come from her new neighbors.

Florence went into labor on July 23, 1888, and gave birth the same day. She named her baby boy Raymond Thornton Chandler, giving him her own maiden surname as a middle name. He was christened shortly after and, as part of the experience, taken to G. W. Varney, a nearby photographer, where he posed for his first photograph in his christening gown.

Sadly, we know very little about Ray's earliest years. The two photographs from this period suggest a relatively normal childhood but they lack context. One, taken when he was around eighteen months old, shows a chubby-cheeked little boy wearing a traditional gown, perched awkwardly on a chaise longue in a photographer's studio. In his hand, he is clutching a doll, a favorite toy, called Alfred. This picture shows early evidence of the shyness from which Ray was to suffer throughout his life: his gaze is drawn away from the camera and he is looking nervously at someone out of shot who was perhaps trying to reassure him and elicit a smile. The photograph was probably taken as a memento for

Maurice because Ray and his mother were about to make their first trip away together. It was time, Florence felt, to visit her mother in Ireland.

Ray and Florence left Chicago some time in the summer of 1890,* when Ray was just two years old, and made the long rail journey to New York. From there they took the boat to Queenstown in Ireland and then on to Waterford. Taking a very young child on such a long journey was brave but it appears that, this time, Florence could at least afford the luxury of a cabin to make the crossing a little easier.[14] The food was better—meat and vegetables served at the table in a dining room, rather than the thin soups she had endured on her last journey—and a cabin also provided greater privacy, an obvious advantage for a young mother. Nonetheless, the journey was still a hard one.

Why did Florence and Ray make that long journey back to Ireland? There is no evidence to suggest a family emergency. Florence's father was already dead and there is no reason to believe her mother was ill. If there had been a crisis, we can also assume that she would have traveled with her sister. Did Florence travel because her mother demanded it? Anna was an exacting woman and may have insisted on seeing her grandson. But the trip had other advantages, too. Aside from introducing her family to her beautiful baby boy, Florence could show her mother what a success she had made of her life and make clear to her family that she was now no longer Miss Thornton but Mrs. Chandler.

At some point during the crossing, Alfred, Ray's doll, fell overboard. It must have upset the young child to lose such a precious toy, and the loss probably put extra pressure on Florence, who must have been expecting the visit to be a challenging one. Miraculously, though, Alfred reappeared once they arrived in Ireland, as Ray recalled years later. Perhaps this was a good omen.

Florence always felt the weight of her mother's disapproval keenly and, though she must have hoped that the presence of baby Raymond would help mitigate her mother's choler, it is unlikely that Anna was anything other than her usual bad-tempered self during the visit. As her later behavior suggests, Anna was not a woman who forgave easily, and the reunion with her daughter

---

*This was a good year for Chicago. In February the city found out that it had won the lucrative bid to host the World's Fair Columbian Exposition in 1893, which would put it on the world stage, and though Ray was very young in the year that it was announced, as he grew up, he would have become increasingly aware of its presence.

may have been uncomfortable for everyone involved. But Florence's prepared-
ness to face Anna is characteristic of the bravery she showed in her late twenties. There is little doubting her resilience.

The young boy's own thoughts about this first visit to Ireland are not
recorded. Ray seems to have remembered very little of his experience during
the trip other than the loss of Alfred and his miraculous recovery at a hotel.
While his mother and grandmother tried to reconcile, it is probable that Ray
kept his own quiet counsel, spending his days as he would have done in Chicago, playing with Alfred and his other toys, toddling about under the supervision of a servant, making his chubby-cheeked way around the Waterford
house, and getting to know his uncle Ernest and aunts.

Their stay came to an end in late October when Florence and Ray headed
home, boarding the SS *Servia* at Queenstown and landing in New York on
the 27th. They headed straight back to Chicago. It would be nice to imagine
Maurice waiting for his wife and son at LaSalle Street Station, where the
trains from New York terminated, but it is more likely that he was away working and that Florence and Ray made their way back to their Langley Avenue
home on their own. While they waited for one of his brief visits, Florence
no doubt tried her hardest to settle into the life that she had just sold to her
mother as happy and successful.

The following summer in Chicago was extraordinarily hot, and seventeen
people died in the heatwave.[15] Florence made the decision to take Ray to stay
with her sister, who had now moved to Plattsmouth, Nebraska. It was the
first of what was to become a series of annual vacations lasting until 1895.
It is clear that Ray enjoyed the time he spent there. Semirural, slightly back-
ward Plattsmouth, sitting on the banks of the Missouri River, was a complete
change from the stench and noise of Chicago. Wild grapes grew on roadsides
and residents gathered them to make wine. At night, fireflies buzzed brightly
through the evening sky while people sat out on rocking chairs, gossiping
with neighbors.[16] During the day, Ray was left to play with his cousin, Muriel
Fitt, who, despite being two years older, seems to have let Ray take charge. In
fact, some of their games were surprisingly adult—he once admitted pulling
down her underwear and admiring her firm bottom.[17] Plattsmouth was not
quite a paradise, though, and Ray characteristically recalled his happy times

there being interrupted one day by the appearance of a dead body floating down the muddy river.[18]

Florence enjoyed Plattsmouth too. She was able to relax and, for the first time, share the responsibilities of childcare with someone else. She must also have enjoyed spending time with her sister and brother-in-law. Their adult company would have made a welcome change from the duties of her day-to-day life. Ray also seems to have benefited from being among grown-ups. He would sit at the feet of his uncle and aunt as they told stories about their families that fired his young imagination:

> My . . . uncle's (by marriage only) name was Ernest Fitt. . . . He used to come home in the evening . . . put the paper on the music rack and improvise while he read it. . . . He had a brother who was an amazing character. He had been a bank clerk or manager back in Waterford . . . and had embezzled money . . . and with the help of the Masons, escaped the police net to . . . Europe. In some hotel in Germany his money was stolen, or most of it. When I knew him, long after, he was an extremely respectable old party, always immaculately dressed, and of incredible parsimony.[19]

There was also an uncle who was a crooked politician and yet another who invented a machine "to take on mail without stopping, but somebody beat him out of it and he never got a dime."[20] Ray later said he should write a book about them, which does raise the question of how much he embellished these stories but, regardless, it seems clear that the original versions fascinated him. It is easy to imagine the young Ray listening to his uncle's tales as they unfolded, noting as he did so that being a storyteller brought plenty of attention.

Of course, summers in Plattsmouth had to come to an end, and Ray and Florence spent the rest of each year in Chicago. At some point, Ray underwent some education there and certainly had friends in the city: according to his own account, he was part of a gang, though it was "not criminal in any way."[21] He would also have seen the construction of the site of the Chicago World's Fair that was emerging steadily. He may have watched as a strange, enormous wheel-like structure, designed by William Ferris, was raised against the sky, but whether or not he ever visited the exhibition after it opened in 1893 and saw the first Ferris wheel, the first shredded wheat, or the first zippers, we do not know.

In Chicago, Florence found life difficult. Whatever had originally drawn her to Maurice did not last. His long absences depressed her, but his rare visits home depressed her even more. And, as Ray grew up, he became increasingly aware of the domestic problems his mother and father faced. During the 1890s, his parents' marriage was steadily unraveling and they had no other children after Ray. Their slow but inevitable breakup would leave a serious psychological scar on Ray, but blame for the end of the marriage lies largely with Maurice.

On his son's birth certificate, Maurice describes himself as a civil engineer. Ray rarely spoke about his father but, in the 1950s, at some of his lowest points, he began to open up to his friend Natasha Spender. He told her that his father used to be in charge of a track-laying team.[22] We know that this means Maurice would often have been out in the wilderness with a gang of trackmen working under his supervision. It was their job to lift and then lay the track and sleepers, while Maurice directed them. For the men doing the lifting, it was hard work (twelve-hour shifts were not uncommon), and it was dangerous and badly paid to boot (the trackmen on the Sante Fe line received a little over $1.20 a day for their work[23]). Managing them would scarcely have been any easier. The situation would not have been helped by the differences between the trackmen and the well-off, college-educated engineers who ordered them around. Trackmen usually had little or no education—the only qualification they needed was the ability to hit a metal spike with a heavy hammer. They came from the poorest families, often had criminal backgrounds, and were well known for their insubordination.[24] Engineers had the difficult task of corralling these motley crews into working to the tight schedules demanded by the railway companies. It often meant coercing them to extended periods of hard labor. Earning the respect of these often violent and thuggish men was imperative, and being away from the eyes of civilization opened up certain options to men like Maurice: more often than not, they resorted to the timeworn method of sheer, brute force. In the end, Maurice Chandler was probably just another one of the many Mr. Kurtzes whose violent conduct was tolerated by the railway companies as long as it was effective.

Maintaining control in the wilderness through violence and oppression must have put Maurice under tremendous strain. And, like many others, he found relief in drink which, for the sake of the manual laborers, would have been readily and cheaply available in very large quantities. Maurice became a heavy and frequent drinker, swigging his way to oblivion to alleviate the stress of work, and before long he was a full-blown alcoholic. His alcoholism, along with day-to-day violence and the constant company of men, had a disastrous effect on his visits home: Maurice could not adjust to the quiet domesticity of Florence and Ray, and the peaceful atmosphere was shattered when he returned.

Chicago was an ideal city for a drunk. Distilling was the city's second industry after meat packing. At one point, it was estimated that the drinks trade in Chicago was worth a million dollars a year and, in 1865, the city produced 7 million gallons of beer, or 39 gallons for every man, woman, and child in the city. By the 1880s, there was one bar for every two hundred residents, and the city's extensive pleasure districts were not only tolerated but also actively protected by the police. Temperance societies boomed and one of Burnham and Roots's early skyscrapers was the Women's Christian Temperance Building, the tallest building in the world in 1890. Groups promoting abstinence created a lot of noise but had little effect on the city's drinking habits: alcohol was everywhere and always available to a man like Maurice with money and a thirst.[25]

Faced with a drunken husband, Florence remained strong. She had learned to stand up to her mother's bullying and was not ready to be subdued by Maurice. They argued fiercely but Maurice did not stop at verbal confrontation: he began to beat Florence. If she complained, he hit her again and kept doing so until she was quiet. It is hard to know quite how much of this domestic violence Ray saw. He could never bring himself to write about his father's behavior and only when he was drunk could he bring himself to speak about Maurice at all. As a result, according to Natasha Spender, his accounts were not consistent: sometimes he claimed to have seen his father beat his mother, while on other occasions he denied it. He must certainly have known what was going on. Though he was perhaps only four or five when the beatings started, he could not have missed the bruises on his mother's body or the change in her manner. As a small child, however, he was utterly powerless to do anything about it. How long Florence endured the beatings is impossible to guess but, by 1895, she and Ray had left Langley Avenue, and Maurice.

At around this time, when he was seven years old, Ray developed scarlet fever: "I remember principally the ice cream and the pleasure of pulling loose skin off during convalescence."[26] Florence had been reduced to living in boarding houses and cheap hotels. Without Maurice's financial support, her options were limited. With no money and no job she headed to Plattsmouth to live with her sister.

Ray was enrolled in a school in the East Fourth Ward of Plattsmouth, where his teacher was Lettie C. Smith.[27] His grades there were good but not remarkable, despite his intelligence. This may be explained by a complicated home life which put him under some strain. Mrs. Smith was not Ray's teacher for long. Her notes tell us that he was taken back to Chicago as a result of what would be the first of several attempted reconciliations between his mother and father.

Maurice and Florence had not given up on their marriage entirely. Florence must have hoped that things would be different and, at any rate, was perhaps concerned that her young son needed his father, and she thought the sacrifice worth it. Over the next few years, they were to go back and forth from Chicago to Plattsmouth several times. This must have been an unsettling and difficult experience for her, but especially so for Ray. Whatever hope kept drawing her back to Chicago and to Maurice eventually died. Florence began to accept that the relationship could not be saved.

She left Chicago for good, possibly as late as 1900, returning to Plattsmouth one last time. This decisive move was to deny Maurice any further sway over their son.

Ray never forgave his father and, once he and Florence had fled, made a concerted effort to cut Maurice out of his life. He all but wrote Chicago out of his own story, too, and avoided mentioning his father at all, preferring to let his friends imagine him growing up in rural Plattsmouth, surrounded by eccentric uncles. It is not clear what happened to Maurice. He disappears from the records and Ray made no effort to find him. When, in 1917, he joined the Canadian army to fight in World War I and was asked if his father was still living, he wrote, "I don't know."[28] Still, whether Ray acknowledged him or not Maurice was to cast a long shadow over his life.

The consequence of witnessing domestic violence was to wire into Ray's brain a desire to protect women, starting with his mother. As this trait emerged in him, the personality of his great creation, the detective Philip Marlowe, also began to form. The phrase "shop-soiled Galahad," used by Ray to describe Marlowe, also suggests how he viewed himself: chivalrous, a protector of women, but not in a purely abstract, romantic sense.

Maurice may have spurred his son's creativity but his despicable conduct also laid many emotional landmines for him to negotiate in the future. Ray's writing betrays a preoccupation with the idea that vices and moral weakness might be inherited. Would he, like his father, become a violent alcoholic?

Florence, meanwhile, had to look to Ray's future. He needed a home and an education. After some serious consideration, she decided that, for the sake of her son, she was happy to sacrifice her own happiness by returning to Ireland and her family. She knew her mother would not accept her divorce and would make her life difficult, but Ireland was the only way forward for the two Chandlers. There, at least, she would be out of Maurice's reach and could more easily resist the temptation to go back.

CHAPTER TWO

"I WAS RAISED ON LATIN AND GREEK"

Ray was twelve years old when he and his mother made the long trip back to Waterford, leaving behind them domestic violence and drunkenness, only to submit themselves instead to the class-ridden, intolerant, bullying atmosphere of the Thornton family home. It was a journey through time as well as space, which saw them turn their backs on the bright novelty of Chicago and Plattsmouth, and enter, instead, the chilly embrace of Victorian Britain.

Queen Victoria had only a few months left to live when the Chandlers landed in Ireland, but the Thorntons were resolutely Victorian in their values. Unsurprisingly, news of the divorce did not go down well with them. At the end of the nineteenth century, divorce was still considered an exceptional and rash act, and one that brought with it social censure. As far as the Thorntons were concerned, no matter how brutally Maurice Chandler had treated Florence, leaving him was a step too far, and Anna Thornton would never forgive her daughter for bringing shame upon the Thornton family.

As would any good Victorian matriarch, Mrs. Thornton dominated her family and their house, as certain of her class and position in society as ever. It is hard to imagine today just how sharply class boundaries were drawn but, in nineteenth-century Britain and Ireland, social position was everything.

Anything that might undermine that structure had to be dealt with swiftly. To be Anglo-Irish was to be tied to the ruling elite and—as far as Anna Thornton was concerned—separate from and superior to the Catholic classes. Anna's prejudices infected the entire household: her children, grandchildren, and servants could not escape them. The family housekeeper, Miss Groome, refused to employ Catholic servants at all.

Miss Groome was the daughter of a Church of England canon, which qualified her for the occasional afternoon tea at the house of Miss Paul, a local spinster, who lived in one of the large houses outside the city. Miss Paul was, Miss Groome liked to point out, "country," which put her in a class above the Thorntons, and her effect on the housekeeper was considerable. Ray later recalled how nervous these tea parties made her.[1] She would make a fuss for days in advance and clearly enjoyed the kudos more than the event itself.

The housekeeper is one of the most prominent characters in Ray's letters about this time. He was attracted to the habit she had of both undermining and reflecting his family's social prejudices. For example, she always looked down on Ray's uncle Ernest because he was a mere solicitor. Ray recalled her observing that "there are only four careers for a gentleman: the Army, the Navy, the Church and the Bar. A barrister was a gentleman, but not a solicitor."[2] Ernest knew how she felt about him and responded in kind:

> Sometimes when the dinner did not suit him he would order it removed and we would sit in stony silence for three quarters of an hour while the frantic Miss Groome browbeat the domestics below stairs and finally another meal was delivered to the master, probably much worse than the one he had refused.[3]

Miss Groome undoubtedly helped add to the uncomfortable atmosphere in the house, but it was the relationship between Ernest and Anna that caused most tension. Having chosen her son's career for him, she continued to meddle in his personal life and in his law practice. Their bizarre relationship, combined with his distaste for the law, soured the mood of the house. It makes it easy to understand why, when Ray remembered his uncle, he did so in the simplest of terms as "a man of rather evil temper."[4]

Despite all of this, Ray seems to have made friends and to have enjoyed living there. He found himself being pushed into the company of nearby cousins and they soon became friends. Ray remembered playing cricket with one of them, though even that was not without its social conflict:

> . . . one of the boys was a Catholic . . . he came in to the game in an elaborate chariot with grooms in livery; but he was not asked to have tea with the rest after the game. He wouldn't have accepted of course.[5]

Ray struggled with this prejudice for most of his life: "I grew up with terrible contempt for Catholics, and I have trouble with it even now."[6] It just goes to show quite how deep the attitudes of Anna Thornton and the Waterford household could penetrate.

Ray makes no mention of his education in Waterford in letters or other writings, probably because he did not remain there long enough to attend school: before long, the decision was made to send Ray and Florence to London. It is not clear who was best served by this. It may have been that Anna sent her dishonorable divorcée daughter away out of a sense of embarrassment; or perhaps Florence wanted to save her son from a childhood like her own, under Anna's stern influence. For whatever reason, the Chandlers packed their things again and set off for London and yet another new home.

It was not, in the end, much of an escape. They moved to Whitefield Lodge at 77 Alleyn Park, in Dulwich, South London, where they were joined by Ernest, another sister, Ethel, and a servant, Rose. Ethel was the odd one out among the Thornton girls; she was considered less attractive than her sisters and, perhaps as a consequence of this, never married. She was also the only Thornton child to feel any affection towards their mother. It must then have pleased Ethel, if no one else, that Anna Thornton would be making regular visits to the Dulwich house, perhaps even relocating there. It was, in effect, to be a continuation of life in Waterford, and Florence suffered there just as she had in Ireland, the victim of constant slights and disapproval. Ray remembered vividly, for example, occasions when Anna refused to serve wine to her divorced daughter.

Unsurprisingly, London came to depress Florence. Starved of affection, she put all her energy into her relationship with her son, and the two became utterly dependent on each other. This brought him a greater emotional maturity than would be usual for a child of his age, burdened as he was with the full knowledge of his mother's difficulties. In turn, this close relationship with Ray left her unable to establish or maintain a serious relationship with any men because she worried about how they would treat her son. Years later, Ray regretted this. He was aware that she had affairs—or rather, men paid court to her—and knew, too, that he was the reason why they never developed into lasting relationships. This knowledge, combined with his own increasing awareness of her dependence on him, would eventually put a serious strain on their relationship.

Despite the atmosphere at home, Ray thrived in London. He fell in love with it. There was something about even suburban Dulwich that seemed to inspire him. It was quiet, calm, and neighborly, a world away from Belgravia, Mayfair, and St. James's, though still part of the great imperial capital. Piccadilly was a mere five miles away and, on a clear day, the grubby, grey dome of St. Paul's was visible on the skyline. It was where bank clerks and civil servants lived in double-stucco-fronted houses; where Sundays were reserved for gardening and gossip; where people led quiet, careful lives. It was nothing at all like Chicago and was very, very British.

As Ray explored his new home Ernest and Florence discussed the boy's future. Ray needed an education and it was decided that he be sent to nearby Dulwich College as a "day boy." Ray was extraordinarily lucky that his uncle Ernest was willing to foot the bill for a private education. Ernest's feelings towards his nephew are unclear—his support has been described by previous biographers as grudging—but there is no doubt that his decision, reluctant or otherwise, changed Ray's life and gave him opportunities that he would not otherwise have had.

Dulwich College is, perhaps, more famous than it should be. It is, as Ray liked to say, not "out of the top drawer"[7] as far as public schools are concerned and does not rank among the socially elite schools such as Eton or Harrow. Like Charterhouse and Marlborough, however, it is a *good* school. It was then, as now, a school for the children of civil servants, solicitors, and bankers, rather than for the heirs of aristocratic families. It has become particularly famous for educating some of the best-known writers of the twentieth century, a testament to its literary and artistic ethos. P. G. Wodehouse, seven years older than Ray, graduated in 1900, the year Chandler joined the College, and Dennis Wheatley and C. S. Forrester studied there after he had left. In the latter half of the twentieth century, its pupils included Graham Swift and Michael Ondaatje. When Ray started, however, this literary reputation was yet to be established. Dulwich College was then known for educating the children of the empire and as a training ground for its imperial servants. It was, in short, a school for the middle classes.

The College had been established in 1619 by a contemporary of Shakespeare's, actor-manager Edward Alleyn. In 1857, Victorian public school reform resulted in the College being split into two—the Lower School became simply Alleyn's, while the Upper School retained the name of Dulwich College. It was also in the mid-nineteenth century that it outgrew its original buildings and was resited on Dulwich Common. Today, modern buildings sit alongside Victorian structures, but any Alleynian of Ray's generation would still recognize the long avenue lined with leafy chestnut trees leading up to the magnificent Italianate "palazzo" designed by Sir Charles Barry. They would recognize, too, the lush, well-maintained grounds at the front of the school, dotted with rugby posts and cricket squares, often filled with the noise of sport.

Ray joined the school as Pupil 5724 on September 18, 1900. Shortly after that date, the family moved from Alleyn Park to Mount Cyra, a tall, red-brick house on Auckland Road, Upper Norwood, just south of Dulwich. He was then a small, thin boy with an angular face, a high forehead, and a knifelike nose. Each morning, dressed in a black jacket, waistcoat, and a thickly striped blue-and-black tie, he walked to the College.

Ray stood out from his peers for several reasons. As a day boy he was immediately set apart from a sizeable proportion of his contemporaries. Boarders had after-school adventures, such as breaking out of the grounds after ten o'clock to smoke cigarettes, while day boys simply sloped off home to be with their mothers, and so were never quite fully integrated into the life of the school.

Then there was the accent. Ray spoke with a mild American twang. Had he attended preparatory school ("prep") not only might he have lost that accent but, in the normal run of things, he would have picked up some schoolboy slang and idiom. Since he had not done so, he found it hard to shake off American manners, and his ignorance made him feel uncomfortable. For example, he hated the way that public school etiquette reduced his name to R. T. Chandler. Sir Alwyne Ogden, a contemporary of Ray's, remembered that he was desperate to be called Raymond but this simply would not take. In a world where small victories and defeats mattered, this would have been troubling for the boy.[8]

Public schools were places where boys were kept in perpetual competition. Everything counted, from the cut of a boy's uniform to the profession of his father. In this last instance, Ray was in trouble. He could only look on quietly as the other boys swapped stories about "pater." Had Maurice been dead, Ray might have gotten away with it—several boys in his year had lost their fathers in battle, and there was a certain pride in that, but Ray had nothing to be proud of when it came to Maurice.

Finally, having lived in households dominated by women, with only the occasional male influence from Maurice, Ernest, and his Plattsmouth uncles, Ray had not really learned how to get along with other men. He was simply not prepared for this aspect of life in a public school. This singled him out even more. Some boys cope well in such situations, but not Ray, and so his first few years at Dulwich were a strain. Interestingly enough, although he accepted the ethos of Dulwich College and of the public school system in general, he rarely mentioned his very early years at the college in his letters, perhaps indicating that it was not a period he liked to remember.

A typical school day started at around eight in the morning with prayers at chapel; then he went straight into lessons. There was a break at a quarter to eleven every day and then lunch at one. In the afternoon, lessons ran from two until four. Once they were over, the boys would run to the sports fields for two hours of Games—rugby in the autumn and winter terms, cricket in the summer. After Games, Ray would have slipped away to make his way home, like other day boys. For the first time in his life, Ray's life had structure and routine, which he relished.

The curriculum at Dulwich was broad. In his first year, Ray received a grounding in the Classics, studying Ovid, Aeschylus, and more. He also studied "English subjects," studying Africa and Australia, in an attempt by the school to instill a sense of British imperial superiority and destiny. Patriotism was a key tenet of the Dulwich way of life and every day a toast was made: "To my country, right or wrong." It suited Ray and, academically at least, he did very well in his first year at Dulwich, finishing second in his form.

During the summer vacation Ray and Florence were sent to Waterford. It would not have been an experience either of them looked forward to, but they were living at Ernest's expense and had little choice. Ray would spend the next four summers there, and this shifting between London and Ireland is, in some ways, symbolic of the much greater pressures that were beginning to shape his young mind. He was always proud of being Irish but bridled at being mistaken for an Irish Catholic. Simultaneously, at school, he was brought up to be British and, while the Anglo-Irish were part of the imperial project, in the eyes of his school contemporaries they remained alien and inferior. And, as he was reminded regularly, he was American, too. This hodgepodge of nationalities left the young Ray facing a challenging question: was he Irish, British, or American? In the end, he settled this conflict by wholly embracing Britishness, adopting all the trappings and manners of an English public schoolboy.

In September 1901, Ray returned to Dulwich and joined the "Modern" side of the curriculum. This, he later explained, was "intended most for boys who expected to go into some sort of business."[9] In other words, it was for boys who were not expected to go to university, and it taught them mercantile skills. The Classics were dropped, much to Ray's disappointment, and replaced by modern languages such as French, German, and Spanish. The focus of these lessons was tight: they studied conversation and correspondence, to the exclusion of literature. Despite the shift, Ray still did well, winning prizes for overall achievement and mathematics. He stayed on the modern curriculum for two years and, had he continued, he would have gone on to study political economy, commercial history, and geography in his final years. Fortunately for Ray, however, his true talents were recognized. By his own admission, having "[gone] up the Modern side to the top," he then "switched down to the lowest form in the senior school on the Classical side."[10]

This move came in the spring of 1903, and Ray was being honest when he admitted to joining the lowest form. In fact, in this year he was not given a form ranking at all, which suggests that he struggled to catch up on three years of lost time studying Classics. It did not help that, in the same year, he suffered several bouts of tonsillitis, each of which kept him away from school for a period. He was kept back for the autumn term of 1903 so that he could consolidate his learning and make up for lost time. For a boy with academic ambition, this must have been frustrating, but he pushed on with his studies so that, in the new spring term, he was allowed to move up to the next form.

That year, he pursued a mixed curriculum, taking German and mathematics from the Modern side and Greek and Latin from the Classical side. He read widely, including the sort of stuff that most adolescent scholars try to avoid: the *Aeneid*, Livy, and Ovid in Latin; Thucydides (or "Thick-sides" in public school slang), Plato, and Aristophanes in Greek; the Gospel of St. Mark (in Greek) in Divinity; and *Henry V* and *Comus* in English. He came to think in later years that he owed his success to this kind of education:

> A Classical education saves you from being fooled by pretentiousness, which is what current fiction is too full of. In this country [America] the mystery writer is looked down on as sub-literary merely because he is a mystery writer, rather than for instance a writer of social significance twaddle. To a classicist—even a very rusty one—such an attitude is merely a parvenu insecurity.[11]

His extracurricular reading, as far as we know, was more limited. Dulwich College library records show that Ray checked out only a few books during his time there. He obviously enjoyed Thackeray, borrowing both *Vanity Fair* and *The History of Henry Esmond*; and he liked to be intellectually challenged, too—Charles Lamb's *The Essays of Elia* and Carlyle's *Sartor Resartus* are also on the list. He was not always so intellectual in his reading and also borrowed a melodrama called *Last of the Barons*. But perhaps the College library lending information is not the best way to judge his adolescent tastes: it is possible that, like P. G. Wodehouse, he preferred to visit the bookstall at West Dulwich station, where he would find magazines containing the latest installments of thrilling serials by authors like Sir Arthur Conan Doyle.

Dulwich did not only encourage scholarly prowess but was famous also as a sporting institution. The 1903 College football team, for example, was wildly successful, defeating the older, more experienced students of Merton College, Oxford, in one match. Ray enjoyed school sports, playing rugby and cricket, though he admitted to playing neither particularly well:

> I played rugger a bit, but was never first chop, because temperamentally I was the furious type of Irish forward and didn't have the physique to back it up. I never weighed more than about ten stone in those days and you have to be made of steel springs at that weight to survive.[12]

He learned that he "didn't have the physique to back it up" the hard way, by breaking his nose in a game. In later life, that gave him a look of toughness that he did not quite deserve.

Dulwich also sought to provide a moral education. When Ray arrived at the College, the headmaster was Arthur Herman Gilkes, and under his influence Ray's moral sense took a firmer shape. Gilkes was a famous man in his own right for his work at the College and was in office at Dulwich for over thirty years in total. He modeled the school on Thomas Arnold's Rugby and drew praise from Thomas's son, the poet Matthew Arnold, who said that Dulwich College was the sort of school he had "long desired, and vainly desired, to see put at the disposal of the professional and trading classes throughout this country." Gilkes was an impressive man, having taken a double first at Oxford and a blue in football. Standing six feet five inches tall and sporting a long white beard, he must have seemed like a god to the boys in his charge. A. H. Gilkes took a hand in the boys' moral teaching himself, guiding them through their confirmation classes. He loathed pretension and would even reprimand teachers in front of their pupils if they displayed anything close to this sin, often to the great delight of the boys. And perhaps it was under his tutelage that Ray developed a similar intolerance, bolstered by his study of the Classics.

But it was not just the teachers that helped Ray develop, it was the atmosphere of the school itself. There is some evidence that the English public school system that emerged in the nineteenth century contributed to a new interest in chivalry that had otherwise died out long ago. Rather than being monastic institutions where cloistered students studied diligently, public schools were more like the tilting yards of Arthurian legend. Mock battles, in the form of sports, were essential as was the hierarchical system of squire and knight that was refigured in schools as fags (younger boys who did the older boys' bidding) and prefects (senior pupils who could impose school rules and administer punishments for any breaches).[13] Indeed Victorian culture was awash with chivalry, from the Pre-Raphaelites to Tennyson, who celebrated a romantic medieval past in their art. It made sense that figures like King Arthur were revered: they offered a less sexual view of heroism (Lancelot and Guinevere being the exception) that contrasted sharply with the fleshy pleasures indulged in by the classical heroes. Of all the heroes celebrated, Sir Galahad, one of the knights of the Round Table who found the Holy Grail, was perhaps the most suitable for a public school. His sexless purity represented the public school ideal of spotless self-sacrifice and was celebrated at Dulwich College in the school library, where a photograph of G. F. Watts's Galahad hung on the wall. This painting of an ethereal, angelic Sir Galahad would have been familiar to Ray in his last years at school and a strong memory of it lodged deep in his mind. At school he may have seen himself as something of a Galahad, seeking to emulate the knight's legendary purity. When Gilkes asked him if he masturbated, he responded in the negative, "thinking it dirty."[14]

Ray faced a crisis in 1904. From early in his school career, he had wanted to be a barrister, perhaps recalling Miss Groome's views on suitable careers for a gentleman. That, however, would require a university education. Dulwich had allowed him to move between the modern and classical curriculum, and he must have held some hope that his uncle would recognize his obvious academic ability and agree to fund a law degree. When Ray approached Ernest, however, the solicitor refused, and Ray found himself winding up his Dulwich education in a class known as the Remove. It was where boys who were not planning to go to university went to hone their skills before entering the world of business. Ray was still studying the Classics at this time and his form tutor, H. F. Hose, was one of the masters. The two obviously got on and they corresponded for many years after. Nonetheless, Ray, once again, was not placed in his form at the end of the year, which suggests that the seventeen-year-old was suffering from another of his periodic bouts of illness, and it must have frustrated him to leave Dulwich without making his mark in the final year.

Still, when he left Dulwich in 1904, Ray could look back on his school career with pride. He had taken a considerable amount from the experience, in the process adopting the ideal of the public school. He emerged, by his own account, as sexually pure, possibly refigured in his own mind in the image of Sir Galahad, with the strong moral code of a Victorian institution. He was no longer an awkward immigrant but rather a Dulwich man of some considerable intellectual caliber.

The disappointment of missing out on a place at university frustrated him though, particularly when he considered that those pupils who were staying on in preparation for entrance exams were not more intelligent than he, only wealthier. It is to literature's benefit that Ernest Thornton never relented, but he did, however, take steps to mollify his nephew by offering to send him to Europe for a year, where he could improve his French and German and complete his education. Ray seized this opportunity and headed off to Europe to start the next phase of his life.

CHAPTER THREE

"A MAN WITHOUT A COUNTRY"

In 1905, Raymond Chandler set off for France and a culture a world away from that of Dulwich and South London. For the first time, he was entirely on his own, his life no longer ruled by school or family. At seventeen, he was tall and striking, with a broad head and sharp, hazel eyes, a young man rather than a child. In Paris, he would experience adult independence but also indulge adolescent irresponsibility.

Foreign travel was part of the Victorian system in which he had been brought up. Leaving school did not mean the end of Ray's education: Dulwich provided him with the tools—"a habit of mind" John Henry Newman called it—to continue to learn and improve his character. Development of the personality was a key idea in the nineteenth century. It was the Victorians who coined the term "adolescence," seeing it as a period between childhood and adulthood when character was formed. In other words, this period of freedom was an essential part of a young man's moral growth.

Although Ernest Thornton did not want to foot the bill for Ray to go to university, he did want to ensure that his charge's schooling was finished properly. Ernest sought success for his nephew for various reasons, chief among them a desire to pass financial responsibility for Florence on to him. The best way to ensure this was to put Ray in a position to take a good job, and a tour of Europe would give him an advantage by augmenting his language skills and broadening his horizons.

Despite his enthusiasm for the adventure, Ray found it tough to leave home. It was the first time that he and Florence had been separated for a prolonged period since he was a very young child, and they were still close. As a day boy at Dulwich he had never had to spend time away from her, and she was always ready to welcome him home and provide him with maternal affection. Their farewell at the station must have been difficult for both of them. He no doubt missed his mother in his first weeks away, that feeling balanced, if not overridden, by his excitement at the freedom he was to enjoy.

On arriving in Paris, he took a room at the Pension Marjollet at 27 Boulevard Saint-Michel in the Latin Quarter and received his first taste of real city life. The Boulevard Saint-Michel is one of the long, wide, tree-lined streets built in the nineteenth century by Baron Haussmann as part of his renovation of the city. Pushing out from the Seine, it marks the line between the fifth and sixth arrondissements, forming one of the two main streets in the Latin Quarter. With the Sorbonne and several museums nearby, he was at the heart of the city's academic community, surrounded by students and conspicuously intelligent conversation. (The Latin Quarter derives its name from the large number of people who spoke Latin while wandering its streets.) If Ray was not to study at university, living in this part of Paris would be the next best thing. Unlike other districts, this enclave on the Left Bank had retained a network of narrow medieval streets. It was raffish and artistic—a place where high culture came into contact with low—and there were plenty of cafés, bars, and restaurants, as well as museums and libraries. It could not have been further removed from the Victorian suburban atmosphere of Upper Norwood.

Ray's room at the Pension Marjollet was cheap and probably small. Breakfast was included in the price but, at lunchtime and in the evening, he would have had to fend for himself. That was part of the fun.

In 1905, Paris was a city with art running hotly through its veins. Names such as Monet, Manet, Degas, and Pissarro, which would have sounded so strange to the ears of a seventeen-year-old public schoolboy from London, were heard everywhere. The success of Impressionism and then Post-Impressionism made Paris both a center and a subject for artists, and in the city's cafés and bars, a new generation of intellectuals and aesthetes debated what constituted art. Ostensibly, Ray was there to study French, and he enrolled in a school to further his knowledge of the language, with an emphasis on its commercial application. Outside school hours, however, he was his own man. Ray's pension was above the Café Vachette, a haunt of many famous Parisian writers and artists. Somerset Maugham described, in his novel *Of Human Bondage*, the sort of scene that Ray would have encountered each morning: "here little family groups, there a knot of men with odd-shaped hats and beards talking loudly and gesticulating . . . Americans loudly arguing on art."[1] Art was in the air; Ray could not escape it.

And it was not only the plastic arts that thrived in Paris—literature was healthy too, with half of all Parisians visiting the theatre at least once a month, and newspapers and periodicals booming. Mass literacy hailed a new age for the novel, and the late nineteenth century had seen the appearance of literary journals. Writers like Émile Zola, Gustave Flaubert, and Honoré de Balzac had put French literature on the map, but it was small presses and daily newspapers like *Le Petit Journal*, with its serialized novels and crime stories, that most Parisians enjoyed reading.

Ray reveled in this atmosphere, lapping up all that was on offer. "I was a young man," he wrote, "and very innocent, and was very happy wandering around, with very little money, but a sort of starry-eyed love of everything I saw."[2] Towards the end of the Boulevard Saint-Michel, he would have found the Jardin du Luxembourg, a beautiful landscaped park built around the Luxembourg Palace, where he would have been able to see paintings by Monet and other Impressionists.

At school, Ray had excelled in math and languages, but in 1905, his artistic sensibility flowered. He hung around in artistic cafés, claiming to have drunk Pernod at the Dôme, a famous bar popular with artists in Montparnasse. In places like this he would have been exposed to debate and argument unlike anything he had experienced at home or at school. At Dulwich, the Master of the school, A. H. Gilkes, was said to rail against his charges when they used vulgar abbreviations like "exam" and "quad."[3] Similarly, the language of Ray's family home had been conservative and staid. In Paris, though, words were used with passion, conviction, and power. Ray started to look seriously at language and, after years of ancient Greek and Latin, found new languages easy to learn. He became fascinated by French slang. Years later he told a friend:

> I have always been a great admirer of French colloquial slang . . . there is a wonderful precision and daring about French slang. I don't think it quite has the reckless extravagance of ours, but it seems to have more endurance.[4]

His interest deepened quickly and he started to look at other, more obscure tongues, both ancient and modern. He wrote that he "once hoped to be a comparative philologist . . . and dabbled in such strange lingos as Modern Greek . . . Armenian, Hungarian, besides the simpler and more obvious Romance tongues and the Germanic group."[5] Ray even tacked "a chart of the 214 key ideographs of the Chinese Mandarin language" above the wall at the head of his bed.[6] He spent hours poring over books on the languages, threading together alien sounds. Words and what they expressed became an obsession. His French developed well enough that, years later, he would be able to keep up a decent correspondence with Gallic fans. It was almost certainly in Paris that he first began to explore the idea of becoming a writer.

There were distractions from language though and, the more he thought about foreign words, the more conscious of his own foreignness he became. At the Pension Marjollet he contemplated his roots, or rather his lack of them. In Britain, Ray had felt isolated by his nationality. He certainly continued to feel sensitive about his American past, and criticisms leveled at his countrymen in the mid-1900s irked him. He once said in a letter to Hamish Hamilton that he "resented the kind of ignorant and snobbish criticism of Americans that was current at that time" but that he still "had no feeling of identity with the United States."[7] In Paris though, for the first time since he left Plattsmouth, Ray came across fellow Americans:

> During my year in Paris I had run across a good many Americans, and most of them seemed to have a lot of bounce and liveliness and to be thoroughly enjoying themselves in situations where the average Englishman of the same class would be stuffy or completely bored.[8]

Despite encountering several of his countrymen, he did not feel any kinship with them and, if anything, the sort of Americans he met in Paris left him feeling less connected to the country of his birth than ever before. These were not the genial Midwesterners of his childhood but cosmopolitan, wealthy Americans who could have leapt from the pages of a Henry James novel. And they were not the sort to make Ray a member of their club. In the same letter to Hamish Hamilton, he went on to write: "I wasn't one of them. I didn't even speak their language. I was, in effect, a man without a country."[9] This left him in a complicated position. He was neither British nor American; he was neither poor nor rich; he was disconnected and free-floating. Though he later came to see the benefit in this freedom and would use it to shape his personality as he wanted, this lack of self must have troubled the teenage Ray.

As an adolescent male, Ray could be forgiven for taking an interest in sex. A year abroad would usually be seen as an opportunity for a young man to indulge in the pleasures of the flesh, and being away from home and unsupervised facilitated many a young man's deflowering. Paris was very open about sex. The city tolerated street prostitution, which shocked Ray, who was, in his own words, "very innocent." Indeed, his pension was seedier than he had first understood: there were girls there who hoped to make some money from naive young men like Ray: "I [was] so innocent that I didn't realize that there were two girls at the pension that couldn't keep their feet off mine and were offering themselves to my innocence and I never even knew it."[10] By modern standards it might seem unusual that Ray would react so ingenuously to such approaches. Though we must take into consideration that this letter was penned by "gallant" Ray writing to a future fiancée towards the end of his life, the fact is that nothing in it was out of character. When it came to sex, Ray *was* unusual.

The girls in Paris were hardly genteel beauties, and he was upset by "the whores at the door of the apartment building."[11] Libido was always an uncomfortable subject for him. At school the discussion of sex made him feel awkward and years later he would write that he regarded "the gift [of sex] as a delicate and almost a sacred thing. . . . I always think of myself as the recipient of a royal favor. Women are so damned vulnerable to all sorts of hurts."[12] To Ray the bodies of men and women were pure until sex entered the equation.

The act of intercourse defiled the body, leaving it vulnerable. It was a view that might have aligned him with Sir Galahad himself.

Nor can we forget that Ray's attitude to sex was molded, in part, by his mother's experiences. She had found that, in effect, sex led to violence and abuse. In some respects, Florence was a typical Victorian woman and, after Maurice, refused to pursue other relationships to their consummation for fear of harming or displacing her son. Effectively, she became celibate, sacrificing her sex life for her son's sake and so, in his eyes, became an elevated example of purity. Women were to be revered, and those who gave themselves up as easily as the painted women on the streets of Paris appalled him. When he came to write poetry a few years later, time and time again, he presented women as immutable goddesses. The narrator of a poem called "When I Was King," a godlike monarch of immense power, speaks of a time when he "trod Valhalla / And chose my goddess out"; he builds her a temple as testament to his love, but she does not want to let him fall for her because to do so will risk his crown and heroic status ("Scarce would she let me love her / Lest I forgo my crown . . ."). But the King is not the sort to give up, so he shows her "bit by bit" the temple of his "manhood," and as if the poem were not overt enough, she proceeds through a door in his temple where he waits "Erect and calm as Thor." Unfortunately, the result is not what the narrator had hoped for because "Her worship fell to scorning, / And lifted nevermore," and he becomes her "broken god." Sex here is a dangerous thing and to suggest to a woman that you might want to sleep with her is to be diminished in her eyes. To young Ray, to love purely was to love without sex.

But if he did not have sex in Paris, he may at least have found romance. In a letter in the early 1950s he wrote:

> What about the time I spent under the shadow of the Saint Sulpice in that short but intoxicating affair with a demoiselle from Luxembourg—the one that afterwards became known the world over—but no, this is dangerous ground. Even in Luxembourg they have libel lawyers . . .[13]

There cannot be many women from Luxembourg who were famous the world over, and perhaps the shy and nervous Ray did indeed somehow meet a beautiful woman from that country and pursue a romance. It seems more likely, though, that he was joking. The letter came about as a response to an overblown author biography that was to appear on a dust jacket for one of his books. He called this sort of thing "a miracle of overstatement"[14] and played with the idea a little himself, picturing one of his much-loved Parisian haunts, the Jardin du Luxembourg, as the scene for an imaginary affair.

In his letters, Ray gave different accounts of how long he stayed in Paris. Sometimes he said six months, sometimes a year. Certainly he wished he had stayed longer. His Paris education did not give him quite what he wanted. Yes, the classes provided a good grasp of the language, but he discovered that, despite his talent and hard work, he would never be able to speak it quite well enough: "French one never speaks well enough to satisfy a Frenchman. Il sait se faire comprendre is about as far as they will go. Or Il parle très bien le français mais (a shrug) l'accent—horrible!"[15]

After Paris, Ray went to Munich, the capital of Bavaria and, since German unification, one of Germany's largest cities. Like the Latin Quarter in Paris, it was a home to artists and intellectuals. The poet Rainer Maria Rilke had studied in Munich a few years before Ray arrived, and the novelist Thomas Mann lived there. Next, Ray moved to Freiburg im Breisgau, another university town, on the western edge of the Black Forest, surrounded by some of Germany's most spectacular scenery. There he worked on his German with a private tutor. He much preferred this to being taught in a school, and it seems this method had a real impact on his understanding of the language: "I could speak German well enough . . . to be taken for a German."[16]

He had his photograph taken in Freiburg. The picture shows a young man wearing a high-lapelled jacket and tie, holding a book. He wanted to impress upon his mother that he was working hard and show himself to be a literary man. It also shows how handsome he was becoming. Florence, who kept this picture with her for the rest of her life, must have felt very proud.

Other than the photograph, we have very little information on what Ray got up to during this period. One small detail comes in the same letter in which he jokes about the affair with the famous woman from Luxembourg: "What about the six months I spent in the Höllenthal, trying to persuade a funicular railway to run on the level?"[17] Again, a joke, but one that points to Ray visiting the beautiful Höllenthal valley in Northern Bavaria during his visit.

It is not clear how long Ray remained in Germany. He seems to have spent several months there and may have spent a large part of 1906 moving around Bavaria. But, at some point, his European travels had to come to an end and, after months of exposure to Europe, he headed back to Britain a more mature man. Ray always looked back on his time in Germany with affection but, as early as 1906, he could feel the drums of war starting to beat:

> I did like the Germans very much, that is, the South Germans. But there wasn't much sense in living in Germany, since it was an open secret, openly discussed, that we would be at war with them almost any time now. I suppose it was the most inevitable of all wars. There was never any question about whether it would happen. The only question was when.[18]

By early in 1907, Ray was back in London. On his return he had discovered that his grandmother had died. His reaction is not recorded but it is unlikely he much mourned the woman who had made his mother's life so difficult. By this time, Florence was living in Streatham. It seems that Ray's uncle, who owned property across South London, would often let his charges stay in empty houses until tenants could be found. Streatham is around five and half miles south of central London and blossomed in the mid-1850s when the first railway station opened, linking what was previously a small satellite settlement to the metropolis proper. Though very definitely a few degrees south of Dulwich on the social scale, it was not so down-at-heel as is sometimes suggested. The house that the Chandlers moved into was situated at 35 Mount Nod Road, around ten minutes' walk from Streatham Hill station. It was—and still is—a quiet suburban road of stout, squat, red brick houses. Some of the houses on the road seem to have been built by men with grand visions and two have ugly turrets attached to them—the kind of pretentiousness Ray would not have liked. The new home had one advantage: Florence and Ray were living alone, without interference from relatives.

Victorian men did not come of age until they were twenty-one, and it appears Uncle Ernest was willing to support his sister and nephew even after

Ray's return. In 1907 Ray had three years left before he could be considered independent. Ernest nonetheless wanted his nephew to begin a career so that he could start paying his way. What else had that expensive education been for? Work was important to Victorians like Ernest—part of a man's identity, and a noble pursuit through which he would achieve happiness and fulfilment. All the freedom Ray had enjoyed in Europe now came to a sudden end. Ray needed to find work, and fast. He went to discuss his options with his old teacher, H. F. Hose. Ray had learned a lot during his period abroad and he hoped to do something with his love for language. Being a writer was never likely to prove secure or profitable and it is possible that Hose made this point clear to Ray. His former master probably suggested teaching, a career that, unlike comparative philology, would not be hindered by the lack of a university education. Either Hose or Ernest also suggested the Civil Service, which evidently struck a chord. It offered a steady and secure career, and for a bright boy, all that stood in the way of a job was the entrance examination.

There was a problem, however: as an American, Ray was not eligible to apply. He and his family were determined, though, and so set about arranging for him to be naturalized. Since Ray was the son of a British-born mother and had lived in Britain for more than five years, the formal investigation into his claim was brief. Aside from swearing an oath of allegiance to the British crown, all Ray remembered was that he had a short conversation with a Scotland Yard detective. He received a certificate of citizenship on May 20, 1907. Ray must have found the whole experience rather amusing: he was hardly a threat to the Empire and, in fact, very much a product of it. As if to accentuate this fact, he went out and bought himself a silver-tipped cane with which he would strut around the West End.

The Civil Service entrance exam was a challenging one and required those sitting for it to have a familiarity with math, English, German, Greek, English history, and French. It could be a grueling experience and took six days to complete. Ray, always fluent with his pen and with a newly acquired command of European languages, came third out of the six hundred candidates, and even managed to come top in the Classics exam. With such glittering results, he must have wondered what would have happened had he gone to university after all. He was offered a position as Assistant Store Officer, Naval

Stores Branch, at the Admiralty. Florence once again had reason to be proud and Ernest cause to feel relieved.

For the next six months, Ray took the train into Whitehall every morning, where he passed his days working steadily from nine in the morning to four thirty in the afternoon. Despite having done particularly well in the Classics section of the exam, and despite his knowledge of French and German, Ray filled what was essentially a clerical accounting role. His task was to monitor and record the movement of naval supplies, from potatoes to bullets, across the country and the Empire. Having always excelled at mathematics, he must have found this an easy task.

Perhaps because of the unchallenging nature of the work, Ray was not happy. After six months, he found himself wanting to escape the Service and eventually resigned. He disliked the routine drudgery, and the years ahead must have looked bleak. The Civil Service had seemed the best option, but in reality, he had felt forced down that route and away from his true ambition: "I wanted to be a writer and that would not have gone down at all well, especially with my rich and rather tyrannical uncle." He would later say:

> I thoroughly detested the civil service. I had too much Irish in my blood to stand being pushed around by suburban nobodies. The idea of being expected to tip my hat to the head of the department struck me as verging on the obscene.[19]

But the truth was almost certainly more complicated than that. For one thing, Chandler's wish to pursue a literary career was not at odds with his working for the Civil Service. It was almost the perfect day job for a writer because of its untaxing hours and its holidays. In fact, there were plenty of writers who balanced the two, Anthony Trollope being perhaps the most famous example. And Ray's own argument that his colleagues' inferiority was too much for him to stomach—though it contains a measure of truth—is one of his many thinly veiled attempts to elevate his own status in the eyes of his friends later in life. In this, Ray was a typical public schoolboy, anxious to establish his own class credentials and bitter towards those who failed to recognize them. In other words, he wanted to prove that he had always been a cut above middle class, and always more than a mere clerk.

If Ray could have been both a writer and a civil servant, and if we assume that colleagues were not perhaps as bad as he later suggested, why else would he want to leave? It is certainly true that the instinct to write was strong in him. From at least 1907—but probably much earlier—until his death, he wrote regularly and habitually. He was willing to undergo a lot to achieve his ambition of becoming a writer and sometime in 1908 went as far as moving into a small flat in Bloomsbury, giving up the security and safety of the house he shared with his mother. But we must also take into account the looming threat of taking financial responsibility for Florence. The two were always close and their relationship developed under adversity and in close proximity. It cannot have been entirely healthy. Though Ray always adored his mother and felt a strong urge to protect her, there may have been something darker in their relationship. Mothers do not appear often in his fiction, but when they do, they rarely come out well.[20] In *The High Window*, Mrs. Murdoch is painted with particular venom:

> She had a lot of face and chin. She had pewter-colored hair set in a ruthless permanent, a hard beak and large moist eyes with the sympathetic expression of wet stones. There was lace at her throat, but it was the kind of throat that would have looked better in a football sweater. . . . Her voice had a hard baritone quality and sounded as if it didn't want any nonsense.

"Ruthless . . . hard . . . unsympathetic"—Mrs. Murdoch is a repulsive human being, not remotely motherly, and one cannot help but wonder if, when Ray described her, some buried feelings about Florence leaked out. Though it is dangerous to read too much into such clues, we do know that, later, their relationship deteriorated. His time on the Continent, though all too brief, must have given him a taste of what it was like to live without Florence. The job in the Civil Service tied him to her. Was the desire to write also a desire to escape responsibility and to be free?

Chandler's first taste of literary success came when his poem "An Unknown Love" was published in *Chamber's Journal*, a decent literary magazine, in December 1908. It is not a good poem, as Ray knew (he thought his pre-1913 poetry was "B grade Georgian at best"). That said, he was only nineteen when he wrote it. Inspiration came one Sunday afternoon, when he was in the bath. This is the opening stanza:

> When the evening sun is slanting,
> When the crickets raise their chanting,
> And the dewdrops lie a twinkling on the grass,
> As I climb the pathway slowly,
> With the mien half proud, half lowly,
> O'er the ground your feet have trod I gently pass.

It is a poem of adolescent longing, directed at a dead girl with whom the speaker was in love but who he never actually met. "Could they understand the union / Of two hearts in dear communion / Who were strangers in the world of flesh and blood?" The narrator is in the mold of Ray's later heroes: he is passive as his ardor is "stormed" by its subject taking advantage of his "weak position." Then, having been conquered, he becomes a devoted "pilgrim," trapped in a relationship that can never happen. Strip away the awful rhymes and the Georgian situation of the verse, examine the bare bones, and you have the framework of a Marlowe story: a seductive woman and a man trapped. The important thing to Ray at the time was that this was his poem, in print. It may not have been a work of genius—how many nineteen-year-old's poems are?—but it was exactly the sort of thing that the readers of *Chamber's Journal* wanted. It was the first indication that he had some ability in the field, and it must have emboldened him in his decision to pursue literary ambitions.

Ray said that his uncle was "livid with rage" when he heard he was giving up his career in the Civil Service, though he may have been twisting the facts to present himself as a literary rebel. This did not, however, necessarily mean the end of Ernest's plans for his nephew. Ray was still young, after all, and it was not unheard of for young men to give up one job only to find another much more stimulating. He would have been able to take some crumbs of comfort from Victorian novels: did not David Copperfield abandon a law office position that had been purchased for him only to become a parliamentary reporter and novelist, finding in that career a decently Victorian moral satisfaction?

Ray's literary career began in earnest when he joined the *Daily Express* as a reporter. Unfortunately he found life hard at the paper: "I was a complete flop; the worst that they had ever had. . . . Every time they sent me out on a story I would get lost. They fired me."[21] Now, despite his frustration, Uncle Ernest stepped in and once again gave his support, arranging for Ray to meet Rowland Ponsonby Blennerhasset, a man whose name would fit a character in a Wodehouse novel and who happened to be as wealthy as Bertie Wooster. Ray described him as "a barrister with a House of Lords practice, a wealthy Irish landowner . . . [and] a member of one of these very ancient untitled families that often make earls and marquesses appear quite parvenu."[22] Blennerhasset in turn introduced Ray to J. A. Spender, a man who would keep him busy for the next few years and provide him with enough pay to live on.

J. A. Spender was one of the great newspaper editors of the early twentieth century. He ran the *Westminster Gazette*, an afternoon paper, for twenty-five years. He was, like Ray, a classicist but, unlike him, had received a university education, at Balliol College, Oxford. Journalism was, for Spender, a noble calling, and his rise in the industry was little short of meteoric. He started as a freelancer before assuming the editorship of Hull's small *Eastern Morning News* in 1888. Evidently he did a good job there because in 1892 he was asked to become assistant editor of the *Pall Mall Gazette*, a Liberal-leaning London paper. Shortly afterwards, he moved to the *Westminster Gazette* in the same position, before rising to the editorship in 1895, when he was only thirty-three years old.

The *Westminster Gazette* was a paper of opinion rather than news. Its distinctive green pages were filled with argument and debate and it had only a small circulation. It was nonetheless a highly influential organ, and if not read by the masses, it was certainly read by people with influence. In the first decades of the twentieth century, Kaiser Wilhelm II of Germany read it, believing it to be a window into the mind of the British political leaders. The Saturday edition included a lively literary section edited by Naomi Royde-Smith. She, along with Spender, helped Ray on his way, though he later claimed never actually to have met her. Spender asked Ray to contribute occasional articles to the paper and encouraged him to trawl through foreign newspapers looking for articles to translate and republish. He even went so far as putting Ray up for membership of the National Liberal Club so that he might have access to the reading room. Royde-Smith, meanwhile, published his verses, which at the time, concerned fairies, legends, and other common late Victorian subjects.[23] They can be divided into two loose groups.

First, there are the male hero poems, which tend to have titles like "The Quest," "The Perfect Knight," and "The Pioneer" and focus on pure male heroes and their journeys. The men in these poems are tough: one has "strength . . . higher than the mountain" ("The Perfect Knight"), while another makes "the hearers wonder / That a man could e'er be weak" ("The Pioneer"). But they have points of vulnerability. In "The Quest," this vulnerability is a woman. The knight at the center of the poem is searching for enlightenment, figured in the poem as the voice of his master ("the cities of the east and west . . . the moorland and the fen . . . [when] there seemed naught undiscovered to my ken"). However he fails to hear his master's call and it is only when he gives up and falls for a woman—against his "wisdom"—only to be let down by her ("She spurned the love which all my soul possessed") that he finally does hear his master's call. In other poems the flaw is isolation, such as in "A Pilgrim in Meditation" or "The Reformer."

It is easy to see qualities this clutch of early poems share with Ray's later work—lonely men with weaknesses, and dangerous women. Some of these women are seductresses ("I left my learning for a maiden's breast, / I scorned my wisdom to become her thrall," from "The Quest") and they tend to abandon men:

> I must leave thee, love?
> 'Tis I must go?
> Then as you wilt,
> For thou must know.
> ("A Woman's Way")

These poems anticipate Carmen Sternwood in *The Big Sleep* and Helen Grayle in *Farewell, My Lovely*, in that they present the destruction of good men by beautiful but dangerous women.

The second variety of poems are more esoteric. They have titles like "Art" and "The Bed of Roses." In these poems the poet and artist are cast as the hero. The artist can create art:

> But a poet waits unnoticed
> Anear the trampled bed [of roses],
> And waters it and watches
> Till a rose-bud lift its head.
> And then he plucks it quickly,
> And quickly steals away,
> For the yokel cometh lusty
> For another harvest day.
> ("The Bed of Roses")

These show a different side to Raymond Chandler but are still laced with the same sentimentality as his later work.

The poetry is a world away from the writing that made his name but it was the sort of poetry he had been encouraged to write at Dulwich and that was popular with the paper's readers. Royde-Smith thought that "attention to fairies and their concerns has always been a poet's business,"[24] while Spender himself, who would one day cut his nephew, the late modernist poet Stephen Spender, out of his will for writing a poem containing a suggestion of homosexuality,[25] was similarly keen on traditional poetry:

> I have spent a great deal of time puzzling out [T. S.] Eliot's poems. . . .
> But the fact that they have to be puzzled out, and in a manner quite unlike the puzzling out of Browning or obscure Greek poets, kills the poetry for me.[26]

This is an early example of Ray's ability to write to a market. He may have slavishly mined all the tropes of Georgian poetry but that is what readers wanted. Modernism was being born in the minds of men like Ezra Pound and James Joyce but could only emerge, in part, as a reaction to the huge market for Ray's type of poetry.

Chandler was not always an assiduous journalist. For one thing, he had very little training, and put simply, he did not always know what he was doing. For example, he would be sent proofs to check for errors and to ensure that his copy would appear as he intended it to. Unfortunately, it seems, no one told Ray that, so he simply ignored them. The only time he would venture into the office was on pay day, when he would turn up to receive his money. He would have fixed a stamp in a large book and signed his name across it to confirm he had been paid, and it is easy to imagine the pride with which he would have first done so: at last, he was the poet "receiving payment in gold and silver."[27]

Ray estimated that he received around three guineas a week from the *Westminster Gazette* when he was at the height of his productivity. Unfortunately, it is difficult to determine exactly how much he wrote because so much of his work was printed without attribution.

As most fledgling authors will recognize, getting the attention of an editor can be difficult, but Ray had a unique approach. Rather than sending his work to them speculatively, he would write to the owners and express interest in buying the paper. His first attempt saw him approach Sir George Newnes, the owner of *Tit Bits* magazine, a lowbrow if rather profitable weekly publication. Ray was invited into the offices, no doubt slightly trepidatious about agreeing to discuss an offer he could not hope to fulfill. Thankfully for him, he was received by a wise secretary, "definitely public school," who assured him that the magazine was doing just fine but that his approach "had at least the merit of originality." Ray must have been relieved that he had not landed himself in hot water but disappointed that he had gone to such effort and received nothing in return.

He kept trying, though, next approaching *The Academy*. Started in 1869, *The Academy* was a periodical devoted to literature. Originally, it was a monthly publication, but as literary discussion grew more popular in the latter half of the nineteenth century, it became a weekly.[28] As a rule, it published unsigned reviews to promote honest debate and, until the turn of the century, was modestly successful. In 1902 it merged with another periodical, *Literature*, and became *The Academy and Literature*, but this did not lead to great success, and through the 1900s, it changed ownership several times. In 1907, Lord Alfred Douglas, best known as Oscar Wilde's lover, became its owner and editor, but by 1910, a man called Cecil Cowper had taken over and it was he who agreed to a meeting with Ray. According to Ray, Cowper "was not disposed to sell an interest in his magazine, but pointed to a large shelf of books in his office and said they were review copies and would I care to take a few home to review."[29]

His book reviews started appearing in the magazine throughout 1911 and 1912. Ray tended to be given books by lesser-known authors, suggesting that he was still an apprentice at the time, though it also indicates the sheer volume of material being printed in the second decade of the twentieth century. At the same time, he contributed occasional essays on diverse literary subjects. Like his poetry, Ray's essays were convoluted disquisitions that reflected the fashion at the time for overblown, rather circuitous prose. One, "Realism and Fairyland," compares two forms of writing—realism and idealism—with the latter winning out, though, if the truth be told, it is hard to unpick the thread of its argument, giving it the quality of a precocious adolescent's essay. It concludes in this lofty fashion:

> . . . any man who has walked down a commonplace city street at twilight, just as the lamps are lit, can reply that such artists are not realists, but the most courageous of idealists, for they exalt the sordid to a vision of magic, and create pure beauty out of plaster and vile dust.[30]

Another contribution, "The Genteel Artist," anticipates Ray's later work in the way it contrasts established, society artists with the struggling writers working on Grub Street. He suggests that rich artists are inferior to the poor artist:

> Other things being equal, one feels that a great poem is more likely to be written on a deal table than on an article of inlaid rosewood. The genius in the garret may have an uncomfortable time in many ways, but he has one great advantage over his more luxurious rivals—he is compelled to throw himself body and soul into his work.[31]

No doubt this position was in part informed by Ray's own experience—in his eyes he was the genius in the garret—but also it foreshadowed later, more mature essays like "The Simple Art of Murder" and "Writers in Hollywood" in the way that it attacked the establishment. "The Genteel Artist" concludes as follows:

He [the genteel artist] turns out a novel or a painting as neatly and as coldly as the machine turns out the packed ounce of tobacco, and probably in the general scheme of things the three products are of similar value.[32]

The art created by the established author is, artistically speaking, of less worth than that created by an impoverished artist. This is the intellectual position of the outsider, the excluded "other" railing against the establishment of which he feels he is not a part. And this is how Ray saw himself. It is little wonder since his sense of self was forged at home, where he and Florence were made to feel like second-class citizens, and hardened at school, where Ray's absent father and American heritage set him apart from his fellows. This sense of otherness became an intellectual position rather than a personal one because, at the same time, he sought to belong. He adopted the public school regalia; he wrote in the style of his Edwardian contemporaries; he was desperate in some way to fit in. In other words, a deep fissure ran through Ray. On the one hand he was the public schoolboy with his silver-tipped cane and Dulwich College tie; on the other hand he attacked the established way of doing things. It was a hard balance to maintain.

In 1912, Ray was offered an opportunity that would have allowed him to write regularly:

I think my most startling experience in those days was the result of an introduction to Horace Voules, then editor of *Truth*, who's chucker-out (*Anglice* bouncer) was a suave Cantabrigian in a cutaway coat and the usual striped pants, and this gentleman advised me to write newspaper serials at six guineas a week. Said it was easy, you just kept on until they made you stop and then you started a new one. Imagine me then in a blue-chalk-striped flannel suit cut by a West End tailor, wearing an old school tie and an old school band on a natty straw hat, carrying a cane and gloves, and being told by this elegant fellow to write what then appeared to me the most appalling garbage ever slung together in words. I gave him a sickly smile and left the country.[33]

Ray's response shows the difficulty of his position. On the one hand, he and the "suave Cantabrigian" were cut from the same cloth (evidently striped), but on the other, Ray's intellectual stance separated them. Ray's eagerness to belong lost out to his unwillingness to compromise intellectually. He did not want to become part of the institutions that he thought produced the most artless of art, preferring to remain on the outside even if it meant missing out on the rewards that might be available. Though this was a very difficult position to maintain, it was a noble one and showed a self-sacrifice of which even Sir Galahad might have approved. Ultimately, it was an intellectual stance that helped make him the writer he eventually became.

Unfortunately, the extra work that *The Academy* brought in did not help alleviate his money worries. After 1909, he seems to have given up his Bloomsbury flat and returned to live with his mother, who now had a house in Forest Hill. This must have felt like a step backwards for an ambitious young man. The drive that had encouraged him to quit the Civil Service was beginning to evaporate. In 1910, he decided to go into teaching. He got in touch with his former master, H. F. Hose, and sought out work at Dulwich College. He was employed as a substitute teacher from Michaelmas term 1910 to July 1911 and earned £53 6s. for his efforts, which was a pittance compared to what his full-time colleagues were earning. Hose, for example, earned £333 a year. The income kept him afloat while he continued submitting essays and poetry to magazines, but put paid to his dream of living by his pen. He would still walk around the West End in a sharply tailored suit, sporting an old school tie, with his silver-tipped cane, but did not have the money for the lifestyle to match. Life began to depress him.

It can only have deepened his despair to know that fellow writers were also suffering. Richard Middleton, an acquaintance of Ray's, committed suicide in Brussels in 1911. Middleton was a poet and writer of short stories who, unlike Ray, managed to hold down a day job, at the Royal Exchange Assurance Company. Unfortunately this made him very unhappy, and to compensate, in the evenings, he joined the Bohemian demimonde. He was never particularly successful, though his work lived on in anthologies after his death. Exactly when or where he and Ray met is not clear, but Ray described his death as a "suicide of despair"[34] and seems to have empathized with Middleton:

> The incident made a great impression on me, because Middleton struck me as having far more talent than I was ever likely to possess; and if he couldn't make a go of it, it wasn't very likely I could.[35]

The realization that someone more talented than him had been pushed to suicide led Ray to contemplate his ambitions. He decided that, despite his education, his confidence in his ability, and his increasingly impressive connections, he was stuck. He had no job and no private income, and without those, being a professional writer was more than just a struggle—it was impossible.

He was, however, still part of literary London and witnessed the beginnings of a new movement. Ray reacted to the emergence of modernism by parodying it in a poem entitled "Free Verse," though he did not submit it for publication:

> But I find somehow I require
> A little more liberty,
> To express my immortal soul
> (That is, if it is immortal, which one rather doubts
> After reading Freud).

It is hardly subtle with its modest attack on linguistic experimentation:

> I like
> To put a word like that down
> And just look at it
> With my head on one side,
> And run around it
> Until I get a bit dizzy,
> And then sit down and
> Babble a bit
> About any old thing that comes
> Into
> My head. Finally I gather it up
> With my poetic gift, a sort of shovel, you know,
> And spatter it whimsically on a

Few
Sheets of paper,
And there you are.
A poem more or less.

Though Ray looked on the nascent movement with scorn, he kept himself informed of the latest trends and ways of thinking. He preferred traditional poetry, and it is ironic that a man which such disdain for experimentation in the form would later so shake up the tradition of the detective novel.

Since 1908, Ray had tried his hardest to succeed as a writer. He worked at it for nearly four years, but though his poetry and essays were adequate and of their time, his output in this period little hinted at the greatness to come. He had failed. Like so many others before and after him, he began to look to the United States with hope. Although he already knew America better than most, it nonetheless promised him the same opportunity that it did to so many true emigrants—the chance to reinvent himself.

Throughout his letters and descriptions of his time in London, Ray seems to come up against the same obstacle over and over again: class. In his mind, he was an upper-middle-class public schoolboy, and this was the image he liked to project to the world around him. Despite the obvious privileges of his upbringing, his situation was much less clear-cut. He had the contacts but he lacked a private income. He dressed in the uniform of his school contemporaries, yet he was different from them. At best, he was an Anglo-Irish American; at worst, a "man without a country." This division was difficult for Ray. It left him isolated and positioned him as the outsider looking in. This, along with the failure of his literary career, contributed to his decision to leave Britain. The United States offered him the opportunity to start from scratch without that class burden and to join the ranks of the self-made men.

He summoned up his courage and approached Uncle Ernest with an offer: if Ernest would lend him £500, he would take himself to America and off his uncle's hands. Ernest agreed, and so Ray used the money to buy himself a first-class ticket and set out for the country of his birth. He left London as a failed British writer and arrived in America as a new man.

CHAPTER FOUR

WELCOME TO LOS ANGELES

On July 10, 1912, Raymond Chandler boarded the SS *Merion* at Liverpool. He was wearing a tailored suit, carrying his silver-tipped cane, and had forty dollars in his pocket. He was heading to America. On the one hand it was to be a homecoming; on the other, he was turning his back on his mother and the life he had known so far. The journey must have been an exciting one but it was also no doubt clouded by the knowledge of what he was leaving behind.

The journey proved to be a fortuitous one. As Ray made his way through the first class portion of the ship, he came across a young family by the name of Lloyd, and in doing so, made one of the most important connections of his life. At the head of the family was Warren. He was an inch or two shorter than Ray, and his grey eyes, set in a tanned, oval face, were striking. His wife, Caroline (Alma to her friends), was almost as tall and had blue eyes and soft brown hair. Together they made a dashing couple and, to Ray, offered an example of a different kind of American from those he had met in Paris. Warren had a degree from Berkeley and a PhD from Yale and was taking his family home after a two-year tour of Europe. The Lloyds were intelligent, cultured, glamorous, and very, very rich. Ray quickly became caught up in the young family's life. The Lloyds, for their part, welcomed Ray—their daughter, Estelle, developed a mild crush on him—and together they talked about France and Germany, Europe and America. Warren and Alma told Ray about the city they were heading back to, their home, and a place that would forever become associated with Raymond Chandler: Los Angeles, California.

They were obviously proud of Los Angeles and, at one point, suggested that Ray might want to move there. Was he tempted? It is not clear, but certainly he filed the suggestion away. For now, though, he had other plans. The SS *Merion* arrived at Philadelphia eleven days after leaving Liverpool, and the Lloyds and Ray went their separate ways, but not without swapping addresses.

Ray would later recall disembarking at New York, but he was surely embellishing the truth, hoping to add romance to the story of his departure. From Philadelphia he headed to Omaha, where his Aunt Grace and his other Uncle Ernest still lived. Ray had spent his first summers with the Fitts but had not seen them since 1900, and they must not have known quite how to treat the handsome young man who appeared before them in 1912. In later years, he liked to gloss over his status as a returning American, preferring instead to present himself as an exile from England, but the Fitts would have seen Ray's arrival as a homecoming.

Grace and Ernest welcomed their nephew and introduced him to their friends and family. It seems likely, though, that Ray did not fit in. It was not simply that he had been brought up in another country; it was that he was quite the snob. Years later, Ray recalled meeting a distant cousin, Harry Fitt, who worked in a hardware store in Omaha. His description of the experience reveals a haughtiness that would have distanced him from his family: "I was fresh out of England at the time and a hardware store was 'trade' [so] I could hardly be expected to get on terms of anything like familiarity [with Harry]."[1]

He would later tell friends that, after landing in New York, he had worked in Missouri as a clerk enduring the bitter cold of a St. Louis winter. While this may have been true, his vivid recollection of life in Omaha squares better with the existing travel records, and it seems possible that his Missouri trip was invented to conceal a group of relatives who did not fit in with his own self-presentation. Whatever the case, he did not stay with the Fitts for long. By December 1912, only six months after arriving in Omaha, he had again packed his bags, this time heading for San Francisco.

Ray's departure from England had left Florence on her own. Separated from her son and isolated by her family (her younger sister had by this time moved to Edgware in North London, to live in another of Ernest Thornton's many properties), she must have felt lonely, even abandoned. It came as a relief when her son wrote to tell her he had settled in San Francisco and that he was ready for her to join him. This was almost certainly part of the plan: it seems likely that, in exchange for Ernest's loan, Ray agreed to support his mother. In December 1912, he was ready to do so and in preparation took a house in Berkeley, on the San Francisco Bay.

Though the Lloyds' idea that he move to Los Angeles had not yet taken a firm root, it was clear that Ray, having made it to California, was edging nearer. By the time Florence arrived on the West Coast, Ray was working long hours in menial jobs to earn what money he could. At one point, he worked on an apricot ranch, which meant ten-hour days picking fruit. Later, he joined the staff of a sporting goods store, where his role was restringing tennis rackets at $12.50 a week. It was an unglamorous life, though perhaps Ray saw it as an extension of his Grub Street existence: he was no longer a genius in the garret but a poet-farmer, a literary racket stringer.

Despite the hardship, Ray continued to keep up appearances, strutting around San Francisco in his London finery. Bill Townend, a Dulwich contemporary, and a friend of P. G. Wodehouse, was also in San Francisco in 1912 and 1913. Like Ray, he was given to wearing a straw boater with Dulwich College colors, and one day he was walking through the city when he felt a tap on his shoulder. He turned around and there before him was Raymond Chandler. Though they had not known one another at College, they struck up a fast and enduring friendship. Townend remembered that despite having "no money at all" Ray still had expensive tastes and was keen to impress:

> Raymond asked me to lunch at one of the expensive restaurants and I firmly said no. He was hard up and I was hard up, so I said we had better have a meal at a fairly cheap place, which we did.[2]

Ray clearly wanted to show that, despite his situation, he remained a good host, as one would expect from a true Dulwich man. However, Ray was a lonely man, recently arrived in the city, eager to make a connection. He was also unsure about Americans in general and openly admitted to feeling "contempt for the natives"[3] when he first arrived, so it is little wonder that he was so eager to establish a connection with a fellow Englishman.

When he was not working, Ray continued to write, but he seems to have given up on the idea of doing so professionally in San Francisco. Money was tight and stringing rackets was little more than a stopgap. He knew that he had to put himself on a more secure financial footing and started to look for other opportunities. He had always had a facility with numbers and decided to take a course in bookkeeping. Later, he would remember the experience with characteristic arrogance:

> As I knew nothing about bookkeeping I went to night school and in six weeks the instructor asked me to leave; he said I had done the three years' course and that was all there was.[4]

However he might have sneered at it, the accounting course converted Ray's rather abstract, very English education into a certificate to which an American employer would pay attention. Application of the new qualification had to wait, though, because in 1913, Ray made a big decision. Bored and frustrated by eking out an existence in San Francisco, he decided to take the advice of the kind family he had met on the SS *Merion* the year before and move to the City of Angels.

Today, Los Angeles is one of the most extraordinary cities in the world, but in 1913, when Raymond Chandler first stepped into the bleached, bright sunshine he would one day come to define in the public imagination, it was just a small town close to the West Coast of America. Los Angeles was built from nothing. It grew out of a dry desert where there were few natural resources to hand. Carey McWilliams, a local historian, wrote in 1946:

> Virtually everything in the region has been imported: plants, flowers, shrubs, trees, people, water, electrical energy, and, to some extent, even the soils. While potentially a rich and fertile region, the land required a highly developed technology to unlock its resources and to tap its amazing fertility.[5]

The leading men of Los Angeles knew that the key to their city was people, and they set about selling the city to the world. Before long, it was the most advertised city in America,[6] and people poured in. Though Los Angeles would later be indelibly linked with the automobile, it was the railroads that first brought the visitors. The companies that controlled the rails set up lectures, showcases, and tours, culminating in the grandest publicity stunt of all—the excursion party. This saw thousands of Midwestern Americans board trains to Southern California for short trips. Once there, they were given the freedom to explore the region while the city's promoters sold them the dream of relocation. Excursion parties were massively successful and people settled by the thousands into this seemingly snakeless Eden, drawn in by the warm climate, where fruit and vegetables grew in abundance and where work was plentiful.

Nineteen thirteen would prove to be a seminal year in the city's history, seeing not just the arrival of Ray but also of something of even greater importance: water.

Without water, Los Angeles could not have survived to become the city it is today. In 1900, it had just enough capacity for around one hundred thousand souls.[7] For a city with big plans, this was not enough. In 1904, a search for water in the surrounding area led surveyors to Owen's Valley. William Mulholland, chief superintendent of the Los Angeles Department of Water and Power, and Fred Eaton, former mayor of the city, visited the Valley, and agreed that they had found the answer to their prayers. The only problem was getting the water from Owen's Valley to Los Angeles. To overcome this obstacle, they planned to construct an aqueduct.

Mulholland and Eaton chose to keep their plan a secret, revealing their intentions only to a small cabal of wealthy Los Angelenos: Harry Chandler, editor of the *Los Angeles Times* (no relation); General Harrison Gray Otis, *Times* publisher; banker Joseph F. Sartori; railroad magnate Henry E. Huntington; railroad executive E. H. Harriman; E. T. Earl, publisher of the *Los Angeles Express*; and railway director M. H. Sherman. These men formed a syndicate in 1905 and, financed by Harry Chandler and others, bought up great chunks of the San Fernando Valley at low prices. With the land under their control, they approached the city with their plan, and unsurprisingly, they had the support of Mulholland and M. H. Sherman, who was himself on the city's water board. The plan was approved, only it would not take the water to Los Angeles but would instead terminate in the San Fernando Valley, where excess water would be used to irrigate the previously worthless land.

In 1910, the plan's sponsors controlled over 108,000 acres there, and by 1913, when the aqueduct was complete, they were able to sell the land at vastly inflated prices. Some estimates put the profit of these sales at $100 million but whatever the sum, it was a swindle of vast proportions. The City of Los Angeles had stumped up $25 million to finance an aqueduct that filled the pockets of private individuals. Though the water was essential to Los Angeles's growth, it was built on a crooked deal: in many ways it summed up the city itself.[8]

The Lloyds welcomed Ray and Florence Chandler with open arms. They were charmed that Ray, the intelligent, part-British intellectual, had followed their advice. Indeed, they were so delighted that, in an astonishing display of generosity, they invited Ray and Florence to live with them.

Their house was at 713 Bonnie Brae Street, near MacArthur Park, then the westernmost point of the city. If you chose to travel a little further west, you would hit Hollywood, then a small cluster of houses, and Beverly Hills, a tiny country village. Where Pico and Olympic Boulevards run today there were barley fields, and the occasional cars on the roads were far outnumbered by horses and buggies. Los Angeles was yet to sprawl. In 1913, MacArthur Park (then known as Westlake Park) was a luxurious district, home to the leading men of the city. It had green and lush grass thanks to irrigation from an artificial lake, originally built as a drinking water reservoir, and on weekends, families would promenade through the park and rent canoes. It was an elegant place with elegant people, surrounded by so many hotels and luxury residences that it came to be known as the Champs-Élysées of Los Angeles. Ray's silver-tipped cane fit right in.

The Lloyds proved to be supportive friends and took Ray and Florence under their wings. Not only did they provide shelter but they also helped Ray find a job in the city. Warren arranged for him to work as an accountant and bookkeeper at the L.A. Creamery, where he had connections (he was the company's legal counsel, and his first cousin was married to its treasurer), and for the first time in several years, Ray had a steady, secure wage.

On top of everything else, the Lloyds also provided a social life for the Chandlers in a city where they would have otherwise been on their own. Every Friday evening, the Lloyds threw the doors of their home open to musicians and intellectuals, who would spend the evening talking, writing, and sharing ideas. This circle of friends, for reasons that remain unclear, was known as "the Optimists," and an intellectual like Ray was made very welcome. With his elegant, well-cut suits and English manners, he added color and an international flavor to the group, who were fascinated by Indian philosophy, psychology, and spiritualism. Evenings of cocktails and conversation would sometimes end with Warren Lloyd sitting down at a Ouija board to conduct a séance. Florence, though she could be a prude, was a rebel at heart and probably enjoyed observing such goings-on, even if she did not join in.

Lloyd was a fascinating character—a corporate professional but also a Bohemian, a lawyer but one with a PhD in philosophy. He had also found the time to coauthor a book called *Psychology, Normal and Abnormal*. Ray, both poet and bookkeeper, writer and bureaucrat, had a similar personality, though more reserved. Did he look to Lloyd as a father figure? They certainly had an easy relationship founded, in part, on a shared sense of humor. On occasion they would head to a cinema, sit on opposite sides of the auditorium and laugh at inappropriate points to see if they could get the rest of the audience to join in. This was, Ray argued, a psychological experiment, though it may have also been a bit of an adolescent prank.

Alma Lloyd loved singing and the Friday evening salons often had a musical element. One night, she invited a pianist called Julian Pascal, his wife, Cissy, and Gordon, Pascal's son from an earlier marriage, to come along to a meeting of the Optimists. They were a popular family and the Pascals quickly became part of the circle of friends.

Julian had been born Goodridge Bowen in the West Indies, and had taught music at the Guildhall School of Music in London before moving to New York. He had adopted the name Julian Pascal for professional reasons, and when he married Cissy in 1907, she had taken his professional name as her own. Julian always suffered from poor health and had been drawn to Los Angeles because of its warm climate but also because, as a growing city with artistic ambitions, it offered him an opportunity to further his musical career. His wife, who was also an accomplished pianist, may have hoped for an acting career when they first moved west but found herself concentrating instead on keeping house for Julian and Gordon. Gordon was a few years younger than Ray and hoped to be an actor one day, too. He was a pale boy with brown eyes and dark hair, and he and Ray became good friends. Meanwhile, Florence found a new friend in Pascal's wife who was, after all, only nine years her junior.

Despite the Lloyds and the Optimists, Los Angeles must still have been a lonely place for Ray and Florence. They could not live with the Lloyds forever and, until they found a more permanent home, were just as they had been for years: transient and dependent on others. In his novels, Ray has Philip Marlowe express so many poignant moments of loneliness, and this was clearly Ray's overriding impression of the place. The trouble with Los Angeles is that everyone comes from somewhere else, and it can seem a city of strangers, where neighbors on the same street or in the same block might never exchange a single word. Migration works both ways, too, and hard-won friends often leave as easily as they come.

As a result of this condition, Angelenos developed ingenious ways to meet one another. State societies were one such solution. They were clubs for migrants from the same state and emerged as early as 1882 when G. C. Haskins called together all the Pennsylvanians in Los Angeles. Several similar clubs followed, and the Iowa State Society became one of the biggest and most important. By the time Ray arrived in the city, the picnics organized by the Iowa State Society were attracting fifteen thousand people. These were not just casual gatherings of friends but well organized events with music and catering. The societies were also beginning to exercise increasing political influence. Ray, of course, struggled to identify which society he ought to join. Was he a Chicagoan and so a natural member of the Illinois State Society? Or was he too British to fit into any of the state societies? Once again, he did not have a place and, had it not been for the Lloyds, both Chandlers might have had a very different experience of California.

The Lloyds continued to encourage Ray that his dream of being a writer was within reach. He would often sketch poems for the other Optimists, and on June 14, 1914, "on the road between Hollywood and Burbank," he, Estelle, and Warren Lloyd wrote one together. It was called "To-Morrow," and perhaps like its audience, it was suitably optimistic. "To-morrow," always just out of reach, was the day when all would come good:

> We shall find the Secret,
> That mocks us from the shade,
> And tell the gods of heaven
> Just how the world was made.[9]

Ray may have preserved this poem for reasons other than merit. It represented a time of pure happiness and freedom, but things were about to change. Exactly two weeks after he had written it, Gavrilo Princip, a seventeen-year-old who had been schooled in Bosnian nationalism and terrorism, walked up to a stalled car in Sarajevo and shot dead the Archduke Franz Ferdinand, heir to the throne of the Austro-Hungarian empire. That event shook the whole world. Germany, which had long been jealous of the British Empire, and which was also beginning to feel threatened by its neighbor, Russia, took advantage of the situation and by August 4, 1914, was at war with France, Russia, and Great Britain.

These international events reached even sunny Southern California. Though America would not enter the war until 1917, the Optimists, with their European connections, were immediately affected. Ray, who had visited and loved the south of Germany, knew all too well that many former Dulwich boys would have signed up to fight. Patriotism was a key tenet of a Dulwich education. Alleynians who had fallen in battle were venerated at the College and Ray may very well have shared his old school friends' eagerness to fight. There can have been talk of little else than the war in the Lloyd household. Alma Lloyd in particular felt divided loyalties—her mother was German and her father French. (In fact, he was from Alsace, a territory over which France and Germany have fought many times, and which has changed hands almost as often.) They were very aware of the situation in Europe which steadily worsened until, by the end of August 1914, seventy-five thousand Frenchmen had been killed. The first dark clouds were gathering over the sunny atmosphere of optimism and intellectual exploration.

But life did continue. At some point, the Chandlers made the decision to move out from under the feet of the Lloyds. They took a house in Bunker

Hill, somewhere close to Angel's Flight, at the top the little funicular railway that took residents into downtown Los Angeles. Ray described Bunker Hill in 1942's *The High Window*, painting a portrait of decay:

> Bunker Hill is old town . . . [it] was the choice residential district of the city, and there are still standing a few of the jigsaw Gothic mansions with wide porches and walls covered with round-end shingles and full corner bay windows with spindle turrets.

There are hints here of the Bunker Hill he knew when he first lived there with Florence, before it started to turn.

It is impossible to imagine Los Angeles, which is today swamped with cars, as a city serviced by trams and railways, but in the 1910s, it had one of the most advanced public transport systems in the world. Ray would have taken the railway to downtown Los Angeles, where his office was situated, and part of him must have been reminded, even in the bright Californian sun, of traveling through South London into Whitehall. Despite his move to America, he was still commuting to a clerical job and supporting his mother. Not much had really changed.

Ray and Florence moved restlessly around the city, never settling for long. At some point in 1915 they moved to a small, furnished bungalow at 311 Loma Drive. By 1916, thanks to a promotion, they were in Santa Barbara County, at 1419 De La Vina, a mile or so north of the beach. It was a long way from Los Angeles, and Ray was suddenly cut off from the few friends he had managed to make. He was now completely alone with Florence.

Meanwhile, the war was coming closer. In February 1917, Germany changed the rules of engagement for its U-boats. Until 1917, German submarines had operated "cruiser rules" under which, should they come across commercial traffic in British waters, they had to surface, board the ship, and inspect the vessel's cargo. If they wanted to sink the ship after this inspection, they had to allow its crew and passengers to get into life rafts before launching torpedoes. To do otherwise—to sneak up and send a silent torpedo gliding towards a ship that might be carrying women and children—was seen as barbaric. Winston Churchill, in 1914, even went as far as to say that he could not imagine anyone employing such tactics. In 1917, though, Germany was starving and blamed the British for their lack of food. They wanted to show that they, too, could inflict great damage and began to sink merchant vessels without warning, without surfacing, and without allowing passengers to disembark. The effect was not what the German high command had hoped for: Britain endured, and America was spurred into joining the war.

At the beginning of June 1917, the American government started to register all men between the ages of twenty-one and thirty-one in an effort to strengthen its army before heading to Europe to join the now global conflict. Ray was twenty-eight and suddenly faced with the possibility of being sent to fight, but he worried as much about his mother as himself. Who would look after her while he was away? What would happen to her if he were killed? Later, he would tell friends that he tried to sign up for the US Armed Forces but that they would not take him because of his bad eyesight. This was a lie. Ray did not sign up because he did not dare leave Florence. When the draft board called him up, he explained that he had a dependent who was unable to work, and was excused. He could equally have argued that he was ineligible to join the US Army as a British citizen but, on his draft registration card, claimed to be a "declarant" in the process of applying for US citizenship.

But Ray was no coward; his concern was his mother. The army would not support her if Ray went to war, so he started to look for other options. He clearly had a desire to fight and discovered that the Canadian Army offered an allowance to soldiers' dependents. In August, the Chandlers headed back to Los Angeles, moving to a house on 127 South Vendome Street, which they shared with Julian and Cissy Pascal. There, Ray and Gordon talked about war, and Ray may have convinced his young friend to join him. They signed up together, each witnessing the other's attestation form.

Ray's form reveals one particularly interesting fact: under the heading "trade or calling" he describes himself as a journalist. Despite working in accountancy since his arrival in Los Angeles, he did not identify himself as such, not at heart. The Canadians were not really interested in his career, though. They assigned him to the Fiftieth Regiment of the Canadian Expeditionary Force (CEF) and sent him to Victoria, in Canada's Pacific northwest, for initial training.

Unusually for a man of his education, Ray was made a private. Considering his frustration at being required to doff his cap to superiors in the Civil Service, it is likely that he resented this lowly position. Thankfully, Gordon was at hand for moral support. Both would fit in well with the Canadian Army because, unlike the US Army, it was filled with international troops. F. A. McKenzie, a news correspondent with the CEF, described the Canadian Army as being "as cosmopolitan as Canada itself" with men "drawn from a score and more of nations . . . welded together in one great whole."[10] There were Englishmen, Canadian-born men of British descent, and entire "Scottish" regiments with direct connection to the old Highland regiments.

In Victoria, Gordon and Raymond met another young soldier who would become a firm friend. His name was William Lever. Like Ray, he was a British citizen, having been born in Northampton. He had come to America to make shoes and, in his attestation papers, lists his address as the San Francisco Y.M.C.A. He was twenty-two years old and stood at five foot five, with light brown hair and grey eyes. Like Ray and Pascal he had no previous army training, and the three men must have felt drawn together during initial orientation. For all three, it was to be an important friendship. A picture taken at this time shows Ray wearing the khaki kilt and tam-o'-shanter of the Gordon Highlanders, with which regiment the Canadian Fiftieth were twinned. His grin suggests a certain wry amusement at this getup. The war must have felt, at this stage, like "dressing up" and hardly real. It was soon to become very real indeed.

On November 26, 1917, Ray and his comrades left Halifax, Nova Scotia, setting sail for Liverpool, where they arrived eleven days later. The following day, December 8, he arrived in Seaford, a small town in Sussex, where he joined the First Canadian Reserve battalion. For only the second time in his life, he spent Christmas without his mother, no doubt missing her but focused on his imminent dispatch across the English Channel. He left for the front on March 16, 1918.

The Canadians had been fighting since 1915 and had had a bloody time of it throughout 1917 in particular, first at Vimy Ridge and then Passchendaele. It had been a tough winter for the troops. With Russia's withdrawal, German divisions that had been on the Eastern Front were suddenly marching west, bristling with confidence. American troops were still being trained and Germany had the advantage. General Ludendorff decided to attack in what was expected to be a final, overwhelming push that would leave Germany victorious. Though the assault was well disguised, it was predictable: Germany had no choice but to make their move in the brief window between the end of the war with Russia and the arrival of the Americans. The Allies had been preparing for such an attack since late 1917.

Ray reached the front line just days before the big German push. He had, by this time, been absorbed into the Seventh Battalion, part of the First Division of the CEF. They were stationed on the front line at Lens, protecting Northern France's last accessible collieries and several communication centers. Ray had fond memories of France from his youthful visit, but the country he arrived in was not the one he knew. It had been scarred by battle, churned up, littered with the detritus of war. His arrival coincided with some unusually good weather, and he probably found himself involved in the construction of two hundred tunneled machine gun emplacements or the laying of the three hundred miles of barbed wire intended to protect the line.

When the attack came on March 21, the Canadians breathed a sigh of relief: the Germans struck at the Third and Fifth Armies to the south of the CEF lines. Still, they were far from safe, and Field Marshall Haig ordered them to take up the reserve positions ready to step in where the battles were most fierce and the stakes the highest. On March 23, the First Division was placed in First Army reserve and then, on March 27, they were moved again, this time to the Third Army reserve. It was through this series of moves that Ray found himself behind the lines, south of Arras, with his battalion stationed on either side of the Arras-Cambrai road.

Here, as the war continued nearby, Ray saw for the first time a new contraption that the Allies hoped would give them the advantage: the tank. The fighting that opened the war belonged to the nineteenth century. At that time, the generals thought the battle could be won with tactics that had served well in the past; but whereas in the Crimean War the Light Brigade had at least been able to reach the Russian guns in their cavalry charge, in 1914, an infantryman's rifle could pick off a horse at a range of a mile. Artillery could take out cavalry at three miles. The generals quickly learned that the old gambits would not work against the hailstorm of machine-gun fire.

By 1918, the practice of advancing troops in waves had been ditched in favor of small parties, darting from shell hole to shell hole, taking it in turns to provide covering fire. Ray and his fellow recruits in the Seventh had to learn these tactics; they had to get used to fighting alongside tanks and dealing with the realities of war.

As March became April, the Germans began to find that they were over-stretched, and hopes of a decisive victory fizzled out. The First Division was redeployed from the reserve position to the front line at Scarpe, where they relieved the British Fourth Division on April 8. The next day, the Germans launched a second massive offensive in Flanders, again missing the Canadian lines, but with gains in the south and increasing success in the north, the position of the Canadian Corps worsened. This was Ray's first real experience of being on the front line, and though he was lucky to escape the fiercest fighting, he found himself amid violence and danger. As the situation in Flanders intensified, the Canadians were left on a perilous salient that jutted into German territory. The only way they could survive, according to their commander, Lieutenant General Sir Arthur Currie, was to take an aggressive attitude.

Ray and his comrades raided the German trenches and witnessed artillery bombings and gas attacks. He would go on to describe his experiences in a descriptive writing exercise, "Trench Raid," in the 1930s. He portrayed rat-infested trenches with sometimes ad hoc defences—dirty sheets blocking dugout doorways offering scant protection from German gas:

> The strafe sounded a lot heavier than usual. The candle stuck on top of his tin hat guttered from something more than draught. The rats behind the dugout lining were still. But a tired man could sleep through it. . . . [Outside] the sky, in which the calendar called for a full moon, was white and blind with innumerable Verey lights, white and blond and diseased like a world gone leprous. The edge of the parados, lumpy with the dirt from a recent housecleaning, cut this whiteness like a line of crazy camels against an idiotic moonrise in a nightmare.[11]

Ray's battalion was on the front for a month, moving back behind the lines in May, but this brief period had a great impact on him. The endless noise and the constant anxiety about surviving the day, or even the hour, are unimaginable to those who did not go through it. He described the sheer exhaustion of listening for bombs:

> He began to concentrate on the shells. Always concentrate on the shells. If you heard them they never hit you. With a meticulous care he set himself to picking out the ones that would come near enough to be reckoned on as a possible introduction to immortality. To these he listened with a sort of cold exhausted passion until a flattening of the screech told him they had gone over to the support lines.[12]

The telling phrase "exhausted passion" reveals the sheer terror of it all. The passion to stay alive mixed with the exhaustion of the day-to-day monotony —the same fight-or-flight reactions to the same events, over and over again.

Eventually, Ray was promoted to sergeant, put in charge of a platoon, and expected to lead his men into battle and embody Lieutenant General Currie's "aggressive attitude." Despite taking part in frequent raids, he later claimed not to have been at all afraid:

> As a platoon commander very many years ago I never seemed to be afraid, and yet I have been afraid of the most insignificant risks. If you had to go over the top somehow all you seemed to think of was trying to keep the men spaced, in order to reduce casualties. It was always very difficult, especially if you had replacements or men who had been wounded. It's only human to want to bunch for companionship in face of heavy fire.[13]

It is interesting to see an expression of the practical side of his mind in a passage where he seems to suggest that he took comfort from following rules and procedures. As usual, though, when we read something Ray has written after the fact, and especially when it is addressed to a woman, we need to take into account his tendency to self-mythologize. In fact, some of his war stories are known to be unreliable. He once wrote:

> I know from my own knowledge that in the first world war [*sic*], during the final German retreat from the Hindenburg line the machine gun crews left behind to hold up the advance as long as possible were

almost always bayoneted to the last man, even though they rose up out of the ground and tried to surrender.[14]

But Ray was not part of the Allied push in the late summer of 1918, he had left to join the Royal Air Force. Frank MacShane's 1976 biography repeats another of Ray's tales:

> In June Chandler's service in France ended abruptly when an artillery barrage of eleven-inch German shells blew everyone up in his outfit, leaving him the sole survivor. The explosion concussed him, and he was taken behind the lines and shortly afterward was returned to England.[15]

This is a typical Ray story, one that casts him as a hero against all odds, and it is the sort of thing he liked to tell his fans. There are two problems with it, though: by June, Ray would have been part of the army reserves, well behind the front, where falling bombs, though not unheard of, were rare; and, more tellingly, his casualty form, the document that tracked his assignments, promotions, and injuries, makes no mention whatsoever of his being blown up and concussed.

That is not to say, however, that he did not witness some terrible things. What he saw affected him physically as well as mentally. A picture taken during his RAF training shows him to be sallow and hollow cheeked, like a walking ghost. His bright grin, familiar from earlier photographs, has lost its energy. Later he wrote:

> Once you have led a platoon into direct machine-gun fire, nothing is ever the same again.[16]

What he went through was horrific and changed him in a multitude of ways, some of which would not be evident for years. In 1918, he was definitely drinking, though it is not clear if he drank in the trenches. Alcohol was widely available, though, and many men turned to it to soothe their shredded nerves. In his play, *Journey's End*, R. C. Sheriff's character Stanhope, a once brave soldier, is dependent on alcohol to get through the day. It is impossible to know how many men traveled down this same path. Ray wrote to one friend:

When I was a young man in the RAF I would get so plastered that I had to crawl to bed on my hands and knees and at 7:30 the next morning I would be as blithe as a sparrow and howling for my breakfast. It is not in some ways the most desirable gift.[17]

It is possible—perhaps even likely—that it was during this period that the link between alcohol and relief was forged in Ray's mind.

By June Ray had made the decision to join the Royal Air Force. In some ways, it was inevitable that he, with his lingering fantasies of courtly gallantry would become a pilot—a so-called knight of the sky. Pilots of both sides were viewed as the noble jousters of the First World War, taking to the skies to do battle in gentlemanly fashion. When Manfred von Richthofen, the Red Baron, was shot down and killed on April 21, 1918, the Allied military authorities gave him a hero's funeral with full honors. Chandler would have been familiar with the buzz and swooping acrobatics of the Allied aircraft as they flew over the trenches on bombing raids and surveillance missions. He would also have seen dogfights taking place in the skies over the field of battle. Despite the Germans' faster-firing machine guns, the Royal Air Force (which had been known as the Royal Flying Corps until April 1918) often took the fight to them, reflecting a daredevil ethos. The Germans, though they recognized the value of air superiority, preferred to keep their aircraft in reserve and deploy them only when they might achieve the maximum effect.

When Ray watched Allied planes loop and buzz overhead, he must have wondered if any were piloted by his old friend Gordon Pascal. He had signed up to the RFC back in Canada. Apparently CEF recruits made fine pilots and one of the key players in the defeat of the Red Baron was a Canadian. Pascal's letters might have described a culture Ray recognized: that of the English public school. Here is a letter from one young pilot to his parents:

Last night I was just getting into my bed when a sponge full of water came along the room. At once the place was in a fine mess. I threw a jug of water, but the same was returned with interest. Next the place got so full of water that I ran into the garden, falling into a big hole full of mud. I managed to obtain two onions on my way back, and with these attacked the mob. All our beds were wet through. However, at last all got right again and we got our sleep. It was great sport.[18]

After signing up, Ray was sent to train in Waddington, near Lincolnshire. The training was dangerous in itself: of the 14,166 pilots who died in the First World War, more than half were killed in training. Ray got far enough into it to be able to fly an aircraft competently. It must have been exhilarating and a role to which he was, in his own odd way, well suited. Unlike fighting in the trenches, flying demanded isolation and self-sufficiency. A pilot was on his own in the sky, and it did not do for him to become too attached to his comrades.

In November 1918, Armistice came and the war ended. Ray's training was cut short and he returned to Canada, where he was demobbed in February 1919. It is not clear what he did immediately after, but it seems likely that he returned to Los Angeles.

In early 1919, he appears to have reached a decision that would have far-reaching consequences: he accepted that he had fallen in love with Cissy Pascal, his best friend's mother.

CHAPTER FIVE

RAYMIO

Cissy Pascal was the central figure in the second part of Ray's life, just as his mother had been in the first. Cissy, though, is more of an enigma than Florence, standing in the shadows, a shimmering presence refusing to be brought into the light and into focus.

She was born Pearl Eugenia Hurlburt in late 1870, probably in October, in Perry Lake, Ohio.[1] Her father, Eugene, was a carpenter and her mother, Maria, kept house. The family were peripatetic during the rest of that decade: they moved two states over to New Jersey, where Leona, Cissy's sister, was born in 1872; and, at some point after that, moved again, this time to Chester Valley in Pennsylvania, where Pearl's second sister, Lavinia, was born in 1879.

Pearl became a striking girl with beautiful red hair, a handsome face, and clear, bright eyes. She was also intelligent and grew up playing the piano, learning languages, and reading. Eventually, though, she kicked against the small-town environment of Chester Valley and in the early 1890s fled to New York City, where she settled in fashionable, bohemian Harlem.

According to an 1893 edition of the *Harlem Monthly Magazine*, "the center of fashion, wealth, culture, and intelligence, must, in the near future, be found in the ancient and honorable village of Harlem."[2] The extension of the elevated railroad and the promise of the Lexington Avenue subway expansion prompted builders to throw up prefabricated houses and apartment buildings in the area. When Pearl arrived, she would have seen polo fields on the site where the New York Giants later built a stadium, and heard piano music playing in almost every bar.

She took an apartment in a red brick building at 333 Lenox Avenue, close to the Apollo Theater. There, her first act was to ditch the name Pearl (too provincial), in favor of a new, sophisticated, more cosmopolitan moniker: Cissy.

Cissy had an interest in art and so sought work as a model, posing for artists across the city. She quickly became absorbed into their world, a fact that Ray would make much of after they were married. Only one photograph remains from this period of Cissy's life. It shows her styled as a Greek goddess, posing atop a low table with a rather dull fleur-de-lis background. Her hair seems darker in this picture than it would in later years, but the small-set mouth is recognizable. She looks remarkably attractive.

It is difficult to separate fact from fiction in Cissy's life story. Most of the rumors about her seem to emerge in the 1940s, and it may be that Ray was trying to add spice to her biography. One such rumor was that she made a nude appearance in a painting hanging in a New York hotel, but if this is true, no one has been able to track the picture down. Ray also claimed to carry a naked photograph of her in his pocket. There were stories about Cissy indulging in opium at wild parties as a young woman, and New York was certainly the kind of place where she might have done so.

Cissy married a man called Leon Brown Porcher on December 28, 1897. With his deep brown eyes and thick black hair he was rather handsome. Porcher worked as a traveling salesman and was a native of New York City. He was twenty-one when they married, six years younger than Cissy, although she was at the time claiming to be only twenty-three herself, presaging a later habit of obfuscating her age. Ray never wrote or spoke on record about this early marriage of Cissy's, but he certainly knew about it, and he kept the marriage certificate until his death.

The ceremony took place at the Church of the Transfiguration, an Italianate building nestled on Twenty-Ninth Street between Fifth and Madison Avenues. This choice of venue might be telling: it was a church famous for marrying runaways, actors, artists, and the poor. Founded in 1848 by the Reverend Dr. George Hendric Houghton, it always welcomed the poor and the needy, and gave shelter to African Americans during the Civil War. Its association with the theater began in 1870 when the rector of a nearby church refused to perform a funeral service for an actor called George Holland—actors at the time were social outcasts—but suggested that "the little church around the corner" probably would. Joseph Jefferson, a fellow actor who was trying to organize Holland's funeral, exclaimed, "God bless the little church around the corner," and the nickname stuck ever after.[3] In 1914, P. G. Wodehouse would marry there, and afterwards, used it as a setting for several weddings in his fiction. He celebrated the Little Church Around the Corner and its willingness to marry the young and rash in this lyric:

> Dear little, dear little Church 'Round the Corner
> Where so many lives have begun,
> Where folks without money see nothing that's funny
> In two living cheaper than one.

Cissy and Leon's wedding was strange and clandestine. On the marriage documents, both listed their home addresses as those of their parents, while Cissy took things a step further, listing her parents under her mother's maiden name, Gray. Lastly, the two witnesses to the marriage—Howard Burton and Fanny Gettings—also witnessed several other weddings in the preceding weeks, suggesting they were habitual witnesses at impetuous, unplanned weddings.[4]

By 1900, the Porchers had settled in the city and had a small apartment on West 138th Street. Leon took a more settled job as a clerk in an insurance firm while Cissy kept house. The marriage did not last long, however; after seven years, they divorced. The agreement stated that Leon had not "appeared, answered, or demured to the complaint" and goes on to say that Cissy was legally entitled to remarry as if Leon were dead, whereas he was unable to marry until Cissy actually was dead, suggesting that she was the injured party. With that document, Cissy was free to marry again. Leon Porcher seems to have stayed in New York, where he did well, becoming an office manager, before being called up to fight in the First World War. There is no record of him after that.

Six years after her divorce, Cissy was living a few streets away from her first marital home, on West 135th Street. She kept her ex-husband's name, though she would have been legally entitled to revert to her maiden name, and shared a flat with a nurse called Elizabeth Foley, also divorced. Cissy had decided to pursue a career in art and, in the 1910 census, lists her occupation as watercolorist. It cannot have brought in much money.

A few months later, she left Manhattan to marry another young man. Julian Pascal was born in Barbados in the late 1860s or early 1870s to an English father and a white West Indian mother.[5] They gave him the name Goodridge Bowen but he changed it to Julian Pascal. He was a talented pianist. His reputation grew across the island, and he began to consider moving away to work in America or Europe. In 1892, he married an older, very beautiful Englishwoman called Annette, possibly in England. Certainly this is where their children, Gordon and Elsa, were born. Later, following Julian's career, they moved to New York City, where he had considerable success as a teacher and performer. He was quite an attraction in society, playing private concerts in several Fifth Avenue drawing rooms. He also played for charity and gave concerts at the Bowery Mission, where a favorite seems to have been "My Dearie," sung by Edward Strong to Pascal's accompaniment.[6]

After a time, Julian and Annette divorced, and she set up home with her children on East Nineteenth Street. It is not clear why the marriage ended, but Annette severed all ties with Barbados, and when she applied for a passport in 1915, rather than admit to being divorced, told authorities that her husband had been killed in the war. In fact, he had moved to West 135th Street, no more than a block or two from Cissy.

Cissy already had some musical training, and it is possible that the couple met because she wanted him to teach her the piano. The successful musician from Barbados must have cut an attractive, glamorous figure. They had a quick romance which led to an early engagement. This time, she did not want to keep her marriage a secret, and the event took place in Greenwich, Connecticut, on April 15, 1911, overseen by one Truman R. Radget. This was no childish elopement, and Cissy, keen to make up for her earlier, hasty marriage, asked her mother, Maria, to witness the event. The newlyweds did not stay in Greenwich for long and within a year had left New York for California. Various reasons have been put forward for their move, including that Cissy hoped to become an actress in Hollywood, and perhaps this formed part of their motivation. But one contemporary source gives a convincing argument that they moved for Cissy's health.[7]

The musical circles Cissy and Julian mixed in soon led them to Ray's friends, the Lloyd family, who introduced them to the rest of the Optimists. Julian and Annette's son, Gordon, wanted to work as an actor and followed his father to California a few months later, where he also found himself part of the group. It seems that there were natural pairings among the Optimists: Cissy and Florence got along easily together, as did Ray and Gordon. Warren and Julian were keen chess players, and on Sunday afternoons, silence descended on the house as the two men faced one another over the chess board.

This is how things continued in Los Angeles until 1917 when Gordon and Ray signed up to fight in the war. When the young men went to Europe, the Pascals welcomed Florence into their home, and amid the constant worry, the two women seem to have become close. It is unlikely that Florence knew the workings of her son's heart, and his return to America, though very welcome, was no doubt marred by the revelation that he was in love with Cissy. For her part, Cissy seems to have responded in kind. She was overheard saying that though she loved Julian, she loved Ray more.

While the news understandably led to tensions between Florence and the Pascals, the Lloyds seem to have taken it in their stride and encouraged Ray, Cissy, and Julian to talk things through. Eventually, Cissy and Julian agreed to divorce. Surprisingly, Ray did not remain in Los Angeles during the proceedings and instead headed first to Seattle, where he spent time with an old army buddy, and then to San Francisco, where he took a job in a bank. It has always been assumed that, after the war, Ray was reluctant to return to Los Angeles and stayed out of the city in an effort to quell his romantic feelings for Cissy, not returning before Christmas. Cissy, however, initiated divorce proceedings in the summer of 1919, with an early agreement reached in September, suggesting that she and Ray had started their relationship shortly after his return from Europe.

The terms of the Pascals' separation favored Cissy. She was allocated an allowance of one hundred dollars a month along with all of the furniture in the household, except what was in Julian's studio, and one half of the couple's war bonds. Julian did not appear in court to hear the settlement read.[8] Was their separation then as amicable as has previously been suggested? Ray's own departure from Los Angeles may be best explained by his wish to avoid antagonizing his former friends during a difficult divorce.

Ray spent only a short time in San Francisco. He was not suited to a career in banking, and having worked in two establishments (the Anglo and London Paris National Bank and then, later, the Bank of British North America), he decided that he did not have the correct temperament for the industry. In particular, he objected to working with the English people who staffed the banks, finding their sort of Anglophilia tiring and objectionable, which seems, perhaps, a little odd, given his own British affectations.

Throughout this period he continued to write. He almost sold a pastiche of Henry James to the *Atlantic*—how frustrating it must have been to have come so close—but it was poetry that consumed him, much of it addressed to, or directed at, Cissy. Between 1919 and 1920, Ray wrote her several poems, one of which, "Lines with an Incense Burner," was a Christmas gift in 1919. It reveals much about the tenor of their relationship. The poem compares the speaker's memory to prayers and other religious utterances:

> Of such my memory is, of such my vision,
> Of faint, sweet things that time will not put by,
> The secret and the silence and the perfume
> Of dreams long wither'd that will never die.[9]

His love is figured as religious devotion to its subject, a frame of reverence that was a regular feature of Ray's poems for Cissy, cropping up time and again. In "Erotic," for example, during an imagined postcoital embrace, the speaker confesses that "a song without music is aflame in my soul," which casts the experience in a holy light. Meanwhile, "Improvisation: Vistas" features a moment of pure obedience when the narrator, imagining himself in various guises including as a man of power, submits himself to a goddess-like woman:

> Still would I come to your presence
> And kneel in the way of your footsteps,
> Gazing into your eyes

> For the things you have not said,
> Seeking the touch of your fingers . . .

Other poems written during this period suggest that Ray was struggling with his separation from Cissy. In an untitled poem, the narrator's world is left in black and white without the woman he loves to add color:

> I have seen wonderful valleys . . .
> I have seen white statues aglimmer . . .
> But all these visions were lonely,
> Lacking the words you would say of them,
> The glances your eyes would give to them . . .

Not only was Cissy to be worshipped, but she was now viewed as a vital part of Ray's existence. Having left his job in San Francisco, he headed back to Los Angeles to be with the subject of his poetry. There was one obstacle, though: Florence Chandler.

Florence was furious when she learned of Ray's love for Cissy. Having lived with the Pascals, she may have looked on Cissy as more her friend than Ray's. Florence and Cissy were certainly similar in age, with approximately nine years between them, as opposed to the eighteen between Cissy and Ray.

Considering their respective ages, it is tempting to leap to the conclusion that Ray had fallen in love with a substitute for his mother. Florence and Cissy had both been through similar experiences, had seen loved ones go to war, and been divorced after failed marriages in their twenties, afterward living with the social stigma. And they were both intelligent women who had no doubt been underestimated by the men in their lives. But they were also very different. Despite their similar ages, they were of different generations. Florence Chandler was a Victorian at heart, albeit a rebellious one. In Los Angeles, where clothing was notoriously loose and the body was often on display, she wore the dark uniform of the Victorian *mater familias*: a long black dress, an unflattering velvet bodice, and for outings, a wide-brimmed black hat. Cissy, on the other hand, was a runaway and a bohemian—a twentieth-century woman. She was a beautiful redhead with clear white skin, almost like porcelain, and the shapely, firm body of a much younger woman. She dressed to show her femininity and like modern Californians, Cissy took toning her body seriously, and what is more, did so naked.

The Mensendieck System of Functional Exercises was the busy woman's dream because it allowed her to exercise while doing everyday tasks like ironing, vacuuming, and dusting. American Bess Mensendieck invented the method while living in Paris and studying art in the late 1800s. She was so appalled by the posture of the models she was supposed to draw that she took up anatomy instead. Her method took everyday movements and turned them into a fitness regime. She produced a book full of illustrated routines, which the body-conscious Germans were first to publish. Soon, women across Europe were carrying out household chores naked to allow maximum freedom of movement, using the toning exercises prescribed to shape their bodies. Cissy may have picked up the method in New York, and in California she was a committed practitioner. Ray certainly noticed her doing the housework nude.[10]

Ray would later claim that he rescued Cissy from an unhappy marriage, but because Cissy's point of view is not recorded anywhere, his assertions are the only evidence. He was undeniably attracted to her sexy sophistication but there must have been more to their relationship than this. Ray was a handsome war veteran and an eligible bachelor. The Lloyds may have had hopes that he would marry their daughter, but instead, he chose to romance a woman a good deal older than he was. Was there something specific about her maturity that appealed to him? Cissy was at an age where menopause was setting in and her body and sex drive were changing. She would almost certainly have been unable to bear children. To Ray, whose own attitude to sex was complicated, this may have made Cissy seem much less threatening or demanding and, in an odd way, purer. At the same time, it also offered the possibility of a guiding, experienced hand to counter his own sexual innocence.

But what did Cissy see in Ray? He was handsome but sexually confused. The English public school system had marked him ("devastated him," one friend said[11]) with an aversion to sex and he was, in all probability, in 1919 at the age of thirty-one, still a virgin. But he was charming, wrote poetry, and spoke in anglicized Americanisms, which must have lent him a patina of exoticism and sophistication. He was certainly nothing like either of Cissy's previous husbands. Perhaps his most attractive quality was the flipside of what attracted him to her: he was a man who still lived with his mother and whom she would have to guide through their courtship. For the first time, she would be in charge.

It is likely that she took the lead in the escalation of their romance. Though Ray was smitten with her and had told her how he felt, would he have had the confidence to kiss Cissy on the mouth for the first time? In his novels, Marlowe is often the recipient of kisses, but rarely the active party. For example, in both *The Big Sleep* ("She put her hands up and took hold of my head and kissed me hard on the lips") and *The Long Goodbye* ("She pressed herself hard up against me and her hair brushed my face. Her mouth came up to be kissed"), it is often women who initiate sexual contact.

Cissy and Julian were formally divorced in October 1920, by which time Cissy was living on her own several blocks west of the Chandlers, who had moved to 1507 South Figuero. She and Ray must have seen each other regularly during this period, at either the Lloyds' or in restaurants, where they would have been chaperoned. Pictures from this time show Ray happy and relaxed, enjoying the Southern California lifestyle. In one, he is lying on the beach in a striped swimming costume, grinning. But there were still clearly tensions with his mother. Another picture taken around the same time shows a happy Ray lying in the shade of a tree, his tie loosened, enjoying a pipe, while Florence sits leaning up against the trunk in a black Victorian dress, complete with a cloche hat. She looks as if she is from another world, let alone another generation. These tensions showed no sign of easing either, for Ray was committed to Cissy and his code of conduct would never allow him to renege on his promise to her.

Ray was about to enter an extraordinary period of his life in Los Angeles: he was living and working downtown and, though he did not yet appreciate it, was at the center of one of the world's most exciting cities. From then on, he would absorb Los Angeles like a sponge, picking up its atmosphere and peculiarities. He also benefited from the proximity of friends like William Lever, whom he had met during his training with the Canadian Expeditionary Force. Lever was now back in the city working as a cutter in a shoe factory and living near the Los Angeles Creamery offices in lodgings on South Olive Street. He and Ray grew particularly close during this period, and Ray must have relished being able to escape Florence and enjoy the company of someone nearer his own age and outlook.

Now that Cissy was divorced from Julian, married or not, she was Ray's responsibility. It became increasingly clear that his Los Angeles Creamery salary was not going to be enough to support both Cissy and Florence. He managed to survive on it for two years, but the strain soon became too much, so he approached Warren Lloyd for advice. In many ways, Ray could not have timed things better, because in the early 1920s, Los Angeles suddenly found itself at the very center of an oil boom.

Gasoline was originally a cheap by-product of the oil-refining process. It was used as a solvent for cooking stoves while coal was used to power engines. Things changed at the turn of the century when western railways ditched the coal-fired steam engine in favor of one that burnt oil, leading to even more fuel oil finding its way into the homes of millions. An even bigger change came with the popularity of the motor car, which needed gasoline to power its engine. "Gas" quickly went from a minor by-product to being the primary reason for drilling, pumping, and refining oil. In 1899, there were only eight thousand cars in the United States; by 1919, there were nearly eight million, and they accounted for 85 percent of all gasoline used.[12] This was great news for the city of Los Angeles because, in 1920, it was discovered that Southern California sat atop vast reserves of oil. The first strikes came at Huntington Beach. Standard Oil had drilled a series of speculative "wildcat wells" in an area not previously known to hold oil, and one of them, on Reservoir Hill, struck a modest deposit that produced forty barrels a day. This was quickly followed by a much more significant strike at a site on the edge of the Gospel Swamp peat bogs. It started with an explosion that was heard fifteen miles away, and with that, the well roared into life, producing an initial flow of twenty thousand barrels a day. Five months later, at Royal Shell's Signal Hill site, a low rumble preceded a massive spurt of flowing oil that reached 114 feet in the air. The Californian oil rush was on.

Signal Hill soon became dotted with oil derricks, earning it the nickname Porcupine Hill. Everyone wanted to get into the game. Derricks started to spring up across the southern part of the state, appearing in the most unlikely of places, including backyards. People started speculatively buying up lots with the hope of leasing them or selling them to oil companies, turning oil into cash without the trouble of drilling for it. One encyclopedia company even gave away plots of land close to oil deposits with their books as a sales gimmick. This was oil fever.

The Lloyds had a hand in the Southern Californian oil industry from the start. Warren Lloyd's father, Lewis M. Lloyd, was involved with a company called the Ventura Land & Water Company and, in 1913, had drilled for oil in the Simi Valley, at a ranch owned by the company. Later, Lewis Lloyd and his son Ralph, Warren's brother, formed a partnership with Joseph B. Dabney and created a company called the Dabney Oil Syndicate. Born in Iowa in 1858, Dabney was an extraordinary character with a reputation for putting in wildcat wells that paid off and struck oil. Their lands in Ventura County, despite early failures, produced very generous royalties once they were leased out to larger producers.

Warren Lloyd, knowing that Dabney needed a bookkeeper, put Ray forward for the job. He joined the company in 1922, working at their offices on Olive, at the Bank of Italy building, not far from the Los Angeles Creamery office. He spent some days at the Signal Hill oilfields but was usually downtown at the center of the action in a city where oil was everything.

Ray enjoyed this job. For someone who had never previously settled in a career, this must have been a pleasant surprise. The sort of lead-footed drudgery that had turned him off the idea of writing serials in London was nowhere to be found in the oil industry. For the first time, he found that the assortment of skills he had picked up over the years had value, especially his facility with numbers.

Ray's happiness was marred, in August 1922, by the sudden death of Warren Lloyd. It came as a huge shock to everyone, not least because the event that led to his death was a mere shaving cut. The cut became infected with septicemia,[13] and Lloyd was taken to the Good Samaritan Hospital, where after a six-day illness, he died. Ray's greatest supporter and close friend was no more. First his father and now Lloyd—the emotional impact of being "abandoned" by these influential men was enormous, and it forms one of the most consistent themes in Ray's work. The event that energizes the plot of *The Big Sleep* is the disappearance of Rusty Regan, and late in the novel, Ray has the General express the pain of being left behind:

I'll pay you another thousand dollars to find Rusty. He doesn't have to come back. I don't even have to know where he is. A man has a right to live his own life. I don't blame him for walking out on my daughter, nor even for going so abruptly. It was probably a sudden impulse. I want to know that he is all right wherever he is. I want to know it from him directly, and if he should happen to need money, I want him to have that also. Am I clear? . . . I guess I'm a sentimental old goat . . . And no soldier at all. I took a fancy to that boy. He seemed pretty clean to me. I must be a little too vain about my judgment of character. Find him for me, Marlowe. Find him.

This is a man yearning for a son-in-law who has become a true son to him. It is a scene that only Ray could write. He would later come back to these emotions in *Farewell, My Lovely*, where Marlowe talks openly about his "strange" liking for Moose Molloy, in a scene that has often been taken as hinting at repressed homosexuality. Marlowe seems to constantly hanker after a real connection with another man and regrets that such a thing seems impossible to achieve. In Marlowe's experience, male friends always leave or betray him, as is made most clear in *The Long Goodbye*. In this late novel Marlowe really does seem to have made a friend in Terry Lennox, but in the end, Lennox double-crosses Marlowe, finishing their relationship.

To get over the loss of Warren Lloyd, Ray threw himself into his work. He was promoted rapidly, though some of his success was due to sharp eyes and good fortune. Very early in his career he showed the strength of his moral code—which would later be echoed in the character of Marlowe—when, in October 1923, Ray stumbled on an internal scandal.[14] The company's auditor, W. A. Bartlett, was embezzling funds, and Ray blew the whistle on him, leading to Bartlett's arrest. He had squirreled away some $30,000 of company money. If he didn't know who Raymond Chandler was already, Dabney certainly did after this. Ray later claimed that he was involved with the prosecution team, prompting the DA to ask the right questions ("The damn fool didn't know his own case").[15] Ray was rewarded with the post of assistant to the new external auditor, John Ballantine. The two men got on well, their affable relationship in some part boosted by the fact that the older man was, like Ray, an outsider in Los Angeles, and a Scot at that, who understood and sympathized with some of Ray's idiosyncracies.

Even as Ray's oil career was taking off, his mother's health was rapidly declining. She had cancer. Florence was very ill throughout 1923 and died on September 26. It was a gruesome ordeal for Ray, who watched her die slowly over a period of ten hours. She had been given enough morphine to both kill the pain and end her life. She was unconscious throughout. She had been the one constant in Ray's life, and regardless of any tensions between them, he loved her. He had always tried to protect her, first from Maurice Chandler, and later from her own mother, but in the end, Ray was helpless to prevent her dying. He made few references to her death in writing, but in a letter to his literary agent in December 1950, he said: "how much better if it took two seconds—if it had to be anyhow?" He found dealing with the loss difficult and turned to Cissy for support. Florence was cremated the day after she died.

It took several months for Ray to come to terms with his mother's death. He moved from the house he had shared with Florence to 723 Stewart Street, and eventually, with Florence no longer able to object, Ray and Cissy married. The ceremony took place on February 6, 1924, overseen by Carl S. Paton, a local minister, with Cissy's sister Lavinia as witness. It must have been a small event attended by work colleagues, friends from the war, and possibly Alma Lloyd. It was Ray's first marriage and Cissy's third. Characteristically, she knocked a decade off her age, telling the pastor she was forty-three. By now, Ray was thirty-five, and we have to wonder whether he knew how old Cissy really was. Years later, in an act of generosity, he would echo her action at their wedding, changing the year of her birth on her death certificate to maintain the lie.

The newlyweds moved to 2863 Leeward Avenue, where it is possible that Cissy was already living, and set up home together. Their marriage was certainly unusual. Cissy, who may have entered or passed through menopause, had a waning appetite for sex. Ray, on the other hand, was in quite the opposite situation. Cissy was probably the first woman he ever took to bed, and she would have had to guide him through the basics as he finally indulged an urge he had suppressed for so long. Cissy certainly tried to *be* sexy during their marriage, dressing in the clothes of a younger woman and making sure that their bedroom was an overstuffed, overtly feminine pink boudoir—the sort of thing that might have come straight out of the movies. Ray always described his wife as "pretty hot" and "highly sexed" but what did "hot" mean to a man who, in his friend John Houseman's description, was "sexually devastated" by his schooling? On the few occasions that Ray describes his and Cissy's sex life, veneration was more apparent than lust:

> You can never cheapen a woman. No man of my sort thinks of her exactly as she thinks of herself. After all, her body is to her a familiar thing; but to some men it is always a sort of shrine.[16]

Before his death Ray wrote a column on sex for the *San Diego Tribune*, and in it he goes yet further:

> After thirty years of marriage, I suppose I should understand this— but somehow I never thought about it [sex] in those [biological] terms. . . . If you love a woman as completely and forever, as I did, you somehow don't think of it in that way. You think only of the wonder and the glory . . .[17]

Ray's poetry written around this time expresses a similar sentiment, but at the same time, it suggest that sex might even be threatening. A second poem titled "Erotic," presented to Cissy after their marriage, demonstrates this:

> Kiss me again with lips too lazy . . .
> Then hold me still in the deep of the pillow,
> Suddenly solemn, and half-afraid.

On balance, it seems likely that sex was a very minor element in their relationship. More prominent was romance, in which they indulged whole-heartedly. Cissy gave Ray the nickname "Raymio" very early on, and this fixes him as the sort of chivalrous hero he had always wanted to be. They also spent a lot of time on "dates," often at supper clubs where they would have dinner and dance, courting like a much younger couple.

At this stage of their lives they could afford to live well because even though they rented and Ray was parsimonious with money, he had been promoted at work. This came about, unfortunately, when the Scottish auditor

John Ballantine had a heart attack at the office and died. Ray had to call the police and was involved with the paperwork surrounding his colleague's death. After the funeral, Ray was appointed chief auditor of the company, and his career continued to develop quickly. It gave him the opportunity to observe the fascinating and often dark business world of Los Angeles that he would eventually document in his stories and novels. At the Bank of Italy building, he quietly soaked up the atmosphere, the characters, and the milieu.

Los Angeles in the 1920s was a dark place, where the seeds of hard-boiled fiction found fertile soil. America was undergoing a second revolution and Los Angeles took a leading part. The 1920s were an age of dangerously short-skirted flappers, wild parties, automobiles, and, beginning on January 16, 1920, illegal alcohol. Hollywood stars like Clara Bow set an example of casual sex, free drinking, and frequent parties, all of which was recorded and disseminated in a new invention, the tabloid newspaper. It was "the greatest, gaudiest spree in history," according to F. Scott Fitzgerald.[18]

Los Angeles, having sprouted out of the desert, was not just the trail-blazer, but also the most at risk. The city was in such a hurry to *be* that the institutions to protect it and its citizens could not be established quickly enough to keep up with the rapid growth. Despite being illegal, alcohol was freely available in the city's speakeasies, underground bars, and backstreet stores, whether home-brewed or smuggled. Prostitution was rife, and more girls arrived day after day in the hope of seeing their names in Hollywood's lights, only to provide ripe fodder for pimps when their dreams failed. Gambling was common throughout the city until it also became illegal, at which time it moved just beyond city limits, still very much within reach.

At the heart of these criminal enterprises were a group of underworld bosses—a syndicate—who went about their business with a low profile. These men were the real rulers of Los Angeles, and though the individuals that made up the syndicate may have been anonymous, its existence was common knowledge, and it was referred to as "The System." This group of powerful men controlled the police and would get officers to help collect the "take"—the tax the underworld bosses creamed off criminal enterprises in their areas. They controlled Los Angeles's politics, and in 1921, Charlie Crawford, a System kingpin, conspired to get George Cryer elected mayor of the city. He kept him in office until 1929. A man under the System's protection could literally get away with murder. "It was the most lucrative, the most efficient, and the best-entrenched graft operation in the country," according to a contemporary journalist.[19] It was little wonder that wide-eyed Midwesterners who had come to Los Angeles seeking a better life quickly became disillusioned.

One of the biggest scams of the age—and one that would touch Ray directly—was the Julian Petroleum scandal. It began in 1921 when a young man called Courtney Chauncey Julian arrived in Los Angeles and failed, at first, to strike it rich. He was a penniless Canadian with plenty of ambition and, like everyone else in the early 1920s in Southern California, a fascination with oil. He started out in the city selling leases on oil properties, but when that venture did not work out, he took out leases himself and, in 1922, started to construct a series of wildcat wells in Sante Fe Springs. He needed money to fund their construction and decided to take advantage of oil fever by purchasing a series of advertisements in local newspapers. Julian would prove to be a genius at enticing small-time investors to his cause, deploying folksy turns of phrase to bring in the dollars. One of his most famous ads ran in big bold type:

Julian Refuses to Accept Your Money Unless You Can Afford to Lose! Widows and Orphans, This Is No Investment for You!

Angelenos in the 1920s regularly displayed a desire to get as rich as possible, as quickly as possible, with the least amount of effort, and Julian's ads, which soon became part of the daily fabric of Los Angeles life, appealed precisely to those people. But Los Angeles was also full of Midwestern hopefuls who had come to the city hoping for a better, easier life, and the ads, with their insistence on hard work and determination, tempted them, too:

Come on, folks, you'll never make a thin dime just lookin' on. I've got a surefire winner this time, a thousand to one shot. We just can't lose. We're all out here in California where the gushers are and we just ought to clean up. Come on, folks, get aboard for the big ride.

The money came rolling in. Julian went on to take out advertisements showing just how much: "Sixty thousand dollars in six days," read one, "seventy thousand dollars in seven days," read another the following day. When all four Sante Fe Springs drills seemed to come up as gushers, his appeal increased all the more and Angelenos bought into Julian in droves. It helped of course that, at first, he could pay out profits on their investments. The oil was coming in—Julian expanded his drilling operation—and being sold on profitably. Julian was a Hollywood celebrity in his own right, and when he got into a spat with Charlie Chaplin that ended with the latter knocking Julian down, the event made the papers.

Capitalizing on his appeal to the little man, Julian Petroleum even opened up a series of gas stations cleverly named "Defiance." But something was terribly wrong with "Julian Pete": there was just not enough money coming in from the sale of oil to keep Julian's promises to his investors. He took a similar approach to Charles Ponzi and, more recently, Bernie Madoff, using newly acquired investment money to pay out "profits" to earlier investors. In other words, C. C. Julian had to keep selling stock to keep paying out.

In 1925, Julian Pete was taken over by S. C. Lewis, a lawyer from Texas, and his sidekick, Jake Berman, who was also known as Jack Bennett, "the boy Ponzi of the Pacific coast." They saw a golden opportunity to make a fast buck at the expense of hundreds of thousands of investors and quickly got rid of Julian himself, shifting the fraud into a higher gear. They started to take over brokerage houses, which would then falsely sell shares and stock. They also created "rings" of investors, starting with the wealthy and riding on their names to encourage other, smaller investors. In the end, something like forty thousand people from Los Angeles, in all walks of life, invested in Julian Pete. Guy Finney, a journalist in Los Angeles, wrote of these investors:

> They knew their city was galloping at dizzying speed. The easy money carnival spirit gripped them. They sang it from every real estate and stock peddling platform, in every glittering club and cafe, in bands and at newsstands. . . . The dollar sign was on parade. Why marvel then that like epidemic measles among the young it spread from banker to broker to merchant to clerk to stenographer to scrubwoman to office boy, to the man who carried his dinner pail. . . . The

mass craving wanted its honey on the table while the banquet was on. It simply couldn't wait a soberer day.[20]

The company kept getting bigger until Friday, May 6, 1927, when the bubble well and truly burst. Trading of stock was suspended when an audit finally revealed that Julian Pete had overissued its stock, with the result that, overnight, thousands lost their savings. Los Angeles's residents woke up to find that they had been fleeced out of $150 million and all of Julian Petroleum's Midwestern, folksy honesty had been a con.

The citizens were furious and wanted blood, but in Los Angeles, even cons this large could be swept under the carpet. A grand jury issued indictments against Lewis, Berman, and several others, but when the district attorney, Asa Keyes, finally got them before a judge and jury in January 1928, he shocked everybody by recommending the charge be dropped. A scandal ensued that would eventually lead to Keyes losing his position after twenty-four years as a public servant.

Two of Julian Pete's victims were Raymond Chandler and his good friend William Lever. When the company was consolidated into the Sunset Pacific Company, they both received shares, but Ray wrote in the 1930s, "the stock is not dealt in and can hardly <u>ever</u> produce a value beyond the mortgage indebtedness of the company. The oild [*sic*] business in California has long since passed the sudden wealth stage."[21] It was not the only time that Ray's life would be touched by Julian—more of that later—and goes to show that even intelligent, well-connected men who knew the industry could be victims of such a con. When he came to write about the city, Ray would use this corrupt, get-rich-quick world as a backdrop.

Another scandal to hit Los Angeles in the 1920s was that of Aimee Semple McPherson, a charismatic evangelical preacher, who established the Angelus Temple at a cost of $1.5 million. It was a remarkable building with five thousand seats and a $75,000 broadcasting suite. McPherson was an extraordinary woman who captured the imagination of thousands of Angelenos with her beguiling sermons that were as much entertainment as theological exposition. In one, she chased the Devil around the stage with a pitchfork. In another, she acted out the destruction of Sodom and Gomorrah. In yet another, she rode around a crowd of worshippers on a Los Angeles Police Department motorbike, dressed in police uniform. This wonderful entertainment was delivered in her trademark husky voice with a distinct hint of sex, and she had a profound effect on her followers, whipping them into a frenzy. She had a reputation as a faith healer, and in a city where the second question after "Where are you from?" was "And how do you feel?" she found a willing audience. The men and women who had flocked to Los Angeles were hungry for God, and Aimee Semple McPherson was one of the many in a position to sate that hunger through her radio show and temple. And then, on May 18, 1926, she disappeared.

She had last been seen in a bathing suit on a beach near Ocean Park, and it was quickly assumed that she had drowned. Thousands gathered there to pay their respects to their vanished sister in God. A specially chartered plane flew over the site of her disappearance to drop flowers across the beach and water, and, on May 23, one ardent follower drowned in an attempt to find her body. Then, three days later, she reappeared in Arizona, claiming that she had been kidnapped and had walked for thirteen hours through the desert to escape her captors. The press lapped up her story, and her return to Los Angeles was as dramatic as her disappearance. She alighted from the train that brought her into the city on to a bed of roses, and one hundred thousand people lined the streets to cheer her as she drove through Los Angeles accompanied by a white-robed silver band, an escort of twenty cowboys, and squads of policemen.

The tabloid papers, which she courted, were fascinated and decided to examine her disappearance more closely. They traced her movements from her vanishing and discovered that, during her absence, she had been spotted in Carmel-by-the-Sea with a man, a former radio operator at her temple. McPherson was arrested, charged with having given false information designed to interfere with the orderly processes of the law, and placed on trial. But, as with Lewis and Berman, the charges were dropped, and she returned to her ministry.[22]

As in the Julian Pete scandal, it was the population of Los Angeles who felt the greatest disappointment in McPherson. They had been let down by those in whom they had placed their trust. Los Angeles, despite its perfect weather and its Edenic image, was exposed as dark and dangerous, a city whose leading lights could not be trusted.

There was concern, too, that the very institutions intended to protect the citizens were not fit for the purpose. The men behind the Julian Pete scandal escaped trial, as did Aimee Semple McPherson, and something else took place in February 1929 to compound the feeling among Los Angeles's citizens that their protectors were failing them. Though Ray was not personally involved in those events, they would reverberate through his fiction for the next two decades.[23]

In the early hours of February 17, 1929, police were called to Greystone in Beverly Hills, the home of Edward "Ned" Doheny Jr. The house was an imposing building that had been completed at great expense the year before as a gift from his father, the oil tycoon E. L. Doheny Sr. Its grounds contained several greenhouses, a sixty-foot swimming pool, badminton and tennis courts, and a waterfall that cascaded down an eighty-foot-high hillside to fill an artificial lake dotted with white water lilies. The interior was no less grand, with a two-lane bowling alley, a gymnasium, a walk-in fur and jewelery vault, a cinema, and a billiard room with a hidden bar that retracted behind a wall at the touch of a button. The mansion got its name from the three-foot-thick grey Indiana limestone walls which rose above Sunset Boulevard on a promontory giving magnificent views of the city and Santa Monica. This being Los Angeles, the house was built on oil profits, some legitimate, some more dubious.[24] What the police discovered that morning were the bodies of two men.

A young investigator from the district attorney's office, Leslie White, was sent to find out what had happened. The scene that he discovered was gruesome. The dead men lay in pools of their own blood in a luxurious bedroom. One, the owner of the house, Ned Doheny, had a bullet hole through his skull, running from ear to ear. He was on his back and his face was covered in blood. Hugh Plunkett, Ned's secretary, lay on his stomach with his brains spattered on the wall. He was holding a half-smoked cigarette in his hand, and when his body was moved, a .45 Colt revolver was found underneath him.

Doheny had been brought up as rich as Plunkett had been poor. Plunkett had worked in a garage owned by Doheney's wife's family, and they had met when the rich man came in to have the tires changed on one of his many cars. They eventually struck up an unlikely friendship. Plunkett became one of the family chauffeurs and signed up to fight in the First World War on the same day as Ned. On their return from Europe, Hugh helped oversee the construction of Greystone and became essential to Ned, signing checks and running his household. On the night of their deaths, Plunkett had turned up at Greystone and dragged Ned from his bed to have a conversation in a separate room. An hour or so later, gunshots were heard. According to witnesses, Plunkett had been behaving oddly for a few days but had refused to be admitted to a sanatorium. Ned had called his doctor to come and help persuade his secretary to be committed, but according to the doctor, when he arrived, Ned was already dead, and after the doctor had tried for several minutes to get into the room, Plunkett then took his own life.

This was the story supported by every witness in the house, family and staff alike, but something did not ring true to Leslie White. For one thing, there were powder burns on Ned's body, but not on Plunkett's, suggesting that while Ned had been shot from less than three feet away, the suicidal secretary had somehow managed to kill himself by firing from a greater distance. And then there was the half-burned cigarette which suggested Plunkett had died while smoking it, an implication at odds with the suicide theory. White was convinced that the story was the wrong way round—that Doheney was the killer and suicide case, not Plunkett—and confidently submitted his evidence to the DA, Buron Fitts. Fitts, however, was politically astute and knew not to cross a man as wealthy as E. L. Doheney. He decided that it would be wrong to dig too deep into the events of February 17, 1929. At a press conference he announced: "My office has concluded beyond all doubt that Hugh Plunkett, while insane, shot Ned Doheney and then turned the gun on himself." There was no inquest and no autopsy, and with that, the case was closed.[25]

For Ray, this summed up all that was wrong with Los Angeles. A terrible crime had been committed, and the blame for it had been laid at the door of an innocent man. Ray would have known it was a cover-up because, despite a day of sensational newspaper headlines, coverage stopped dead the following day. Doheney Senior's power ensured that. Years later, Ray and White would meet at a dinner for contributors to the pulp magazine *Black Mask*, the publication that had given Ray his first break, where White took a famous picture of Dashiell Hammett and Ray together at what was probably their only meeting. Ray had read White's book, *Me, Detective*, and would have sympathized when White wrote:

> I entered the district attorney's office with an "open mind"; I knew practically nothing about the complexities of a great office of that kind and I was hungry to learn. I soon found out that "we"—the dicks in the bureau—were no mere policemen. Some of our work was so involved with politics that it was vitally necessary to be constantly aware of the fact that we were part politician. We were hybrids— sired by law and "damned" by politics.[26]

The grisly events at Greystone leached into Chandler's books in several ways. There have been suggestions that White may have been one of the models for Marlowe, who, like White, was once one of the DA's investigators. The manor itself appears as the Sternwood residence in *The Big Sleep*, the location clearly recognisable from the description of Owen Taylor's journey. It is also reclothed in *Farewell, My Lovely* as the Grayle residence: "The house itself was not so much. It was smaller than Buckingham Palace, rather gray for California, and probably had fewer windows than the Chrysler Building." And the incident comes up again in yet another novel, *The High Window*, when Marlowe talks in great detail about "the Cassidy case," a thinly disguised version of what happened at Greystone. Marlowe neatly states one of Ray's great themes towards the end of this passage when he asks:

> Did you ever stop to think . . . that Cassidy's secretary might have had a mother or a sister or a sweetheart—or all three? That they had their pride and their faith and their love for a kid who was made out to be a drunken paranoiac because his boss's father had a hundred million dollars?

This expresses one of the central ideas of hard-boiled fiction: that the average guy gets suckered by the city. Los Angeles disenfranchises its people again and again because of politics, money, and the law. In the Julian Pete scandal, the Doheney-Plunkett murder, and the disappearance of Aimee Semple

McPherson, it was the little people who were conned, their dreams crushed, while the rich prospered. Ray wrote in *The Big Sleep* that in Los Angeles "the bright gardens had a haunted look, as though wild eyes were watching . . . from behind the bushes, as though the sunshine itself had a mysterious something in the light." That "thing" was the jaded, tarnished spirit of Los Angeles and its people. It was something Ray sensed, smelled, and tasted in the city's air.

Though the elements of his later literary success were beginning to coalesce, Ray remained, at this time, as far from being a writer as ever before. He was enjoying his life as an executive, his marriage, and his friends, and he continued to be promoted. In 1926, he felt flush enough to buy himself a Chrysler, which he and William Lever "broke in" together. By the late 1920s, he had risen to being "director of three companies and president of three," though, as he reminded people, he was "simply a high-priced employee."[27] He was a popular guy, always known in the office as Ray, never Mr. Chandler, and by his own account was thought of as "the best office staff in Los Angeles."[28] It seems he ran a fairly modern office, claiming that his "door was never closed."[29] He also paid his staff "higher salaries than they could have got anywhere else"[30] and this caused some conflict with senior management. Typically, Ray was adamant that his way was the best way, and two examples show how his determination drove company policy:

> I always somehow seemed to have a fight on my hands. At one time I employed six lawyers; some were good at one thing, some at another. Their bills always exasperated the Chairman; he said they were too high. I always paid them as rendered because they were not too high in the circumstances.[31]

Ray showed quite how determined he could be during one incident involving lawyers. His company was sued after a car crashed into a length of pipe sticking a long way out of a company truck on the road near Signal Hill. The driver and passengers of the car claimed that, contrary to the law, the pipe had not been illuminated by a red lantern, so they did not know how far it protruded. Ray, however, was sure that the lantern had been both present and illuminated; so when the insurance company said it wanted to settle because to defend the action would be too costly, he hit the roof. To Ray's mind, the only option was to fight the case in court, because the drivers and passengers were in the wrong. It offended his moral code to back down and let cheaters win. He told the insurers that his company would defend the case and, if it did not get their support, would sue them for costs. He wrote:

> We defended the action, with the best lawyer we knew, and we proved that the pipe trick had been properly lighted and then we brought in various bar men from Long Beach (it took money to find them, but it was worth it) and [proved] that they [ie, the drivers and passengers] had been thrown out of three bars. We won hands down, and the insurance company paid up immediately about a third of what they would have settled for, and as soon as they did this I canceled the policy and had it rewritten with another company.[32]

Fierce determination like this made Ray a success in business, but it is also interesting to see his moral code in practice: right and wrong were sharply defined in his world. His reaction on another occassion shows quite how strange he sometimes found the world of business:

> I knew a banker once from Aberdeen, Washington, who served two or three years in federal prison for making unsecured loans from the bank's funds to the ranchers on whom the bank's business was built. He was a perfectly honest man, he didn't make a cent out of what he did. . . . The banker undoubtedly broke the banking laws. He admitted it. But who was he defrauding? The stockholders of the bank? He was one himself and the others were all men of property in the neighborhood. The stock was not traded in. He was attempting by the only means he saw to keep the bank's source of income from collapsing. He was tried and convicted and the bank closed its doors. . . . There is something tragically wrong with a system of justice which can and does make criminals of honest men and can only convict gangsters and racketeers when they don't pay their income taxes.[33]

Business was inherently corrupt in Ray's eyes. It did not make much sense and he always believed that "big business left to itself will always be crooked."[34] This was not a statement born out of any left-wing beliefs but rather a frank recognition that, in Los Angeles, and America more generally, the institutions built to protect the citizenry were not up to scratch. He made a direct comparison in the early 1930s once Prohibition had been repealed:

> The typical racketeer is only very slightly different from the business man in many of the more tricky kinds of business such as oil, real estate, sports promotion, theatrical ventures, nightclubs and hotels and restaurants.[35]

It is a view of a perfect world corrupted, and one that Ray could only develop working in a city as strange as Los Angeles, where businessmen and criminals rubbed against each other daily, in plain view.

Ray's business life was on the up in the 1920s, but it was also during these years that he developed a serious alcohol problem. He had drunk heavily during the war, but somehow, drinking does not really seem to have affected his life until the mid- to late 1920s. At that time, heavy drinking became dependence and started to upset the balance of his life. There were probably many reasons why Ray drank: the memory of the war, perhaps; the pressure of work; but, in the end, alcohol was simply so much a part of the warp and weft of his life that dependence was practically inevitable. His father had been a drunk, and Ray himself had a high tolerance for drink, a dangerous combination of factors. He may have been able to escape alcoholism had he not been surrounded by booze, but drink was ever present.

For example, he would go to watch football games with "the Dabney gang"—Milton Philleo (treasurer), Louis Knight (insurance man), and Orville Evans (another colleague)—at the University of California Los Angeles (UCLA) or at the University of Southern California (USC). Sometimes he went up to Palo Alto or to Berkeley to watch the big game between Stanford and the University of California. These trips would always include plenty of hard drinking, but for Ray, liquor was not just part of the fun—it was essential if he was to relax in the company of other men.

Even tennis matches, a regular feature of life for the Dabney gang, involved drinking before, during, and after matches. Surrounded by young people, especially the attractive young wives of his friends, Ray found himself drinking more and more so as to be able to relax in their company. And herein lay the problem. While Ray's drinking usually reduced his inhibitions and allowed him to mingle more easily, as soon as he had had too much he could turn all too quickly from charmer to grump. Once, he turned up at Milton Philleo's home to play tennis but found that Philleo's wife, Evelyn, was unwell and that the game could not go ahead. Ray was disappointed, and it appears that drink made him act in a way he later regretted: he marched upstairs and tried to drag Evelyn from her bed, convinced she was putting it on so the couple could avoid him. Milton was understandably furious and insisted his friend leave the house immediately. Instead, Ray went to the living room, pulled out a gun and threatened to shoot himself. It was melo-dramatic, strange behavior—as typical of drunk Ray as it was at odds with his professional persona. The incident demonstrates that, despite his apparent self-control and success, he was finding life in the 1920s a strain.

Another point of tension was his marriage. Ray may have become aware of Cissy's real age once they were married. At the very least, he was aware that she was not as young as she claimed. In an early draft of one poem he tactlessly mentioned the age gap only to regret doing so, scribbling the inference out. Being surrounded by younger, attractive people can only have made the age gap more obvious to Ray. It was, of course, a vicious circle: he drank because he was troubled, and drinking put their relationship under further strain, which led to more drinking. Another colleague at Dabney, John Abrams, was sure that Ray was a loner who drank to forget about his home life: "At the annual oil and gas banquets of a thousand rollicking oil men at the Biltmore, Chandler was a shadowy figure, stinko drunk and hovering in the wings with a bevy of showgirls, a nuisance."[36]

The other women in Ray's life were no doubt enticing. Now sexually experienced, at least to a limited degree, and with an unusual erotic life with Cissy, he felt drawn to younger, more available women. The alcohol he con-sumed to get over his nerves before approaching them only made rejection more likely, which, in turn, just led to more drinking. Ray did have some suc-cess with women, though, and embarked on an affair with one of the Dabney Oil secretaries. It was a torrid liaison that may have been based more on a mutual problem with alcohol than any real attraction, romantic or sexual.

They were given away by shared absences from the office and meek, hungover reappearances.

Perhaps he had, after all, begun to think of Cissy more as a mother figure. She and Florence were of similar ages and the kind of relationship they offered—in which Ray played the part of devoted follower, a knightly savior, almost Galahad-like in his purity—was the same. The tabloid press was filled with stories of promiscuity and perhaps these began to influence his sense of missing out on life. Ray knew he was good-looking and yet it was not to his benefit. Years later, in *The Lady in the Lake*, he wrote: "You know how it is with marriage—any marriage. After a while a guy like me, common no-good guy like me, he wants to feel a leg. Maybe it's lousy, but that's the way it is."

Ray and Cissy had been moving house around Los Angeles every year, usually sticking to East Los Angeles, close to downtown. In 1929, they were living at 1024 South Highland Avenue. Ray's drinking put enormous pressure on their marriage, and by 1930, Cissy was sick of his boozing and absences. She was a tough, experienced woman, able to put up with a lot, but this was too much: she walked out and on March 3 a separation agreement was drawn up. The separation was not a divorce but a legal document which made clear that the couple had decided to live apart after "unfortunate differences had arisen."[37] The document each signed does not make it clear what these differences were but it is easy to see that the settlement was largely weighted in Cissy's favor, suggesting the fault was on Ray's side. The man for whom she had turned her back on Julian Pascal had chosen the bottle and other women over her. She got to keep the furniture, the car, and the revenues due from any of the three life insurance policies Ray had taken out. He also agreed to pay her $300 a month split into two portions of $150, which would continue until and unless Cissy remarried. It was a good deal for Cissy and allowed her to live alone and essentially continue with her life as before.

Ray, meanwhile, was on his own, and homeless. He checked into the Mayfair Hotel very close to his offices and started to drink even more heavily. He continued to work but at some point began to call Cissy repeatedly, threatening to jump from a window. Somehow, she talked him down from the ledge.

It is not clear how long the couple were separated, though the fact that they signed a Memorandum of Agreement shows that it was a serious breach, one that would most likely end in divorce. However Cissy did not give up on Ray completely. At some point, there was an emotional reconciliation between the two, and they found a way to live together again. There must have remained some bitterness between them, though. How could Cissy have lied to him about her age? And how could Ray turn into such a womanizer? What had happened to her Raymio? And Ray would not give up drinking.

Despite his alcoholism and marital problems, Ray's job at Dabney's seemed secure. He was a trusted employee, and in 1927, when the Julian scandal came back knocking on Dabney's door in the form of Arthur Loeb, it was Ray who was trusted to deal with it. Loeb was a fascinating character who, like both Ray and Dabney, had lost money investing in Julian Petroleum. However, his grudge against the company was made a lot more personal when, at a shareholders' meeting, his eye was gouged out during a struggle. Loeb was furious that nothing was being done about the Julian fallout and so found a top attorney in the form of Guy Crump, a former superior court judge, and tried to take it to trial. The two men presented their case to Ray, who almost immediately advised Dabney to join their cause. It led to a $15 million lawsuit being brought by a collection of Julian shareholders, including Loeb and Dabney, and would eventually lead to blackmail, murders, and kidnapping.[38] It is little wonder that when Ray turned to write about crime, he used the city of Los Angeles as his backdrop: he had witnessed it at its worst throughout the 1920s.

The case was filed on October 8, 1929, but other events would soon overtake the people involved. Three weeks later the United States was struck by a terrible financial crisis. Overnight, share values plummeted, heralding the arrival of the Great Depression. It was like a punch to the solar plexus for America. Confidence evaporated, bankers started to throw themselves from window ledges, and the country found itself in turmoil. That Ray survived this black period as a Dabney employee goes to show quite how useful he was to the company and to Joseph Dabney in particular. Personal problems, drinking, and womanizing could be forgiven, it seemed, as long as his work was good. But it was not to last.

Trouble hit Ray in 1931. John Abrams was a colleague at Dabney who took a particular dislike to him. Ray, it must be said, was no longer the affable and popular office manager. He had become increasingly rude to his expensive attorneys and sharp with his staff. Abrams took matters into his own hands and called Joseph Dabney to tell him what was really going on. Dabney asked Abrams to come up to his lake house, and he arrived to find the old man shirtless, his round belly sticking out prominently, his feet resting on the veranda rail. Abrams explained his grievances. As a result, Ray was given a warning. He considered suing Abrams for slander but, for whatever reason, could not bring a case together, perhaps because Abrams's accusations were too close to the mark. The warning did not alter Chandler's behavior, or satisfy his colleague, and a few months later, in June 1931, Ray was fired.[39]

Chandler was devastated. A couple of years later, he wrote to William Lever explaining that he had been "intrigued" out of the company. He did admit to a share of the blame, though, saying, "I tried to make a big business out of material that didn't warrant that kind of play," but ultimately felt personally let down by Joseph Dabney. Here, again, was a man whom Ray had respected and to whom he had grown attached, who had cruelly abandoned him:

> If Dabney had been a little bigger man I might have made him a figure in the oil business and I might have made myself a rich man. I had the ability to organize, but the old codger couldn't let the business get to a point where he couldn't understand it. Also as he got older his business judgment got worse and worse, until towards the end his success looked like a pure fluke rather than a result of any kind of ability. Towards the end his affairs got badly involved, his assets frozen up, his investments terribly compromised.[40]

In the end, Ray concluded that he was happier out of the oil business: "I lost a job that was paying me too well (for Dabney's peace of mind) without really getting me anything but physical breakdown and moral disgust. I'm well out of it, much better and much happier."[41] But he always harbored a grudge against Dabney; when Warren Lloyd's son Edward, who had first met Ray back in 1913, sued Dabney for misappropriation of funds from oil revenues from the Ventura Avenue fields, a tract of land that had belonged to the Lloyd family, Ray dished as much dirt as he could remember on the old man's financial dealings. The Lloyds were grateful for what he had done and rewarded their friend with an allowance of one hundred dollars a month, which came in very useful now Ray was out of work.

Losing a job can do terrible things to the kind of man whose identity, hopes, and dreams are tied to a career. Ray was such a man, and when he woke up one morning without an office to go to, he did not know what to do with himself. Everything he had worked for had crumbled and he no longer had any purpose. In 1931, Ray was forty-three, and he found himself having to piece his life back together again. He found a glimmer of hope in a forgotten ambition and the thing he loved most, and said to William Lever: "I'm on the threshold of getting the only place I ever wanted with all my heart to get. I'm making a start as a writer."[42]

CHAPTER SIX

MAKING A START

Shortly after Ray was sacked, he and Cissy loaded up their Chrysler and drove up the Pacific coast for a tour of the Northwest.[1] The first years of the 1930s had been challenging ones and the Chandlers had been bruised by a series of events. Disorientated by Ray's sudden ejection from Dabney, the couple must have hoped that some time out of Los Angeles would do them good.

Ray would later claim that it was on this journey that he became familiar with the pulps: "In 1931, my wife and I used to cruise up and down the Pacific Coast, in a very leisurely way, and at night, just to have something to read, I would pick a pulp magazine off a rack."[2] Certainly it was on this trip that Ray set about trying to write again. Since he had come to California his literary output had been, by and large, poetry. Aside from a pastiche of Henry James, he does not seem to have tackled fiction and his inexperience was immediately clear. The few short pieces he wrote in the cooler, wetter climes of Washington State he considered to be "ineffectual efforts."[3] He soon realized that he had a long way to go before becoming a proficient writer of fiction but, this, he understood, was another advantage afforded by the pulps: "I might be able to do this stuff and get paid while I was learning."[4] After several weeks without direction, his compass was now set to a new pole.

The Chandlers' return to Los Angeles was an ignominious one. Many of their former friends had stopped returning their calls, and under the pressure of recent events, Ray's health started to suffer[5]—it would take a year for him to regain his strength. Still, having made the decision to write again, he started to explore the options available to him. First and foremost he had to address his lack of knowledge, and, rather as he had taken evening classes in bookkeeping on first arriving in California, Ray signed up to a correspondence course in short story writing: "I had to go back to the beginning and learn to write all over again," he wrote to William Lever after his first story was published.[6]

The course, it seems, was fairly basic. Tasks included "create a scene" and "create a character," which Ray's existing knowledge must have stretched to. Evidently he was successful and received steady grades—As and Bs throughout—though he had clearly not shaken off his fascination with the world of knights and castles. One exercise opened, "The walls of the Castle of Innifrath were vast and grey with that greyness which remembers dark deeds and a moon too pale to be friendly." Other pieces written during this period show that Ray wrestled with several influences, with other authors' stylistic tics resurfacing again and again. Henry James was one, but Ray eventually settled on Hemingway as his model. He dedicated one story to Hemingway—"Beer in Sergeant Major's Hat, or The Sun Also Sneezes"—calling him "the greatest living American novelist."[7] Throughout the story, Papa's impact is clear:

> Hank went into the bathroom to brush his teeth.
>
> "The hell with it," he said. "She shouldn't have done it."
>
> It was a good bathroom. It was small and the green enamel was peeling off the walls. But the hell with that, as Napoleon said when they told him Josephine was waiting without. The bathroom had a wide window through which Hank looked at the pines and the larches. They dripped with faint rain. They looked smooth and comfortable . . .
>
> Hank unscrewed the top of the toothpaste tube, thinking of the day when he had unscrewed the lid off the coffee jar, down on the Pukayuk River, when he was trout fishing. There had been some larches there too. It was a damn good river, and the trout had been damn good trout. They liked being hooked. Everything had been good except the coffee, which had been lousy. He had made it

Watson's way, boiling it for two hours and a half in his knapsack. It had tasted like the socks of the Forgotten Man.[8]

Despite the Papa-esque flourishes, there are elements that are unmistakably Ray: the bathroom with its peeling green enamel was exactly the kind of detail he would pick up on.

By the time Ray completed his course, his financial situation was dire. The Chandlers had managed to live on what little they had put aside, but they were soon forced to sell their possessions. At one point, all they had left was their furniture and their car and they were living on twenty-five dollars a week.[9] Despite these hardships, Ray and Cissy were happy. Adversity had brought them closer together and had helped smooth over the cracks and fissures that had emerged in their relationship over the last few years. Still, despite their newfound contentment, money was at the forefront of Ray's mind, and it was for this reason that he turned to the pulp magazines. He had already noted that they would provide a reasonable way to both learn to write and to get paid, so he set about picking apart a story by Erle Stanley Gardner, one of the most prolific and popular pulp writers. The story he chose was almost certainly either "The Glove Mystery," "Between Two Fires," or "The Invisible Ring," and the aim was to learn the mechanics of the form by stripping it back and rewriting it:

> I simply made an extremely detailed synopsis of your story and from that rewrote it and then compared what I had with yours, and then went back and rewrote it some more, and so on. It looked pretty good.[10]

Ray could hardly have chosen a better time to start writing for the pulps. In the early 1930s, in the shadow of the Great Depression, pulp magazines were enjoying their heyday. Two types of magazine existed at the time: the slicks, printed on luxurious, glossy paper, but with a moderate cover price subsidized by pages of advertising; and the pulps, printed on cheap, off-white paper, quickly produced and sold in vast quantities for next to nothing. Though cheap, the pulps were rich in diversity, publishing a range of stories from crime and westerns to spy stories and romance. As the readership developed so did the demand for writers. Titles such as *Underworld, Dime Detective, Dime*

Western, *Adventure*, and *Love Story* relied on a network of authors who could churn out lots of stories very quickly. Though the quality was not always high, pulp writing required a certain skill, whether stories featured detectives, cowboys, or spies, and as such the best writers were in constant demand.

Pulp stories were also uniquely American and took as their inspiration the heroes of the West. By the nineteenth century, successive generations had pushed their territory further and further into the West, and this shift brought Americans increasingly far away—both literally and metaphorically—from the European roots of the original settlers. As these pioneers brought their civilized behavior to the untamed wilderness, they drew from the wilderness itself both strength and individuality.[11] In other words, the American psyche was forged in the clash between order and unfettered nature. Cowboys, who often appeared in the proto-pulp magazines known as "penny dreadfuls," embodied this new America. They were tough men, at home in the wild, but who also imposed the rule of law. Expressions of this new American psyche could also be found in more respectable novels like *The Last of the Mohicans*, written by James Fenimore Cooper and published in 1826.

By the twentieth century, the push west was complete. Instead of the frontier, pulp writers relocated their stories to urban environments, but they continued to employ the tropes and characters of western frontier tales. The stories tended to revolve around a central male character who, more often than not, operated alone. Toughness was an essential virtue, as was a strict moral code that divided the world into good and bad, right and wrong. And the stories were characterized by simple, muscular, almost brutal prose.

The most famous of the pulp magazines was *Black Mask*. It was set up in 1920 by H. L. Mencken and George Jean Nathan, who wanted to take advantage of the huge popularity of the genre to support *The Smart Set*, a glossy that was good at attracting modernist authors but bad at turning a profit. From the start, *Black Mask* claimed it offered "the best stories available of adventure, the best mystery and detective stories, the best romances, the best love stories, and the best stories of the occult." The fact that it came into being in 1920, a short year after Prohibition, meant that its authors were never short of source material: tales of organized crime could be found all too easily in the daily newspapers. *Black Mask* soon became very successful.

In 1923 the magazine was sold to newspaper magnate Eugene Crow and his business partner, Eltinge "Pop" Warner, then head of the Warner Publishing Company. With their business manager, Phil Cody, they set about bolstering the list of contributors, bringing in the likes of Dashiell Hammett and Erle Stanley Gardner. Though there were hundreds of other authors, these two in particular became associated with the magazine. Hammett had worked as an investigator for the Pinkerton Detective Agency, while Gardner was a practicing lawyer. Both men drew on their professional experiences to write realistic, hard-hitting stories that proved extremely popular with the magazine's readership. Realism quickly became an essential part of the *Black Mask* aesthetic, and Hammett stressed in his letters how close his stories were to reality:

> About the story ["The Vicious Circle"[12]]: None of the characters is real in a literal sense, though I doubt that it would be possible to build a character without putting into it at least something of someone the writer has known. The plot, however, is close to earth. In the years during which I tried my hand at "private detecting" I ran across several cases where the "friend" called in to dispose of a blackmailer either went into partnership with him or took over his business after getting him out of the way. And I know of at least one case where a blackmailer was disposed of just as "Inch" disposed of "Bush."[13]

As this letter suggests, though realism was important to Hammett, so too was humanity and character. In this, he blazed a bright trail for Raymond Chandler, showing that rich, human detail did not smother action. In "House Dick," an early *Black Mask* story, the narrator is a man with whom the reader can connect:

> From behind me came a scream and a thud as the maid fainted. I wasn't feeling any too steady myself. I'm no sensitive plant, and I've looked at a lot of unlovely sights in my time, but for weeks afterward I could see those three dead men coming out of that clothespress to pile up at my feet: coming out slowly—almost deliberately—in a ghastly game of "follow your leader."

Here the narrator's toughness is stripped from him, leaving instead the recognisable shell of a man. It is a powerful moment and, in early *Black Mask* stories, a rare one.

Despite his artistic aspirations, however, Dashiell Hammett was a pragmatist, and to him, pulp writing was also about paying his bills: "The trouble is that this sleuth of mine has degenerated into a meal ticket."[14] Hammett showed Ray both the creative possibilities in pulp fiction and its potential rewards. For Ray, the latter was essential. He had made the decision to write, but he had also chosen to focus on something that could be commercial, and Dashiell Hammett was proof that a man could live on his writing without entirely compromising his artistic integrity.

In 1926, *Black Mask* took another important step into its future when Joseph Shaw was appointed editor. It was under Shaw that the magazine really hit its stride. He was the perfect man for the job: athletic (he was a fencer and invented a parry with the épée sword against which there was no defence[15]), intelligent, and, essentially, heroic (during the war, he had been a captain known affectionately as "Cap"). Later, he claimed to have known very little about pulp writing before his appointment as editor but, even were this true, there can be little doubt that he was the man who identified the magazine's real strength: not westerns or romances, but crime.

When Shaw started at *Black Mask*, he immediately identified Hammett's writing as the sort around which he could build the magazine. Shaw wrote that Hammett had the "requisite spark and originality," telling his stories "with a new kind of compulsion and authenticity."[16] This was what Shaw wanted for the whole magazine and he wrote to Hammett to outline his vision. Hammett responded enthusiastically: "That is exactly what I've been thinking about and working toward. As I see it, the approach I have in mind has never been attempted. The field is unscratched and wide open."[17] Under Shaw, with Hammett as a model, *Black Mask* developed a reputation for more than just the run-of-the-mill pulp fiction, and though there was still plenty of murder and brutal violence in its pages, it was seen as being a cut above the competition.

With Shaw's encouragement, writers were able to branch out from the pulps and turn to novels. Hammett's first, *Red Harvest*, was published in 1929 by Alfred A. Knopf Inc. after he sent it speculatively to the company, having chosen them because of their Borzoi Book imprint, which specialized in mystery and crime fiction. Blanche Knopf, the wife of the company's founder, bought the book and helped Hammett make the leap from pulp hack to novelist. Now a published author, he could develop the literary aspect of his writing:

> I'm one of the few—if there are any more—people moderately literate who take the detective story seriously. I don't mean that I necessarily take my own or anybody else's seriously—but the detective story as a form. Some day somebody's going to make "literature" of it (Ford's *Good Soldier* wouldn't have needed much altering to have been a detective story) [sic], and I'm selfish enough to have my hopes, however slight the evident justification may be.[18]

In this, Hammett was Ray's progenitor, showing him what could be done within the relatively restricted confines of pulp fiction. Though Ray did not realize it ("I doubt that Hammett had any deliberate artistic aims whatever," he would one day mistakenly write[19]), Hammett had created a fertile climate for Ray's own books.

This then was the world Ray set about entering in 1932. He chose to use the pulps as a way of learning a craft, but implicit in this was his ambition to write serious fiction, too.

It was not that he did not enjoy reading the magazines, though. He wrote in 1939, in the early days of his writing career: "I should never have tried to work for *Black Mask*, if I hadn't, at one time, got a kick out of reading it."[20] Given the choice, however, he would have preferred to write in a more literary vein but later came to understand that:

> . . . no writer ever in any age got a blank check. He always had to accept some conditions imposed from without . . . [and] try to please certain people. It might have been the Church, or a rich patron, or a generally accepted standard of elegance, or the commercial wisdom of a publisher or editor, or perhaps even a set of political theories. . . . No writer ever wrote exactly what he wanted to write, because there was never anything inside himself, anything purely individual that he did want to write.[21]

For now, though, Ray was learning by rewriting the work of others. In method, it was very similar to the one used by him in studying Classics at Dulwich College.[22] Back then, he had copied out hundreds of lines of Latin and Greek poetry and then translated them, laying bare the architecture of each work. As Ray put it: "It would seem that a classical education might be a rather poor basis for writing novels in a hardboiled vernacular. I happen to think otherwise."[23]

As well as structure, Ray also had to learn a new language. Dulwich had not equipped him with the vocabulary for pulp fiction, but it had given him a facility with languages. He treated American English and pulp style like any other foreign tongue, making lists of strange slang that he found in newspapers, storing them in a notebook for later use. He came to love the new vernacular:

> All I wanted when I began [writing] was to play with a fascinating new language, and trying, without anybody noticing it, to see what it would do as a means of expression which might remain on the level of unintellectual thinking and yet acquire the power to say things which are usually only said with a literary air.[24]

Language aside, Ray was also drawn to the pulps because they offered an appealing image of manliness. The pulps sold a very specific idea of what a man should be, one that was reflected in the advertisements that appeared in the magazines. Ads included Charles Atlas's bodybuilding system, workmen's denims, and night school classes. One exhorted men to study electricity, offering a more secure future:

Stop Gambling With Your Future and LEARN ELECTRICITY TODAY Where Jobs Hunt Men at $50 a Week and UP

The almost entirely male readership of *Black Mask* wanted to be like both the men in the ads and the heroes of the stories: tough, strong, and able to survive against all odds. Since his father had abandoned him and his mother, Ray had always felt a great sense of responsibility for the women in his life, which had only developed further during his relationship with Cissy. He recognized the ideal of the tough man in the pages of these magazines, adding to it his own fascination with chivalry. In this, he had a lot in common with the audience for which he would now be writing.

Once he felt confident with the mechanics and language of the pulps, Ray tackled his first story. The pulp world relied on a high turnover of material, but the fast pace was incompatible with Ray's work ethic. His pulp debut, "Blackmailers Don't Shoot," took more than a year to write.[25] It was only when he felt entirely happy with it that he sent it off to Joseph T. Shaw.

Ray committed a small faux pas with his first submission, setting his pages with the right-hand margin justified, mimicking the Linotype layout of a magazine publication. This strange-looking manuscript puzzled and amused Shaw,[26] but he read the story and, evidently impressed, immediately sent it to another one of his contributors, W. T. Ballard, with a note that said that the author was either a genius or crazy. Shaw decided it was good enough to appear in the magazine and offered $180, paying at the very lowest rate of a cent per word. The story that had taken so long to write,[27] and which had needed at least five revisions, appeared in the December 1933 edition of the magazine. Ray was once again a paid writer.

Compared with his later work, "Blackmailers Don't Shoot" is a mess of a story, but it found a deserving home in *Black Mask*, where it stood apart from many contemporary pulp tales. Ostensibly, the story revolves around a private detective who is in Los Angeles to track down the blackmailers of Rhonda Farr, a Hollywood actress. But a combination of a large cast, clichéd names (like Costello and Slippey Morgan), and lots and lots of guns make the plot difficult to follow. Nonetheless, the compelling tropes of the hard-boiled crime story keep the reader engaged. There is the oversexed starlet, who mixes toughness with femininity:

> Rhonda Farr was very beautiful. . . . [She wore] a white wig which, meant to disguise her, made her look very girlish. . . . Rhonda Farr lifted her face and gave him a look as hard as marble.

There are corrupt cops; and a nightclub-owning hoodlum, Mardonne, who seems to have a distant hand in the story's events. Several scenes involve graphic, gratuitous violence, and the descriptions revel in the savagery in a way that was bound to appeal to *Black Mask* readers:

The lanky man stopped smiling. He ducked sidewise very fast, and a gun jumped into his hand. Roar filled the room, a great crashing roar. And again a roar.

The lanky man's duck became a slide and the slide degenerated into a fall. He spread himself out on the bare carpet in a leisurely sort of way. He lay quite still, one half-open eye apparently looking at Macdonald . . .

Macdonald put his other hand up to the door-frame, leaned forward and began to cough. Bright red blood came out on his chin. His hands came down the door-frame slowly. Then his shoulder twitched forward, he rolled like a swimmer in a breaking wave, and crashed.

The major flaw in the story is that each scene feels as if it was created in isolation, polished individually, with little thought put into how they would thread together. This is how Ray had been taught to write on his correspondence course, and his chief concern when imitating other pulp writers seems to have been creating the right effect, rather than plot. But it is in those effects that we see his potential. For example, the passage quoted above ends like this: "He crashed on his face, his hat still on his head, the mouse-colored hair at the nape of his neck showing below it in an untidy curl." A rather ugly, corrupt cop suddenly becomes human in this sentence, and the reader feels for his death, a haunting moment in an otherwise blunt, rather unimpressive text. Fifteen years later, Ray wrote about the importance of creating moments like this:

> . . . when I was writing for the pulps . . . The things they [the readers] really cared about, and that I cared about, were the creation of emotion through dialogue and description; the things they remembered, that haunted them, were not for example that a man got killed, but that in a moment of his death he was trying to pick a paper clip up off the polished surface of a desk, and it kept slipping away from him, so that there was a look of strain on his face and his mouth was half open in a kind of tormented grin, and the last thing in the world he thought of was death.[28]

From the very outset of his pulp career, Ray was trying to satisfy his literary urge, undercover. As he wrote to Alfred Knopf, the man who would publish his first novel, this was sometimes a matter of slipping something past his editor:

> From the beginning, from the first pulp story, it was always with me a question (first of course how to write a story at all) of putting into the stuff something that they would not shy off from, perhaps even not know was there as a conscious realization, but which would somehow distill through their minds and leave an afterglow.[29]

This afterglow was paramount to the sort of story that Ray wanted to write, and there are several examples in "Blackmailers Don't Shoot" that suggest the path he was to follow. One example is the name of the story's hero, Mallory. Would any other pulp writer have named a character after Sir Thomas Malory, author of the Arthurian romance *La Morte D'Arthur*? With this, Ray was suggesting that his protagonist was a man who shared the knightly qualities of Sir Lancelot or Gawain. This kind of allusion, even if it slipped past the editors and over the heads of his readers, was key to the kind of hero he wanted to create—good in a chaotic world, pure despite temptation. Though this story never comes close to the great writing of his later stories and novels, it prepared the ground for Marlowe, and not only by anticipating his name.

The beginnings of Ray's distinctive prose style can be glimpsed here, too. Unlike other pulp writers, rushing from one fight to another, he lingers over the details—"the ceiling was remote and vague, like the dusk of a hot day." Getting these touches past the blue pen of the editor must have pleased him immensely. He told William Lever that "one misguided soul" had gone so far as to call it the best story to appear in that magazine.[30] Though self-deprecating, he was clearly also proud. There are also early examples of the atmosphere of shallow emptiness that would later define the Los Angeles of his novels:

> The two bored men gave her [Rhonda Farr] an interested eye. The dark woman brooded glumly over the task of mixing herself a highball that would have floored a horse. The man with the fat sweaty neck seemed to have gone to sleep.

Ray was not surprised that the story was accepted and well received by readers. Even before it was published he wrote: "I knew I would, because I knew what effect I wanted to get, and I wouldn't send out a line until I got it."[31]

It is possible that, in his original plan, "Blackmailers Don't Shoot" was to be the first in a series featuring Mallory, which could eventually lead to a novel. The story ends with Mallory saying, "I might stick around. . . . One of the studios made me a proposition." The next story he wrote begins with Mallory employed by a film studio to help with another blackmail case. He summarized this period in a letter to his friend William Lever: "I'm making a start as a writer. . . . You'll laugh when I tell you what I write. Me, with my romantic and poetical instincts. I'm writing sensational detective fiction."[32] He goes on to justify why he chose to write this type of story:

> It is not anything like a success of course, but it is the foundation for one. You can write prettiness and clever-clever stuff and sell it now and then to a highbrow magazine and starve on the proceeds. But if you can do detective fiction with involved plots and plenty of action you can <u>always</u> make a living. Two or three of the boys who write for the magazine I'm writing for now have graduated into $100,000 a year movie jobs, and one sold the rights to a single story for $25,000. Of course I'm years from anything like that, but I'm headed that way. And I'd rather have a couple of hundred dollars a month writing than five times that much as an office hack or a salaried executive.[33]

As the long labor pangs for "Blackmailers Don't Shoot" demonstrate, Ray was willing to work hard, not only to write well but also to make a living. But he did not just want to scrape by—he wanted to live well. Crime fiction offered commercial reward. He did not like the action, "the blood and guts,"[34] he called it, but excused it because it took him to the "threshold of getting the only place I ever wanted with all my heart to get."[35] His ambition had outweighed any misgivings about the genre in which he was working. And, anyway, as far as Ray was concerned, though action was necessary, it was incidental to what he wanted to achieve. Except . . . what did he want to achieve? He had not quite worked that out: "It's the best I can do and get <u>paid</u> for just now. It won't I hope always be."[36]

CHAPTER SEVEN

A PULP WRITER

Blackmailers Don't Shoot" may have been the product of uncertain times, but it was not the product of unhappy ones. Losing his job actually initiated a period of stability and happiness for Ray. In the immediate aftermath of his being fired, Cissy and Ray's life together was in flux but, by 1933, things seemed to have settled as they took up residence in Silver Lake, at 1639 Redesdal Avenue. Silver Lake is a hilly part of Los Angeles, northwest of downtown, and appears in Ray's writing as Gray Lake. In "Finger Man" (1934), he described the area as typical of Los Angeles—a place where the road surface is more expensive than the flimsy homes that line it:

> Gray Lake is an artificial reservoir in a cut between two groups of hills. . . . Narrow but expensively paved streets wind around in the hills, describing elaborate curves along their flanks for the benefit of a few cheap and scattered bungalows.

Ray and Cissy liked it. They had a small home with a lawn and a garden and, importantly, "good air and a view of the mountains."[1]

Fresh air aside, they still had nothing "except the furniture"[2] and were living on twenty-five dollars a week. In his intimate letters to William Lever, Ray says that, despite all the difficulties, he and Cissy were "better than we ever were before."[3] He found that he was able to cut down on his drinking and, though he never achieved total abstinence, his consumption of alcohol became manageable. Besides, he wrote, "I have ceased to get much kick out of it unless I take more than is good for me, and then I get sick," and a sick man could not focus on writing.

Ray also drew strength from Cissy. They had separated once, leaving him desperate and unhinged. He had no desire to repeat that experience. In "I'll Be Waiting," a story from 1939, the character Eve Cressy says, "Redheads don't jump, Tony. They hang on—and wither." Cissy was a redhead and certainly had the ability to hang on during tough times. In March 1933, an earthquake with an epicenter offshore from Long Beach shook Los Angeles with several tremors. On the first night of quakes, the couple slept in their clothes. Ray leapt out of bed every time he felt a tremor, running into the kitchen to cut the power. Cissy, though, was unfazed by the experience, leading Ray to write that "Cissy didn't care anything about it, but Cissy scares harder than anybody I ever knew. You can't frighten her."[4]

Their life together developed a pleasant rhythm. Ray would get up early to write and would break his day with afternoon tea. The Chandlers would sit down together to enjoy this quaint and strangely formal event. Ray would pour the tea and they would talk. In the evening, Cissy would prepare dinner. She was a competent cook and assiduously collected recipes, which she annotated and stored for later use. After dinner, they would turn on the radio and sit with a cocktail listening to the *Gas Company Evening Concert* of classical music. It was a simple life, but a good one, and they were very happy during this period. They bought a cat, Taki, a big Persian ball of black fluff, which gave them both great pleasure. Ray also began to collect small glass animals—simply fashioned elephants, swans, and cats—that he called "amuels." To Cissy, Ray was Gallibeoth, a nickname that alluded to his knightly hero Sir Galahad; she was his "Double Duck" or, simply, "Momma."

Ray would later exaggerate the poverty he experienced, claiming once to have lived for five days on nothing but soup,[5] but there is no mention of this kind of extreme hardship in contemporary correspondence between himself and William Lever, though money was certainly short. An apartment in L.A. could be rented for fifty dollars a year,[6] so the hundred dollars or so a month the Chandlers lived on, though a step down from the large sums he had earned only a few years earlier, was adequate and allowed him to continue writing.

Though Ray was not a prolific writer he was a steady one and, on the back of his first success, he had the confidence to write regularly, improving with each new story. His second, "Smart-Aleck Kill," was much better than the first. For one thing, the plot is easier to follow. It appeared in the July 1934 edition of *Black Mask*, more than seven months after its predecessor and again featured Mallory who must discover who killed actor Derek Walden.[7] The pulp tropes were back (an alcoholic blonde, a corrupt house detective, and a dirty councilman) but whereas each scene in "Blackmailers Don't Shoot" seems to have concluded with a shooting, a double cross, or a death, "Smart-Aleck Kill" resists serious violence until the very end. When it finally does come, it is a lot more measured. Some characters even survive. Mallory, too, is a much more considered character. He is now tired of the city he is working in, of the violence and the corruption:

> "Get up off the floor, Johnny," he [Mallory] said wearily. "Get up and tell a poor dumb dick how to cover this one up—smart guy!"

The story ends with Mallory and Captain Cathcart sharing a drink:

> "What'll we drink to?" the captain asked . . .
> Mallory said: "Let's just drink."

Mallory needs to forget the part he has played in the mess. Expounding his ideas around the archetype of the hero detective in an essay called "The Simple Art of Murder," Ray would later write that "down these mean streets a man must go who is not himself mean, who is neither tarnished nor afraid." Though this statement came years later, the thought that led to it was beginning to crystallize in 1933 and 1934, and Mallory, in this second story, is as much a product of it as Philip Marlowe. The detective survives the story, weary of the world of which he is part, but not tainted: "It was the job—and that's all a guy can say."

It was in his next story, "Finger Man," that Ray really hit his stride. This was his first *Black Mask* story told in the first person, and we begin to hear brief snatches of the voice that would eventually become Marlowe's. "Finger Man," like "Blackmailers Don't Shoot" and "Smart-Aleck Kill," took time to write, but the effort was rewarded. It achieved the ultimate accolade, being chosen as the cover story for the October 1934 issue. With only three stories under his belt, Ray had raced to the front of the pack and, like Hammett before him, was making a name for himself. He was justly proud of this achievement:

> I got my name on the cover recently. This won't appear to you a very great honor in the circumstances, but it means a lot to a writer to have what is called a "cover" name. It means he is a drawing card to the magazine's particular clientele.[8]

Ray could now see a serious future in writing: "it is fairly clear that it is only a question of time until I really get somewhere."[9] As a story, "Finger Man" is yet another notch up from his previous efforts. First person suited him, making action scenes easier to write, but also allowing him more opportunity to convey emotion. Ray was still polishing each scene to perfection and, in "Finger Man," used first person narration to expand on the note of weariness he had sounded in "Smart-Aleck Kill."

"Finger Man" revolves around Lou Harger, who wins a large amount of money at a crooked roulette wheel. Harger goes missing, and Miss Glenn, his beautiful redheaded assistant, asks the unnamed narrator to find him. Following up a lead, the detective finds himself involved with Frank Dorr, a politician behind a lot of the crime in the city of San Angelo. Dorr is a key element to the story because he represents a fictionalized version of "The System," the network of powerful people involved in crime and politics in the real Los Angeles. The detective can never truly win: the crime he is investigating is only a small part of a whole that he can never completely see or understand. He does his job, such as it is, but cannot defeat the evil behind the crime in the city. It is a curiously modern, paranoid vision from a time before conspiracy theories seized the popular imagination. This idea was to become an important recurring theme in Ray's fiction.

The city of San Angelo presented in "Finger Man" is a thinly veiled portrait of Los Angeles and gave Ray his first opportunity to paint a recognizable version of a place that he had come to know intimately—to write about the pimps and the players, the pretty boys and girls, the con men and nymphets.

He had his detective react with convincing feelings to such a glittering, sordid world, as when he first learns that Harger is dead: "I leaned against the wall of the booth and felt my eyes getting haggard." The word *haggard* echoes Harger's name and suggests the feeling of tiredness and submission the detective feels on hearing the inevitable news of his friend's death. It would be much harder to achieve this level of emotional poignancy in the third person.

The story's conclusion shows the detective's realisation that his mission to fight crime will never end:

> I had a little trouble, but not much. Fenweather [the DA] pulled too much weight. Not all of the story came out, but enough so that the City Hall boys in the two hundred-dollar suits had their left elbows in front of their faces for some time . . .
>
> Miss Glenn made a clean getaway and was never heard from again. I think that's about all, except that I had to turn the twenty-two grand over to the Public Administrator. He allowed me two hundred dollars fee and nine dollars and twenty cents mileage. Sometimes I wonder what he did with the rest of it.

The last line teases the reader, hinting at continuing corruption, but we can also take comfort in the fact that the detective remains pure. He is one of the little people, doing his job, but up against the might of the political and criminal forces that run the city. Ray does not make this point in a heavy-handed way, but he conveys the detective's position and emotional state through subtle use of language.

The success of "Finger Man" marked the beginning of an increase in activity from Ray. Despite describing himself as a slow worker—which he was, compared with other pulp writers—his writing was getting bolder and better with each story. He was reading a lot on the side, particularly thrillers, from which he tried to pick up technique, though a slightly tongue-in-cheek remark to Lever does suggest that he also enjoyed reading them: "Naturally, to me, much of the pleasure is seeing how the effects are obtained; a purely professional interest."[10] In the next series of stories, he further developed the idea of a detective battling against a large and corrupt organization loosely modeled on "the System." He did not have to look far for further inspiration, and the atmosphere he was able to create drew considerably on events in Los Angeles in the 1930s without making direct reference to them.

In 1934, the novelist and eccentric vegetarian Upton Sinclair came very close to winning the gubernatorial election as the Democratic Party's nominee. His successful run, against the odds, was linked to the aftershock of the Depression, which pushed California to a dangerous crossroads where it risked having to choose between communism on the one hand and fascism on the other. California took longer than some states to feel the full force of the Depression because its economy was not based on heavy industry, but when it did arrive, the Depression was devastating and hit the Los Angeles middle classes with astonishing severity. The very cycle of saving and investment, in real estate and oil speculation, that had fueled Los Angeles's growth was undermined in a moment, creating hysteria and bankrupting many. The Julian Pete scandal had shown how fragile confidence could be, and in the early 1930s, the Depression brought home this point to millions of small-time investors who saw their investments and savings vanish.

Because the middle classes felt the effects so strongly, the crisis took an unusual turn. In 1934, when Upton Sinclair was pushing for election, he campaigned on the EPIC program (End Poverty in California), which advocated production for use, not profit. The movement's motto was "I Produce, I Defend," though it is not clear exactly what the movement defended against. Sinclair had a utopian vision of California that he outlined in his manifesto-cum-novel, *I, Governor of California and How I Ended Poverty—A True Story of the Future*. It included heavy property taxes and the development of communes, where the unemployed could grow or build products to exchange with each other and the state. It all smelled suspiciously like Bolshevism to the right-wing elements in Californian politics, but the vision appealed to large chunks of the middle class, who had suffered most in the Depression.

A force of right wingers, including some of the most powerful studio moguls in Hollywood, came together to disrupt Sinclair's campaign in 1934. They recognized that the middle-class vote would decide the 1934 election. Irving Thalberg, the production chief at Metro-Goldwyn-Mayer, worked with the Hearst organization to produce a series of fake newsreel shots for free distribution across the state. In them, some of Hollywood's prettiest office girls and most convincing business executives told the camera why they should vote for Sinclair's Republican rival, the incumbent Frank Merriam, while a succession of heavily accented, scruffy and bearded men—sinister foreigners—came forward to explain why they were voting for Sinclair. The trick worked: Sinclair was stained with communism and lost the election. Worryingly for the right, however, he gained a respectable share of the vote, prompting further action.

While Sinclair was developing and promoting his idea of a Californian Utopia, there were a series of clashes between striking workers and authorities across the state. Trouble flared in the Imperial Valley, in early 1934, when groups of lettuce pickers went on strike in an attempt to increase their wages to thirty-five cents an hour.[11] The response was astonishing in its ferocity. A paramilitary organization was established to quash the strike. It consisted of the farm owners at the very top (organized as the Imperial Valley Growers and Shippers Protective Association); the Anti-Communist Association, whose leading members took on ranks such as Commander; American Legion units; and a string of county commissioners and local police chiefs. The strike leaders were harassed, arrested, and imprisoned, charged with vagrancy, disturbing the peace, trespassing, and resisting arrest. The coming together of this alliance of potent interest groups was, in the words of one historian, what "even a moderate conservative might label as fascist."[12]

This trend became yet more obvious when, in 1936, Chief Davis of the Los Angeles Police Department dispatched 126 of his officers to sixteen crucial highway and railroad entry points across the state to turn away transients who could not prove residence in California. In this astonishing act, one portion of one city attempted to seize power over the entirety of California, which had essentially become a police state. Transients had long been recognized as a problem, and structures akin to concentration camps had been built to house them, but this reaction, and the public's acceptance of it, marked a new level of anxiety about invasion from beyond state lines. In Los Angeles in particular, with its lack of heavy industry and its investment in the make-believe of Hollywood, there was a feeling of paranoia which made the city a darker place than usual. The City of Angels, with its permanent summer weather and surface beauty, was in fact home to a people who were disenfranchised by their political overlords and prey to an acute sense of threat—a belief that the menace of the Depression, in the form of transients, was turning the city into an urban hell.

James M. Cain, another pulp writer, picked up on this threat in his 1934 novel, *The Postman Always Rings Twice*. In it, a drifter arrives at a gas station, the Twin Oaks Tavern, and falls in love—or, perhaps more accurately, in lust—with the owner's wife. The two become lovers and conspire to murder the husband. The tale turns into an exploration of sexual desire and guilt. The opening unfolds as follows:

> They threw me off the hay truck about noon. I had swung on the night before, down at the border, and as soon as I got up there under the canvas, I went to sleep. I needed plenty of that, after three weeks in Tia Juana, and I was still getting it when they pulled off to one side to let the engine cool. Then they saw a foot sticking out and threw me off. I tried some comical stuff, but all I got was a dead pan, so that gag was out. They gave me a cigarette, though, and I hiked down the road to find something to eat.

Readers of the time would have immediately recognized this sort of man. His disconnection from society and his desperation give him the unsettling amoral outlook that allows the story to move forward.

Though Ray never examined these political problems directly, stories he wrote between 1934 and 1938 explore feelings of paranoia and disillusionment that were exacerbated by the political situation. The System, previously hinted at, is more fully realized in stories like "Nevada Gas," "Spanish Blood," "Guns at Cyrano's," and "The Man Who Liked Dogs," all of which appeared in *Black Mask* between 1935 and 1936. In "Nevada Gas," a corrupt lawyer called Hugh Candless is brutally killed by the brother of a client he crossed. Lawyers—who rarely come out well in Ray's stories—are shown to be a dangerous bunch, and the justice they seek is compromised by personal interest. In "Spanish Blood" that justice is given a perverted twist when a lawyer—an assistant DA called Imlay—seems to have assassinated the leading member of the System, Donegan Marr. This is complicated by the fact that the main character in the story, Sam Delaguerra, a police officer in the LAPD, says: "I was a close friend of Donegan Marr once." This friendship leads to Delaguerra being framed, but in an effort to clear his name, the detective uncovers something even nastier about the murder: Marr's wife, also Delaguerra's friend, is the killer. The detective has little option but to try and cover up the true identity of the killer, and this leaves him feeling dirty: "It's my first frame-up . . . I hope it will be my last . . . Got the badge back . . . It's not quite as clean as it was. Clean as most, I suppose." Ray makes the point that this sort of corruption is contagious and that, no matter how pure the detective is, he cannot help but be tainted.

The story had added resonance because it was loosely based on true events. In 1931, Charles Crawford, a leading member of the Los Angeles criminal and political system, was shot to death by a prosecutor and potential judge called Dave Clarke. Clarke admitted killing Crawford but explained that he had done so because Crawford was pressuring him to stop attacking underworld figures as part of his campaign to be judge. Crawford arranged to meet with Clarke, which resulted in the former pulling a gun. Clarke claimed he had shot the man in self-defence and was acquitted at trial. But it was clear that Crawford was trying to pull Clarke into his web and, though Clarke refused to be part of it, he ended up a criminal nonetheless.

In the midst of all this new work, Ray and Cissy decided to move away from Silver Lake and down to the coast. In March 1935, they rented a house at 943 Hartzell Street, in Pacific Palisades.[13] The better houses in the area looked out over the Pacific, but Ray and Cissy's home was further back, near where the foothills began to rise. They had a sun room and a garden that they loved. It was typically Californian, with two peach trees, a grapefruit tree, and a "very prolific" lemon tree. Ray and Cissy started to learn to grow flowers, which gave them a huge amount of pleasure.[14] It has been said that the 1930s were a restless period for the Chandlers, but this is simply not true. Since Ray lost his job they had lived in Silver Lake, then in Pacific Palisades, and would move one more time during the decade. Though three moves may be less common for a couple at the midstage of their lives, to describe this period as unsettled goes too far. Taki, their Persian cat, and the two goldfish they also kept, added to the small but childless family unit. Together, they would pack the Chrysler and take day trips out of the city, Ray reveling in driving fast whenever he could.

Ray's letters from this period repeatedly mention Cissy's happiness: "Cissy is very well and happy . . . and sends her love."[15] Exclusively written to William Lever, they are very different from the majority of letters on record. These are intimate, friendly exchanges between two men who had been through a lot together, and convey an honest sense of Ray and Cissy's contentment. In 1935, Ray wrote Cissy a poem for her birthday. In it, he admits he has given her "Lean years slinking by at the edge of the dusk, / Gaunt with memories,"[16] but, in return, she has stood by him:

> And of them you have made jewels to wear in your hair.
> This is what love is, this is what love is.
> When love is this, how can there be despair?[17]

It seems that despite the troubles caused by Ray's drinking, she had forgiven him.

Part of the stated reason behind their moving to Pacific Palisades was that both were bored of Los Angeles. Indeed, Ray was even starting to think about returning to England. He had lived in California for more than twenty years and was beginning to tire of it. The "bucolic atmosphere"[18] of Pacific Palisades offered an antidote to urban life but still lacked something. England, to Ray, became a distant paradise. Cissy was herself a bit of a snob—nobody in her home sat on a sofa, always on a davenport—and probably shared her husband's view that England was a place of culture and sophistication far preferable to Los Angeles's grubbiness. It would remain a dream, however, as long as they struggled to find enough cash to live on.

Ray was now beginning to make a name for himself. By 1936, he had had several stories published, with all but the very earliest appearing on the cover. Buoyed by this success he started to plan something more serious. He wanted to try and get a story in what he called the "upper crust" magazines, and by that he meant a magazine like the *Saturday Evening Post*. The *Post* was a bimonthly magazine that published illustration, opinions, and short fiction by leading writers such as William Faulkner and F. Scott Fitzgerald. In 1933, Ray had claimed that he was bored by "almost all the fiction" in it,[19] but this might have been sour grapes. He always made it clear that writing for the pulps was a way of learning but that he hoped for better.

The stories written during this period suggest that he was trying to pull away from the pulps. "The Man Who Liked Dogs" continues the theme of corruption but moves the action away from Los Angeles to a coastal part of California, possibly Santa Monica. In the story, the detectives of the unnamed city are involved in a plot to hide a wanted criminal from the authorities, first in a clinic for alcoholics and then, when Ted Carmady, the private detective narrating the story, discovers this, on an offshore gambling ship. Ray returned to first-person narrative for this story and used it to express the sort of anger that would eventually become typical of Marlowe:

> I said disgustedly: "Just what kind of sap did you and your gang take me for? Your clean little town stinks. It's the well-known whited sepulchre. A crook sanctuary where the hot rods can lie low—if they can pay off nice and don't pull any local capers—and where they can jump off for Mexico in a fast boat, if the finger waves towards them."

Significantly, Ray would use large portions of this story to build his second novel, *Farewell, My Lovely*, and it again shows how the first-person narrative mode allowed him to express his increasing anger at the corruption he could see around him. This is how the story ends:

> By that time the County Grand Jury had indicted half the police force of the little beach city. There were a lot of new faces around the City Hall, I heard. One of them was a big redheaded detective-sergeant named Norgard who said he owed me twenty-five dollars but had had to use it to buy a new suit when he got his job back. He said he would pay me out of his first check. I said I would try and wait.

Ray always liked an offbeat ending, but this one is unusual because it reveals the gentle side of the detective who is pleased to see a friend deservedly rewarded. Ray had recognized from the beginning that to be a writer of serious fiction he needed to focus on character and explore it in the best language available to him. His first stories had developed characters but they always had to fulfil the demands of the genre. "The Man Who Liked Dogs" is the first example of his successfully moving beyond these demands and shows the way that his mind was beginning to turn.

"Noon Street Nemesis" and "Goldfish" followed. "Noon Street Nemesis" (now generally published under the title "Pick-Up on Noon Street") is an uncomfortable story for modern readers because it is set around Central Avenue, Los Angeles, home to the city's black population, and the language Ray uses is clearly offensive. Black characters are invariably referred to as "the negro" while the heroic protagonist is called Pete Anglich, a name which seems to deliberately evoke Anglo-Saxon whiteness. Ray's perspective on issues of race has dogged his reputation for years, of which more later.

Ray ended this group of stories with "The Curtain," which would eventually be used to form parts of both *The Big Sleep* and *The Long Goodbye*. It is, in many ways, the best story he wrote in the run-up to his career as a novelist, bringing together all the ideas and techniques he had learned so far. The story opens with detective Ted Carmady being woken very early one morning by his friend Larry Betzel, who tells him that the supposed disappearance of the former bootlegger Dud O'Mara is not what it seems, and that there has been a murder. When Betzel is killed immediately after leaving Carmady's apartment, the detective decides to take up the case. He pays a visit to General Dade Winslow, O'Mara's father-in-law, and is eventually asked to find O'Mara. The story, in usual pulp fashion, features a climactic gun fight and murder, but the way this is handled is very different from the usual *Black Mask* approach. Carmady returns to the Winslow house to report and finds himself being shot at by O'Mara's stepson. He realizes this boy was in fact the killer and that he is mentally disturbed. Though readers of crime fiction were familiar with twists, designed to keep them guessing at the killer's identity until the end, Carmady's reaction and his conversation with Mrs. O'Mara would have seemed quite new:

> "Why in the hell," I groaned, "didn't you take the guns away from him?"
>
> "He's worse than you think. That would have started something worse. I'm—I'm almost afraid of him myself."

"Take him away," I said. "From here. From the old man. He's young enough to be cured, by the right handling. Take him to Europe. Far away. Take him now. It would kill the general out of hand to know his blood was in that."

Instead of a simple criminal act, "The Curtain" looked at how wealth could corrupt a family and its malevolence transmit and evolve. It is important that at the end of the story the child is not killed or punished—he can be cured after all. The Winslow family has been twisted by money, and the account of Carmady's encounter with the General stinks of the family's decay, represented by the contents of the house: "High over the huge marble fireplace hung two bullet-torn—or moth-eaten—cavalry pennants crossed in a glass case." And this is how the General is described:

Nothing lived in his face but the eyes. Black eyes, deep-set, shining, untouchable. The rest of his face was the leaden mask of death, sunken temples, a sharp nose, outward-turning ear lobes, a mouth that was a thin white slit.

The General's daughter, Mrs. O'Mara, who appears to be trying to avoid her father's fate, can only do so by existing in a sterile environment, literally drained of color and life:

"This room had a white carpet from wall to wall. Ivory drapes of immense height lay tumbled casually on the white carpet inside the many windows. . . . Mrs. O'Mara was stretched out on a white chaise-longue . . ."

To convey the family's complete corruption Ray employs some obvious literary techniques that would not normally be found in a pulp story. He had clearly come a long way from the debut writer trying to slip this sort of thing past his editor.

Again, Los Angeles is depicted in some detail:

Beyond the estate the hill sloped down to the city and the old oil wells of La Brea, now partly a park, partly a deserted stretch of fenced-in wild land. Some of the wooden derricks still stood.

But Ray takes things further, specifically tying Los Angeles to the corruption and decay of the Winslow family, as in this passage:

> Some of the wooden derricks still stood. These had made the wealth of the Winslow family and then the family had run away from them up the hill, far enough to get away from the smell of the sumps, not too far for them to look out of the front windows and see what made them rich.

These sumps, Ray makes clear, contain—literally and metaphorically—dark things. The money that they generated is the cause of the Winslows' decay, of which the murderous and malevolent youth who killed Dud O'Mara is the ultimate product. The story is a much fuller expression of the way that corruption works, and how it can be transmitted, than any of his previous attempts. He had identified a subject to explore and refined his writing enough to do so with confidence.

Ray published two further stories, "Try the Girl" (*Black Mask*, January 1937) and "Mandarin's Jade" (*Dime Detective Magazine*, November 1937), in which he continued to explore the theme of corruption. He liked them enough to reuse them both as source material for *Farewell, My Lovely*, but it is suggestive that his output slowed down considerably in 1937. This was partly because Joseph Shaw had been dismissed as editor of *Black Mask* magazine. According to Frank Gruber, a fellow pulp writer, the management decided he had become too expensive,[20] and anyway, the pulp market was slowly beginning to decline. Ray thought this meant it had "gone sissy"[21] and switched his allegiance to *Dime Detective*, which he thought still had the sort of edge needed for his work. He wrote three stories for them, two of which were published in 1938, and earned $1,275, a decent amount of money for the genre, though hardly oil executive money. With a degree of financial security, he began to think seriously about writing his first novel. After five years of hard work he was ready to take on the next challenge.

CHAPTER EIGHT

WRITING THE BIG SLEEP

*T*he *Big Sleep* was not Raymond Chandler's favorite of his own novels but it is certainly the most famous. Along with *The Maltese Falcon* and *Double Indemnity*, it has come to represent the high peak of the hard-boiled genre. And of those three novels, it is by far the best. Most people know the book's title and, with some thanks to the 1946 movie starring Humphrey Bogart, it has enjoyed a life well beyond the confines of literature.

The first draft of *The Big Sleep* was complete by May 1938. Ray and Cissy had moved to Big Bear Lake that month, intending to spend the summer there, and probably the autumn also. Ray had been suffering from a bad cold that he had struggled to shake and hoped that the mountain air would do him good. They took a cabin high up in the mountains in a village called, rather romantically, Pine Knot. It was a welcome change from Los Angeles, according to Ray, which was "too crowded, too hot, and the streets are always jammed with cars."[1] The air there was clean and dry and the weather was warm. It was, in short, exactly what they needed. Their cabin was well furnished, but it lacked a gas stove, and the couple were confined to cooking on one that burned wood, which they had to collect themselves. Evidently, despite these minor hardships, they were very happy. Ray wrote that "Cissy [seems to have] bathed in the fount of perennial youth and blooms like the early roses. I can hardly imagine a time when either of us will be old, though mathematically speaking it seems inevitable."[2]

With the benefits of seclusion and serenity, Ray was able to take the time to focus on the second draft of *The Big Sleep*. He had taken two stories— "Killer in the Rain" and "The Curtain"—and merged them to create a stronger, more substantial narrative. He was not happy with the first draft, though, and Ray, having labored over his first pulp story until it was perfect, prepared himself to do some serious work, for as long as it took.

Writing a novel was the necessary next step for Ray. He had achieved all he could in the short story form, and though he would keep writing them, he was never able to surpass the heights of his work for *Black Mask* in the mid-1930s. The stories that he contributed to *Dime Detective* were among his best, but they were not revelatory, just more of the same. In 1937, he had hoped to make an entry into the "upper-crust" magazines like *Collier's* and the *Post*,[3] but by 1938 he had changed his mind. Getting into the slicks, he came to realize, could do him more harm than good; he considered the sort of material they published to be "the unfreeest of all forms of writing."[4] He worried that success would lead to his acquiring "a fresh set of inhibitions," and this would not do.[5] This was hardly surprising for a man who been trained to reject pretentiousness. His schooling in the classics had made him cautious of posturing, and he was beginning to understand that the language of the pulp novelette could be far more expressive than conventionally "literary" language. He looked at novels like *The Maltese Falcon* and *The Postman Always Rings Twice* and saw that they were close to offering what he thought was possible but that, in the end, they fell short. Ray set out to "grow into a style of [his] own," confident that this would allow him to use language in a new way and to produce something he himself would like to read.[6]

Though the book was based on earlier writing, Ray still decided to start afresh, recalling whole passages from memory. He also ditched Ted Carmady, Sam Delaguerra, Mallory, and the others in favor of a new detective-narrator: Philip Marlowe. The origins of his name are obscure. It has been suggested that they allude to a house at Dulwich College, though when Ray was at the school the house system had not been introduced.[7] Another theory is that Sir Philip Sidney and Christopher Marlowe were sources, while some point to Joseph Conrad's Marlow, the narrator of *Lord Jim, Chance,* and *Heart of Darkness*. It is more than likely that Chandler would have been familiar with all of these writers, and a case can be made for each but, perhaps significantly, if any one of these was the root of his hero's name, Ray never acknowledged it. For someone who obviously put a lot of thought into the names of his earlier characters, it is frustrating not to be able to pinpoint a source for Marlowe. But, then again, perhaps that is the point. Marlowe is a name that hints at a scholarly playwright and a heroic past, but never takes on a significant form and remains elusive, rather like the character himself. Whatever the case, he was a step forward from the characters of the pulp stories—a fully realized man rather than a vehicle for action. Ray wanted his hero to be recognizably human, as well as tough, and funny. Here is how Marlowe enters the canon:

> It was about eleven o'clock in the morning, mid October with the sun not shining and a look of hard wet rain in the clearness of the foothills. I was wearing my powder-blue suit, with dark blue shirt, tie and display handkerchief, black brogues, black wool socks with dark blue clocks on them. I was neat, clean, shaved and sober, and I didn't care who knew it. I was everything the well-dressed private detective ought to be. I was calling on four million dollars.

In this opening paragraph, we get an immediate sense of the sort of man Marlowe is. He is smart and eloquent, but there is also a strong hint in the line "I was neat, clean, shaved and sober" that he is a drinker. We also know he has a sense of humor and that he knows how to behave in polite company, though it is not, perhaps, usual for him to have to do so. It is a powerful piece of prose, and reading it aloud gives a sense of its remarkable rhythm and balance.

Rhythm was important to Ray, and he took an unusual approach to ensure his novels had it. He would take a sheet of yellow letter paper, eight and a half inches by eleven inches, cut it in half, and roll it into a typewriter "turned up long ways."[8] Then, triple spacing as he went, he would write around 125 to 150 words on each piece of paper. He believed that this method of writing, in short sharp bursts, kept his prose lean and punchy: "If there isn't a little meat on each [page], something is wrong."[9] Looking carefully at *The Big Sleep*, it is sometimes possible to see quite clearly each 150-word chunk of text. Critics have pointed out that the differences between the two source stories and *The Big Sleep* offer a clear illustration of how much more ambitious his prose had become in treating essentially the same material. True as that is, it also implies that Ray was simply "gilding the lily," when, in fact, in rewriting, he did so much more. He chose to amplify elements from the original stories and add new details but by using a largely ready-made plot, he left himself free to focus on what were, to him, more important things like character and effect.

When Ray began writing crime novels, most mystery writers were interested in plot, in teasing the reader through the story. Even writers like Dashiell Hammett, who sought realism and did think about character, gave plot and action at least equal billing. Ray was different. He always considered the mystery less important than character, and that was the key to his success.

To give Marlowe the depth Ray sought, he developed the relationship between the detective and the elderly client. General Winslow from the short story became, in *The Big Sleep*, General Sternwood, a name that suggests a man of solid severity, and what had been hinted at in "The Curtain" was made explicit in the novel. In the story, Carmady is keen to save General Winslow the pain of knowing his grandson murdered his son-in-law because he respects the old man but, in *The Big Sleep*, Marlowe does not just respect Sternwood—he develops affection for the old man, too: "You can say anything you like to me [General] and I wouldn't think of getting angry. I'd like to offer you your money back. It may mean nothing to you. It might mean something to me." And, equally, it seems that Sternwood likes Marlowe. Or at least the butler, Norris, thinks he does:

> "He's not as weak as he looks, sir."
>
> "If he was, he'd be ready for burial. What did this Regan fellow have that bored into him so?"
>
> The butler looked at me levelly and yet with a queer lack of expression. "Youth, sir," he said. "And the soldier's eye."
>
> "Like yours," I said.
>
> "If I may say so, sir, not unlike yours."

It is an oddly tender moment that would seem incongruous in a pulp story, even one of Ray's. In those, the heroes are driven by a desire to defeat the bad guys but, here, Marlowe is motivated by a desire to protect the General. In the scene where Marlowe and Sternwood first meet, they bond over their drinking and also over their shared fluency in the language of boot-leggers, adventurers, and criminals. In the end, they develop an ambiguous father-and-son relationship, with Marlowe desperate to impress the old man and to take the place of Rusty Regan, the much-loved missing son-in-law. The detective is seen in a new light, as a lonely man in dire need of a real con-nection. He goes well beyond his duty to General Sternwood, but that ends badly, and the only real connection Marlowe seems to make is with Eddie Mars's wife. He kisses Vivian Regan, but only as a detective trying to root out the answer to her husband's disappearance; he also kisses Mars's wife, nick-named Silver-Wig, but in a very different way. In the last lines of the novel, Marlowe mourns the loss of that connection in an odd parody of a wake: "On the way downtown I stopped at a bar and had a couple of double Scotches. They didn't do me any good. All they did was make me think of Silver-Wig, and I never saw her again." The final image is of a desolate man mourning what he has lost. It is a haunting snapshot of a lonely life and is much more unsettling than the neatly tied-up endings of most mystery novels of the time.

In *The Big Sleep*, Ray also found the chance to elegantly use the language of the criminal world he had assiduously collected throughout the preceding decade, not only for color but also to convey character. There is plenty of slang littered throughout the book: "Take the air . . . Dust. I got enough chinning with you. Beat it." He liked the pliancy of this kind of language but also liked to play with the reader a little and, in one scene, writes of a character with "the elaborately casual voice of the tough guy in pictures." "Pictures," Marlowe observes, "have made them all talk like that." People did not only come across criminal slang in cinema, though—they also learned it by reading pulp stories like Ray's. By using slang in *The Big Sleep*, he makes a sly, circular reference to his own art form. In 1949, with a few more novels under his belt, Ray wrote:

> Do [Americans] not see the strong element of burlesque in my kind of writing? Or is it only the intellectuals who miss that? It is as though the public, most inconstant in its own emotions, expected a writer to be utterly constant in his. . . . There is a strong element of fantasy in the mystery story; there is in any kind of writing that moves within an accepted formula. The mystery writer's material is melodrama,

which is an exaggeration of violence and fear beyond what one normally experiences in life.[10]

Ray's point was that his novels were exaggerated versions of real events and, by pointing out the artifice of the hoodlum's apparently authentic street talk, he is daring to make the same point in fiction, in his very first novel.

His use of language went beyond literary tricks. It also allowed him to create brilliant dialogue, the kind of exchanges between characters that were far from typical for mystery novels of the time. Ray wrote: "Give me two people snotting each other across a desk and I am happy. A crowded canvas just bewilders me."[11] He had written scenes where two people argue in his short stories, but in *The Big Sleep*, he first succeeded in creating the tone he wanted. Take this conversation between Vivian Regan and Marlowe:

> She took the photo out and stood looking at it, just inside the door.
> "She [Carmen Sternwood] has a beautiful little body, hasn't she?"
> "Uh-huh."
> She leaned a little towards me. "You ought to see mine," she said gravely.
> "Can it be arranged?"
> She laughed suddenly and sharply and went half-way through the door, then turned her head to say coolly: "You're as cold-blooded a beast as I ever met Marlowe. Or can I call you Phil?"
> "Sure."
> "You can call me Vivian."
> "Thanks, Mrs. Regan."
> "Oh, go to hell, Marlowe." She went on out and didn't look back.

This is "snotting" at its most vivid, and Ray uses it not just to ramp up the tension between Marlowe and Vivian, but also to tell us about their characters. Vivian appears in this exchange to be as much of a sexual predator as her sister, though she is more subtle about it, while Marlowe comes over as a witty but rather reserved man.

One of the biggest steps Ray took in writing *The Big Sleep* was to focus on the city of Los Angeles itself. In the pulps, the city had shimmered ethereally in the background, occasionally slipping into a blurry almost-focus in later stories but, in *The Big Sleep*, Ray's perception of it becomes more concrete. We have already explored the way the System played an increasingly prominent role in his stories and, despite this being a relatively domestic novel, it still makes its appearance:

> "You ought to stop some of that flash gambling," I said.
> "With the syndicate we got in this county? Be your age, Marlowe."

Marlowe and Bernie Ohls are discussing Eddie Mars's illegal casino in Las Olindas, and it is clear that Mars is part of the underworld that connects the powerful in Los Angeles. Another example of the same theme is Geiger's pornographic book store, which is tolerated by a corrupt police force that has a stake in keeping it open. In the short stories, it is clear that the corruption which led to this situation develops because the people in Los Angeles are corrupt or corruptible. In *The Big Sleep*, however, Ray turns the city itself into a corrupting influence, rather than an empty vessel. Los Angeles is not just a city in *The Big Sleep*, but a poisonous place; it is not merely a home to lonely people, but actually makes them lonely. Marlowe's experience with Silver-Wig underlines this point: "I was driving hard along the highway through the rain, with Silver-Wig in the corner of the car, saying nothing, so that by the time we reached Los Angeles we seemed to be utter strangers again." Within the city boundaries, there can be no connection.

In the same manner, the corruption of the Sternwood family is shown to be a product of the pernicious influence of Los Angeles. The Sternwoods are inextricably tangled up in the city. The General's grandfather fought in the Mexican war, a struggle that resulted in Mexico ceding the Alta-California territory, and ultimately led to the formation of the state of California in 1850. They are also an oil family, part of the industry on which the city was built. At one point, Marlowe looks out of the mansion and observes old, semi-retired derricks in the distance:

> The Sternwoods, having moved up the hill, could no longer smell the stale sump water of the oil, but they could look out of their front windows and see what had made them rich. If they wanted to. I don't suppose they would want to.

The parallel Ray draws between the city of Los Angeles and the Stern-wood family is made explicit in this passage. Both have built their fortunes on oil, and the city, like the Sternwoods, has tried to detach and segregate the oilfields. Oil, in Ray's view, is the essence of corruption, and that has infected the whole family, generation after generation. The General is no better than his daughters, as he makes clear: "Vivian is spoiled, exacting, smart and quite ruthless. Carmen is a child who likes to pull wings off flies. Neither of them has any more moral sense than a cat. Neither have I. No Sternwood ever had." And just as the General and Vivian share their coal-black eyes, they share blood which "was always wild blood, but . . . wasn't always rotten." Once wild, now rotten—just like Los Angeles. That is echoed in continual references to the expansion of the city and its consequences: "This is a big town now, Eddie. Some very tough people have checked in here lately. The penalty of growth."

Ray was certainly not the only author to pick up on the dark side of the city. In *The Day of the Locust*, Nathanael West mines similar seams. In West's novella, published in the same year as *The Big Sleep*, Tod Hackett's talent as an artist is gradually destroyed by the glittering world of Hollywood. Everything in the city is flat and shallow and fake.

> The house was queer. It had an enormous and very crooked stone chimney, little dormer windows with big hoods and a thatched roof that came down very low on both sides of the front door. The door was of gumwood, painted like fumed oak and it hung on enormous hinges. Although made by machines, the hinges had been carefully stamped to appear hand-forged. The same kind of care and skill had been used to make the roof thatching, which was not really straw but heavy fireproof paper colored and ribbed to look like straw.

Ray picks up on the same kind of fakery in *The Big Sleep*: "About the only part of a Californian house you can't put your foot through is the front door." The flatness produces a strange boredom in the city's inhabitants, as Nathanael West explains:

> [In Los Angeles] they discover that sunshine isn't enough. . . . Nothing happens. They don't know what to do with their time. . . . They

watch the waves come in at Venice . . . but after you've seen one wave, you've seen them all. The same is true of the airplanes at Glendale. If only a plane would crash once in a while so that they could watch the passengers being consumed in a "holocaust of flames," as the newspapers put it. But the planes never crash.

Their boredom becomes more and more terrible. They realize that they've been tricked and burn with resentment.

The Sternwoods suffer from the strange flatness and boredom of the city just as do West's more recent arrivals. Carmen, in particular, struggles: her boredom results in a desperate nymphomania and, ultimately, violence. Los Angeles corrupts by offering a hope of excitement that is crushed by the dullness of reality.

Ray's lasting achievement in *The Big Sleep* was the creation of Philip Marlowe. When Dashiell Hammett was writing *The Maltese Falcon*, he deliberately distanced Sam Spade from his readers in two ways: first, by using the third person; and, second, by describing Spade as a rather odd, alien type of man:

> Samuel Spade's jaw was long and bony, his chin a jutting v under the more flexible v of his mouth. His nostrils curved back to make another, smaller, v. His yellow-grey eyes were horizontal. The v *motif* was picked up again by thickish brows rising outward from twin creases above a hooked nose, and his pale brown hair grew down— from high flat temples—in a point on his forehead. He looked rather pleasantly like a blond satan.

The strange eyes, the abstract *v* motif, and the fact that he looks like Satan makes Spade seem barely human. Marlowe, by contrast, is attractive, and very human. He is also witty.

It is in Marlowe's voice that we find the metaphors and similes for which Ray's prose is most famous. They rarely appeared in the pulp stories but *The Big Sleep* is littered with them: "The General spoke again, slowly, using his strength as carefully as an out-of-work showgirl uses her last pair of stockings." Here is another: "She approached me with enough sex appeal to stampede a business men's lunch." These are just two examples—there are many more. These descriptive elements fulfill an important function: Marlowe is not a hero just because he is tough, or because he has a gun, but because he knows how to express himself.

Marlowe is also appealing because he can be hurt. He is no superman, not like Mickey Spillane's Mike Hammer, the kind of pulp hero who can endure any number of beatings without suffering. Nor can he drink without consequence: he gets hangovers. He gets depressed. Marlowe is sickened by the behavior of Carmen and Vivian just as the reader is, and he is able to put it into words:

> I got up feeling sluggish and tired and stood looking out of the windows, with a dark harsh taste of Sternwoods still in my mouth. . . . You can have a hangover from other things than alcohol. I had one from women. Women made me sick.

Ray wanted some death scenes to touch the reader emotionally ("The things they really cared about, and that I cared about, were the creation of emotion through dialogue and description"[12]) and, by describing Harry Jones's death through Marlowe's eyes, he surely does so:

> I wiped sweat off my face. I walked to the far corner of the office and stood with my face to the wall, patted it with a hand. I turned around slowly and looked across at little Harry Jones grimacing in his chair.
>
> "Well, you fooled him, Harry," I said out loud, in a voice that sounded queer to me. "You lied to him and you drank your cyanide like a little gentleman. You died like a poisoned rat, Harry, but you're no rat to me."

The accomplishment of this scene is not just conveying the sadness of Jones's death but that Marlowe is hurt by it. Unlike, say, Hercule Poirot, Marlowe is not the same man at the end of the story as at the start, and he articulates the change he goes through more like the narrator of a literary rite of passage novel than a crime story.

His opening gambit, delivered when he sees the stained-glass panel in the entrance hall to the Sternwood house, shows Marlowe's innocence and instinct to gallantry:

There was a broad stained-glass panel showing a knight in dark armor rescuing a lady who was tied to a tree and didn't have any clothes on but some very long and convenient hair. The knight had pushed the vizor of his helmet back to be sociable, and he was fiddling with the knots on the ropes that tied the lady to the tree and not getting anywhere. I stood there and thought that if I lived in the house, I would sooner or later have to climb up there and help him. He didn't really seem to be trying.

He is a knight, prepared to save the innocent damsel in distress. Towards the end of the novel that self-view has soured: "Knights had no meaning in this game. It wasn't a game for knights."

The very conclusion of the book makes clear just how much he has changed:

> What did it matter where you lay once you were dead? In a dirty sump or in a marble tower on top of a high hill? You were dead, you were sleeping the big sleep. . . . Oil and water were the same as wind and air to you. You just slept the big sleep, not caring about the nastiness of how you died or where you fell. Me, I was part of the nastiness now.

There are some unsettling moments in *The Big Sleep*. Marlowe's attitude to women is disconcerting and something not previously seen in Ray's writing. When Carmen Sternwood pays a late-night visit to Marlowe's apartment, looking to seduce him, he throws her out and returns to his apartment where this happens:

> I went back to the bed and looked down at it. The imprint of her head was still in the pillow, of her small corrupt body still on the sheets.
>   I put my empty glass down and tore the bed to pieces savagely.

Marlowe's reaction is strange and violent, almost psychotic. Note that he is not reacting to her body but to its imprint, and it is this apparently inanimate element that provokes him. Later on, he sees a condom and it, too, provokes a disgusted reaction, albeit more subdued: "In a shadowy angle against the scribbled wall a pouched ring of pale rubber had fallen and not been disturbed. A very nice building." It is odd that these mere reminders of sex seem to anger Marlowe so much, and there has been plenty of discussion about what this implies. Does it mean, as some have suggested, that Marlowe—and, by extension, Ray—was a closeted homosexual? Ray liked a domestic environment and, for him, home was not somewhere tainted by sex. In a revealing letter to his friend James Sandoe, he wrote: "I find it impossible to respect a woman who lives with a man. She can sleep with him all she pleases and with whomever she pleases and in whatever place she pleases, but the tawdry imitation of domesticity gets me down."[13] As Judith Freeman has pointed out, for Ray, it wasn't "sex that cheapened a woman. It was playing house when she wasn't married." An imprint on the bed should symbolize a long relationship, the bed being worn through years of companionship. In this case, it represents the opposite—cheap, impure, loveless sex. This explains, in part, the more uncomfortable passages of *The Big Sleep*, but it does not explain why Ray made the most dangerous people in his novels women, or why Marlowe seems only to feel real affection for other men.

By the end of 1938, Ray had completed his final draft of *The Big Sleep* and was happy with it. He sent it first to an agent, Sydney Sanders, who was familiar with the sort of pulp writing that *Black Mask* produced. Sanders loved the novel and immediately recognized that Ray should be placed at Alfred A. Knopf Inc. who had so successfully published Hammett and Cain. These two writers had, more than anyone else, established a wide audience for the hard-boiled novel. Both *The Maltese Falcon* and *The Postman Always Rings Twice* had succeeded because they did not appeal only to readers of detective fiction but to readers of more literary fiction too. Founded in 1915, Knopf had a strong literary reputation, publishing authors such as Theodore Dreiser, D. H. Lawrence, and Sigmund Freud. It also had a small imprint called the Borzoi Mysteries overseen by Alfred A. Knopf's wife, Blanche. It is likely that Sanders would have submitted *The Big Sleep* straight to her, and she certainly worked on the manuscript. This marked the beginning of a new friendship, and the Knopfs, who often visited California, would try to meet up with Ray whenever they came.

In the lead-up to publication, Knopf decided to invest heavily in publicity. In autumn 1938, he took a full-page advertisement on the cover of *Publisher's Weekly*, the main organ of the American book trade. The first three lines were:

In 1929 Dashiell Hammett
In 1934 James M. Cain
In 1939 Raymond Chandler

He was signaling that he had signed a new star, the heir apparent to the hard-boiled tradition. Unfortunately the advert, with its dates and names, also has something of the gravestone about it and, for Ray, this was a sign of things to come. Yes, he was a writer of hard-boiled crime fiction, but he was not only that. This advertisement and other publicity fixed him in the public mind as a certain type of writer and, thereafter, he struggled to shake off the hard-boiled label.

Still, in 1939, in his fifties, Ray had finally achieved a lifelong ambition: he could describe himself not only as a writer but as a novelist. He had made it.

CHAPTER NINE

"A FEW DROPS OF TABASCO ON THE OYSTER"

By the beginning of 1939, Ray, Cissy, and their Persian cat, Taki, were living in Riverside, California. It was a decent-sized town, with a temperate, almost Mediterranean climate, and made for an agreeable change from the cooler conditions to be found at Big Bear Lake, where they had spent their last few months. One of the beauties of the Californian climate is its sheer variety, and they took full advantage of this, entering into a rhythm where they spent winters on the warm coast and summers in the cool, dry mountain air. This was largely for the benefit of Cissy's lungs, which were starting to be a real problem. On coming down from the mountains, the Chandlers really wanted to stay in La Jolla, a small town north of San Diego, but possibly because it was expensive, they only stayed there for a short time choosing the cheaper, less glamorous Riverside as their temporary base.

At Riverside, Ray had a lot on his mind. *The Big Sleep* was published in the States in February and, as any new writer would be, he was nervous about how it would be received. He had a lot riding on the two-dollar hardback with its bold cover in red, white, and blue. It represented an effort not of months, but of years, the culmination of a plan that had been faintly sketched back in 1932 when Ray first started writing for the pulps.

The reviews came through in a trickle and, at first, they were not encouraging. For a start the book usually appeared in the regular crime fiction roundups, something which frustrated Ray deeply. And, when they did appear, the reviewers could be cutting, as in this from the *New York Herald Tribune*:

> In our opinion, though, Mr. Chandler has almost spoiled it with a top-heavy cargo of lurid underworld incident, and he should therefore be stood in a corner and lectured upon the nature and suitable use of his talents.[1]

A review in the *New York Times* made Ray remark that it had "deflated me pretty thoroughly."[2] To Chandler, *The Big Sleep* was a "detective yarn that happens—from my point of view . . . to be more interested in people than in plot, to try to stand on its own legs as a novel, with the mystery a few drops of Tabasco on the oyster."[3] To most reviewers, though, it was just another crime story. There were some positive reviews. The *New Republic* said: "If you have any feeling for subtle workmanship, don't give it the go-by."[4] The *Los Angeles Times* described Ray as the man who could "out Cain James M. Cain," which cheered Ray up enough for him to write to a friend: "I don't feel quite such a connoisseur of moral decay as I did yesterday."[5] But it is fair to say that reception was mixed and that Ray did not achieve the recognition that he had hoped for.

Having completed one book, he started to plan for the next, in the hope that crime fiction would lead to something more:

> I should probably do a minimum of three mystery novels before I try anything else.[6]

Crime writing, to Ray, was a waypoint on the route to something else, and he had an idea of what that something else might be. A little more than a month after *The Big Sleep* was released, he sat down and started to map out his future, asking Cissy to type his plan onto one of the stiff card-like pages he could clip into his leather notebook. The page started, "Since all plans are foolish and those written down are never fulfilled, let us make a plan, this 16th day of March 1939, at Riverside Calif." For the rest of 1939, all of 1940, and the spring of 1941, he would focus on detective novels, and he made brief sketches of these books next to potential titles: *Law Is Where You Buy It* ("theme, the corrupt alliance of police and racketeers in a small Californian town, outwardly as fair as the dawn"), *The Brasher Doubloon* ("a burlesque of the pulp novelette . . . mostly new plot"), and *Zone of Twilight* ("A grim witty story of the boss politician's son and the girl and the blending of the upper and underworlds . . ."). And then he went on to outline another book, *English Summer*, which would be the one he had always wanted to write. This would be the novel that he hoped would send him to England and would be very different from the four preceding. It was based on a short story he had written as a very young man (no more is known than that) and had kept with him ever since. He had a very clear ambition for the story:

> A short, swift, tense, gorgeously written melodrama, based on my short story. The surface theme is the decay of the refined character and its contrast with the ingenuous honest utterly fearless and gener-ous American of the best type.[7]

In Ray's scheme, *English Summer* was going to be the book that would let him move on from mystery writing into something different. It was not that he wanted to abandon crime writing altogether but, rather, that he did not want to become trapped by it: he did not intend crime fiction to be the sum total of his career.

What should we make of this map of the future? It is difficult to believe that Ray himself put much faith in it, as his preface indicates. Cissy, too, seems to have had concerns about her husband's plans, adding a short note to the end of his entries:

> Dear Raymio, you'll have fun looking at this maybe, and seeing what useless dreams you had. Or perhaps it will not be fun.

It was a prescient coda—Ray never would get to "forget mystery writ-ing"—one that might also seem a sharp, almost mean thing to write to a husband. To see it in this light, though, is to take it out of context. This is not an example of Cissy's cruelty but rather shows how close she and Ray were. The list was Ray at his most ambitious. It is a glimpse of the man who could travel to America with a cane and a good suit and expect to make it; of a man who had moved to Los Angeles when it was little more than a settlement in the desert; of the man who could drive along a deserted coastal road, pick up a cheap magazine, and be inspired to believe he could become a writer. Cissy instinctively recognized her husband's flighty excitement and understood these ambitions had the fuzzy nature of dreams, rather than the solidity of resolutions. At around the same time, Ray listed a series of potential book titles. One, *Sit With Me While I Dream*, he noted could be the title for his autobiography. Cissy worried, though, that her overambitious Raymio was running ahead of himself: he had only published one book, after all.

Every journey had to start somewhere and, eager to get going, Ray decided that the best way to prepare for the next book was to reread the last one. He found *The Big Sleep* to be "unequally written" with scenes that were still redolent of the pulp magazines he had cut his teeth on but, at the same time, he knew it was a step in the right direction. As he prepared to start his next book, he took a degree of comfort in the sales figures. The American edition of *The Big Sleep* sold around ten thousand copies, netting Ray $2,000 in royalties. Though sales of Dashiell Hammett's *The Thin Man* outstripped sales of *The Big Sleep* by a factor of ten to one,[8] Ray's novel was considered a modest success. Knopf was encouraging and wanted him to keep writing. Similarly, the English edition of the book, which had been published in Britain by Hamish Hamilton in March 1939, was highly regarded by publisher Jamie Hamilton and, like Knopf, he was keen to see another book.

Ray was buoyed by the support he was receiving but it had its downside: suddenly he found his head fizzing with ideas. In late March he settled down to write, starting with the first novel on the list, *The Law Is Where You Buy It* but, within a few days, had given up. Years later, he could not remember why he had abandoned this early idea, only that it had "died" on him. Instead, he took up a different idea, one that would eventually form the kernel of *Farewell, My Lovely*. The tentative title was *The Girl from Brunette's* and progress was steady. By April 12, 1939, Ray had written 10 pages; by April 23, he wrote "First lap—'The girl from Florians'"; and five days later, had filled 127 pages of the short, yellow pieces of paper he wrote on. He made headway until May, when he suddenly changed his mind:

This story is a flop. It smells to high heaven. I think I'll have to scrap it and try something new.[9]

Briefly, he picked up a short story, "Tony Gets Out," which became "I'll Be Waiting," but found he was unable to concentrate on that either, so he returned to *The Girl From Florians*. By the end of the month, he had given it up again, picking up yet another new idea. It is not clear if he returned to *The Law Is Where You Buy It* or if he started afresh but, for the next few weeks he continued to write. His notes revealed that the character he had focused on was called Adrian Fromsett, who would later appear in *The Lady In The Lake* (though her name would be spelled as Adrienne), and he was therefore perhaps working on the idea that would evolve into that 1943 novel throughout June 1939. Again, he made progress but hit a block:

Tragic realization that there is another dead cat under the house. More than three-quarters done and no good.[10]

The flurry of activity, carefully detailed in his diary, and recounted years later to his lawyer, sheds an unusual amount of light on Ray's writing method, revealing the patterns in his approach. He wrote his books scene by scene and rarely, if ever, knew where the plot would take him. His use of stories helped provide a framework for a book, but it was not a rigid one. Sometimes an old pulp story would provide a scene or character, sometimes more, but they rarely provided a conclusion. This was the problem in trying to entwine two plots. Sometimes it worked, as in the case of *The Big Sleep*, but not always. This lack of direction caused Ray endless problems, the most difficult being the necessity of stitching together a lot of unconnected events to make a seamless whole. Time and experience would eventually help him refine this method but, in early 1939, he was still feeling his way as a writer. He did not yet fully understand his strengths or his weaknesses and, in a morass of half-formed ideas, he struggled to identify a clear way, which caused him to fret, further hampering his ability to concentrate.

Issues of plot and construction were not the only things weighing on his mind in mid-1939. Chief among his worries was the distant rumble of war in Europe. He was following events there closely, and the importance of the annexing of Austria and the invasion of Czechoslovakia were not lost on him. Having fought in one war against Germany, he could easily imagine what a second Great War would mean, and could not stop worrying about it. In one letter to Blanche Knopf, he said: "The effort to keep my mind off the war has reduced me to the mental age of seven."[11] The more he worried about events in Europe, the less energy he found he had to work.

In Riverside, the daytime temperature was starting to get too hot for the Chandlers, so they packed their bags and headed for the cooler air of the mountains. They arrived back in Big Bear Lake sometime in the summer, certainly before August, and, among the trees and the soft noises of the local fauna, Ray tried to regain some focus. Things started out well enough. In July, he picked up again the draft of the book that would eventually become *Farewell, My Lovely* and started tinkering with it. In fact, his earlier dissatisfaction seems to have evaporated entirely by the end of August, when he wrote to Blanche Knopf, saying that he only had twelve thousand words left to write and promising her a manuscript the following month. On September 15, he wrote again to say that he had completed a draft, but he would not be able to deliver a clean version for at least another six weeks. By this point, Germany had invaded Poland, leading France and Britain to declare war. For Ray, who had relatives in London, albeit now distant ones, the confirmation of news that had long been expected was devastating. On September 29, he tried to enlist in the Canadian Army again. He saw little point in remaining neutral about the war, and the patriotic urge instilled at Dulwich pushed him towards doing his duty. Had he been younger, he may have found himself fighting German soldiers once again but, at fifty-one, he was rejected out of hand. Rather than relief, he felt frustration, and his work suffered. *Farewell, My Lovely*, which only two weeks before he had thought close to completion, was quietly filed away while he tried to distract himself with other projects.

Without a new book, money was tight, so Ray returned to writing short stories. For some time, his agent, Sydney Sanders, had been pestering him to write a story that could be sold to the slick magazines, but Ray had resisted in the firm belief that "good serials seldom make good novels."[12] Faced with financial pressures, though, he relented, and sent Sanders "I'll Be Waiting," a story he'd been toying with since the summer. Sanders placed it in the *Saturday Evening Post*, where it appeared on October 14, 1939.

"I'll Be Waiting" is markedly different from Ray's pulp work and was a great success. Just as in previous short stories, he tried to leave his readers with an afterglow, a feeling that lingered long after the reading was over. The central character, Tony Reseck, sneaks a criminal out of the hotel he works in, but this action inadvertently leads to the death of a friend. The power of the story comes from our recognition of Tony's loss and the part he played in the killing. Towards the end, Tony receives a call. Expecting it to be his friend Al, he picks up, but a different voice comes on the line:

> "We had a little business with a guy in your place. Picked him up scramming. Al had a hunch you'd run him out. Tailed him and took him to the curb. Not so good. Backfire."
>
> Tony held the phone very tight and his temples chilled with the evaporation of moisture. "Go on," he said. "I guess there's more."
>
> "A little. The guy stopped the big one. Cold. Al—Al said to tell you goodbye."
>
> Tony leaned hard against the desk. His mouth made a sound that was not speech.

It is a powerful moment. Tony's world is instantly eviscerated and, as the ending makes clear, there is only the slimmest of chances that he will be able to recover. It is a powerful example of what Ray could do and, indeed, how far he had come since 1932, but he continued to feel uncomfortable with the slicks. He wrote that its strictures left the story "artificial, untrue and emotionally dishonest,"[13] and though this is perhaps an unnecessarily harsh judgement that focuses too much on the story's weaknesses, it indicates that the emotional quality of his work, the richness of his characters and the realism of their actions, was paramount in his mind at this time. Even though a career in the slicks might have helped bring in a steady, almost comfortable income, Ray refused to be swayed and returned instead to the plan he had drafted at the start of the year.

So far his attempts to write a new novel had been frustrating, but he continued to tinker with other ideas, such as a story called "The Bronze Door," the title of which first appeared on a list in his notebook in 1938. It was not to be a crime story, but a fantasy. Ray continued to work on the story throughout 1939, completing it sometime in the early summer. It was published in November of that year in a pulp magazine called *Unknown*. Its editor, John W. Campbell, who also ran *Astounding Science Fiction*, had a keen eye for stories that involved the weird and wonderful—for example, he once commissioned a story about a swimming team coach who recruited a mermaid to help. When "The Bronze Door" landed on his desk, he quickly bought up the rights to publish.

What motivated Ray to write a story of this type? In many ways it was a natural step for him to take. He always saw himself as a highly experimental writer and this presented a unique challenge: was it possible to show an unrealistic thing within the confines of a realistic world? Where crime writing had become work, this was fun, as well as providing a much-needed break from constantly dwelling on the corruption of Los Angeles.

"The Bronze Door" is set in London. The main character, James Sutton-Cornish, is an unhappily married man with a drinking problem, who returns home one day—he is drunk, of course—to an angry wife who is in the process of leaving him:

> She looked at him horribly, turned again, said over her shoulder: "This is the end, James. The end of our marriage."
>
> Mr. Sutton-Cornish said appallingly: "Goodness, m'dear are we married?"
>
> She started to turn again, but didn't. A sound like somebody being strangled in a dungeon came from her. Then she went on.
>
> The door of the room hung open like a paralyzed mouth. Mr. Sutton-Cornish stood just inside it, listening. He didn't move until he heard steps on the floor above. . . . He sighed. . . . Then he crept downstairs, into his long, narrow study beside the entrance hall, and got at the whiskey.

Were there echoes here of arguments between Ray and Cissy when he himself was drinking heavily?

Sutton-Cornish's life takes a strange turn when, on leaving his house, he tries to call a hansom cab and the driver does not seem to know about World War I ("Wot war, guv'nor?"). It gets decidedly weirder when, in an auction room, he comes across a strange bronze door that has the power to make the people who pass through it vanish into thin air. Intrigued and fascinated, he buys the door and, inevitably, uses it to make his wife and her annoying dog disappear. Sutton-Cornish meets his comeuppance, though, when a police officer from Scotland Yard starts to investigate. Having failed to push the policeman through the door, Sutton-Cornish ends up vanishing himself.

It is a strange story, but it is presented in a thoroughly natural way, and that is the key to its success. Here is the moment when Sutton-Cornish first discovers the door's powers:

> He straightened, and with a pleasantly idle gesture thrust his stick forward through the opening. And then, for the second time that evening, something incredible happened to him. . . .
>
> Mr. Sutton-Cornish looked down at his gloved right hand. There was no stick in it. There was nothing in it. He stepped to one side and looked behind the door. There was no stick there, on the dusty floor.
>
> He had felt nothing. Nothing had jerked at him. The stick had merely passed part way through the door and then—it had merely ceased to exist.

Ray worked hard to make the story feel real. In his original plan, he had noted that each of the fantastical stories he intended to write would have a different effect. They were experiments in method and a continuation of the fascination with the mechanics of writing that he exhibited when learning the art of crime writing.

Despite having grand plans for his fantastical stories, he rarely managed to inject much life into them and, more often than not, they remained locked away in his notebook. "The Bronze Door" was a rare exception. It marked a first attempt in a different genre, and perhaps Ray would have explored the fantastic further had he not been drawn back to *Farewell, My Lovely*.

By October 1939, Ray and Cissy were starting to think about their next move. The weather at Big Bear Lake was becoming too cool, which signaled that it was time to head back down the mountain. Ray had worked fitfully through-out his time in the country and had produced fragments of two novels, neither of which were in a state to be published. The Chandlers first choice was La Jolla, where they had briefly stayed in previous years. It is a small town that sits on a bulge of land shaped like a clenched fist jutting into the Pacific. The beach and the ocean were easily accessible to residents, and the climate was usually warm and languid. Ray described it as combining "good manners" with "the perfect climate both winter and summer" and "the finest coastline on the Pacific side of the country."[14] It was a place he would settle in, if he could ever afford it.

They had briefly spent time there in 1938 and had fallen in with the local literary crowd ("It has a few writers, not too many, no bohemian atmosphere (but they will let you take a drink)"[15]) but, a year later, things were different. The writers had left or, worse, had got rich:

> The literary colony here has undergone a few modifications since we were here last year. That is, those of the boys who are making any money are now playing their tennis at the Beach Club. The old cast system is at its dirty work again. I don't think the beach club is very expensive but a few bucks off his whisky ration plays hell with a writer's imagination.[16]

La Jolla now seemed somehow less vibrant, less literary and, above all, less like somewhere they wanted to settle. Ray's dream had been to live in La Jolla during the winter and have a cabin in the mountains in the summer but, to his surprise and frustration, La Jolla now depressed him. He was getting sick of the regular moves and, though part of him craved stability, it was clear that La Jolla was not the place for them:

> We haven't had one [a home] for so long that I look back with a touch of nostalgia to any place we have stayed in as long as six months. I don't think we shall be here long either. Too dear, too damp, too elderly, a nice place, as a visitor remarked this afternoon, for old peo-ple and their parents.[17]

It is likely that the average age of inhabitants of La Jolla had a nega-tive effect on the Chandlers, too. When Ray said to Blanche Knopf that "advancing age" drove him away from La Jolla,[18] though he was referring ostensibly to himself, he was perhaps also alluding to Cissy, who was now approaching seventy but had always battled hard to stay young. Then there was the weather. They had moved down from the mountain to get away from the cold but arrived to find the town damp, which played havoc not only with Cissy's health but also Ray's—he started to develop rheumatism in one arm. In the end, they stayed for Christmas and moved on after New Year's—and what a restless year 1940 would prove to be.

From La Jolla they headed to Monrovia, in the foothills of the San Gabriel Mountains and north of the city of Los Angeles, but the neighbors were loud and Ray could not focus on his work. After only a few weeks, they headed three miles west to Arcadia, another small town in the Los Angeles basin, where they took an apartment in a bungalow complex. This was now the Chandlers' most unsettled period since they had married, and the stress was beginning to take its toll. Ray found it difficult to work on the new draft of his book and this, in turn, began to create pressures of a different kind:

> I had to throw my second book away, so that leaves me with nothing
> to show for the last six months and possibly nothing to eat for the
> next six.[19]

But in Monrovia, at last, Ray rediscovered the urge to write. Perhaps, in part, this was out of sheer necessity, though he could have survived financially by producing the occasional pulp story. For the first time in several months, he found himself able to focus properly on the manuscript for his nearly completed Marlowe novel and, after a few short weeks, had a draft ready for Blanche Knopf.

By the time he sent the book to his publisher, the title had changed several times and, with each change, it is clear Ray's attitude to his writing was evolving. One of the earliest titles, *The Girl from Florian's*, is redolent of the pulps. A later title, *The Second Murderer*, a reference to *Richard III*, was an improvement but, by deploying the word *murder*, it declared loudly its roots in the mystery genre. It is little wonder, then, that the team at Knopf liked this title immensely and actively encouraged Ray to keep it. From their perspective, this made a lot of sense: it sounded like a murder mystery and would easily find a home in a bookshop alongside the likes of Agatha Christie or Rex Stout. Ray, however, was beginning to have second thoughts, and suggested *Farewell, My Lovely* instead. It took him a lot of effort to convince Blanche Knopf (she "howled like hell about the title"[20] because it was "not at all a mystery title"[21]) and she must have worried that the book's audience would be turned off by something so enigmatic. Ray's instincts were right. *Farewell, My Lovely* is a beautiful title that, unlike *The Big Sleep*, does not find its source in the story. In fact it is not clear who the "Lovely" referred to might actually be, but that is part of its secret. The combination of the spondee of "Farewell" with the amphibrach "My Lovely" gives it a haunting quality quite different from contemporary hard-boiled titles. It points to a kind of romantic weakness at the center that is rather appealing. It is certainly very different to the other titles advertised on the cover of the first edition: *The Glass Triangle* by George Harmon Coxe and *Journey into Fear* by Eric Ambler have a hardness to them that pales in comparison with the nuance of *Farewell, My Lovely*. The title suggests the book is something grander than a mere mystery novel. Despite Blanche Knopf's protestations, Ray was convinced he had the best understanding of what his readers wanted:

> I have never had any great respect for the ability of editors, publishers, play and picture producers to guess what the public will like. The record is all against them. I have always tried to put myself in the shoes of the ultimate consumer, the reader, and ignore the middleman. I have always assumed that there exists in the country a fairly large group of intelligent people . . . who like what I like.[22]

In the long run, he proved himself right.

Ray worked on the proofs throughout July. They were a mess and he went to great efforts to untangle some of the errors his copy editors had dropped in. He was very specific about points of grammar ("When I split an infinitive, God damn it, I split it so it stays split," he told a copyeditor who had the temerity to correct his language), and the emendations took time. He had originally planned to deliver the completed book in August, but it was delayed with his extra edits. In the end, it was published in October 1940 in both America and Britain. Despite its troubled genesis, Ray had completed two novels in a little under two years. He was right to feel proud.

Farewell, My Lovely was, for a long time, Ray's favorite of his own books. Nearly a decade after its publication he wrote to Dale Warren: "I think *Farewell, My Lovely* is the top and that I shall never again achieve quite the same combination of ingredients."[23]

If *The Big Sleep* announced Ray's intentions to the world, then *Farewell, My Lovely* was the book in which he showed the extent of his skill. It starts on Central Avenue, downtown Los Angeles, with Marlowe on the hunt for an inconsequential Greek barber. The barber is quickly forgotten when Marlowe runs into Moose Malloy, recently released from jail and on the hunt for a former lover. He is huge—"not wider than a beer truck"—and gaudily dressed:

> He wore a shaggy borsalino hat, a rough grey sports coat with white golf balls on it for buttons, a brown shirt, a yellow tie, pleated grey flannel slacks and alligator shoes with white explosions on the toes. From his outer breast pocket cascaded a show handkerchief of the same brilliant yellow as his tie. There were a couple of colored feathers tucked into the band of his hat, but he didn't really need them. Even on Central Avenue, not the quietest dressed street in the world, he looked about as inconspicuous as a tarantula on a slice of angel food.

Things take a violent turn when Malloy drags Marlowe into a Central Avenue bar, where Malloy proceeds to kill a man in a sudden and brutal murder and then runs away. Marlowe, quite by chance, finds himself under interrogation by the police, even though his part in the murder is limited to being in the wrong place at the wrong time. The police take advantage of Marlowe's position and push him to find out more about Malloy, but he has already made up his mind to investigate—"Nothing made it my business except curiosity." Before long, he is pursuing a jewelery thief, a mysterious quack psychic, and a gangster.

In the plan Ray had inscribed into his notebook, *Farewell, My Lovely* was outlined as "the corrupt alliance of police and racketeers in a small Californian town, outwardly as fair as the dawn,"[24] but the novel that resulted was much more than that. To give the book a backbone, he wove together elements of his stories "Mandarin's Jade," "The Man Who Liked Dogs," and "Bay City Blues," setting the bulk of the novel in Bay City, a thinly veiled allusion to Santa Monica. Incidentally, though it has been said that Ray hated Santa Monica, he moved there shortly after the publication of *Farewell, My Lovely*, so this seems unlikely. Ray's intention appears to have been to explore that relationship between the police and racketeers, but what started out as a book about a corrupt town became one about how a town corrupts. Ray explored that by comparing the experiences of two very different police officers. On the one hand, there is the cop Marlowe nicknames Hemingway, who says of Bay City: "A guy can't stay honest if he wants to. . . . You gotta play dirty or you don't eat." On the other hand is Red Norgaard, a man who did try to stay clean but got kicked out of the force for doing so. Hemingway is the man that Red could have become if he had let his morals slip—outwardly successful but inwardly disappointed. Red is spiritually content but reduced to hunting for honest, casual work, and finding very little.

But Bay City's corrupting influence is broader, and the novel uses it as an example of a wider problem particular to Southern California. To live in the region means breathing the noxious fumes of an all-pervasive, inescapable corruption, and even Marlowe finds his own assumptions challenged. For example, at one point he suspects that Lindsay Marriot was murdered because he was involved with a gang of jewel thieves and organized crime but, in fact, the reason Marriot ended up dead was much simpler: he was the weak link in a chain that pointed to the real identity of Mrs. Lewin Lockridge Grayle and, to stop that being revealed, he had to be killed. Though there was a connection between some of the characters in the book, they were not tied together by murder, but murder was the inevitable result of corruption: just as metal rusts in the sea air, people are corrupted in Bay City. Mrs. Grayle was not destroyed by a conspiracy but, rather, her killing Marriot was the natural result of living in a poisonous place.[25]

Farewell, My Lovely represents a deeper engagement with Southern California than *The Big Sleep*, and it shows how his thinking about the area was changing. Evidently Ray had thought long and hard about the place where he had lived since 1913. He had spent years working at the heart of Los Angeles, both literally (downtown) and figuratively (in the oil industry), and could draw on the deep well of his own experience. At the same time, he was able to root the novel in the city's recent history. Knopf chose to draw attention to this in their promotion, with one attention-grabbing advertisement describing the book as "realism that *is* realism."[26]

One example of the book's closeness to life is the gambling ship featured in the closing scenes, which Ray based on the SS *Rex*, a vessel owned by former bootlegger and "gambling entrepreneur" Tony Cornero.[27] In the 1930s, gambling was illegal in California and so, to get around the law, ships anchored three miles off the coast, where they could claim to be in international waters. In 1938, Cornero opened the *Rex*, making sure it was a clean, safe ship; that it was open twenty-four hours a day; that there was good food and drink; and that the ferry from the mainland was cheap and efficient. This system made sure that ships like the *Rex* got a steady supply of high rollers but also, importantly, that they attracted a different kind of customer: the middle classes. As soon as the *Rex* opened, Cornero ran into trouble with the law, and Buron Fitts, then district attorney, unsuccessfully tried to have the ship shut down, but it was not until 1939 that California attorney general Earl Warren was finally able to do so, and only then after a standoff that saw the crew turn a fire hose onto police officers attempting to board. With the *Rex* out of action, Cornero moved to Las Vegas, Nevada, taking the business model with him and establishing the sort of casinos that are still familiar today.[28] In the end, Cornero never faced prosecution and the *Rex* was eventually put into service during the war, later to be sunk off the coast of Africa by a German U-boat. Ray was suspicious of the public attempts to close down the casinos ("Others had tried (or pretended to)") but came to the conclusion that Warren had solved the problem "very simply, and no doubt quite illegally."[29] This was a typical Southern California situation in which the good guys acted no better than the bad—a theme that would come up time and again in Ray's fiction.

Ray was right to be suspicious about the local police and their connection to the *Rex*. A few years after *Farewell, My Lovely* was published, he recounted a tale that made it clear that they were as corrupt as the local gangsters:

The other day I thought of your suggestion for an article of a studied insult about Bay City (Santa Monica) police. A couple of D.A.'s
investigators got a tip about a gambling hell in Ocean Park, a sleazy
adjunct to Santa Monica. They went down there and picked up a
couple of Santa Monica cops on the way, telling them they were
going to kick in a box, but not telling them where it was. The cops
went along with the natural reluctance of good cops to enforce the
law against a paying customer, and when they found out where the
place was, they mumbled brokenly: "We'd ought to talk to Captain
Brown about this before we do it, boys. Captain Brown ain't going
to like this." The D.A.'s men urged them heartlessly forward into the
chip and bone parlor, several alleged gamblers were tossed into the
sneezer and the equipment seized for evidence (a truckload of it) was
stored in lockers at local police headquarters. When the D.A.'s boys
came back the next morning to go over it everything had disappeared
but a few handfuls of white poker chips. The locks had not been
tampered with, and not a trace could be found of the truck or the
driver. The flatfeet shook their grizzled polls in bewilderment and the
investigators went back to town to hand the Jury the story.[30]

There is a weary resignation to the circumstances evident in this letter, the
epistolary equivalent of a knowing shake of the head, which masks a genuine
anger at the sort of corruption that was rampant in the 1930s. That anger is
better articulated through the voice of Philip Marlowe, with his sharp, biting
sarcasm:

It's a nice town. It's probably no crookeder than Los Angeles. But you
can only buy a piece of a big city. You can buy a town like this all
complete, with the original box and tissue paper.

If *Farewell, My Lovely* marks a different attitude to Southern California, it also marks a new level of depth to Ray's characters. Shortly before
he died, Ray was interviewed on BBC radio by Ian Fleming and, when the
conversation turned to villains, he said: "In my own mind I don't think I
ever think anyone is a villain." This interview took place in 1958 and, over
the years, Ray's view of his characters changed, but, nonetheless, it seems safe

to suggest that his approach to writing about criminals crystallized between the writing of *The Big Sleep* and *Farewell, My Lovely*. In the former, Carmen Sternwood is entirely bad—the distillation of pure evil, inherited from her father and unmediated by any natural goodness, as the frequent references to her animal nature suggest. In *Farewell, My Lovely*, the two central criminal characters, Moose Malloy and Mrs. Grayle, are presented with far greater complexity. Both are murderers and yet both also try to redeem themselves. Malloy, who Marlowe "strangely likes," is treated throughout with an unusual dignity despite being a double murderer and, right at the end, Marlowe says of him "*he* was a long way from being a rat," as if his actions had somehow been excusable and understandable. Similarly, before she dies, Mrs. Grayle shows a great deal of compassion towards her husband, something which she had failed to do before:

> Maybe she saw a chance—not to get away—she was tired of dodging by that time—but to give a break to the only man who had ever really given her a break.

Ray had been working on creating complex detective characters for some years; his willingness to add shade and depth to his villains was another big step. He had become interested in their motivation and wanted real characters, not just one-dimensional, functional bodies for Philip Marlowe to react against.

Despite its considerable successes, *Farewell, My Lovely* has always been a controversial work, attracting critical comment for two main reasons. First, there is the heavy charge of racism, and there can be no denying that the book has a number of objectionable passages. In the opening chapter, Ray describes Malloy's ejection of one of the bar's customers:

> The doors swung back outwards and almost settled to a stop. Before they had entirely stopped moving they opened again, violent, outwards. Something sailed across the sidewalk and landed in the gutter between two parked cars. It landed on its hands and knees and made a high keening noise like a cornered rat. It got up slowly, retrieved a hat and stepped back on to the sidewalk. It was a thin, narrow-shouldered brown youth in a lilac color suit and a carnation. It had slick

black hair. It kept its mouth open and whined for a moment. People stared at it vaguely. Then it settled its hat jauntily, sidled over to the wall and walked silently splay-footed off along the block.

No matter how deeply you drill into Ray's life and his private writings, nothing excuses his repeated use of the word "it" to describe a black character. If we compare the way that he deploys the word "rat" in the book, we see an uncomfortable judgment behind the writing: the murderer Malloy is described as "a long way from being all rat"—a man with dignity, despite being a killer; the character ejected from Florian's, on the other hand, is "like a cornered rat." The implication is unmistakable: a white man can kill and yet keep his dignity whereas a black man, who has committed no crime, belongs to the lowest rank of animal.

It is easy to pass this sort of language off as being nothing more than a reflection of the environment. Certainly Ray was working in a genre where race was a frequent topic. *Black Mask* magazine at one point ran an editorial that promoted debate about the Ku Klux Klan and, though it was careful to avoid calling outright for readers to support the KKK, its airing of the subject might indicate the thinking of its readership and editors. Even if Ray was trying to fit into the constricts of a genre, or was reflecting his era, there can be no denying that the way he presents his black characters throughout the novel is racist. On one of the few occasions that one of his black characters is given a voice, he speaks as a stereotype: "Yessuh, this liquor has been keepin' the right company." It is a far cry from the sophisticated vernacular put in the mouths of the white people in the book. Quite simply, Ray does not present his black characters with the same vitality or care as his white characters. And when combined with his repeated use of "it," not to mention "nigger" to describe a black character, the charge of racism is hard to refute.

It was not only in fiction that Ray expressed his racism and, a few years after *Farewell, My Lovely* was published, having had trouble finding someone to help at home, he wrote the following to a friend:

> Everyone has colored people and they are no damn good to us. My wife simply will not put up with their dirt.[31]

That views like this were common currency in the 1940s makes no difference—Ray's statement is indefensible.

Farewell, My Lovely has also been pored over by critics looking for evidence that Ray was gay. Certainly the novel manifests some of the most homoerotic language that he ever deployed. Here, for example, is Marlowe's description of Red:

> I looked at him again. He had the eyes you never see, that you only read about. Violet eyes. Almost purple. Eyes like a girl, a lovely girl. His skin was as soft as silk.

However, the reason for this sort of language is perhaps more complicated than it may at first appear. In this novel, Marlowe makes two strong connections, one with Red and another with Malloy. These are real relationships that ultimately fail because Malloy dies, and Red has to return to the job he lost as a Bay City police officer. That does not take away from the fact that Marlowe could have found a real and lasting friend in either man. In contrast, the relationships in *The Big Sleep* were always going to be impossible to sustain. It is true that Marlowe makes a connection with the General but, because the old man is dying, it can never be a lasting friendship. Marlowe's loneliness has a real chance of being addressed in *Farewell, My Lovely*. His way of describing these men is loaded with homoeroticism because this is the only language with which he can fully express a desire for a connection.

Many have used this language to suggest that a latent homosexuality makes itself known in Ray's fiction. He reached maturity in a very tightly organized public school, where sexual desires were sublimated through sports and other activities, and where chaste male friendships were encouraged and prized above all others. The English public school novel, one of the oddities of the late nineteenth and early twentieth centuries, was aimed at young men who had been through the school system. These books were sepia-tinted re-creations of happy school days and, in many, the boys formed extremely close friendships that, though sexless, were loaded with romantic allusion and imagery. In *Tim*, a novel by H. O. Sturgis published in 1891, the title character has developed a close friendship with a boy called Carol, which reads as wholly romantic:

> Listening to the history of the two friends long ago, [Tim] felt his
> love for his friend almost a religion to him. . . . "What woman could
> love him as I do?" thought Tim, as he looked to the seat where Carol
> sat. At that moment a sunbeam from some hole high in the roof fell
> on the golden curly head, which seemed transfigured; and as Tim's
> hungry eyes rested on the face of his friend, he turned towards him
> and smiled upon him in his place.[32]

Public school novels often feature boys apparently infatuated with other
boys, and this was usually depicted by feminizing the object of love. There is
no direct evidence that Ray read these books, but they were so common, so
widely read, and he was so invested in the public school system that it seems
unlikely he did not. Ray may have missed any homoerotic subtext, taking
on board their use of romantic language and the idealized relationships they
portrayed. This is not to say that he did not feel attraction to other men but
rather that there is another explanation for his use of romantic terms to frame
male relationships in his work.

Farewell, My Lovely was published in October 1940 in both America and
Britain. Knopf had high hopes for the book, printing seven thousand copies
on the assumption that it would outsell *The Big Sleep*. They were hugely disappointed when it did not. The critical reaction was almost identical on both
sides of the Atlantic, where the book was reviewed in the roundups of crime
fiction like any other hard-boiled novel—"Mr. Chandler is a near crafts-
man and writes like a breeze. A good time will be had by all."[33] Though he
had grown accustomed to this, it was still deeply frustrating. Blanche Knopf
blamed the lack of sales on the title. Ray was not impressed:

> I am terribly sorry about the title and all that, and because the advance
> sales disappointed us, but you must remember that I didn't refuse to
> change the title, I just couldn't think of another one, you gave me no
> time at all, and although I said I liked the title, that should not have
> made you go against your business judgement.[34]

Ray and Knopf did not fall out over this, but Ray clearly felt let down by
his publisher. He could not understand why that "fairly large group of intelligent people" had yet to discover him.

Shortly after he had sent the final manuscript to Knopf in May 1940, he and Cissy left Arcadia and once again headed to Big Bear Lake to enjoy the cooler summer weather, although Ray was now beginning to tire of the place. The Phoney War in Europe was over and the Battle of France had proven to be a bloody one. At the end of May, the German Army had managed to split the British Expeditionary Force from the bulk of the French Army, and they threatened to take over the ports before any evacuation could begin. The German Army, however, halted, which allowed Allied troops to begin an evacuation. On June 14, German troops entered and occupied Paris and, three days later, Philippe Pétain, the French chief of state, asked for an armistice, which was signed on June 22 and went into effect on the twenty-fifth. France was lost.

Although shocked by the speed of the German advance, Ray was still confident that Britain was strong enough to repel an invasion. Shortly before he left for the mountains, Ray wrote to his friend George Harmon Coxe explaining how difficult the Germans would find an attack on England:

> The English Channel, even at its narrowest point, is worth fifty Maginot lines, and the English troops are at least equal to the Germans and the British colonials are far better. The job of landing in England enough shock troops, tanks and guns to overrun the country is probably a military possibility, but it is infinitely more difficult than anything the Nazis have yet attempted. Probably Hitler would rather have destroyed or captured the British army than anything else in the world, and he had all the cards.[35]

In the same letter he went on to explain how the threat of bombing might play out:

> As for bombing it will be bad, but it will work both ways. If Hitler uses gas on England, it will be used on Germany. If he bombs London, Berlin will be bombed. And the British have made a speciality of night bombing for twenty-five years. And on top of all this the English civilian population is the least hysterical in the world.[36]

Ray's conclusion makes it clear that he still associated himself with the English, even though he had not lived there for nearly forty years, and it also shows how romantic his view of them remained. Imperialism and its trappings had, in Ray's eyes, produced a nation of stoics. This fits the widely held stiff-upper-lip stereotype and shows how unfamiliar he was with modern Britain—how perfect he still hoped it would be.

At Big Bear Lake, the creative spirit which had been so elusive on their last visit proved less tricky this time, and Ray started work on a new story. It may have been money worries that prompted him to return to the stories, as neither *The Big Sleep* nor *Farewell, My Lovely* had set the world alight just yet, and pulp stories were a good source of ready cash to keep the Chandlers afloat. It was probably also that, being between novels, he wanted something to keep his mind busy, and even struggling with a pulp story was better than nothing:

> I'm trying to write a pulp story just to feel I'm doing something, but I no longer seem to be any good at it.[37]

The war weighed heavily on Ray's mind, though, and threatened to derail his progress. Rather than let this happen he decided to incorporate the war into the story. "No Crime in the Mountains" would be his last pulp story and probably would not stand out if it did not touch on the war effort. In it, a Los Angeles detective is called up to Puma Point, a version of Big Bear Lake, where he helps uncover a German counterfeiting operation. It comes to a climax when the detective, Evans, and the local sheriff are trapped with the counterfeiter in a mountain cabin. Having realized his operation has failed, the German, Luders, kills himself in a Nazi fashion:

> Very slowly his [Luders's] face drained of all expression and became a dead grey mask. He lifted the gun, and at the same time he lifted his right arm stiffly above shoulder height. The arm was as rigid as a rod.
> "Heil Hitler!" he said sharply.
> He turned the gun quickly, put the muzzle in his mouth and fired.

Though the story does not make it explicit, Ray was taking sides. He felt that Nazi Germany was a threat to the United States, though not necessarily an immediate one. He wanted America to be wary. There was a fierce debate in 1940 about how the United States should respond to the fighting in Europe.

On the one hand, President Franklin D. Roosevelt, who was running for a third term in office, was campaigning on a promise to keep America out of the war, while remaining privately sympathetic to Britain. On the other, the Selective Service Act, which congress passed in September, initiated the first peace-time draft in American history. It commanded that all men between the ages of twenty and thirty-six had to register, and from that pool, nine hundred thousand would be drafted into the army for a year's service. This sent a very different signal from Roosevelt's pledge. "No Crime in the Mountains" was Ray's contribution to the debate, and though he thought Germans "fundamentally just as decent" as Americans,[38] Nazis were a different matter, and he sought to illustrate this in his story.

By and large, the mainstream media offered a similarly mixed message. The most popular song of 1940 was "When You Wish Upon a Star," sung by Jiminy Cricket in Walt Disney's *Pinocchio*; it was practically a hymn to escapism. Consider also the movies released in 1940, which included *Citizen Kane*, *The Grapes of Wrath*, *Of Mice and Men*, and *The Philadelphia Story*, all purely American and making no reference to Europe. But, equally, Charlie Chaplin did satirize Nazism in *The Great Dictator* (released around the same time as *Farewell, My Lovely*), and several thrillers, including *Confessions of a Nazi Spy* (1939) and *The Mortal Storm* (1940), lobbied subtly for American intervention. Ray was part of this early push. As he explained to Blanche Knopf, "I am not neutral and don't pretend to be."[39]

By now, Ray and Cissy were desperate for some stability in their lives. In October they moved yet again, to an apartment on San Vicente Boulevard in Santa Monica, where they hoped to stay for at least six months, even bringing some furniture out of storage.[40] In February the following year, though, having found Santa Monica too loud, they moved to a small house with a garden on Iliff Street, in Pacific Palisades.[41] Ray was working on a new novel, tentatively titled *The Brasher Doubloon*, which had been sketched out in the March plan. He first imagined it as a burlesque on the pulp novelette, featuring a Golden Age detective in a pulp world, based on the story "Pearls Are a Nuisance." The story featured Walter Gage, a well-spoken, effete, amateur detective with a vicious punch, and Henry, a hefty, hard man straight out of a typical pulp story. Told by Walter in the first person, it represents a coming together of two very different styles and would have been a challenge to categorize, had it ever been written. The burlesque idea, however, seems never to have progressed beyond the notebook, perhaps because the effort required to sustain Henry and Walter over the course of a novel would have been just too great.

Instead, Ray chose to stick with Philip Marlowe and, if nothing else, the exercise had inspired enough of a plot to make him think he could write a new novel without relying on previous stories:

> I don't think I'll beat my brains out trying to use material from old novelettes any more. It's really frightfully hard work.[42]

Progress throughout 1941 was slow, but Ray received a financial boost when RKO bought the movie rights to *Farewell, My Lovely* for $2,000. By September, Ray had finished his first draft of his novel and, by the following March, was arranging for it to be typed and sent to Blanche Knopf:

> I'm afraid the book isn't going to be any good to you. No action, no likable characters, no nothing. The detective does nothing.[43]

This is not fair. *The High Window* may not be among his best fiction but it is not as bad as Ray suggests. It tells the story of a missing gold coin, of a type known as a Brasher Doubloon. Marlowe is called in to investigate its disappearance by Mrs. Murdock, a fat, port-sodden woman, who is worried that the nightclub-singer wife of her dandy son has run off with the coin. It opens in Pasadena, the wealthy enclave to the northeast of Los Angeles, and introduces a very different set of wealthy people to those in his previous two novels. In *The Big Sleep* and *Farewell, My Lovely*, the Sternwoods and the Grayles represent old money, whereas the Murdocks are quite the opposite. Their house is ramshackle and decorated in bad taste:

> The room beyond was large and square and sunken and cool and had the restful atmosphere of a funeral chapel and something of the same smell. Tapestry on three blank roughed stucco walls, iron grills imitating balconies outside high side windows, heavy carved chairs with plush seats and tapestry backs and tarnished gilt tassels hanging down their sides. At the back a stained-glass window about the size

of a tennis court. . . . Marble topped tables, with crooked legs, gilt clocks, pieces of small statuary in two colors of marble. A lot of junk that would take a week to dust. A lot of money, and all wasted.

The Murdock family represent a different type of Los Angeles resident: the Midwesterners who had arrived and struck it rich within a generation. Similarly, *The High Window* takes us to parts of Los Angeles that Ray had not touched before:

> Bunker Hill is old town, lost town, shabby town, crook town. Once, very long ago, it was the choice residential district of the city, and there are still standing a few of the jigsaw Gothic mansions with wide porches and walls covered with round-end shingles and full corner bay windows with spindle turrets. They are all rooming houses now, their parquetry floors are scratched and worn through the once glossy finish and the wide sweeping staircases are dark with time and with cheap varnish laid on over generations of dirt. In the tall rooms haggard landladies bicker with shifty tenants. On the wide cool front porches, reaching their cracked shows into the sun and staring at nothing, sit the old men with faces like lost battles.

It is a striking portrait of a district Ray had known well and it establishes his intention to explore new aspects of life in Los Angeles.

The High Window marked itself apart in other ways too. Whereas the two preceding novels had explored different forms of corruption, *The High Window* examined the chimerical nature of Los Angeles and its inhabitants. Throughout the novel, there are examples of how appearance and reality do not match. Leslie Murdock might have the "smile of a bored aristocrat" but he is not wellborn, as his mother demonstrates. Then there is Lois Magic:

> From thirty feet away she looked like a lot of class. From ten feet away she looked like something made up to be seen from thirty feet away.

In Southern California, looks can be deceiving. This is, in part, due to the influence of the movie industry, as the character of Alex Morny demonstrates. This onetime B-movie actor who specialized in playing heavies has become one in real life, but, to Marlowe at least, he is still just an actor:

Morny lifted his cigarette away from his lips and narrowed his eyes to look at the tip. Every motion, every gesture, right out of the catalogue.

In Ray's analysis, the movie business is not the only reason for the illusory, false nature of Los Angeles; rather there is something in the very nature of the city that encourages this behavior. The newness of everything, including the people, means that any suggestion of history or heritage is a lie. It is telling that there are several references to aristocracy in the novel, from Leslie Murdock's smile to the Mornys' chauffeur, who rubs down his cars as if he is working at a stately English home in the previous century:

> He looked like an overgrown jockey and he made the same kind
> of hissing as he worked on the car that a groom makes rubbing down
> a horse.

The chauffeur's posed behavior points to a lineage that is not there: everyone can own a car, but only the rich would employ a groom to brush a horse. It is as if by assuming some of the outward signs of aristocracy, the impression will be given of deep roots in the Los Angeles soil when, in fact, the Mornys and Murdocks are relatively recent arrivals, both to the region and to their social class. They are playing parts. Similarly, George Anson feels that wearing the garb of the private detective (he even steals the Pinkerton logo for his business card) will make him one. He learns to his own cost that this is not so.

In Los Angeles, money buys power, and therefore the ability to control events, or at least how they are presented. In the book, Marlowe describes "the Cassidy case" in which it is thought a young secretary has killed his boss, the wealthy young Cassidy, before shooting himself. This, though, is just how the story was spun to the public; the reality, as Marlowe knows, was quite different:

> The D.A. knew it wasn't so and the D.A.'s investigators were pulled
> off the case within a matter of hours. There was no inquest. But every
> crime reporter in town and every cop on every homicide detail knew
> it was Cassidy that did the shooting, that it was Cassidy that was
> crazy drunk, that it was the secretary that tried to handle him and
> couldn't and at last tried to get away from him, but wasn't quick

enough. Cassidy's was the contact wound and the secretary's was not. The secretary was left-handed and he had a cigarette in his left hand when he was shot. Even if you are right-handed, you don't change a cigarette over to your other hand and shoot a man while casually holding the cigarette.

This is an important moment in the book and sees Marlowe distance himself from the sort of moral corruption that riddles the police force. What is not made explicit, though every Angeleno reading would have known it, is that the Cassidy case was based on a true story—the 1929 death of Ned Doheny, the son of a megawealthy oil baron, and his secretary, Hugh Plunkett. In both *The Big Sleep* and *Farewell, My Lovely*, there had been cover-ups, but they were private ones (the Sternwoods choose to deal with Carmen themselves; Mr. Grayle tries to protect his wife from the police) whereas the Cassidy (Doheny) case made public institutions complicit. The failure of the police, the DA, and even the newspapers to uncover what happened leaves Marlowe disillusioned and without trust:

> Until you guys own your own souls you don't own mine. Until you guys can be trusted every time and always, in all times and conditions, to seek the truth out and find it and let the chips fall where they may—until that time comes, I have a right to listen to my conscience.

When the institutions that protect the citizenry fail to uphold the truth, the nature of truth comes into question, and this is why Ray referred to the Doheny case in *The High Window*, seeking to show that the corruption within the institutions of Los Angeles contributed to the way its people behaved. When they cannot tell fact from fiction, truth from lies, the city becomes a dangerous place.

By the end of the novel, there are multiple versions of the Murdocks' Brasher Doubloon and only an expert, Teager the forger, can tell the difference. The Murdocks, however, fail to reclaim their stolen item, happily retaining their fake while Teager is released, having not technically committed a crime. How, then, do you value the Brasher Doubloon? Is it, as the Murdocks suggest, worth $10,000, or only as much as the gold it contains? Marlowe appears to have an answer: in an environment where reality and fiction are easily blurred, he trusts only his own sense and his own judgement. To make this point, Ray has Marlowe look in the mirror throughout the book, as if to confirm to himself that he still exists. To underline it, the novel concludes with a powerful scene:

> It was night. I went home and put my old house clothes on and set the chessmen out and mixed a drink and played over another Capablanca. It went fifty-nine moves. Beautiful cold remorseless chess, almost creepy in its silent implacability.
>
> When it was done I listened at the open window for a while and smelled the night. Then I carried my glass out to the kitchen and rinsed it and filled it with ice water and stood at the sink sipping it and looking at my face in the mirror.
>
> "You and Capablanca," I said.

These are the final words of the novel. The implication is that the chess grand master Capablanca, through his "implacable" and "remorseless" chess, is like Marlowe. Chess is pure, and Marlowe likes to think he is too. Meaning, then, can only be applied by the pure—by people like Marlowe. It is a haunting conclusion and a very Modernist one at that, regardless of genre.

Partway through the writing of *The High Window*, in December 1941, the Japanese attacked Pearl Harbor and, almost overnight, America was dragged into the war. Unfortunately, very few letters survive from this period of Ray's life, but he must have been relieved. California had experienced a certain type of fascism in the 1930s and Nazi sympathizers were making their voices heard across the country. Charlie Chaplin related this story in his memoir:

> It was strange to listen to slick young Nazis along Fifth Avenue haranguing small gatherings from little mahogany pulpits. One spiel went as follows: "The philosophy of Hitler is a profound and thoughtful study of the problems of this industrial age, in which there is little room for the middleman or the Jew."
>
> A woman interrupted. "What kind of talk is that!" she exclaimed. "This is America. Where do you think you are?"

The young man, an obsequious, good-looking type, smiled blandly. "I'm in the United States and I happen to be an American citizen," he said smoothly.[44]

Ray thought that Germany had suffered much more than it deserved after the First World War and that Hitler had given the country "a tremendous shot in the arm when it needed it very badly. [And] For that he deserves a lot of credit."[45] But he still regarded the dictator as "a nasty little man," surrounded by a "gang of Gestapo," who was fighting a war for "personal aggrandizement." Ray certainly had no truck with American Nazi sympathizers like the one Charlie Chaplin came across in New York.

In early 1942, the Chandlers were living at 12216 Shetland Lane, Brentwood Heights, where they would have been witness to one of the strangest moments of the war. Late on February 24, through the night, Los Angeles's military units went on alert, and the city was put under blackout. There was a rumor that unidentified aircraft had been spotted flying over Los Angeles and, at twelve minutes past three in the morning, antiaircraft guns dotted about the city opened fire, shooting into the air, their ammunition exploding in fiery orange bursts. For a little over an hour, air-raid sirens wailed, searchlights swept, and tracer bullets streaked through the night sky but did not find or hit anything. Los Angeles was enjoying a Hollywood version of the Blitz: reality and fiction had blurred once again. Though, in the end, there were no enemy aircraft, parts of the city were damaged by falling shrapnel, and five people lost their lives—three died in traffic accidents and two of heart attacks. Suddenly, the war was terrifyingly close at hand.[46]

The Chandlers must have been scared by the "air raid," and it may have played some part in the decision to head to Idyllwild for the summer. It was a mountain resort very similar to Big Bear Lake but further south. Ray had got sick of the Lake, but Cissy must have insisted that they leave the city, and Idyllwild would have been an acceptable alternative. In 1901, a sanatorium for the treatment of tuberculosis opened there but did not last long. Eventually, the village became a resort modeled on an alpine village. Idyllwild's alpine roots were evident everywhere, including the names of local businesses. When Ray and Cissy arrived, signs were being rapidly dismantled to avoid offending tourists. It was there that Ray took delivery of an edition of *The High Window*, the design of which he liked. Cissy, though, was not sure: the picture of him on the back flap was not good enough; she thought her husband a lot more handsome.

In October, Ray learned that, yet again, his book had failed to sell as well as his publishers hoped. More than six thousand copies had been printed but it had not sold more than four thousand by October.[47] Though, once more, it was all but ignored in America, it received more attention in Britain, where it was reviewed in the *Times Literary Supplement*. Ray, though, was not surprised at its poor performance in the market: "I'm not disappointed by the sales. I think it did well to get by at all."[48]

He was, however, frustrated by his inability to get away from his *Black Mask* roots. In March 1942, he wrote:

> The thing that rather gets me down is that when I write something
> that is tough and fast and full of mayhem, and murder, I get panned
> for being tough and fast and full of mayhem and murder, and then
> when I try to tone down a bit and develop the mental and emotional
> side of a situation, I get panned for what I was panned for putting in
> the first time.[49]

In this letter he is referring to some of the criticism of *Farewell, My Lovely* as well as anticipating that which would greet the *The High Window*, and it is clear that being boxed into a genre was beginning to irritate him. Later that year, he amplified this sentiment in another letter to Blanche Knopf:

> I hope the day will come when I won't have to ride around on Ham-
> mett and James Cain, like an organ grinder's monkey.[50]

His publisher had lumped him together with Hammett and Cain from the beginning, but Ray was beginning to find this stifling. What he really wanted to do was "turn one out that will have that fresh and sudden touch."[51] In the critics' eyes, none of his previous novels had achieved this. Ray was starting to think that he had lost something since *The Big Sleep*, and it may be for this reason that he decided to return to *The Lady in the Lake*, which he had started writing in 1939.

The Lady in the Lake may have started out as a companion piece to *Farewell, My Lovely*, and Ray was certainly playing with both ideas in the first part of 1939.[52] It's possible, in fact, that they started out as the very same idea. Throughout April, May, and June 1939, he alternated between drafting *Farewell, My Lovely* and *The Lady in the Lake*, switching when he ran into problems, but his annotations to the March plan hint at a connection between the two. In 1939, *The Lady in the Lake* was briefly called *Deep and Dark Waters* and, in his notebook, above *Law Is Where You Buy It*, the original title for *Farewell, My Lovely*, he added by hand "Deep in Dark Water, The Lady in the Lake." The idea that both books might have at one time shared a common root makes sense when you look at the characters in the two novels: whereas *Farewell, My Lovely* shows how the wealthy and powerful are affected by Bay City's corruption, *The Lady in the Lake* focuses on everyday people. Derace Kingsley may have a high-powered job at Gillerlain Company, but he is not a wealthy man, and the power he wields is not felt outside his small world. This makes him very different to the Grayles or even Lindsay Marriot. This is the key: *The Lady in the Lake* is about the everyday experience of corruption and how it affects normal people. It may also be the reason why Ray struggled with this book, as his talent seems really to have lain in observing the rich.

Ray was frustrated that the reviewers did not seem to recognize his skill, so he made *The Lady in the Lake* more obviously a crime novel, deploying the tropes of the genre more freely than before. There are real, old-fashioned "clues" in the book, such as the ankle bracelet that Marlowe uses to identify the murder victim. There is also the confusion over the identity of the body in the lake—the sort of subterfuge common in Golden Age mysteries. Ray had included some of these elements from the very beginning—the anklet was part of the original pulp story that he used as a basis for the novel—but his retention of it in the subsequent book suggests that he wanted to write something that stuck closely to expectations of the genre. This, he may have hoped, would help with sales which, so far, had proved disappointing. Ray was always a pragmatist and, though very willing to experiment, was also keen to ensure that his books were commercial.

Unfortunately, *The Lady in the Lake* is also one of his most misogynistic books. As in *The Big Sleep* and *Farewell, My Lovely*, the killer turns out to be a woman. Muriel Chess (or Mildred Haviland) has killed at least three people before she herself is killed, but this is not the worst of her crimes in Ray's eyes. She is murdered by Degarmo, a former lover who has been ruined by his love for her:

> Webber looked at his thumb. "But he was never married to the girl," he said quietly. Degarmo was. I can tell you she led him a pretty dance. A lot of what seems bad in him is the result of it.

And this is the true evil in the book. Muriel Chess is a manipulator of men, who ruins them to her own ends. Marlowe shows her no sympathy at all, calling her "a cold-blooded little bitch if ever I saw one." Degarmo, a corrupt cop and a murderer, who tries to frame Marlowe, is never treated with the same disgust. Patton, the sheriff at Puma Point, says he "ain't that kind of killer," implying that his crime is somehow less than Muriel Chess's. Even Degarmo's death reserves for him a kind of dignity: he speeds away from the cabin and tries to cross the dam, which is guarded by soldiers who shoot him when he does not stop:

> A hundred feet down in the canyon a small coupe was smashed against the side of a huge granite boulder. It was almost upside down, leaning a little. There were three men down there. They had moved the car enough to lift something out.
> Something that had been a man.

These are the final lines of the book and the implication is that Degarmo's relationship with his wife does not just result in his death but in something much worse: it destroys his masculinity. Again there are parallels with *Farewell, My Lovely*. In that novel, the killer, Mrs. Grayle, is condemned for her crimes, whereas Moose Malloy, also a killer, is judged less harshly. The same happens in *The Lady in the Lake*, and it is hard not to feel that Ray sees crimes by women as much worse than those committed by men.

Ray completed the book in April 1943, and he was relieved to finally have it finished. It had taken four years to produce and, in the end, he still felt that it lacked the magic he had hoped for. It had been a tough four years that had seen him move around Southern California with alarming speed.

He was now eager to settle somewhere but was still worried about money, though, on that front, things were about to take a turn for the better. That year, Knopf decided to sell the paperback rights to *The Big Sleep* to Avon. In the 1940s, paperbacks were still viewed with a certain suspicion, and publishing houses tended to print either hardbacks or paperbacks, rarely both. Knopf had thought Ray too good a writer to be sold in paperback but, with sales not reaching the level he had expected, they gave in. Ray liked what he referred to as the "two-bit edition"[53] and, when he reread it, took some comfort. He found it "both much better and much worse" than he had been expecting but also noted "occasional signs of almost normal sensitivity in the writing."[54] The book was released in the spring with a cover price of twenty-five cents; it sold something like 300,000 copies almost right away, with a further 150,000 being sold as a specialist armed services edition.[55] Four months later, Pocket Book released a paperback edition of *Farewell, My Lovely*.

The plan he had outlined in 1939 had not unfolded as he had hoped. England must have seemed further away than ever, and his ambition to forget mystery writing was looking less attainable. Ray was becoming bored with Philip Marlowe and was eager for a change and, in the summer of 1943, he received a call out of the blue which was to give him just that: though film adaptations of his books had begun to appear in cinemas the previous year, now Hollywood wanted Raymond Chandler in person.

CHAPTER TEN

HOLLYWOOD

Raymond Chandler never courted Hollywood but, in 1943, Hollywood came to him. Movie studios had been curious about his fiction from the start. After the success of John Huston's 1941 adaptation of Dashiell Hammett's *The Maltese Falcon*, starring Humphrey Bogart as Sam Spade, other studios started looking for hard-boiled crime novels to put on the screen. RKO picked up the rights to Ray's *Farewell, My Lovely* but, in what now seems a strange and rather ridiculous move, ditched both Philip Marlowe and the title. *The Falcon Takes Over* (1942) uses Ray's plot, retains Moose Malloy and Anne Riordan, but relocates the action to New York City. Marlowe's place is taken by the eponymous Falcon, a low-rent imitation of the Saint, played in this film by George Sanders. At roughly the same time, the plot of *The High Window* was being casually bent out of shape by an undistinguished screenwriter called Clarence Upson Young and reformed as *Time to Kill*. In that film, Marlowe's place was taken by detective Michael Shayne. Any reputation these all-but-forgotten B-movies have today is because of their connection to Raymond Chandler. In the early 1940s, this, it seemed, was to be Ray's fate: having his carefully wrought novels stripped of their plot and characters by filmmakers desperate for ideas and short on time.

At any rate, to have adapted his fiction with any sort of care—to project the flickering, silvered image of Philip Marlowe onto a big screen and to show the seedy world of sex and corruption he inhabited—would have been impossible in 1943. At that time, Hollywood was in the grip of the Motion Picture Production Code (MPPC). This debilitating convention had been introduced in the early 1920s due to fears that the lewd behavior on-screen would result in lewd behavior off it. William H. Hays, a lawyer and former chairman of the Republican National Committee, was asked by the Motion Picture Producers and Distributors Association (a group of some of the biggest studio bosses in Los Angeles) to develop a set of rules that would ensure films were morally decent. At first, little more than lip service was paid to the Code, but then came Mae West, the woman who made famous the line "Is that a gun in your pocket or are you just happy to see me?" Her brand of smutty humor and licentiousness drove American moralists into a fit of fury. Martin Quigley, the publisher of the *Motion Picture Herald*, wrote of the movie *I'm No Angel*, which West had written herself:

> There is no more pretence of romance than on a stud farm . . . it is vulgar and degrading [and] its sportive wise-cracking tends to create tolerance if not acceptance of things essentially evil.[1]

Some members of the audience were angry about the sort of things they were seeing on their movie theatre screens, too. A group of Catholic bishops formed a Legion of Decency and started to collect the signatures of disaffected moviegoers. Eleven million people signed up to their cause, promising to "avoid pictures that are dangerous to my moral health." Threatened with a declining audience and eager to agree to anything that would protect their bottom line, movie studios came together and accepted the Code. From then on, all screenplays had to be vetted and approved by the Production Code Administration (PCA), popularly known as the Hays Office (and, later, the Breen Office), before they could go into production. If filmmakers failed to do this, their films would be barred from Motion Picture Producers and Distributors Association theatres. In other words, their movies would not make it to their audience. The Code had real teeth and moviemakers were at its mercy.

This was how things looked set to stay until movie producer Joe Sistrom of Paramount Pictures came across James M. Cain's short novel *Double Indemnity*. It had originally run as a serial in *Liberty* magazine in 1935 and was dark, violent, sexy—exactly the kind of story that Hollywood could not film under Hays. But Sistrom liked a challenge. Billy Wilder, the young German émigré who would eventually direct the film, told different stories about how Sistrom discovered the book. In one version, Sistrom told Wilder that his secretary was missing, presumed lost, probably because she was in the bathroom reading "that story."

Though Sistrom and Wilder thought *Double Indemnity* had the potential to make a good film, they were not the first studio men to have that idea. It had been submitted to executives in 1936, shortly after publication, but had run into the same problem time and time again: the Motion Picture Production Code. It is little wonder that *Double Indemnity*, submitted to studios a mere two years after the code came into effect, failed to make it past the new rules. Cain remembered the rejection by the PCA:

> It knocked it in the head . . . it was an uncompromising ban of the story in toto, one of those things that begins "under no circumstances" and winds up "no way, shape or form." The main objection was that the story in part was a "blueprint" for murder, that it would show [the audience] how to kill for profit.[2]

In 1943, when Wilder and Sistrom first read the story, it had not become any less violent or sexy, and the MPPC was not any looser, but, still, the two men believed they could find a way around the rules. It was a courageous decision that would unsettle Hollywood and make space for a new type of movie: just what Billy Wilder had always wanted to do.

Wilder was born in Vienna in 1906 and had worked as a journalist and screenwriter in Berlin between the wars. He was Jewish and fled Hitler's Germany in anticipation of the Holocaust that would later see his mother, grandmother, and stepfather killed in concentration camps.[3] After a brief stay in Paris, where he directed his first movie, he found himself, in 1933, in Hollywood, at the beating heart of the global film industry. His career as a screenwriter in Los Angeles did not take off until senior executives paired him with Charles Brackett, the silver-haired, Harvard-educated scion of an East Coast family. Brackett was everything Wilder was not and, perhaps unsurprisingly, their relationship was not an easy one but, for all its frustrations, it proved successful. Together, they wrote movies like *Bluebeard's Eighth Wife*, *Midnight*,

Ninotchka, and *Ball of Fire,* all of which received acclaim and achieved box-office success. The pair soon realized—as do many writers in Hollywood—that the only way to ensure their stories ended up on screen as written was to direct and produce them, too. Wilder's first experience of this in Paris had been nightmarish but, though he had vowed never to do so again, he was persuaded to take the director's chair, with Brackett as producer. The two of them made a successful team, making two movies together before Wilder came across *Double Indemnity.*

Having settled on *Double Indemnity* as his next project, Wilder wanted Brackett on board as well, but the grey-haired producer refused: he thought the novel "disgusting." Undeterred, Wilder suggested to Sistrom that they try to get James M. Cain himself to work on the screenplay. Wilder had worked with Cain at Columbia and liked him. In fact, Wilder used to share a self-deprecating anecdote in which the older author, arriving in the writers' room at ten o'clock one morning to find a bright-eyed Wilder pounding enthusiastically away at his typewriter, broke the news that no one really started working until around quarter to twelve when the studio boss, Harry Cohen, showed up.[4] Sistrom made the call but discovered that Cain was under contract at Fox. He had another idea, though—what about Raymond Chandler? Wilder once said that Sistrom always had three things in his hand: "a cigarette, a bottle of beer, and a greasy soft-covered book." He was certainly very well read and it is no surprise that a copy of one of Ray's four novels had passed across Sistrom's desk at some point. Cain and Ray had also been yoked together when Knopf launched *The Big Sleep*, so it was hardly a great leap of imagination on Sistrom's part. He gave Wilder some of Ray's books and sent him home to read them. Wilder loved them and, according to film critic Richard Schickel, who interviewed Wilder for his book on *Double Indemnity* in the early 1990s, such was the impact of Ray's prose that the director could still remember some of the lines vividly many years later.

Ray was surprised to get the call from Sistrom. He and Cissy were sporadic cinemagoers at best and, despite living in Los Angeles for so long, he seems never to have considered working in the industry. Still, he was intrigued and sat down to read *Double Indemnity* before meeting Sistrom and Wilder at their offices on the Paramount lot. According to one version related by Wilder,

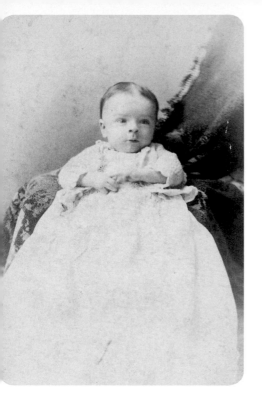

above: Raymond Chandler in his christening gown.

Supplied by the Bodleian Libraries, University of Oxford

above right: Ray as a young boy with his favorite doll, Alfred.

Supplied by the Bodleian Libraries, University of Oxford

right: Ray aged about seven.

© Topfoto

above left: Long before she met Ray, Cissy lived in New York, where among other things, she worked as an artist's model. *Supplied by the Bodleian Libraries, University of Oxford*

above right: In 1918 Ray transferred from the Canadian army to the RAF. His ghostly thin face hints at the horror he witnessed on the front. *Supplied by the Bodleian Libraries, University of Oxford*

Ray and his mother, Florence, sit together in the shade at Cypress Grove, California, shortly after the First World War. *Supplied by the Bodleian Libraries, University of Oxford*

Ray with his colleagues from the Dabney Oil Syndicate accounting department. Ray stands on the far left of the second row. Joseph B. Dabney is in the center of the first row. *Supplied by the Bodleian Libraries, University of Oxford*

below left: Taki, the Chandlers' cat, as a kitten in 1932. He was, Ray said, "all fur with four legs peeping out from under it." *Supplied by the Bodleian Libraries, University of Oxford*

below right: Ray and Taki at the Chandlers' house in Pacific Palisades sometime in the mid- to late-1930s. Taki had put on some weight and some fur. *Supplied by the Bodleian Libraries, University of Oxford*

Ray pictured smoking his pipe with Dashiell Hammett (standing, far right) at a dinner for *Black Mask* writers.

Supplied by the Bodleian Libraries, University of Oxford

The distinctive cover of *The Big Sleep*, first published by Alfred A. Knopf in the United States, in February 1939.

left: Ray with Mr. and Mrs. Anthony Blond at a party in London in 1952.

© Hulton-Deutsch Collection/CORBIS

right: In the summer of 1952 Ray and Cissy headed to London. They had dreamed of visiting Britain for years, but the trip would prove to be a difficult one.

Supplied by the Bodleian Libraries, University of Oxford

left: Ray relaxing in sunny Palm Springs in late 1957.

Supplied by the Bodleian Libraries, University of Oxford

when Ray was asked if he wanted to work on the project, he said "Yes!" adding that he expected $1,000 to do the job and that he could deliver his script the following week. Wilder told the story several times and the details shifted slightly with each telling. Another account of this early meeting comes from H. N. Swanson, who had just sold *Double Indemnity* to Paramount:

> One day I had a call from Joseph Sistrom. . . . He told me about a situation in which he thought I could be of help. Sistrom had signed a contract with Raymond Chandler. . . .
>
> Sistrom said, "Chandler doesn't know a thing about screenplay writing, but it doesn't matter. He knows the kind of people Cain wrote about. He's eager to try his hand at the material and would take the two or three hundred a week the studio would probably offer him. Will you be his agent and get him a proper deal here?"[5]

Both versions have the ring of truth about them and some elements are consistent: from the outset, Ray was enthusiastic about the project, keen to get involved with movies and had no idea what he was doing. Despite his naïveté, Sistrom was keen to sign him up, believing that the experienced Wilder would iron out any wrinkles. Swanson agreed to be Ray's agent and had soon negotiated a ten-week contract at $750 a week.[6] If Ray had expected a $1,000 fee, this sum of money must have seemed astonishing. Having spent the last decade struggling by on the small income from his writing, he must have felt as if he had hit the jackpot.

It was clear to Wilder that Ray was going to need guidance if he was to write a successful screenplay, so he sent his new colleague home with a fresh copy of the novel and his own script for *Hold Back the Dawn*, telling him to make a start that weekend. Ray's first attempt, written quickly, lifted Cain's dialogue and laid it out as he thought a screenplay should look. It contained instructions like "fade in" and "dissolve," which he assumed were part of the process. Wilder was the director and disliked being given instructions by the screenwriter but, despite this rough start, persevered. He respected Ray's ability with language and was keen to have a partner to counterbalance his own writing. He had collaborated on scripts in the past and seems to have liked working that way.

In the end, the relationship between the two men was more complicated than Joe Sistrom had anticipated. In some ways, this is surprising, as they had plenty in common. Wilder, like Ray, was an outsider in California, and a European exile at that. Both men spoke German: Wilder as a native, Ray as an enthusiast. They shared a fascination with the American language— Wilder's preoccupation with idiom burst through in movies like *Ball of Fire,* in which Barbara Stanwyck, as a nightclub singer on the run, hides out in a think tank for the study of the American vernacular. Billy Wilder was also hugely ambitious and once wrote that he wanted to "set Hollywood back on its heels," echoing Ray's desire to revolutionize his own field. Wilder even liked to carry a malacca cane. Despite all that, their relationship soon started to fray at the edges.

Several things contributed to the tension, the first being Ray's shock at the working conditions of a Hollywood studio. When he was writing his novels and stories, he could work when and how he wanted. A life without deadlines was the privilege of the artist, but Hollywood was not looking for artists: it needed people to create documents that gave enough shape and structure to a project to allow a director and production manager to start work. This was an entirely different process to writing a novel and one that demanded regular hours and real discipline. For years, Ray had lived a steady life, seeing friends occasionally, meeting his editors if they were visiting Los Angeles, drifting between the mountains, the desert, and the coast, and spending time with Cissy. That was it. Then Joe Sistrom called and, suddenly, he had an office to go to, with regular meetings and deadlines to face. Ray found himself in a world that should value good writing but which felt more like a factory, and Billy Wilder, who could rewrite the script moments before it was shot if he wanted to, did little to pander to Ray's artistic temperament.

Throughout the summer and autumn of 1943, Ray and Wilder worked together on the Paramount lot. They shared an office in the writers' building, also known as "the campus" because of its cloistered courtyard and strange, literary inhabitants. Theirs was a small room with bare, white walls and the minimum of furniture—a desk, some utilitarian chairs, a telephone, and a well-worn sofa. For a set period each day, Ray had to sit in this cramped room and, if that was hard for him to get used to, the idea of working with someone else was even more so. Hollywood seemed to have swallowed the belief that writing a screenplay was just too complicated for one person alone; partnerships were common but, to Ray, sharing a creative vision seemed strange, if not downright impossible. Wilder had a clear view of how their partnership should work:

> I would guide the structure and I would also do a lot of the dialogue, and he would then comprehend and start constructing too.[7]

This remark was made years after he and Ray worked together. No doubt Wilder was keen to stake his claim after the fact, but it does point towards how the director saw their relationship: as one of guide and acolyte. To a certain extent, this was necessary but, after a while, Ray began to feel frustrated with his partner and his insistence on taking the lead. It is easy to imagine the two of them in their office, Wilder pacing from corner to corner with his malacca cane while Ray sat on the sofa holding a yellow writing pad, scribbling down ideas, burning with irritation. Ray was the subordinate, not only in his relationship with Wilder but, as he would quickly come to realize, in the studio system as a whole. Writers' lives in Hollywood were not easy: calls were monitored, they could be banned from the set, and, sometimes, they were not even invited to the previews of movies they had written.[8] One day, about three weeks into the process, Ray reached breaking point and simply stopped coming to work.

Wilder waited in the office for Ray, who was supposed to have shown up at nine. As the hands on the clock swept round without any sign of him, Wilder became agitated. Finally, he went to tell Sistrom that his partner had failed to arrive, only to find Sistrom sitting hunched over a long, narrow sheet of yellow paper reading intently. It was a letter from Ray. Wilder described the letter like this:

> It was a letter of complaint against me: he couldn't work with me any more because I was rude; I was drinking; I was fucking; I was on the phone with four broads, with one I was on the phone—he clocked me—for twelve and a half minutes; I had asked him to pull down the Venetian blinds—the sun was streaming into the office—without saying please.[9]

Ray never gave his side of the story in relation to this letter of complaint, but it was not out of character. He could be a grumpy, difficult man, and faced with a younger, more knowledgable coworker, a streak of jealousy mixed with frustration meant that he struggled to maintain his sangfroid. Wilder put the outburst down to several factors: "my German accent . . . I knew the craft better than he did . . . I drank after four o'clock . . . [I] was fucking young girls."[10] Wilder certainly had a mild accent but, since Ray had enjoyed his time in Southern Germany and always expressed an affection for its people, even during the war, it seems unlikely that it was Wilder's Germanic roots that made him uncomfortable. Wilder never suggested that Ray was anti-Semitic, a charge that would later be laid at his door as his novels became part of the literary canon. It seems that it was the sex and the power that he resented, particularly in the hands of a younger man. As an oil executive, Ray, too, had enjoyed a position of power and liked to give the impression that he was a benevolent boss, even paternalistic, but he never failed to remind friends that he had been at the top of the business. Later, as a writer, the tricky issues of office politics were forgotten but, at Paramount, they loomed large again. Ray thought that, as a novelist, he was due some respect from his colleagues, but Wilder showed him very little.

There was a further catalyst for Ray's revolt: alcohol. In an interview with his biographer, Maurice Zolotow, Wilder revealed that Ray was sneaking drink into the Paramount office.

> Every time Wilder went to the toilet, Chandler went to his briefcase. He took out a pint of whisky. He always carried his briefcase. It was a capacious brown briefcase with three compartments. Inside was a small writing board and sheets of cut up yellow paper—and some liquor. Chandler was wont to wander around the city and sit at bars looking around.[11]

Gauging the reliability of this story is difficult, as Wilder's recollections could be imperfect and self-serving, but neatly cut yellow pages were precisely what Ray liked to write on. Then there is the photograph of Ray and Wilder taken while they worked on the screenplay: it shows a sprightly Billy Wilder seated next to a bedraggled Raymond Chandler. Ray looks towards the camera wearing a dark-blue tie speckled with polka dots, under a checkered sports coat. His face is marked by a day or two's beard growth. There are deep pouches under his eyes and his skin looks drained and puffy. Billy Wilder's gaze is directed towards his cowriter. He is wearing an open-necked shirt with a light grey tank top. He looks young, vibrant, and energetic, exuding all the confidence of Southern California. Ray seems to be from a different generation entirely. He looks unhealthy and ill; he looks like he drinks.

It has been suggested that Ray gave up drinking after he got sacked in 1932, but that is not true. He drank throughout the 1930s, though, it must be said, without the gusto he had demonstrated during the previous decade. There were still evening cocktails with Cissy, there were glasses of Scotch over ice, and there was wine too. A letter from 1934 suggests the extent to which alcohol still played a troublesome part in his life:

> I find even one cocktail before dinner makes me a bit logey, so that I feel stupid afterwards. I hope there will be good wine after a bit and good Scotch that is not too dear. I'd say offhand that the racketeers have too much hand in the liquor business still, maybe always will have.[12]

This letter was written a year before Robert Smith and William Wilson met and created a blueprint for what became Alcoholics Anonymous. Their timing could not have been better. Prohibition in the 1920s had created a legion of heroic drinkers who, by the 1930s, were struggling to keep their lives in check and their livers in working order. The only solution to heroic drinking, thought Wilson and Smith, was its absolute opposite: complete abstinence.[13] Ray had developed his problem before their "cure" found fame and, rather than giving up completely, he willed himself to reduce his drinking to a manageable amount. This effort of will was partly successful, or at least it was until the early 1940s, when his drinking began to escalate again.

There is likely no single factor that pushed Ray back to dependence on the bottle but, during this period, he was under a considerable amount of strain. Both *The High Window* and *The Lady in the Lake* had been difficult books to write, and the agony that went into them had not netted a return to match his ambitions. He was also beginning to realize that his plan to use Philip

Marlowe as a way of learning to write and then to "forget mystery writing altogether" was slipping further and further out of reach. The trouble he had had writing his last two books had caused him to question his abilities, and he worried that he lacked the necessary skill to write fiction in a different genre. This would have created a crisis of confidence in many writers, but Ray also had to deal with Cissy's continuing illnesses, which were as distressing and debilitating as ever. Working with Wilder, and dealing with the Hollywood studio system, were the final straws. People drink for all sorts of reasons, and alcohol can stimulate as easily as it can calm. In the end, there was a nasty inevitability about his return to excessive drinking.

Ray's sudden refusal to work with Billy Wilder was the first manifestation of how hard he was finding life at the studio. In the short term, Joe Sistrom was in a position to calm him down with soothing words, while Wilder tried to modify his own behavior. In the immediate aftermath of Ray's outburst, Sistrom was successful, Wilder less so, but Ray did come back to work. In Hollywood, where drinking to excess was par for the course, they could do little to stop Ray boozing once he had begun, but at least he and Wilder were back in the same room and could focus again on the screenplay.

Double Indemnity would not have been Ray's first choice for his debut studio project. He was not an admirer of James M. Cain and, before he was asked to adapt the novel, shortly after *The High Window* was published, had written:

> I hope the day will come when I won't have to ride around on Hammett and James Cain, like an organ grinder's monkey. . . . James Cain—faugh! Everything he touches smells like a billygoat. He is every kind of writer I detest, a faux naif, a Proust in dirty overalls, a dirty little boy with a piece of chalk and a board fence and nobody looking. Such people are the offal of literature, not because they write about dirty things, but because they do it in a dirty way. Nothing hard and clean and cold and ventilated.[14]

What Ray valued most in good writing was what he called "honesty." By this he meant that the language used should be at once fresh and authentic. In his view, there was no point in putting low, gritty language in the mouth of a highborn character unless the point was that the character was not highborn. Similarly, the narrator should tell the story using the most natural language possible. In Ray's eyes, Cain failed to do this. Rather than using words in fresh new ways, he turned out stale, half-baked sentences. Rather than giving his characters the language they might naturally use, he gave them the language he thought they should use. When Ray accuses Cain of having a dirty way of writing, he is not referring to the sex or perversion that occur during the story but, rather, to the quality of the prose. To Ray, the apparent simplicity of Cain's prose just showed how phony it was. It was not the language of a real drifter but what a middle-class writer imagined a drifter might say. An entry in Ray's notebook sheds further light on his attitude:

> What is there about this [style of writing] that is beyond disgust to me? Is it the nature faking, or the fact that the attitude has been done to death so that one simply cannot feel any honesty in it? Is it that the minor cadence, the restraint, all the words, the pseudo-simplicity of the thought and so on, suggest a mind either too naive or too phony to be endured, or a cynical imitation of something that might once have been good?[15]

To Ray words were like the tools of a surgeon, "clean and cold and ventilated," and should be used accurately to describe a person and a situation. In contrast, Cain's prose, as Ray saw it, was the sort of dirty, frothy mush that was ultimately meaningless. It was nothing more than a well-conceived trick and certainly not art. Despite all that, Ray enjoyed tackling the screenplay. In fact, he wanted to return to work even though he was struggling with the conditions. Perhaps he was keen to make his own mark on *Double Indemnity*, to show how it should have been done—after all, in the act of adapting the book, he was also figuratively taking it away from Cain. Whereas once it would have been known as James M. Cain's *Double Indemnity,* a successful movie version would be as much associated with Ray and Wilder as with Cain. In other words, it was an opportunity for Raymond Chandler to step out of Cain's shadow and establish himself as a different, superior type of writer. In practice though, it meant that their names and their careers became further entwined. Ray was not quite able to escape James M. Cain.

At first, Ray and Wilder decided that they wanted to keep most of the original dialogue, but Ray quickly alighted on a problem: though the speech read well on the page, it did not convert to spoken dialogue. It was, he said, "impossibly dramatic."[16] A simple typographical trick meant it worked on paper—Cain had removed most of the "he said" speech signifiers, giving the impression of sharp, hard language—but it was an illusion. To make his point, Ray suggested that they bring in some actors to read the lines aloud and, once Ray had overcome Wilder's initial objections, the results were plain to both men. It was simply awful. "The effect was of a bad high school play," Ray wrote, "The dialogue oversaid everything and when spoken sounded quite colorless and tame."[17] This was a break for Ray. Having heard the artificial and uncomfortable words being read aloud, he and Wilder knew that they had to deconstruct the story completely so that it could be built back up, brick by brick, until it would work for the screen. They now had the freedom to craft something better.

They made some significant changes to the original story, particularly in the second half of the narrative. In Cain's novel, the two central characters are called Walter Huff and Phyllis Nirdlinger, but these needed to change to remove the comic aspect and bring in a darker, harder edge, so the central characters in the movie are Walter Neff and Phyllis Dietrichson. Would the movie have had the same impact if Wilder and Ray had not made this change? Probably not. These names could carry greater significance, for one thing. In the name Dietrichson there is a suggestion of the feline sexiness of Marlene Dietrich and, possibly, a joke about her offscreen character (she could be pretty nasty). Film historian David Thompson has suggested that Neff might be a sly allusion to the popular Hollywood architect Wallace Neff. If so, it was an inside joke.[18] They also changed the way the story was told. In the novel, the narrative unfolds through Huff's written confession sent to Barton Keyes, the chief investigator, but this would not have the same impact on screen. Wilder and Ray had the brilliant idea to have Neff use a Dictaphone to reveal his confession, which retained all the urgency of the original but was far more visually satisfying.

They also had to do some careful work with the characters. One of the advantages of first-person narrative is that it tends to get readers on the narrator's side, no matter how nasty he or she is. Would Humbert Humbert be seen with any sympathy at all if *Lolita* was written in the third person? On-screen, the effect is not so easy to re-create; a voice-over can help but the effect is different. So, Wilder and Chandler set about turning Neff into a murderer the audience could like. The tricks are often simple but effective. For example, when Neff first encounters Phyllis Dietrichson he is briefly left alone in the living room while she changes into some clothes. He walks over to the fish tanks and sprinkles a few flakes of food into the water. This is a small moment, and one that marks Neff out as a man an audience could identify with. Walter is a good guy who the audience can like.

The situation was helped by Wilder and Sistrom's choice of male lead, Fred MacMurray. Before entering the movie business, MacMurray had worked on Broadway and, up to 1943, was cast in light comedies and musicals. He was a huge star and was at one time the highest-paid actor in the industry, but had never been offered a role like Walter Neff. An inspired choice, he was able to bring out Neff's nice-guy side and make the audience believe he could be corrupted by a dame with a killer ankle bracelet. In the screenplay, Neff is described as having movement that is "full of ginger,"[19] which gave MacMurray something to play with, allowing him a certain cheeky edge that helped him deliver the lewd lines with enough boyish irreverence to seem charming. In the scene where Neff and Phyllis first meet, they have this famous exchange:

PHYLLIS: There's a speed limit in this state, Mr. Neff. Forty-five miles an hour.

NEFF: How fast was I going, officer?

PHYLLIS: I'd say about ninety.

NEFF: Suppose you get down off your motorcycle and give me a ticket.

PHYLLIS: Suppose I let you off with a warning this time.

NEFF: Suppose it doesn't take.

PHYLLIS: Suppose I have to whack you over the knuckles.

NEFF: Suppose I bust out crying and put my head on your shoulder.

PHYLLIS: Suppose you try putting it on my husband's shoulder.
NEFF: That tears it.[20]

In the mouth of a different actor, with a different script, this might seem salacious, but Ray and Wilder used an oblique metaphor—speeding tickets are not sexy—to make the interaction more playful and, crucially, to get it past the Production Code Administration. On the page, there is nothing of the sexy undertone that the actors were able to bring out. In the finished movie, MacMurray wears a slight grin while Barbara Stanwyck looks sultry, so the scene drips with unspoken attraction. This was clever writing combined with clever acting. It conveyed exactly what the story required and did it within the restrictive confines of the Motion Picture Production Code. It was sheer genius.

If the audience needed to like Neff, they needed to be suspicious of Mrs. Dietrichson. In the original story, she is a quiet, clearly detestable character who has killed three children as well as Nirdlinger's first wife, all without remorse. But Ray and Wilder saw an interesting quality in Phyllis, and they chose to tease out a more complicated character than Cain had originally envisaged. At the outset, she is a bad girl who has used her sexual capital to rise to the top. Her ankle bracelet, a cheap piece of jewelry, suggests her tastes are vulgar, and her perfume, which comes from Ensenada in Mexico, highlights that she is not a natural inhabitant of the calm middle-class outpost of Los Feliz, where the Dietrichsons live. She is supremely confident in her power over men and does not expect someone like Neff to challenge her view of herself. In the scene where she visits Neff in his apartment, her attitude is laid bare:

PHYLLIS: I bought it in Ensenada.
NEFF: We ought to have some of that pink wine to go with it.
            The kind that bubbles. All I've got is bourbon.
PHYLLIS: Bourbon will be fine, Walter.[21]

Why does Neff want pink wine? Because, in his eyes, this encounter is a romantic one, and Phyllis is prepared to let him think that to get what she wants. In reality, bourbon will do because her only concern is to convince a man to kill for her. And yet, despite her pointed seduction of Neff with promises of Happy Ever After in exchange for his murdering Mr. Dietrichson, Phyllis is given a moment of redemption at the close of the movie. In the climactic scene, when Neff confronts her, she pulls a gun and shoots him. Neff, injured, walks towards Phyllis and asks: "Why don't you shoot again. Maybe if I come a little closer?"[22] But Phyllis cannot take the second shot:

NEFF: Why didn't you shoot, baby?
           (Phyllis puts her arms around him in complete surrender.)
NEFF: Don't tell me it's because you've been in love with me all this time.
PHYLLIS: No, I never loved you, Walter. Not you, or anybody else. I'm rotten to the heart. I used you, just as you said. That's all you ever meant to me—until a minute ago.[23] I didn't think anything like that could ever happen to me.[24]

In this beautiful, moving scene, Phyllis realizes that Neff is finally refusing to bend to her will and, in that moment, she falls in love. Of course this does not change the eventual outcome—Phyllis must die—but now her death carries extra weight: she could have been saved from herself had Neff stood up to her sooner. This, in the end, is the tragic quality of the film, that lingers in the minds of the audience long after the final frame has flickered past.

It is impossible to try and work out which elements of the movie were written by Ray and which were written by Wilder and, in any case, their working method suggests the screenplay evolved through discussion and argument and is therefore a genuine collaboration. There are lines, however, that feel as if Ray wrote them: "Walter Neff, insurance agent, thirty-five years old, unmarried, no visible scars." If one element in particular has the smack of Ray's style about it, then it is the relationship between Keyes and Neff. In the novel, Keyes is a relatively minor character but, in the film, deserves equal billing with Neff and Phyllis. He has an inner voice, a "little man" in his chest, who keeps nagging him with uncomfortable questions about the case, and the kind of obsessive personality that, we are told, led him to investigate his own fiancée before his marriage and thus ruin his own chance at happiness. The Neff-Keyes dynamic seems Chandleresque because it is so familiar from his novels and stories: two men share a relationship that is full of possibilities but which is ultimately doomed. Wilder always said that the Neff-Keyes relationship was the real love story of the movie, and it is easy to see why. Several of their exchanges close with Neff saying "I love you" and, while this is supposed to be humorous, when combined with the other elements, it becomes more than that. For example, Keyes never has a match to light his cigar but Neff is always there to produce one, to light it with a flick of his nail, like a boy showing off to a girl. But the relationship goes both ways, and Keyes is disappointed when the insurance salesman refuses to become his assistant, saying: "I thought maybe you were a shade less dumb than the rest of the outfit. I guess I was all wet. You're not smarter, Walter. You're just a little taller."[25] His disappointment at rejection is palpable. Had Neff never met Phyllis, then he and Keyes could have paired up and worked together happily ever after.

The relationship between Neff and Keyes is designed to throw the one between Neff and Phyllis into sharper relief. Walter bonds with Keyes because they are similar: they share tastes and instincts that could make for an almost romantic connection—as the match lighting is supposed to symbolize—whereas his relationship with Phyllis is based on sexual desire and results in murder. These parallel relationships represent an inner conflict as Neff is constantly pulled between the pure and good Keyes and the evil but sexy Phyllis. Indeed, Keyes sits at the moral center of the story and probably fills what would have been the Philip Marlowe role, had *Double Indemnity* been one of Ray's novels.

Shooting started on September 27 and finished on November 24, 1943. Ray seems to have been involved in rewriting parts up until the end, telling Alfred Knopf on November 13 that he would only be done with the movie at the end of the month.[26] He was happy enough with the final film and even had a small cameo in it, though it went unnoticed until very recently. Around sixteen minutes into the film Walter Neff closes the door to Keyes's office and walks past a middle-aged man sitting in a chair, wearing spectacles, smoking a cigarette, and reading a magazine. It was Raymond Chandler.

He later wrote to Cain after the film was finished to say this of the changes:

I don't think any of the changes we made were in conflict with your basic conception. In fact, you would have had to make them yourself. I do not doubt that some of them might have been made better, but they had to be made. The emotional integration is due to the fact that the three guys who worked on the job did not at any time disagree about what they wanted to achieve, but only how to do it.[27]

Cain was very pleased with the outcome. In a conversation with Peter Brunette and Gerald Peary, years after the film was made, he said:

It's the only picture I ever saw made from my books that had things in it I wish I had thought of. Wilder's ending was much better than my ending, and his device for letting the guy tell the story by taking out the office dictating machine—I would have done that if I had thought of it.[28]

According to Wilder, after seeing the film at a preview with the cast and crew, Cain marched up to him and gave him his seal of approval by putting his arms around him and telling him that he had done a "good job."[29]

Cain's praise echoed that of other industry professionals, and the movie quickly gained a reputation for brilliance in terms of both direction and adaptation. Financially, it was less successful. It did not lose money, but nor did it make a great deal.[30] Still, despite a lack of commercial success, it was immediately recognized as a watershed movie due to the clever job Wilder and Ray had done in getting a dark, sexy, and immoral screenplay past the Production Code Administration. This was no mean feat. That said, the PCA came back with remarkably few changes for such a movie. They wanted references to specific poisons removed and the use of gloves to hide fingerprints, because they worried these would give tips to would-be criminals,[31] but did not object to the sexual and sinful atmosphere of the movie. In this, Ray and Wilder had done something unique and important for the industry and, with the passing of *Double Indemnity*, the dark and dirty door that Hollywood had long been told not to open was suddenly thrown wide. There was now a vogue for films in the *Double Indemnity* mold, much darker than earlier attempts at hard-boiled cinema like *The Maltese Falcon*. This, in turn, paved the way for successful adaptations of Ray's own novels.

Industry respect for the movie was bestowed in what has become the traditional way: through Oscar nominations. *Double Indemnity* garnered seven in total, including Best Picture, Best Director, Best Actress, and Best Screenplay, but, on the night of the ceremony, it failed to win anything. It lost out on Best Picture and Director to another Paramount picture, *Going My Way*, a movie long since forgotten, starring Bing Crosby as a priest and directed by Leo McCarey. The ceremony was held on March 15, 1945, at Grauman's Chinese Theatre. Despite *Double Indemnity* being nominated for Best Screenplay, Ray did not attend, for reasons unknown. It was a fitting end to his involvement with the project. In a letter to Hamish Hamilton, he said:

> *Double Indemnity* . . . was an agonizing experience and has probably shortened my life; but I learned from it as much about screen writing as I am capable of learning, which is not very much.[32]

He did not realize at the time quite what a remarkable job he had done.

As the work on *Double Indemnity* was coming to an end, Ray found his mind turning back to fiction. As the Santa Ana winds blew hot and dry through Southern California that year, he started to reconsider his options. The plan that he had outlined in March 1939 with such grand ambition was looking more and more hopeless. It is clear that on more than one occasion, Ray opened his book and reread what he had written shortly after the publication of *The Big Sleep*. Back then Cissy had added her own handwritten addendum, "you'll have fun looking back at this maybe, and seeing what useless dreams you had. Or perhaps it will not be fun," and Ray, in September 1940 and again in February 1941, had scratched next to this entry: "Check." In December 1941 he had looked again and this time written "Double Check." Looking back was not fun at all.

His ambition, though, was not extinguished entirely. He still wanted to write a book that would allow him to "forget mystery writing altogether," but he was also beginning to realize that Philip Marlowe might still have a part to play in that next stage of his career. During his long hours at the studio, he began to turn over a new idea, which he explained in a letter to Alfred Knopf:

> It is to be a story about a murder involving three men and two women, and practically nobody else. It is to take place in Bel-Air, and all these

characters are wealthy except the protagonist of the story. He[re] is my problem. I should like to do a first person story about Philip Marlowe. I wouldn't have to develop him very much more than I have already because he is the sort of guy who behaves according to the company he is in. But the story is not going to be a mystery, and I hope to avoid its being tagged as a mystery novel. Is this possible if I use a character who is already established in fiction?[33]

The wish to move away from crime writing was a familiar one, but here was a new approach. In the past, Ray had wanted to tackle a new location, England, writing in a new genre, what he called the dramatic novel, and, presumably, this would also have required a new central character. The idea of a Marlowe novel set in Bel-Air was a marked shift away from that plan. What prompted him to consider this approach? On the surface it may have been a combination of sheer exhaustion mixed with his recent return to drinking. Eager to get started on a new project, he came up with a hodgepodge idea that played to his strengths and did not require much mental exertion. But equally, Ray was a pragmatist and knew that a Marlowe novel would be less of a risk for a publisher or, for that matter, a reader. But this does not take into account his ambition which, though troubled, was not undimmed. Another explanation might be that he was beginning to question the limits of his literary abilities. He admitted as much to Knopf when he said, "the character will probably turn out to be Marlowe anyway, even if I give him another name."[34] But this would ignore the fact that Ray had just helped write a successful movie, one that did not require him to write about Marlowe at all. Surely this would have bolstered his faith in his skill? Instead this idea may have been a recalibration of Ray's course. Not long ago, he had set out to learn to write detective fiction by imitation; now he wanted to learn to write in a new way but, rather than scrapping everything he had already learned, he planned to use Marlowe as lodestar to guide him along a new course, one that would eventually lead, perhaps after several iterations, to a novel that did not center on crime. In fact, in this letter we catch a glimpse of the hazy and unformed idea of what would, a few years later, condense into *The Long Goodbye*.

The novel he outlined in the letter to Knopf stalled almost immediately. Ray's life was undergoing rapid change during this period, with his new

Hollywood career pulling him in one direction and his literary ambitions in another. Sydney Sanders, Ray's book agent, was probably aware that his client was not likely to produce a new book in the near future and so tried to get Knopf to publish a collection of his early stories. Knopf's reader's response came back swiftly:

> These stories by Raymond Chandler—novelettes really, five of them—are from 10 to 7 years old. They don't do Chandler justice, they don't represent him. They are positively unworthy of publishing in book form.[35]

This was hardly a blow to Ray, who probably shared some of the reader's views. Away from books, his stock as a screenwriter was rising as quickly as that of *Double Indemnity* and, suddenly, he was a hot commodity. Paramount extended his contract and set him to work. And then he hit the earth with a bump. Overnight he went from part of the team behind *Double Indemnity* to being just another novelist in Hollywood, stuck finessing dialogue for somebody else's screenplay.

In 1944 he worked on two films, *And Now Tomorrow* and *The Unseen*. Both were adaptations of novels, so Paramount had at least found a niche for Ray, but the movies themselves were wildly different. *And Now Tomorrow* was an Alan Ladd vehicle in which he played a tough-talking doctor who specialized in curing deafness. He meets the beautiful Emily Blair (played by Loretta Young) and, in his attempt to cure her, falls in love. It has rightly been forgotten and was never going to be the sort of movie that would show his talents in the best light. Ladd's character, Dr. Merek Vance, talks tough and delivers some Chandleresque lines—"Pride isn't even enough for you to live on"—but the story, set in New England, never engaged Ray in the way that stories set in Los Angeles did. Ray's variety of magic failed to cast the same spell when wielded outside his chosen city.

Ray's next movie, *The Unseen* ("more deadly than the *Uninvited*," the movie Charles Brackett had turned down *Double Indemnity* to do), lived up to its name. It was a story of ghosts and ghouls and was easily forgotten. According to the movie's producer, John Houseman, Ray's job was to add toughness. Houseman, who had worked with Orson Welles in New York and played a crucial role in getting *Citizen Kane* made, would become a good friend to Ray. The two men had both attended English public schools (Houseman was at Clifton) and seemed to recognize similarities in each other which forged a connection between them.

Not that Ray was short on friends at Paramount. Despite Wilder's suggestion that he had an acid personality that was hard to like, Ray seems to have been a popular person around the lot, particularly in the writers' building, where the atmosphere was especially relaxed. Notwithstanding the regular working hours and the sometimes dull work, Ray found being at Paramount a surprisingly pleasant experience, as he explained to Carl Brandt some years later: "Paramount was the only one [studio] I liked. They do somehow maintain the country club atmosphere there."[36] And it was the "country club atmosphere" that Ray was especially drawn to. He had started sneaking drinks during the writing of *Double Indemnity* but, in the writers' building, discretion and subterfuge were not necessary. Drinking, if anything, was positively encouraged. Studio bosses had little interest in the sobriety of their writers as long as the scripts were delivered on time, and they even encouraged a drinking culture, providing copious amounts of wine, whisky and champagne in an effort to stimulate their workers' creativity. For a man like Ray, who had never wholeheartedly abandoned alcohol, the temptations were dangerous, and he started to spiral out of control.

Ray may have stood out a little—his tweed jacket and pipe set him apart from the other writers, most of whom were some years younger—but his colleagues were a tolerant bunch and accepted his eccentricities. Some younger colleagues would seek him out for advice on writing. One, Robert Presnell, remembered knocking on Ray's office door to talk about his ideas and observed that "he loved interruptions more than anything else."[37] He was also an important part of the regular drinks and lunches in the canteen or at Lucey's Restaurant on Melrose Avenue, opposite the lot. These lunches could be raucous affairs, where drink flowed as freely as the stories:

> At the writers table [*sic*] at Paramount I heard some of the best wit I've ever heard in my life. Some of the boys are at their best when not writing. I remember Harry Tugend's wonderful crack about _____, when Tugend was trying to be a producer and hating

it. He said: "You know this is a lousy job. You got to sit and talk to that birdbrain seriously about whether or not this part is going to be good for her _____ career and at the same time you got to keep from being raped." Whereat a rather innocent young man piped up: "You mean to say she's a nymphomaniac?" Harry frowned off into the distance and sighed and said slowly, "Well, I guess she would be, if they could get her quieted down a little."[38]

Alcohol was not the only vice that was easy to indulge in at Paramount: the studio buildings ran hot with sexual energy. Is it any wonder when young, beautiful people roamed the lot, sometimes with little to do and even less to distinguish themselves from their competitors? This atmosphere left Ray deeply unsettled. He maintained an absolute vision of what a woman should be, one that involved the usual courtly tropes about purity, chastity, and honor. When that was challenged, he could react strongly, as he did with Betty Hutton. She was an actress who had worked with his friend Harry Tugend, another writer at Paramount, but Ray found her sense of bawdy humor to be vile:

> I do not go to see films with Betty Hutton in them. She was under contract to Paramount when I was there, and I saw a good deal of the lady. She has a lot of bounce and vitality, but she is horribly coarse. It is said that she is wonderful in a night club. I think she would be equally wonderful on a hog ranch.[39]

On the other hand, when he drank, it became increasingly hard to maintain his devotion to his own ideal woman, Cissy, and it was not as if he had stopped noticing other women. He might find their sexual energy uncomfortable, but part of him was drawn to it, too. It was as if Ray had a good angel on one shoulder and a bad angel on the other, the former representing Cissy and chastity, while the other urged him to run riot. Unfortunately, when he drank, the voice of his good angel became quieter than a whisper, giving the bad angel free rein.

The result of this combination of sexual energy and a weakening of Ray's moral position through drink was that he had another affair. Life at home had become difficult. Cissy's health was not getting any better and she did not like it when he drank with his friends. In addition, he was now surrounded by vibrant, energetic, beautiful young women, which only served to highlight Cissy's age. It did not matter what clothes she chose to wear: compared to the women on the lot, she was old. At work, a haggard-looking Ray would complain to colleagues about how unhappy he was with Cissy but would say he could never ask for a divorce because she was too old. His drinking contributed to an unhappy home life and his unhappy home life contributed to his drinking. He sought solace in the arms of an unknown secretary and, just as he had done more than a decade before, ran away with her. When they came back to Los Angeles, she quietly departed from the studio, leaving Ray to keep working. His drinking had once again undermined his marriage and complicated his affairs. It was as if everything he had learned since 1932 had been tossed aside for a brief moment of sexual and alcoholic pleasure. When the madness passed, Ray found himself having to once again reassemble his life and marriage.

CHAPTER ELEVEN

"NO JOB FOR AMATEURS"

At the same time Raymond Chandler was establishing his name as a screenwriter at Paramount, he also entered into one of the most important correspondences of his career. James Sandoe was a librarian at the University of Colorado and a crime fiction enthusiast. In Ray's novels, Sandoe detected a rare spark of brilliance that he felt set Ray apart from run-of-the-mill crime writers. He thought they deserved the same level of attention in the papers as literary novels and wrote to Bernard Smith, an editor at Knopf, to ask why Ray was not receiving the recognition he deserved. Smith was at a loss, saying that he could not understand "why the critics have failed to notice what a remarkable prose writer he is and how acute are his descriptions."[1] He went on to suggest that Sandoe write to the book editors of several newspapers to make the same point. Sandoe did so, contacting people like Orville Prescott, principal book critic at the *New York Times*. If he thought his endeavors would be rewarded, he was wrong. Sandoe did not anticipate how entrenched the views of men like Orville Prescott were; his response was swift, blunt, and completely missed the point:

> I never have time to read them preoccupied as I am with books of more general interest. . . . I have turned your letter over to the man who reviews detective fiction.[2]

It was typical of the replies Sandoe received—detective fiction was either not of general interest or it was not the right fit for the paper—and he was quick to realize the scale of the challenge. Undeterred, Sandoe wrote directly to Ray, who was always pleased to receive fan mail and responded warmly. They shared a common outlook, as one letter made clear:

> You are certainly not without company in your wish that "something could be done about the disadvantages of the redlight segregation of detective stories from 'novels' by the reviews." Once in a long while a detective story writer is treated as a writer, but very seldom.[3]

The two men started to write to one another regularly, exchanging views on a variety of subjects from detective fiction to the art of prose. At first, Ray's letters to Sandoe were stiff and formal but, after a few months, as he relaxed into the friendship, he started signing off his letters "Ray Chandler." He was no longer Raymond, or Mr. Chandler, just Ray—a tacit acknowledgment of their new friendship.

In one of his earliest replies to Sandoe, Ray set out several possible reasons for the segregation of detective fiction from literature:

> (a) Most detective stories are very badly written. (b) Their principal sale is to rental libraries which depend on a commercial reading service and pay no attention to reviews. (c) I believe the detective story is marketed wrong. It is absurd to expect people to pay any more for it than they would for a movie. (d) The detective or mystery story as an art form has been so thoroughly explored that the real problem for a writer now is to avoid writing a mystery story while appearing to do so.[4]

Ray held strong views about the way that detective fiction was written, sold, and published, and his own "Poetics" of crime writing had emerged from his learning to write pulp stories through careful deconstruction of the work of his contemporaries. His letters to Sandoe were a forum to explore and explicate these ideas. At Paramount, too, he was known to outline his theories to those who would listen, especially younger writers; and Cissy must also have heard him thinking aloud, as well as typing up notes to be clipped into the rough leather notebook he used to collect his thoughts. Until 1944, though, his ideas of the principles of crime writing had not been exposed beyond a small group of friends and colleagues but, with increasing fame, came increasing attention. Charles Morton, editor of the *Atlantic* magazine, was an admirer of Ray's and contacted him to request a piece on detective fiction. Here was Ray's opportunity to reach a wider audience, and the article he contributed has become a manifesto of sorts. It helped that he gave his article a brilliant title: "The Simple Art of Murder."

The piece was written in the first part of 1944 and published in the December issue of the *Atlantic*. In it, Ray set out to give an intellectually rigorous defence of the hard-boiled crime novel. He starts by taking aim at a cultural apparatus that undermines the value of crime writing, arguing that the "critical fraternity" and "little clubs" that discuss books and try to promote the cultural value of fiction are, in reality, only interested in sales. Crime fiction cannot work in the same way because it cannot be easily marketed; sales are therefore limited, so it can only achieve an audience through a kind of attrition that Ray describes as "a slow process of distillation."[5] In short, a crime writer only finds an audience by hanging in there long enough so that people eventually notice him. The net result of this is that crime publishers value product over prose, output over art, so that the novels that are released are stale and dull:

> The average detective story is probably no worse than the average novel, but you never see the average novel. It doesn't get published. The average—or only slightly above average—detective story does.[6]

As a natural consequence of this overproduction, the financial rewards on offer are lower than they might be and writers with real talent refuse to waste their time and effort on a second-rate genre when the only reward is a third-rate income. The men and women who could breathe life into crime writing do not because they cannot make a living by writing elegant mystery fiction. Instead, they exercise their talent elsewhere:

> The fellow who can write you a vivid and colorful prose simply will not be bothered with the coolie labor of breaking down unbreakable alibis.[7]

He goes on to pick apart a much celebrated locked room story, *The Red House Mystery* by A. A. Milne, concluding with an oblique comparison of the detectives found in English detective novels with real-life detectives in Los Angeles:

> The detective in the case is an insouciant amateur named Anthony Gillingham, a nice lad with a cheery eye, a nice little flat in town, and that airy manner. He is not making any money on the assignment, but is always available when the local gendarmerie loses its notebook. The English police endure him with their customary stoicism, but I shudder to think what the boys down at the Homicide bureau in my city would do to him.[8]

Ray makes the point that the amateur would be a joke in the real world of murder, trapped in the rusting armor of a genre that is unrealistic in comparison to the tangible presence of the Angeleno detective. The amateur may have extensive knowledge of curare that does not make for realistic fiction and, ultimately, fiction that does not attempt to create realism does not create art:

> The boys with their feet on the desks know that the easiest murder case in the world to break is the one somebody tried to get very cute with; the one that really bothers them is the murder somebody thought of only two minutes before he pulled it off. But if the writers of this fiction wrote about the kind of murders that happened, they would also have to write about the authentic flavor of life as it is lived. And since they cannot do that, they pretend that what they do is what should be done.[9]

This last line contains a sharp sting. Writers of this sort of puzzle mystery cannot do any better so they do not try. This begs the question: who can?

Ray argues that some of the writers who wrote for the pulps, chief among them Dashiell Hammett, had made the first inroads into a new type of detective fiction. They wrote what he calls "realistic mystery fiction" but, importantly, he locates this shift in a larger cultural moment, linking Hammett with the modernist writers who had experimented with their writing at the same time as he was contributing to *Black Mask*:

Hemingway may have learned something from Hammett as well as writers like Dreiser, Ring Lardner, Carl Sandburg, Sherwood Anderson. . . . A rather revolutionary debunking of both the language and the material of fiction had been going on for some time. It probably started with poetry; almost everything does. You can take it clear back to Walt Whitman, if you like. But Hammett applied it to the detective story.[10]

There is a second point here, too: Hammett was not just employing realism, he was using American language, writing in "this style, which did not belong to Hammett . . . but is the American language . . . [and] can say things he did not know how to say."[11] It is this focus on realism and language that made them successful writers. They were much more than the writers of locked room mysteries because they started from a realistic standpoint and they used realistic language. In Ray's eyes they were not mere crime writers, but artists.

But for Ray it was insufficient. Hammett had not gone far enough (he still focused on murder, after all). What Ray wanted to do was depict not just a murder but, rather, the world where such a thing could actually happen. As he sketches out this world he gives us one of the best descriptions of hard-boiled fiction:

> The realist in murder writes of a world in which gangsters can rule nations and almost rule cities, in which hotels and apartment houses and celebrated restaurants are owned by men who made their money out of brothels, in which a screen star can be the finger man for a mob, and the nice man down the hall is a boss of the numbers racket: a world where a judge with a cellar full of bootleg liquor can send a man to jail for having a pint in his pocket, where the mayor of your town may have condoned murder as an instrument of money making, where no man can walk down a dark street in safety because law and order are things we talk about but refrain from practicing. . . . It is not a fragrant world, but it is the world you live in.[12]

The picture Ray draws is of a place where surface and substance are at odds; that offers one thing and delivers another; that stinks of corruption and causes people to become corrupt. This is the Los Angeles he had experienced in the 1920s, and this was the world he chose to re-create.

Of course, such a world requires a hero and, in the closing lines of the essay, Ray looks at the sort of man who can live and work in this environment and, for a brief moment, Philip Marlowe slips into sharper focus:

> In everything that can be called art there is a quality of redemption. It may be pure tragedy, if it is high tragedy, and it may be pity and irony, and it may be the raucous laughter of the strong man. But down these mean streets a man must go who is not himself mean, who is neither tarnished nor afraid. The detective in this kind of story must be such a man. He is the hero; he is everything.[13]

Ray is making two points here. First, his invocation of redemption directs us to the conclusion that he is the better artist, certainly better than Hammett and the other *Black Mask* writers. And, equally, he is starting to give a shape and name to his hero. He must be pure, he must be good and he must resist temptation:

> He must be, to use a rather weathered phrase, a man of honor—by instinct, by inevitability, without thought of it, and certainly without saying it. He must be the best man in the world and a good enough man for any world. I do not care much about his private life; he is neither a eunuch nor a satyr; I think he might seduce a duchess and I am quite sure he would not spoil a virgin; if he is a man of honor in one thing, he is that in all things.[14]

He was not the first author to employ an honorable hero, but his decision to make a sense of honor the very marrow of his hero set him apart from his contemporaries. Ray's ideal protagonist belonged to another time and another place: he is the courtly hero refracted and reformatted in the nineteenth century and relocated to America. The way Ray lingers over the word "honor" points towards his hero's roots in the English public school system. Evelyn Waugh, who was educated at Lancing, wrote that, at school, "'Honour' was a word often on our lips. Dishonesty, impurity, cruelty would have been inconceivable to us."[15] Ray's hero, though he may be American, is, like his creator, a product of the European tradition.

In 1950, "The Simple Art of Murder" became the preface to and title of a selection of Ray's stories and, thereafter, the essay was widely anthologized as one of the best explications of the hard-boiled school of crime writing. Ultimately, it was an extremely useful commission for Ray because, while his four novels were struggling to gain the recognition they deserved, in America at least, "The Simple Art of Murder" identified him in the minds of the readers of the *Atlantic* as more than just a crime writer—as an artist, a thinker and a man of literary ambition. It was the first step towards his eventual acceptance into the literary canon.

Meanwhile, basking in the glow of *Double Indemnity* and enjoying a regular wage for the first time in over a decade, Ray and Cissy decided it was time to stop their regular migrations between the city and the mountains. In October 1944, they took a house west of San Vicente Boulevard and north of Wilshire, at 6520 Drexel Avenue—rented, of course—where they would stay for two years. It was the longest period they had remained in one place for a good while. They started to pull the furniture they had hoarded out of storage so that they could fill the little stucco-walled bungalow. Outside, the couple had a simple garden, where they could work in the warm sunshine while Taki roamed the area. Money gave them the opportunity to settle, but another reason for the decision was that Cissy was increasingly fragile. She had recently injured her foot severely enough that it would require an operation. Packing the car with their belongings and driving up to the lakes in the mountains suddenly became too big an undertaking.

From the house, it was a short drive to the lot at Paramount. Every weekday, Ray would put on a jacket and tie, climb into his car, and head to work. He was popular and successful, but Cissy, aware of his weakness for young secretaries and a good drink, would have worried. It seems that, despite his brief affair, he was able to hold his life together, and his career as a screenwriter developed rapidly. With each new contract he earned a little more money and gained a little more cachet on the lot, though the projects he worked on were not exciting. He was still a script doctor, albeit a good one. No doubt the drink and sociable atmosphere eased the pain, but Ray was creatively frustrated. His most recent attempts at fiction had stalled and the projects he was offered at Paramount were not challenging enough. He yearned for another project like *Double Indemnity*.

For the executives at Paramount, 1944 had been a great year. Despite the war, cinema attendance figures were steady at eighty-five million,[16] and the industry was in good shape. But as 1944 became 1945, a new problem came to light: Paramount's main star, Alan Ladd, was called up to fight. Panic rippled through the studio. As their lead, and the highest-rated male performer in Hollywood at the time, he was Paramount's principal asset. Without him, their movies would not attract as big an audience, and revenues would plunge. They needed to find Ladd a movie to make before he left for basic training. At the next producer's meeting, all of the staff were encouraged to come up with new ideas, but nothing seemed to work. One of the producers at the meeting was Ray's friend, John Houseman. Two days later, he found himself at a lunch with Ray at Lucey's and, after a few drinks, Chandler revealed that he had been working on a new Marlowe story. It had not got very far because he had had to abandon it when he became ground down by the detail. Houseman was intrigued and asked to see more, so the two men headed back to Drexel Avenue, where Ray dug out the abandoned pages. Houseman was impressed by what he read and, forty-eight hours later, Paramount had bought the rights and commissioned Ray to write the screenplay. The story that had been shoved in the bottom drawer would become *The Blue Dahlia*.

In some ways, the war was an opportunity Hollywood was keen to embrace. Not only did it offer new ways to make money, but it was also a chance to change the public perception of cinema. Movie moguls like Darryl F. Zanuck, who ran Twentieth Century Fox, wanted to make the film industry as American as apple pie and to fix it firmly in the minds of the people as a part of the establishment. A few short months after war was declared, movies like *Little Tokyo* and *Wake Island* started to appear in theatres. These Japan-bashing films signaled Hollywood's intention to become the voice of the people. At the same time, stars like Spencer Tracey and Katharine Hepburn were being cast in movies such as *Keeper of the Flame*, in which it was suggested that America was vulnerable to fascist influence. Like the anti-Japanese movies, *Keeper of the Flame* was an attempt to sway public opinion—soft-core propaganda, which Hollywood studios were more than happy to churn out if it meant audiences would keep coming to see their films.

But, over time, the public began to grow sick of this sort of changeless output and the resulting apathy, in part, created a space where movies like *Double Indemnity* could make their name. *The Maltese Falcon* had started a vogue for what would later be recognized as the first examples of film noir, and *Double Indemnity* had made that kind of picture simultaneously grittier and more respectable. Soon, everyone wanted to make the sort of tough-guy thriller Ray and Wilder had been able to produce, and Paramount was no different. They had a star, they had an audience, and now they had a screenwriter with an idea.

Ray immediately started writing. For the first time, he was to be the sole screenwriter. The preproduction process would begin at once so that filming could run parallel to the writing, and George Marshall, a prolific if undistinguished director, was chosen to direct. Alan Ladd and his regular on-screen partner, Veronica Lake, were cast in the lead roles. Ray wrote steadily and quickly realized that *The Blue Dahlia* offered him a unique chance. Rather than contributing to a screenplay as he had done in the past, here he could actually *author* a film. Due to the extraordinary time pressure, the normal process of editing, drafting, and story boarding were either truncated or dropped altogether and so, in effect, Ray was "writing directly for the screen . . . almost under the camera."[17] Very little of his vision could be mediated in this way and so the resulting film would have more of Raymond Chandler in it than any previous efforts.

Ray enjoyed himself at first and the script came fluently:

I am very busy doing an original screenplay which is much more fun than anything I have done in pictures so far because instead of fighting the difficulties of translating a fiction story into the medium of screen, I can write directly for the screen and use all its advantages.[18]

The first half of the film was delivered in around three weeks.[19] Though shooting was rushed, there was something to be said for the process:

What you lose in finish you gain in movement; and movement is what the motion picture has been steadily losing for a long time.[20]

Ray's focus on motion here (he was referring to dramatic movement) reflects his own vision of the filmmaking process. To him, blocking, editing, the use of clever angles, and other directorial tricks blunted scripts to a point where they became something else. He was convinced that the more control he had, the better the resulting movie would be. The pressure was great, tempers frayed, and arguments on set were common—and Ray was at the center of it all, "screaming at the front office to protect the producer"[21] one day, and lending a hand on set the next. He even found himself taking the director's chair for one scene though, unfortunately, we do not know which one.

Then disaster struck. The steady flow of pages coming out of Ray's office started to dry up. Four weeks into filming, the shooting script was getting thinner and thinner each day, with no new material to replenish it. Ray was stuck; he could not work out who the murderer was. He had intended it to be naval veteran Buzz Wanchek, but this idea was rejected by the US Navy, who did not want their boys presented as bad guys, potentially undermining morale in wartime. An additional problem for Ray was that, because the film was being shot as it was written, the trail of clues in the entire first half of the film pointed towards Buzz and could not be changed. He was stymied and the more frustrated he got, the less creative he felt. Before long, Ray's panic had rippled across the studio. No one there knew quite what to do. A series of story conferences were called on the ground floor of the Paramount office block, but Ray struggled to contribute. He was, after all, a writer who had never particularly cared about plot, and the revelation of the murderer in his novels never had the sort of choreographed disclosures common to many of his contemporaries. On April 12,[22] the producers called another story conference and, with Ray, sat around a table trying to work out what was going to happen. In the middle of all this, a young man stuck his head through the window and announced the solemn news that President Roosevelt had died. No one knew what to say. After some minutes, they managed to get back to talking about the story, but it hardly mattered. Ray was barely listening. Instead he sat there, nodding occasionally and contributing nothing.

The following day, Ray received a call from his agent, H. N. Swanson, asking him to call on the head of production early the next morning. If anything was sure to cause him a sleepless night, this was it. He showed up as requested and was ushered in to one of the wood-paneled executive offices. The walls were hung with prints of English hunting scenes and the carpet was cream colored. On the other side of a large desk sat the head of production. Ray must have felt like a schoolboy being called into the office of the head-master. The head of production offered him a bonus of $5,000 if the movie was delivered on time, but also added that he should not mention this to John Houseman. He left the executive's office stunned and lost for words.

Eventually, Ray went home, but he found that he could not sleep, such was his anger. The following day he paid a visit to Houseman in his office. It was clear to the producer that Ray was in a rage[23] and, as he explained what had happened the day before, it emerged quite how much the head of production had misjudged him. Chandler was angry because Paramount did not believe he could finish the movie. It was true that he was struggling, but he had signed a contract to deliver the completed screenplay and, to a man of honor, this should have been enough. The offer of a $5,000 bonus was an insult that may have swayed a hack screenwriter into pulling out his best work but, to Ray, who liked to think he was giving everything to each project, it was an almost unforgivable gesture. And the request that he not say anything to his friend about the bonus was nothing short of offensive. Years later, Houseman described the moment as Chandler explained what had happened:

> These accumulated grievances had reduced Ray to a state of nervous despair, the depth of which it took me some time to realize. But finally, when he assured me that his creative mechanism had been wrecked and that he had no choice but to withdraw from a project to which he had nothing more to contribute, I found myself believing him.[24]

Ray left Houseman's office and went to lie down. Ten days remained before Ladd had to leave for the army, they had almost run out of script, and their screenwriter had just told the producer that he had nothing left to offer. If things had seemed desperate before this point, then the intervention of a front office executive with his misguided offer had turned it into a train wreck.

There were at least two contributing factors to Ray's inability to finish the screenplay. First, he was almost certainly drinking at the office, as he had throughout work on *Double Indemnity*. Secondly, Cissy was not well. Her injured foot was painful and she was starting to develop a recurring chest infection that gave her a rattling cough and made her seem increasingly frail. With her leg bound up, she could not walk far and spent most of her days sitting on the davenport with her feet up. The injury had come at a time when the wound inflicted by Ray's affair was still raw. She was not a happy woman. Abandoning her to go to work each day burdened him with a particularly acute form of guilt.

But, miraculously, as he calmed himself after his meeting with Houseman, he began to formulate a plan that would allow him to finish the film and, at the same, relieve his guilt over Cissy. He explained to Houseman that, after years of alcoholism, he had been teetotal for some time (a lie, of course, but a useful one). Drinking now, he declared, could seriously damage his health, but it could also be the answer to their prayers, because alcohol had always given him energy. Ray's conclusion was that the best way to finish the screenplay was to do so drunk. Houseman was taken aback as the plan was laid before him, but Ray had thought through a lot of the detail and confirmed that he had the support of a reluctant Cissy. He had somehow managed to convince her that this was a necessary step that would ensure the completion of the screenplay and preserve his honor. Since she called him her Gallibeoth, casting him as the willing knight errant in her own romance, she must have understood his need to keep his word at all costs. Ray presented to Houseman a sheet of yellow paper on which he had written his demands:

A. Two Cadillac limousines, to stand day and night outside the house with drivers available for:
   1. Fetching the doctor (Ray's or Cissy's or both).
   2. Taking script pages to and from the studio.
   3. Driving the maid to the market.
   4. Contingencies and emergencies.
B. Six secretaries—in three relays of two—to be in constant attendance and readiness, available at all times for dictation, typing, and other possible emergencies.
C. A direct line open at all times, to my office by day and the studio switchboard at night.[25]

Houseman read through the demands but did not know quite what to say, so he went for a walk to clear his mind. He also paid a visit to Joe Sistrom and asked him what he should do. Sistrom's advice was that, if this was the only way the movie would be made, he should agree to Ray's plan: if not, all hell would break loose. Houseman returned to his office, where he tried to dredge up all of his "Public School fervor and esprit de corps"[26] to tell Ray that he would accept his plan. Chandler, evidently pleased with the news, suggested they go to lunch, where he proceeded to get very drunk, consuming three double martinis before lunch and three double stingers afterwards. It was a moment of alcoholic gluttony, and Houseman must have wondered what he had just agreed to. The producer took him home, where they found the cars and the secretaries waiting, but he was worried and had very little idea of what might happen next. But sure enough, when he visited the house the following day, he found Ray passed out in the living room with a small stack of neatly typed pages sitting next to him, ready to be taken to the studio.

For the next eight days, Ray drank and wrote; the cars sat outside and the secretaries typed; and, occasionally, a doctor showed up to administer him with a "vitamin" injection. The upshot was that the screenplay was completed, and with a few days to spare, too. The effort, though, wrecked his health and exhausted his spirit. It would take him more than a month to recover physically and much longer to regain his energy and focus. Still, he had kept his word and had done so in a particularly heroic fashion that might have impressed Ernest Hemingway. To Ray, sacrifice was a noble thing and, in the writing of *The Blue Dahlia*, he believed he had shown deep courage[27] in compromising his own sobriety for the sake of the film. This is certainly how he wanted the events presented to the world, and John Houseman was a willing accomplice in this, as in his essay "The Lost Fortnight." It has been suggested, however, that the whole business was actually nothing more than a ruse to allow Ray to work from home. The speed with which he delivered the ending indicates that he might have exaggerated the extent of his difficulties in deciding on the identity of the murderer. Still, this theory ignores the awkward corner that Paramount had found themselves in. They needed Ray to write his screenplay and, had he wanted to work from home, they would more than likely have readily agreed without the need for such fuss.

Unlike Ray's first major film, *The Blue Dahlia* has entered film history as much for its difficult birth as for its quality. It is recognized as a good example of film noir but has never troubled the likes of *Double Indemnity*, *The Maltese Falcon*, or *The Big Sleep* for the crown of best in genre. From the start, it is clear that *The Blue Dahlia* is firmly located in Raymond Chandler territory. The opening shot, after the credits have rolled, shows the destination board of a bus reading, simply, Hollywood. The three men at the heart of the story—Johnny Morrison (Alan Ladd), George Copeland (Hugh Beaumont), and Buzz (William Bendix)—are US Navy airmen on a break from the war in the Pacific. They stumble off the coach, blinking in the bright Los Angeles sunlight, and immediately seek comfort in a nearby bar. This, though, is not a happy homecoming: Johnny and the men raise their glasses to "what was," not what will be, and the implication is that they were happier with the certainties of war than they are with the uncertainties of home. Johnny heads to the exclusive Wilshire Boulevard bungalow where his wife, Helen (played by Doris Dowling) is holding a party. Johnny's unexpected return quickly changes the mood in the house, particularly for Eddie Harwood, owner of the Blue Dahlia nightclub and sometime paramour of Helen Morrison, who gets a swift punch to the face from her husband. As the guests leave, Helen finds herself alone with Johnny, and it becomes clear that her fidelity has not been the only thing she has lied about. Their son, Jimmy, who she had said had died from an illness, was actually killed in a car accident she caused by drunk driving. In a few moments, Johnny's life is shattered and he briefly contemplates shooting Helen with his service gun. Instead he throws the weapon down and runs into the wet night. But the next day, when the maid comes in to clean the house, she finds Helen shot to death.

It is worth pausing a moment and considering the scene that Ray lays before his audience. Johnny is coming home from war and it would be right to celebrate his return with a party but, in Ray's story, the Wilshire Boulevard bungalow is not Johnny's home—he has never actually lived there—and the party he walks in on is not for him. In other words, the correct order of things is inverted and the idea of the home is corrupted by Helen Morrison. This is a very Chandleresque situation. In his fiction, Marlowe's home is sacrosanct: when invaded by Carmen Sternwood, he responds violently, tearing his bed "to pieces." To a war hero, the home should be a sanctuary, but it is not, and the story which follows is as much about Johnny Morrison's search for a home, more specifically a bed to rest in, as it is about the murder of his wife.

Johnny's swift departure results in his meeting Joyce Harwood, Eddie's wife, who finds him standing in the rain as she drives past, though she does not reveal who she is. They head to Malibu, where Johnny learns of his wife's death. At first, he has no interest in identifying her murderer; his only concern is survival, and he goes on the run.

Unusually for one of Ray's stories, it is the police who are intent on solving the crime under the guidance of Captain Hendrickson. Unlike those in the novels, there is no whiff of corruption about these officers, who are upstanding, businesslike lawmen. It is the audience, though, who gets the best view of what is going on and has the best opportunity to solve the mystery. We see the police, we see Eddie Harwood, we see "Dad" Newell (the elderly house detective who shifts between parties trying to offer information in exchange for money) and, most importantly, we see Buzz, Johnny's fellow Navy flier. In the opening scenes, it is established that he has a metal plate in his head which makes him very volatile: he nearly beats up an army sergeant for playing music too loudly, and music becomes a discordant riff throughout the movie, causing Buzz to get confused and to black out. On the night of Helen's murder, he had a drink with her, though he had no idea who she was, and the trail of evidence pointing to his guilt begins. He was not her only visitor—Eddie Harwood was there, too—but the audience is left to guess which of the two men is guilty.

Johnny's part in the revelation of the murder is slight indeed: when a photo frame breaks, he discovers a potentially crucial piece of evidence entirely by accident—that Harwood has another name and is wanted by the New Jersey Police for murder. This small event draws him into Harwood's world and he ends up being kidnapped, having to shoot his way out of a hideout in the Los Angeles hills.

The denouement, when it does come, is abrupt and surprising. In the back office of the Blue Dahlia nightclub, the surviving suspects gather, and it seems that blame will fall onto Buzz. He was the last person to see Helen alive and cannot give an account of himself that evening other than that he was angry with Helen, spurred on by the music she played that beat against his brain. Johnny though, for very little reason other than they were war buddies, does not believe Buzz could be the killer and, in a reversal of the traditional detective exposition, pushes his friend to reveal his innocence. As the room starts to empty it seems that no one will work out who the killer is, at which point Captain Hendrickson suddenly reveals that it was "Dad" all along and quickly gets a confession from the old man.

Much has been made of the fact that Ray's original choice for the killer, Buzz, was not allowed by mandate of the US Navy. In many ways, it is to the good of the film that he is not, because the clues as to his guilt are laid with a heavy hand. It may be that a modern audience, more familiar with the tropes of the genre that Ray was inventing as he wrote, pick up on these more easily than would an audience of the 1940s. On the other hand, "Dad," who is not as paternal as his name suggests, is similarly unsatisfying as the killer: he is too peripheral to the story and his reasons for murder too convenient.

None of this really mattered to Ray. His novels show that plot and "who-dunit" were less important to him than atmosphere and character. Though there is plenty of atmosphere in *The Blue Dahlia*, and there are flashes of brilliant dialogue, it is the characterization that really lets the movie down. This was not Ray's fault. He was in the studio straitjacket, having to provide Alan Ladd with a movie in which he could play Alan Ladd. Ray described the actor as "hard, bitter, and occasionally charming, but . . . after all a small boy's idea of a tough guy,"[28] and that is pretty much the role Ray had to write for him. It was hard to explore the character of Johnny Morrison when limited by the talents of an actor already cast in the part. Johnny's most testing times come when he discovers that his wife caused the death of his son and when he realizes his friends think him guilty of her murder, but these moments are too brief. In one of Ray's novels, they would have received much richer treatment.

Joyce Harwood (Veronica Lake) is about as flat as they come. She is neither sexy nor seductive in *The Blue Dahlia*, and her role seems to be limited to that of a perfect woman to put the others in sharper relief. Very early on in the film, Eddie Harwood's business partner says that women "are all poison. Almost all . . ." and the camera pans slowly to a picture of Lake. Later, Johnny says to her: "Every man has seen you somewhere before. The trick is to find you." Clearly she was not meant to be an in-depth portrait of a woman married to a criminal but a pure and perfect woman whose worst crime is a witty phrase. She has nothing interesting about her—no sex, no past, almost no present either. Compared with Vivian Regan or Anne Riordan, she is completely uninteresting. Ray may have been aware of Lake's limitations when he signed on and so made little of her role, not even making her a murderer as he did with so many of the women in his novels. Later he said this of the actress, who he liked to call "Miss Moronica Lake":

> The only time she's any good is when she keeps her mouth shut and looks mysterious. The moment she tries to behave as if she had a brain she falls flat on her face. The scenes we had to cut because she loused them up! And there are three godawful shots of her looking perturbed that make me want to throw my lunch over the fence.[29]

This suggests that the character he originally conceived was more interesting. Later, he would claim that she could not "play the love scenes" and that, as a result, "too much had to be discarded,"[30] laying the blame for the movie's shortcomings at her door. This seems unfair because the script could certainly have been stronger, too.

In the end, the movie will be best remembered not because of its merits as a picture, or because of who wrote it, but because it became associated with a brutal murder. In 1947, a woman called Elizabeth Short was found dead in Los Angeles, her body sliced in half, separating her torso from her hips and legs. Elizabeth could have been a minor character in one of Ray's novels. She was twenty-two and wanted to be an actress. In the popular press, who lapped up this gruesome story, she was christened "the Black Dahlia." She always wore black and her hair was dyed the same color, so either locals who knew her or a crime reporter made a connection with the title of Ray's film. The fact that the murder was so gruesome, that it remains unsolved, and that it has drifted into popular culture in a variety of ways, including a James Ellroy novel, means that *The Blue Dahlia* has become a footnote in the story of the Black one.

The Blue Dahlia experience was very hard on Ray, and on Cissy, too: it caused her to come down with a case of the flu, which no doubt exacerbated the problems with her already sensitive lungs and certainly left her confined to bed. When Erle Stanley Gardner offered Ray and Cissy the run of his ranch in Temecula, Riverside, Ray responded cautiously. In a letter he described himself as "a complete nervous wreck":[31]

> I don't think my wife or myself could hike or ride. She had an operation on her foot about a year ago and it's still weak. We don't know how to ride. I am a complete nervous wreck and theoretically could walk a few miles, but probably not your kind of walking. Haven't got the equipment anyhow. What we hope to do was just to get down to your place around noon and spend a few hours with you. We have some business in Riverside and were thinking of stopping over at the Mission Inn and then driving to Temecula in the morning.[32]

This is Ray at his most awkward. Exhausted by the movie, he clearly wanted some sort of respite but felt that he could not admit to this and so used the excuse of business to see a friend without appearing desperate or old.

Outside of the movie business, events in the world were taking a more positive turn. As Ray was finishing up his script for *The Blue Dahlia* and during its shooting, it became increasingly clear that the war in Europe was coming to an end. He found this to be a huge relief. America suffered during the war in Europe and in Asia: its sons were brutally killed on foreign soil and, at home, rationing made life hard. Ray was always engaged with events abroad and found himself distressed and distracted by the war. To support friends in London, he dispatched regular food parcels. Hamish Hamilton and his wife were one of the recipients of his generosity; his old schoolmaster, H. F. Hose, was another. The war's conclusion was a weight off his shoulders.

Since he was relieved now on so many fronts, the trip to Riverside had some positive effect on Ray because, on his return, he agreed to write a new screenplay. This, he thought, would be nothing like *The Blue Dahlia* because it was an adaptation of his own novel *The Lady in the Lake*. The rights to make the movie belonged to a rival studio, Metro-Goldwyn-Mayer (MGM), but when Paramount was asked whether Ray could work at MGM they made no objection. Rival studios often lent talent to one another, but it is remarkable that

Ray, who had really only worked on a small number of screenplays, was in such demand. It helped that it was his own novel, but it also shows the momentum that his screenwriting career had gathered. In an age when poets, journalists, and novelists were snapped up by the studio, and cinema was still too young to have many writers coming through the ranks with ambitions to write nothing other than screenplays, Ray had a particular talent: he could write natural-sounding, convincing dialogue. Not everyone had this ability. Even great and well-respected writers such as William Faulkner wrote dialogue that was impossible for actors to deliver.[33]

Ray moved to an office on the fourth floor of the Thalberg Building, a white art-deco construction that he later called "that cold storage plant."[34] His producer was a man called George Haight, who would later write for *The Addams Family*. Ray thought him a "fine fellow"[35] and settled down to work on the first draft of the screenplay for *The Lady in the Lake*. He quickly found that his influence at MGM was not what it had been at Paramount. There, he had been able to work in his office, sitting or lying on a sofa and dictating into a machine, but sofas were frowned on by MGM executives who thought that a writer lying on his back was not writing but sleeping. Ray, who was now used to getting his own way, brought out a rug from his car and lay on that instead. When his producer paid a visit to the office and found his star writer lying on a picnic blanket, he immediately called down to the story editor and, according to Ray, "shouted that I was a horizontal writer and for Chrissake send up a couch."[36] Ray must have seemed something of an oddity to his fellow writers, all of whom were couchless, and it is possible that they were jealous of the new arrival. He said that his colleagues formed "coteries" and in the use of that word we sense his exclusion that must have left him feeling lonely. At Paramount, he had been part of a group but, at MGM, he was an outsider once more, and his age and his shyness, which others often took as haughtiness, further excluded him. When he asked if he could work at home, he was told that the studio manager, Edgar J. Mannix, had ordered that no writer be allowed to do that. Ray claimed that he ignored the instruction and left the lot. In a letter, a couple of years later, he said that "a man as big as Mannix ought to be allowed the privilege of changing his mind,"[37] but this seems too neat to be true.

In the end, MGM did not work out. Ray struggled there throughout the late summer and early autumn before finally giving up. Part of the pleasure in writing *The Blue Dahlia* had been that what he wrote was shot pretty much as he intended it and, to a lesser extent, this was what he was supposed to be doing for MGM:

> I found out as I began to send it [*Lady in Lake* screenplay] that they were regarding it as a shooting script (subject to cutting) and didn't want any other writer on it.[38]

Unlike his last effort, though, Ray was treading here on familiar ground, rewriting his own work, and it bored him. In a letter to James Sandoe, he described the process of adapting his own book as "turning over dry bones."[39] He found that he had neither the energy nor the desire to work out the numerous problems of adapting a novel for the screen, and he started to get "more mechanical every day."[40] Despite being offered a much greater influence over the final movie, he could not bring himself to write in any other way, and so suggested that the studio bring in another writer with more energy to fix the problems. MGM said no. Ray knew that what he was producing was not going to make much of a movie:

> What will almost certainly happen, once they have milked me dry, will be that some executive above the producer will say, Look here, we got a lot of high-priced writers here in the studio. For Chrissake put one on this and let him give it what he's got. The writer will then take good care, or as good care as they let him, to make enough changes to put his mark on the thing and get a credit. I don't grudge him the credit, but I do rather resent the waste of my own fading energies.[41]

George Haight was not impressed by the draft and, according to Ray himself, called it "lousy."[42] MGM could not understand why Ray was writing scenes that had not appeared in the book when they wanted a straight adaptation and did not appreciate that he wanted a fresh challenge. He told Charles Morton that he "was already too fed up to do a good job on any script"[43] and, after thirteen weeks, left the project. This probably pleased MGM as much as it did Ray.

The script was completed by Steve Fisher, an in-house screenwriter who would eventually write for *Starsky & Hutch* in the 1970s. The movie starred and was directed by Robert Montgomery. Unusually, it was shot from Philip Marlowe's point of view in an attempt to capture the first person technique of the novel. Ray was not impressed:

> The camera eye technique of *Lady in the Lake* is old stuff in Hollywood. Every young writer or director has wanted to try it; it just so happened that Bob Montgomery was in a technical position where he could make them do it. . . . "Let's make the camera a character"; it's been said at every lunch table in Hollywood one time or another. I knew one fellow who wanted to make the camera the murderer; which wouldn't work without an awful lot of fraud. The camera is too honest.[44]

Ray refused credit on the movie in the end and, in a postcard to James Sandoe in November 1945, mentioned that there were some legal issues that prevented him from being involved with MGM again. It is not exactly clear what happened but, according to Frank Gruber in his memoir *Pulp Jungle*, Ray and Steve Fisher had to go to the Screen Writers' Guild to seek arbitration, which Fisher won.[45] This must have added to Ray's own frustration about the movie and with himself. It was yet another drain on his energy. Despite his misgivings, the movie made money and added to his reputation in Hollywood. The kind of pictures that would come to be known collectively as film noir, and Raymond Chandler, whose name was attached to some of the best of them, were hot properties.

After escaping MGM, it was time for some rest, so Ray took Cissy up to Big Bear Lake, their favorite retreat, where they could get some much-needed time and space. Ray was still struggling with the aftereffects of his MGM experience:

> I went up to Big Bear Lake to get over a case of complete exhaustion such as you will never know, you dynamo. I'd done a script for MGM in 13 weeks and hated every bit of it, especially as it was one of my own stories. I was completely sunk. The only thing I could read was the Perry Mason stories.[46]

Big Bear Lake had the sort of thin, dry air that helped Cissy's ailing lungs, and it was warm enough that they only lit the fire once.[47] There was very little to do there save for chopping wood and, eventually, Ray managed to pull himself out of the hole he had been sunk in. Not for the first time, it was at Big Bear Lake that his mind started to turn to writing fiction again. It may be that he picked up a previously abandoned book or that he had been writing quietly all year but, by November, having come back to Los Angeles, he was writing regularly and relishing it:

> I'm trying to finish a Marlowe story but I'm so in love with mere words and phrases after writing dialogue for jerks that I'll probably forget all about the plot.[48]

This novel would become *The Little Sister.*

While he was up in the mountains, the *Atlantic* published "Writers in Hollywood," an article that Charles Morton seems to have commissioned from Ray at the beginning of the year.[49] Quite when it was written is not clear. Ray's attitude to the movie business had changed steadily throughout 1945, and this article codified a lot of the grievances that he felt during his time at Paramount and MGM. He used the piece to express his disappointment:

> An art which is capable of making all but the very best plays look trivial and contrived, all but the very best novels verbose and imitative, should not so quickly become wearisome to those who attempt to practice with something else in mind than the cash drawer.

This heartfelt plea for cinema to be treated as art, not simply as industry, is hardly surprising coming from Ray, who had faith, despite such little experience, in its power. He had always tried to understand the form he was using, patiently rewriting his short stories to get them right for the pulps, for example, and film was no different. Sitting in an office with Billy Wilder, and then later in his own office at Paramount, he had tried to get to grips with the medium and started to believe that, contrary to the industry hype, "the basic art of motion pictures is the screenplay; it is fundamental, without it there is nothing."[50] This was, in part, Ray yearning for a simpler, imagined time when the writer was the supreme figure. Hollywood was not like this, and writing *The*

Blue Dahlia and *The Lady in the Lake*, in which he came closest to being in control of what appeared on screen, proved such a dream was impossible. He and his contemporaries were the last of a generation of writers brought into Hollywood because they had achieved in literature but, under the studio system, they were not allowed to be real writers. This was down to the way the power was spread through the system, with a producer at the top and the writer at the bottom. What use was it for a writer to have talent if that was then submitted to the will of the studio? As Ray put it, "the essence of this system [is] that it seeks to exploit a talent without permitting it the right to be a talent."[51]

There was a feeling among producers and those in the front office that writers who came from outside the industry needed to be reeducated in the ways of Hollywood, knocking out of them whatever had got them the job in the process. It did not help that screenwriting was not considered an art and that scripts tended to be created by committee. Characters, plots, and situations were hashed out at story conferences and, rather than making them richer and better, this tended to flatten the peaks, replacing anything new with tired clichés. Writers in studios were virtual serfs, whose only ability to influence their careers was in which scripts they accepted, but even this a writer "could only do within narrow limits"[52] because of the contract with the studio:

> There is no present guarantee that his best lines, best ideas, best scenes will not be changed or omitted on the set by the director or dropped on the floor during the later process of cutting—for the simple but essential reason that the best things in any picture, artistically speaking, are invariably the easiest to leave out mechanically speaking.[53]

In talking about his time in Hollywood, Ray chose to be careful about how far he went in attacking some targets. He was careful to say that his own experiences did not justify some of the harsher criticisms of producers, perhaps wanting to keep his option to return to Hollywood open. His conclusion was not as pessimistic as it might have been:

> There is hope that a decayed and make-shift system will pass, that somehow the flatulent moguls will learn that only writers can write screenplays and only proud and independent writers can write good screenplays.[54]

But, if this was to come to pass, writers must be stronger, tougher, prouder:

> And there is the intense and beautiful hope that the Hollywood writers themselves . . . will recognize that writing for the screen is no job for amateurs and half-writers whose problems are always solved by somebody else.[55]

This is a uniquely Chandleresque call for writers to rediscover their honor—to be writers, not showmen, and to take pride in their work. It is an unusual conclusion to a fairly commonplace analysis. Ray was not the first to level such criticism at Hollywood and his colleagues, but he was probably the first to imply that they needed to "man up" to be successful.

Much to his disappointment, Ray reported that the response to his article in Hollywood was a "frozen silence."[56] His agent reported that it had done him some damage with the Paramount producers, and Charles Brackett is said to have remarked: "Chandler's books are not good enough nor his pictures bad enough to justify that article."[57] Ray, who reported all this in a long letter to his editor at the *Atlantic*, responded: "If my books had been any worse, I should not have been invited to Hollywood, and if they had been any better, I should not have come."[58] He was also disappointed by the presentation of the article, objecting to the way that a copy editor had changed the order of his words. In his complaint, it is easy to see how easily he could push people away, demonstrating his attitude towards those he considered to be beneath his literary status:

> It is obvious that somebody, for no reason save that he thought he was improving the style, changed the order of the words. The length is the same, therefore that could not enter into it. I confess myself completely flabbergasted by the literary attitude this expresses. Because it is the attitude that gets me, the assumption on the part of some editorial hireling that he can write better than the man who sent the stuff in, that he knows more about phrase and cadence and the placing of words.[59]

Ray is hardly the first writer to attack a copy editor, but it is worth remembering that he was only an occasional contributor to the magazine and, though a friend of the editor, could not realistically expect the editorial staff to be as careful with his words as he was. This is not to say that he did not have a right to be upset but, rather, that this attitude shows the sort of self-importance he could sometimes exhibit. He did not always strike the right balance between pride and arrogance, probably made worse by approaching old age and continued drinking.

In 1944, Howard Hawks had started production on a film of *The Big Sleep*. It was to star Humphrey Bogart and Lauren Bacall, with whom he had just finished shooting another Hawks movie, *To Have and To Have Not*. Howard Hawks was not a studio man: he worked independently and then sold his ideas to studios, a forerunner of the more modern system of independent producers. He had bought the rights to *The Big Sleep* and took the idea to Warner Bros. who, in turn, saw the value of capitalizing on the trend for gritty, dark crime stories. William Faulkner was asked to write the screenplay alongside a young novelist, Leigh Brackett. Hawks thought Brackett was a man when he first sought her out, having been impressed by her first novel. Rather like Ray being invited to be part of *Double Indemnity*, she landed a plum role on her first screenwriting job.

Her cowriter, the Southern novelist William Faulkner, was a troubled man. Like Ray, he had a drinking problem which had landed him in some difficult situations. Writing for the screen was, for him, strictly a moneymaking exercise, and he took it far less seriously than his own very literary prose fiction.

Brackett and Faulkner started work in August 1944 and wrote through to November, though rumor has it that they turned out the first draft in only eight days.[60] It is probable that Hawks started shooting before he had a final screenplay. He did not like to stick to a rigid script, preferring some improvisation and on-set editing to get something he thought interesting onto celluloid:

> Hawks shoots from the cuff more or less, he tells me, merely using a rough script to try out his scenes and then rewriting them on the set.[61]

Later, Hawks asked Jules Furthman, a journalist turned screenwriter, to be his on-set writer, adding and editing scenes as necessary. In late 1944 and early 1945, Ray seems to have been close to the script in some ways: he had several conversations about it with Hawks and it may be that he would have worked on it, had his contract with Paramount not prohibited him from doing so. His insight could occasionally prove useful to Hawks, but not always. When Hawks asked Faulkner, Brackett, and Furthman who killed Owen Taylor and none of them could answer, they asked Ray if he knew. He did not. John Sutherland has written an essay on "Who Killed Owen Taylor" that suggests that Ray's response was meant to needle Faulkner and that he actually had a very good idea who killed the chauffeur. While his argument as to the killer is plausible, there is no evidence that Ray had any dislike of William Faulkner, or that he resented the writers on the picture.[62] Ray seems to have been very cooperative throughout.

Filming was complicated for various reasons. For one thing, Bacall and Bogart were in the throes of a passionate relationship, having met during the filming of *To Have and To Have Not*, while he was dealing with a drink problem and a troubled marriage. Then there was the war, which was drawing to a close and threatening to leave the studios with a backlog of war movies in production or ready for release. To get maximum value out of them before peace was declared, and for a time afterwards, they started to hold back the release of other types of movies. This meant that *The Big Sleep* was not released in America until 1946. An early version did appear in US cinemas in the Pacific (in army bases and other military outposts) and was seen by a test audience in the United States.

Ray was, in general, full of praise for the film and for Humphrey Bogart:

> When and if you see *The Big Sleep* (the first half of it anyhow), you will realize what can be done with this sort of story by a director with the gift of atmosphere and the requisite touch of hidden sadism. Bogart, of course, is also so much better than any other tough-guy actor that he makes bums of the Ladds and the Powells. As we say here, Bogart can be tough without a gun.[63]

But he goes on to say:

> The girl who played the nymphy sister [Martha Vickers] was so good she shattered Miss Bacall completely. So they cut the picture in such a way that all her best scenes were left out except one. The result made nonsense and Howard Hawks threatened to sue to restrain Warners

from releasing the picture. After long argument, as I hear it, he went back and did a lot of re-shooting.[64]

Now, it should be said that there is no other evidence that Hawks tried to sue Warners over the movie, but there are certainly some elements here that ring true. There was some reshooting and Ray was involved with this, talking through a new ending with Hawks. In it, Marlowe and Carmen are trapped in Geiger's house while Eddie Mars and his gang wait outside; Marlowe knows that if he sends out Carmen, who is, after all, a murderer, she will be shot, and that will give him time to escape; but he cannot face making the decision. After an internal struggle, a prayer, and the toss of a coin, he lets her go to her death.

> She started to leave. At the last moment, as she had her hand on the doorknob, Marlowe weakened and started for her [*sic*] to stop her. She laughed in his face and pulled a gun on him. Then she opened the door an inch or two and you could see she was going to shoot and was thoroughly delighted with the situation. At the moment a bust of machine gun fire walked across the panel of the door and tore her to pieces.[65]

This scene was not used, but a variation of it did appear in the movie with the purpose of killing off Eddie Mars. Adding this scene as described above would have given the movie a different complexion. In Hawks's hands, it is a love story between Vivian and Marlowe, with some comic and some hard-boiled elements. Ray's ending would have aligned it more closely with the novel, where Vivian and Marlowe were verbal sparring partners rather than lovers, and this would have lost some of the enigma and romance of the final version.

The movie of *The Big Sleep*, like the novel, has endured and is a classic of the genre. In 1946, its success added yet more value to Raymond Chandler's name.

The years 1943 to 1945 were important ones for Ray. During this period, he became part of Hollywood and, for the first time in his life, could justifiably call himself rich. None of this, though, made him happy. He was drinking heavily, he had had at least one affair, and his marriage was less settled than it had been during the golden period of the 1930s. He also began to realize that he would never escape crime writing and, though this depressed him, it also helped him. Towards the end of 1945, without the nagging doubt that he ought to be writing something more "worthwhile," he felt able for the first time in years to concentrate on the task at hand. He was about to enter his richest years as a novelist.

CHAPTER TWELVE

"THE LIMITATIONS OF A POPULAR ART"

In 1946, Raymond Chandler had a hangover. He had spent the last year suffering at the hands of Hollywood. Though his time there had taught him a lot, what he had learned above all was to hate it.

The process of writing *The Blue Dahlia* and then *The Lady in the Lake* had left him drained, both physically and emotionally. After giving up *The Lady in the Lake*, he should have returned to his employers at Paramount under the terms of a contract that tied him to two more screenplays, but he could be cantankerous and stubborn. Faced with what he thought would be another unhappy session on the lot, he took a stand and refused to come to work. Ray hoped they would either quietly sack him or offer to renegotiate. John Houseman, who had produced *The Blue Dahlia* and was an advocate of the talented but difficult writer, left Paramount at about this time. Without him lobbying on Ray's behalf, the studio was free to act swiftly, suspending him and taking away his office and secretary. This is pretty much what he wanted, of course, so it was no hardship. Ray made it clear that he wanted his contract canceled, but the studio refused. It is easy to see why they were so reluctant to let him go. They had invested time and money in him and had few films to show for it. Yes, the movies he had written were well regarded in the industry, but this was not necessarily reflected in the box-office takings: the studio expected a far greater return on their investment.

Ray, for his part, did not want to turn his back on movies completely:

What I want is something quite different: a freedom from datelines and unnatural pressures, and a right to find and work with those few people in Hollywood whose purpose is to make the best pictures possible within the limitations of a popular art, not merely to repeat the old and vulgar formulae.[1]

In other words, he wanted to be able to write screenplays with the same freedom as he wrote novels. This, by and large, is how modern Hollywood works—freelance teams coming together to work on a single project—but, in 1946, the studio contract system was still going strong. Writers were members of the workforce, just like carpenters, electricians, and cameramen, and they were expected to behave as such, turning up for work at ten in the morning and putting in a full day's labor.

Ray had some serious concerns about what might happen if he stayed too long at Paramount. In his essay "Writers in Hollywood," he had described how the studio system had a habit of destroying talent rather than nurturing it. In January, he wrote this in a letter to Hamish Hamilton:

I have only a limited number of useful years left and I do not want to use them up destroying what talent I have.[2]

At fifty-eight, it might be said that Ray was overstating his case, but perhaps he was all too aware that his alcoholism might cut short his life. He remained an ambitious man who still hoped to achieve something in literature, and he still had not quite abandoned the plan first written down in 1939.

Having made his stand, he turned to his Hollywood agent, H. N. Swanson, to sort out the situation. Swannie, though, proved less than helpful, largely because he was stymied by the sudden and unilateral action by his client. Disappointed by this lack of support, Ray wrote that "the Hollywood agent, however nice a fellow, is strictly a summer soldier"[3] and, instead, asked his literary agent, Sydney Sanders, to get involved. Sanders got tough, writing to Richard Mealand, head of the story department. Mealand was shocked by the letter and was afraid to pass it on to the manager of production at the studio, and so the problem dragged on. Frustratingly, Paramount then started to get tough themselves, bringing up the sticky issue of Ray having written for himself during his absence, something technically prohibited by the contract. In practical terms, this did not stop him working on *The Little Sister*, but it did mean abandoning any film projects that might have been percolating in his mind. Ray, who was not unfamiliar with contracts, considered the clause in question a difficult one to enforce, but he also knew that should the studio choose to force the issue, it would result in a long and expensive court case.

Ray's spat with Paramount was no secret, and it must have been widely known that while it was being contested, he would not be available for any film work. Even so, the offers kept coming. One producer, an independent, got in touch with Ray asking him to work on a screenplay for "one of the most advertised projects of the year."[4] Ray felt insulted:

Perhaps, in spite of my faults, I still have a sense of honor. I may quarrel, but at least I put the point at issue down on the table in front of me. I am perfectly willing to let them examine my sleeves for hidden cards. But I don't think they really want to. They would be horrified to find them empty. They do not like to deal with honest men.[5]

For Ray, this was one of the central problems with Hollywood: it was without honor, and trust was an alien concept. Ray thought his word good enough and so found contracts stifling and unnecessary, once writing that he was "unable to function as a freeman when tied up in any way."[6] But Paramount was too large a business to rely on a man's word and needed paperwork to back it up.

The argument with Paramount ran on throughout the first six months of 1946. The studio made offer after offer to appease him, and was even willing to let him direct his own pictures if he wanted, but even the considerable power being a director would bring would not allow him to work and write unmolested by producers. By March, he was considering legal action, but concluded that it was too expensive. By April, Ray, his lawyer, and his agent were looking for compromise:

[We] have won a remarkable victory in fact, which can still by the studio's legal department be made to look like a practical victory for the company. And that of course is what they must have for face-saving purposes.[7]

This deal, the details of which are unknown, saw him back on the lot and writing. The project he wanted to work on was the adaptation of *The Innocent Mrs. Duff* by Elizabeth Sanxay Holding, one of the few mystery novelists Ray liked to reread—a rare and serious compliment.[8] At first, translating the story of a high-functioning alcoholic into a screenplay came easily but, perhaps inevitably, it ground to a halt. Despite having chosen his own project, Ray was still stuck with a producer he did not get along with and their relationship quickly soured. The producer would use the names of the studio actors in place of those of the characters, which Ray found especially infuriating. When his output slowed to a trickle, the management brought in another writer to help speed up the process, which, of course, upset Ray even more. The project dragged on through the summer and he was in no mood to compromise. Instead, he continued to work slowly until his contract ran out. Though his plodding output may have been a deliberate attempt to let time take care of the Paramount agreement, he was adamant that the failure of the film should be laid at the feet of the producer:

> If Paramount had had the sense to let me write my own idea of a rough screenplay on Mrs. Duff, without the interference of a producer's ideas, ambition, and eagerness to dominate a project to his own advantage, they would have got something in a comparatively short time, which would have shown them at a glance where the picture was . . . they simply cannot realize that what they want from me is what I write in my own way; they think they can get that and at the same time control almost every move I make and every idea I have. It just can't be done.[9]

During the first part of the year, while in dispute with Paramount, Ray was making slow progress with a new novel. It was to be another Marlowe story and would eventually be called *The Little Sister*. In January 1946, however, it was refusing to settle into any shape. Ray was feeling bitter about writing about Philip Marlowe again after his Hollywood break, and his reliance on that character was starting to feel tedious, but he could not abandon him:

I am in a bit of a quandary about it [the novel]. The practical need to keep that character alive is important for many reasons, among them the threat of a radio program which must eventually mature.[10]

Practical need is not the stuff of which great novels are made. Ray worried that he was starting to lose his passion for crime fiction, and he found that the elements that had given his earlier stories their power were largely absent from this latest manuscript:

I have a suspicion that the quality that finally put these stories over was a sort of controlled half-poetical emotion. That for the story of blood and mystery I seem to have lost.[11]

Despite accepting that his fortunes were linked to Marlowe's, Ray's mind kept turning over ideas that would struggle to find expression in crime fiction. One appears in a 1946 letter to Alfred Knopf:

I have learned a lot from Hollywood. Please do not think I completely despise it, because I don't. . . . But the overall picture, as the boys say, is of a degraded community whose idealism even is largely fake. The pretentiousness, the bogus enthusiasm, the constant drinking and drabbing, the incessant squabbling over money, the all-pervasive agent, the strutting of the big shot (and their usually utter incompetence to achieve anything they start out to do), the constant fear of losing all this fairy gold and being the nothing they have really never ceased to be, the snide tricks, the whole damn mess is out of this world. It is a great subject for a novel—probably the greatest still untouched.[12]

This seems to be the first mention of a new idea beginning to crystallize in Ray's mind. The movie industry would be central to *The Little Sister* and it may be that, at this moment, this central pillar of the story was beginning to take shape. In another letter, he discussed the management of Paramount:

The studio is now under the control of a man whose attitude to pictures-making is that if you own 1600 theatres, all you have to do is grind out the product as quickly and economically as possible.[13]

The man referred to in the letter would contribute later to the character of Jules Oppenheimer, a studio boss in *The Little Sister*:

Fifteen hundred theatres is all you need. A damn sight easier than raising pure-bred boxers. The motion picture business is the only business in the world in which you can make all the mistakes there are and still make money.

In a throwaway comment, he described "his current effort . . . [as a] piece of rather gaudy sarcasm masquerading as a murder mystery,"[14] which pretty much sums up the tone of parts of *The Little Sister*, with its bitterness about the Hollywood experience. Though he knew he had to work with Philip Marlowe, it is clear that he was beginning to consider bringing something deeper and richer to the book, and this was his first attempt to realize his ambition to write something beyond the mystery novel.

Between January and March, he managed to get "pretty well into a Marlowe story."[15] This early progress encouraged him and he was soon writing to Hamish Hamilton to tell him that it would be finished by the summer. But his rhythm was broken when he and Cissy were both struck down by a bout of flu. Cissy, with her weak lungs, suffered quite severely this time, and Ray was worried. Sick himself, worrying about Cissy, and with ongoing troubles with Paramount, work on the novel slowed over the summer and, eventually, *The Little Sister* went into hibernation. By the end of the summer, it had shape, but there was nothing solid to show anyone. As he had done before, Ray may have destroyed an early draft, or perhaps it simply never got past the planning stage.

As he started to wind down at Paramount, his agent wondered about what he could do next and, keen to keep him working, arranged a meeting with Samuel Goldwyn. Goldwyn was not tied to one of the big studios in Hollywood and, like David O. Selznick, operated as an independent producer with his company, the Samuel Goldwyn Studio, having been forced out of the Goldwyn Picture Company shortly before it merged with others to form MGM. Perhaps H. N. Swanson thought that Goldwyn's independence would suit Ray's way of working. That Samuel Goldwyn was keen to meet him shows just how high he had risen in Hollywood, despite a reputation for difficult behavior and alcoholism. Ray was flattered to hear about the meeting but he was not convinced that it would suit him and, even before meeting the great man, was set against the idea:

> I imagine everyone ought to meet Samuel Goldwyn this side of paradise. I've heard he feels so good when he stops. But since the whole thing is predicated on my working for him, and I ain't gonna, is it worth while?[16]

Ray was determined not to work in the movies and for now, at least, was done with Hollywood. There is a hint in a postscript to a letter to Swanson that this was only temporary, though: he gave emergency contact details and added that his idea of an emergency would be "a lot of money for nothing."[17] Tongue-in-cheek as this was, money mattered to Ray, and a big fee or interesting project might just have pulled him out of retirement.

For now, though, Ray wanted out of Los Angeles entirely. He and Cissy took what seemed to be a short holiday to San Diego in August but, while there, decided to settle for a few weeks. By September, they had moved back to La Jolla. Back in 1939, Ray had dismissed La Jolla as "[too] dear, too damp, too elderly, a nice place, as a visitor remarked this afternoon, for old people and their parents."[18] Seven years later, it had not changed, but Ray and Cissy had, and now it seemed to suit them. For the first time in their marriage, at the ages of fifty-eight and seventy-six respectively, they became homeowners, buying a sprawling one-story house with an ocean view, at 6005 Camino De La Costa.

The house was very Californian. It had been built that year and had white stucco walls, a cool shaded courtyard where pots of geraniums flowered, and a small garden, where purple bougainvillea crept up the walls and Taki stalked. There was a large, bright living room with a picture window that looked out over the Pacific towards Loma Point. It was in this room that they put Cissy's piano, and where she would play in the evenings while Ray sat and listened, smoking his pipe. This was Cissy's space more than Ray's; his was the book-lined study on the other side of the house. His office looked out over the garden, which suited Ray, who objected to sea views out of principle. It was here that he spent most of his time, writing through the mornings, until joining Cissy for lunch in the early afternoon. After lunch, he would run errands in town and, after dinner, once Cissy had retired, he would return to his study to read or to write letters, tapping the ashes from his pipe into trays perched on teetering piles of books.

Ray's new study should have been the perfect place to complete his novel but, now the move was over, the energy that had been apparent earlier in the year had dissipated. In September, he wrote to Erle Stanley Gardner:

> Have started trying to write a detective story. I seem to have lost something or perhaps I just used it up.[19]

It is not clear why Ray wrote of starting a new story when he had been writing *The Little Sister* for nearly a year. Perhaps this indicated that he was commencing a new draft, or perhaps he did not want to admit to a writer as prolific as Gardner that it was taking so long to write a new novel. Either way, he was, in his own words, "a tired character, a battered pulp writer, an out of work hack."[20] He was struggling to balance the need to write a new Marlowe story with his own drive for something fresh and new. If he was to keep his name and his fiction in the public eye, he had to push himself to write, but this commercial pressure was sucking the pleasure out of the work:

> The story I am working on seems to me to lack some of the nobler qualities. In addition to which I find it dull. I wonder could I be washed up for good.[21]

In late 1946 and early 1947, after he acquired a Dictaphone into which he would speak late into the night, for a newly hired private secretary to transcribe in the morning, Ray's letters took on a more reflective tone. His loneliness also contributed to the new openness in his correspondence. Ray had a fairly active social life at Paramount and enjoyed the company of other writers, but, though he had friends in La Jolla, it seems that the life he led there was quieter and more cloistered. In this mood, his letters began more often to discuss the features of his writing that, in the past, he had reserved for people he knew better. It is in such letters that some of the causes for his struggle with *The Little Sister* are made clear. *The High Window* had been an experiment in writing new plot without recourse to earlier stories but Ray was not happy with the result and so, for the *The Lady in the Lake*, had fallen back upon old material to form the backbone of the plot. With the early draft of *The Little Sister*, he once again found himself creating new scenes, new plots, and new characters—struggling through unfamiliar and unsteady territory. In a letter to Mrs. Robert Hogan, who had written to Ray with a questionnaire about his writing, he discussed some of his oddities:

> One of my peculiarities and difficulties as a writer is that I won't discard anything. I have heard this is unprofessional and that it is a weakness of the amateur not to be able to tell when his stuff is not coming off. I can tell that all right, as to the matter in hand, but I can't overlook the fact that I had a reason, a feeling, for starting to write it, and I'll be damned if I won't like it. I have lost months of time because of this stubbornness. . . . I always regard the first draft as raw material. What seems to be alive in it is what belongs in the story. Even if the neatness has to be lost. I will still keep whatever has that effect of getting up on its own feet and marching. A good story cannot be devised; it has to be distilled.[22]

Ray was able to write his earliest novels fluidly because some of this distillation process had already taken place in writing the original stories. In the case of *The Little Sister*, however, he tied himself in knots writing new characters and plot, unable to cut anything he had written, leaving both elements muddled. This is what he must have been hinting at when he suggested that this book lacked the "nobler elements" of his previous work.

In the early part of the year, in the midst of wrestling with these problems, he received some other unwelcome news. A novelist called James Hadley Chase had published *Blonde's Requiem*, a work which seemed to be built around large chunks of prose borrowed from Ray and other writers. Chase, whose real name was René Raymond, was an Englishman and former encyclopedia salesman, who had turned his hand to crime writing around the same time as Ray was completing *The Big Sleep*, having read some of the *Black Mask* school and James M. Cain. He is now largely forgotten, but his debut, *No Orchids For Miss Blandish*, was a sensation when first released because of its explicit depictions of sex and violence which, perhaps unsurprisingly, made it a bestseller. After his speedy rise to prominence, Chase ran low on ideas

during the war and turned to his American contemporaries for "inspiration."
He quietly lifted passages from Ray, Hammett, and others, and his publisher
failed to notice this blatant plagiarism. Understandably, Ray was disappointed
when he learned what Chase was doing, but he did not react angrily. Instead,
he wrote to his publishers in America and in Britain and asked what action
they intended to take. Knopf passed the issue on to a lawyer who reported
back, somewhat unhelpfully, that the texts were not similar enough to justify
prosecuting Chase. In Britain, Hamish Hamilton was much more vigorous,
perhaps recognizing his author's displeasure more clearly than Knopf, and
forced Chase to publish a letter in the *Bookseller*, the trade journal of British
publishing, apologizing for the plagiarism.

The Chase incident was a small one, but it indicates the way Ray's
relationships with his publishers were changing. He had become increasingly
close to his British publisher, even though the two had never met, even calling him Jamie in their letters in a nod to their intimacy. Hamilton, for his
part, seemed to enjoy his correspondence with Ray. To Ray, though, the letters were not only enjoyable, but offered a connection outside of La Jolla and,
more specifically, a link to his beloved Britain. By contrast, he was drifting
further and further apart from Alfred and Blanche Knopf. The frequency of
letters between them slowed down, though this was in part because Ray was
not close to delivering his new book yet, and had little else to tell them. Still,
there was something more behind this distance. In May 1947, Ray wrote to
Erle Stanley Gardner:

> If the publisher really was the author's or agent's friend and repre-
> sented him as he should, it would be fine, but I don't think in general
> that the publisher is. My publisher, for instance, made very little real
> effort to sell my books, spent very little money publicizing them, had
> no great success selling them in their original library editions, and it
> was quite a long time before the sale of any of them reached ten thou-
> sand copies. Then when they suddenly began to sell in large numbers
> in reprints . . . he collected from this source as his share, through no
> effort of his own, about twice as much as he ever paid me from the
> books in which he invested his capital and effort.[23]

Here, Ray is talking directly about Knopf and his subsequent experience with the cheap paperback editions of his novels. It is also clear that his confidence had grown considerably since 1938. He had always been sure that his Marlowe novels would sell, and knew that his writing was good, but it was only after working in Hollywood that he began to act imperiously with people to whom he had once been close. The atmosphere of Hollywood had made him feel important, and he had become increasingly able to get his own way; La Jolla amplified what Hollywood had started.

Being physically removed from colleagues and friends meant that Ray relied on letters more and more. In his darkened room, with only Taki for company, his correspondents took the place of more immediate friends. La Jolla was home to a few writers, but Ray does not seem to have mixed with many of them, though he would later befriend Neil Morgan, a young journalist. The people he had known in the late 1930s had moved on and those who had stayed were rich now, to which Ray seems to have objected, despite his own newfound wealth. He also knew that he was not the easiest person to get on with, as he explained in a letter to Charles Morton:

> I am standoffish with strangers, a form of shyness which whiskey cured when I was still able to take it in the requisite quantities. I am terribly blunt, having been raised in that English tradition which permits a gentleman to be almost infinitely rude if he keeps his voice down.[24]

In La Jolla, without regular contact with other people, he drew further into himself, exaggerating his bluntness and his shyness yet further, and he could be startlingly direct in correspondence ("I think you've done wrong, Joe, but the hell with it, nobody's immune"[25]). From 1947 onwards, however, a less formal tone also became more common. Hamish Hamilton was now Jamie, while James Sandoe was addressed as Jim, and Charles Morton was quizzed about his marital status. In one letter to Erle Gardner, Ray unburdened himself about his recent troubles:

> As to me, I am not busy and I am not successful in any important way. I don't get written what I want to write and I get balled up in

what I do write. . . . My wife has been under the weather with flu for ten days.[26]

There was always a pretext for his letters, though—usually business—and it took time for Ray to become familiar with his correspondents. He had been corresponding with Gardner for years but it is only in the mid-1940s that his letters became personal, those of a friend to a friend. And, unlike face-to-face meetings, letters—even intimate, friendly ones—allowed him to maintain a certain distance.

Ray had left Los Angeles but was not done with Hollywood just yet. At the beginning of 1947, he took a new screenplay idea to his agent, H. N. Swanson. It was one of the ideas that had been bubbling away at the back of his mind while he struggled to finish *The Little Sister* and, eager to escape from a book which had been weighing on him for over a year, he decided to shift focus. Like most writers, Ray would sometimes find himself taken with an idea that he could not shake off:

> Once in a while a writer gets what might be called a compulsive idea and I suppose I have had them. . . . I find that I throw them off without any difficulty, or else they start to grow and grow and become confused in ramifications.[27]

Swanson took Ray's idea for a script to Joe Sistrom, the producer of *Double Indemnity*, at Universal International Pictures. The deal Swanson negotiated was extraordinary, as Ray explained to James Sandoe:

> My next job . . . [is] one of the most unusual deals ever made in Hollywood, or so I am told. They pay me a large sum of money and a percentage of the picture [profit] to write them a screenplay, and they only get the picture rights. The unusual feature, which may not only seem striking to you but I can assure you is, is that they do *not* employ me, but merely agree to buy the motion picture rights to something I write in my own way and without any supervision.[28]

Ray was paid the sum of $10,000 for the rights to a story idea[29] and then left alone to write it, working from La Jolla without studio interference. On top of all this, he was paid $4,000 a week, making him one of the highest-paid screenwriters in Hollywood. It is astonishing that a man who had failed to complete his last two screenplays could command such a deal. Two Oscar nominations helped, but there was also the feeling that, if a studio could give him enough space, Ray would eventually produce a great screenplay. The contract was an experiment—for Ray and for Universal International—and everyone involved hoped that it would lead to a good movie. Ray had a lot invested in the agreement: if he could not make this work, he might never work in Hollywood again.

He settled down to write *Playback* in April or May 1947 but, by June, he was writing to Blanche Knopf to complain:

> I am struggling bitterly with a motion picture script for Universal-International, and am not enjoying it at all.[30]

The problem was the plot and, as usual, Ray found himself bogged down with scenes that did not fit together. The original delivery date was August 1, but it was soon clear that this was impossible and he wrote to his agent: "The story is not set and I don't yet even know how to tell it."[31] An extension was agreed and Joe Sistrom dispatched to La Jolla to help Ray thrash out some ideas. Their work was positive enough, and Ray wrote that Sistrom had helped get the story "remolded . . . slightly nearer to the heart's desire"[32] but, despite this, Swanson was worried and advised his client to focus on delivering the material:

> I feel very strongly that for financial reasons, if for no other, you should complete the Universal deal with every ounce of energy in you and then forget it, and be able to move on to do some other writing. I think it has now grown into a Frankenstein. It seems to me the studio wanted a barn painted and you are heroically trying to give them their money's worth but you are using an artist's camel's-hair brush. To hell with the art! . . . I don't want to kid you around this, Ray. I think you should look on this as you did when you were writing a story for *Black Mask*. You were doing it to pay the grocery bill. Let's get this baby delivered quickly and put the money in the bank and live on it as far ahead as it will carry you.[33]

This was, by now, a familiar story—Ray's enthusiasm for a project rapidly dimming in the cold light of the days spent having to write it. Swanson had negotiated a clever deal but it did not go far enough because it still contained a deadline. Unlike with his novels, for which Ray did not like to take an advance until he had finished the manuscript, he could not put the screenplay to one side while he refreshed himself. He was stuck, and the pressure, the endless chasing, and the studio interference, caused his interest to wane. He tried to take Swanson's advice but pointed out:

> As to your idea this job is "painting a barn" and that I am trying to do it with a camel's-hair brush, the fact is I am trying very hard <u>not</u> to do it with a camel's-hair brush. However, I would point out to you that when I was writing for the pulps, I wrote with a camel's-hair brush, and if you don't think it paid off in the long run, look around for some of the boys who painted barns.[34]

This was the problem with the contract and the Hollywood system. Ray's process of writing was slow and required long periods of distillation, patience and dedication. He could never write for the sake of it. When, in October, he finished the first draft, he was suddenly very aware of another limitation of the deal he had signed: yes, he had freedom to write when he wanted to but, in exchange for this latitude, he had agreed to a no-release clause. At Paramount, he had been able to work slowly until his contract ran out but, this time, that was not possible.

In a letter to Hamish Hamilton, he complained about having to write the next draft and explained how painful he expected this to be:

> I finished the first draft of my screenplay and the way I went on anyone would think I was building a pyramid. I loathed it with a great loathing. Now I have to "polish" it, as they say. Which means leave out half and make what is left hammier. This is a very delicate art, and about as fascinating as scraping teeth.[35]

There were further delays as he redrafted, and another extension was agreed on, setting the delivery date back from October to the beginning of 1948.

At this time, it became increasingly clear at the studio that, even when the script was delivered, the movie was going to be a challenge to film for various reasons. It is true that net profits in 1946 were $120 billion, up from $66 billion in 1945,[36] but these figures masked a decline in the number of cinemagoers and an end to Hollywood's boom years. Soldiers who had returned from service in 1945 were busy, in 1946, with young families, or taking night classes—not taking dates to the movies. By 1947, when Ray was working on *Playback*, the impact of these changes was starting to be felt, and Universal International seems to have suffered in particular. At $4,000 a week, Ray's fee was huge, and by October, Universal had already paid out more than $120,000. In addition, the plot, and especially the dramatic closing sequence Ray envisaged, required the movie to be shot on location in a border town. Ray had settled on Vancouver, Canada, a city he knew fairly well, probably because he spent time there either before or after his World War I military service. This would be expensive. There were no existing studios they could use and the weather, unlike in balmy Southern California, was far from predictable. Universal may have gotten themselves a top-notch writer with twin Oscar nominations, but this did not equal a guaranteed profit. Finally, after weighing up the costs and likely proceeds, Universal decided that the margin was too slim: they pulled the plug on the film, and that was that.

Ray was frustrated and disappointed, and it was little comfort that, after all that work and pressure, he could reuse the plot and characters as he saw fit. It is a shame that *Playback* did not see its way onto celluloid. From the beginning, it was set to be an interesting and challenging movie, giving him the opportunity to experiment. Like the best of the novels he had written before 1947, it borrowed from the plot of an earlier story, in this case "I'll Be Waiting" from 1939. In the original story, a lonely woman retires to a tower suite in a hotel to wait for a killer and, in the first part of Ray's early treatment of *Playback*, there are clear echoes of this:

> The crucial week in the life of a girl who decided to spend it in a tower suite in a hotel, under an assumed name, her identity thoroughly concealed with great care, to accept what comes, and at the end of the week to jump to her death.

In the next paragraph, though, it becomes clear that Ray had expanded on his earlier vision:

> During this week the frustrations and tragedies of her life are repeated in capsule form, so that it almost appears that she brought her destiny with her, and that wherever she went the same sort of thing would happen to her.[37]

This new plot was much more ambitious. Ray added characters: Brandon, a wealthy socialite, and a homicide detective called Killaine, an officer of Irish descent who, like Ray, had served in the Canadian Highlanders. The theme of the story—is it possible to escape your own past?—was amplified with these additions.

The film opens on a train, with a meeting between Betty Mayfield, the heroine, and Mitchell, a heel. Mitchell is a user of women and when, after a party in Brandon's hotel room, he is found dead on Betty Mayfield's balcony, Killaine is called in to clear up the murder. Everyone except Killaine suspects Betty of the murder, but he detects some latent courage in her, despite her refusal to talk about her past. The detective is the closest character to Marlowe in the screenplay—the noble detective, describing himself at one point as "Kid Galahad. The King of the White Plume"—but he is more fallible than Marlowe, admitting, albeit obliquely, to having fallen in love with Betty when he is ordered to pull her in:

BETTY:	You can't be in love with me. You hardly know me. I'm not in love with you.
KILLAINE:	I know that.
BETTY:	But even if you *were* in love with me.
KILLAINE *(almost rudely)*:	There's an empty taxi across the street. If you're so anxious, take it. He'll know the way to the police headquarters.
BETTY:	You do things the hard way, don't you?[38]

In some ways this expression of love makes Killaine more sympathetic than Marlowe in his first appearances, and it is possibly the first conscious step away from him that Ray could take, most of his screen work before that time being restricted by source material or, in the case of *The Blue Dahlia*, the actors.

At the same time as experimenting, Ray was also keen that *Playback* be a thriller in the conventional sense—that it should excite audiences. Here again we see the familiar tussle in his mind between art and commercialism, and his determination to find a balance was evident. He had always believed that he could create an effect in the mind of his readers and now he wanted to see whether he could develop an atmosphere on screen. He was clearly thinking about ways to tell the story in October, as he came to the end of the first draft, when, in a letter to James Sandoe, he started to explain the importance of cutting:

> Hitchcock, the only time I met him,[39] gave me a lecture on . . . waste. His point . . . was that Hollywood (and England too) was full of directors who had not learned to forget about the Biograph. They still thought that because a motion picture moved it interested people.[40]

He goes on to describe a scene, a meeting of two "old flames who had not seen each other for years," and the way that an old-fashioned director would shoot it. This is his conclusion on that manner of filmmaking:

> Every bit of this stuff is dead film, because every point, if there is a point, can be made inside the scene itself. The rest is just camera in love with mere movement. Cliché, flat, stale and today meaningless.[41]

Staleness and cliché are exactly what Ray was trying to avoid in the conclusion to *Playback*, which sees Brandon kidnap Betty and try to kill her on board his boat as he flees from the Canadian police. Up to this point, the murderer is well disguised with a trail of false clues to distract the audience. These stage directions describe the actions of Margo, an older woman Mitchell has been bleeding financially, in the lead-up to his murder:

> She hangs up, stands a moment, picks her wrap out of the chair, puts it on, crosses to the desk for her handbag. She opens the bag, pauses, then in slow motion, pulls open the drawer of the desk. CAMERA

IN A CLOSE SHOT, studies her face as she looks down into the drawer of the desk, which we do not see. But we already know there is a gun there. Her body is quite motionless, her expression frozen. When she moves we do not see whether she takes the gun out of the drawer or not. We hear the snap of her bag shutting. Then she turns away, starts across the room to leave.[42]

Here is a clear example of what Ray had understood from Hitchcock: he wanted the audience to realize that the gun was in the drawer because they had seen it there earlier, rather than having its presence pointed out by the camera. The same logic applies in the closing scenes:

REVERSE SHOT BEHIND BRANDON

A fog bank about a mile ahead.

> BRANDON
> (as if to himself)
> Always some fog out here.

He looks up in the direction of the PLANE NOISE which is increasing.

> BRANDON
> There better be.

INT. HUDSON BOMBER—COCKPIT—NIGHT

SHOT THROUGH THE PLEXIGLAS HEAD AND SHOULDERS OF THE PILOT AND Co-PILOT.

The cruiser down on the water is getting rapidly larger, but still cannot be seen who is in the cockpit, or even how many persons. The co-pilot puts a pair of binoculars to his eyes.

EXT. CABIN CRUISER VALKYRIE—COCKPIT—NIGHT

Brandon with one hand on the wheel, the other holding the gun. He is staring up towards the plane. Betty is not in the cockpit. Brandon turns towards where she was, reacts sharply, seeing she has disappeared. An expression of frustration and despair shows on his face for a moment. The NOISE OF THE PLANE in the power dive becomes furiously LOUD. Brandon's head goes around again.

REVERSE ANGLE—THE PLANE DIVING DIRECTLY ON THE VALKYRIE

Brandon sees it. It dives down almost into the CAMERA.

MED. LONG SHOT—FROM WATER LEVEL

The Valkyrie and the plane. At the last moment, the plane pulls out of the dive, only thirty or forty feet above the Valkyrie, and goes into a climbing bank.

MED. LONG SHOT—VALKYRIE—SHOOTING FROM BEHIND

The fog bank is dead ahead. The coast Guard plane is climbing off to the left. The Valkyrie reaches the fog bank, plunges into it, and becomes invisible.[43]

Here, rather than use too much camera work or unrealistic dialogue, Ray employs visual switches between the interior of the plane and the interior of Brandon's boat, the *Valkyrie*, along with the noise of the engine, to build up the threat. This is a dangerous situation and Ray, better known for his dialogue, here uses purely visual, cinematic tools to develop it. It is very well done and, had the movie ever been made, would have been powerful on screen. It shows how confident Ray had become in the medium. As with his detective fiction, he understood the craft of screenwriting well enough to break free from its conventions to great effect. It is not unfair to say that this screenplay represents the high point of his Hollywood career and, though flawed, it is certainly his best original script, far exceeding the quality of *The Blue Dahlia*. Nonetheless, he did not believe in it enough to fight for it once he had learned of Universal International's decision to pull out. He put it away and turned, once again, to his unfinished Marlowe novel.

Though, early in 1948, Ray admitted in a letter to a fan that he still wanted to "write a good motion picture,"[44] having had such difficult experiences with Paramount, MGM, and Universal International, he could no longer see how this would be possible:

I simply don't want to do any more work for Hollywood. There is nothing in it but grief and exhaustion and discontent. In no real sense is it writing at all. It carries none of the satisfactions of writing. None of the sense of power over your medium. None of the freedom, even to fail.[45]

This decision threw up some new challenges for Ray. La Jolla was an expensive town, full of "tired old men and tired old money,"[46] and the Chandlers had grown used to keeping a maid, a secretary, and a cook. His film income adequately covered these expenses but, without it, he started to worry about whether they could afford to live so lavishly. "My expenses," he wrote to Charles Morton, "are terrible and I am not even sure I can make a living writing fiction."[47] Screenwriting may have been hell, but it paid the bills, and more. Without it, Ray was going to have to make some serious changes and, most importantly, get the book finished and on sale, albeit without the pressure of an externally imposed deadline.

At home, when writing fiction, he could keep to his own rhythm. Some days he would write and sometimes he would not but, no matter what, he would never force himself. When an author claimed to be able to sit down and write each morning, no matter how he felt or what he thought, Ray said he took care to avoid their books. He saw the act of writing as an act of physical endurance. In a letter to Alex Barris, a Canadian journalist, Ray harks back to his early inspiration, Ernest Hemingway:

> All writing that has any life in it is done with the solar plexus. It is hard work in the sense that it may leave you tired, even exhausted.[48]

Numerous studio executives had seen just how true this was in Ray's case.

Throughout 1948, he ploughed on with *The Little Sister*, but writing only when he felt he had something to say. To push himself, he set a routine, sitting in his study each morning, the time of day when he felt he wrote best. The deal he struck with himself was that, if he was not writing, he could do nothing else. The boredom, he hoped, would prompt the words to flow. It worked and he began to move forward with the stalled novel.

Ray was aware that Philip Marlowe was a valuable character but so far had received little in the way of return for other people's adaptations. Howard Hawks's version of *The Big Sleep* had paid well enough but some other adaptations had not. Ray had placed the blame for failing to generate secondary income from Marlowe on the shoulders of his literary agent, Sydney Sanders. This, along with a feeling on his part of having outgrown Sanders, led to their parting ways at some point in 1946, with Swanson stepping into the breach.[49] Ray found this stopgap arrangement unsatisfactory and so approached the firm of Brandt & Brandt in New York City. Despite Ray's success and his faith in his own ability, his first letter to Carl Brandt, the firm's founder, betrays some of the shy nervousness he felt when approaching new people:

> Come Michaelmas, or thereabouts, I shall be in need of a literary agent. The purpose of this is to inquire whether your office would be interested.[50]

But Ray knew that he had something to offer Brandt. *The Little Sister* would be his fifth novel and potentially the most valuable so far. *The Big Sleep, Farewell, My Lovely,* and *The Lady in the Lake* had all been turned into movies of varying success, and editions of his books had sold more than two million copies.[51] Still, Ray was cautious about what he told Brandt of his current work in progress, explaining that he had a draft underway but that "something has gone wrong with the story. An old trouble with me,"[52] and that he had plans for another novel "which has a murder in it but is not a mystery."[53] Ray wanted to be clear about the sort of writer he was:

> You are a stranger to me and I can't very well let my hair down, but neither should I want you to be too much in the dark. I am not a completely amiable character any more than I am a facile and prolific writer. I do most things the hard way and I suffer a good deal over it. There may not be a lot of mileage left in me. Five years of fighting Hollywood has not left me with many reserves of energy.[54]

Ray was in a strong position to define the relationship he had with his agent because he was an established author. Sydney Sanders had occasionally tried to steer him in a certain direction, asking him to write "I'll Be Waiting" for a slick magazine, for example, but there was to be no more of that kind of interference.

Brandt must have been surprised to receive Ray's letter and quickly asked to read the half-finished manuscript, which was sent to his office in New York a few days later. Before long, Brandt paid a visit to California. Was it made especially to meet Chandler? If so, it shows quite how eager Brandt was to sign him up, and Ray would have loved that he was being courted. Whatever the case, the meeting was successful. Ray liked Brandt and signed with the company.

By July, Ray was close to completing the first draft of *The Little Sister*. All that was left to write were the final scenes. At this time, he had a sizeable audience of correspondents with whom to share his woes, and so it is possible to piece together the problems he was having. While his fiction technique had developed over time, his approach and method had not. Even though he was now dictating rather than writing on small pieces of paper, he was probably still composing in similar, short sections—a habit only reinforced by working on screenplays. This approach could be very powerful indeed, and each scene would contain multiple instances of the magic he sought and which made the writing enjoyable, but it created its own difficulties. *The Little Sister* proved to be a minefield. He ended up with a surplus of wonderful moments, some of which either did not fit the plot, or added nothing to it. Some writers would have cut this material, but Ray refused. He described this, with the characteristic flair of a classicist, as having "the bed of Procrustes."* The excess scenes appear sporadically through the book and, if nothing else, help convey Marlowe's character and certainly add to the richness of the Los Angeles backdrop. In one, Marlowe meets a studio boss, Jules Oppenheimer, and towards the end of their encounter, Marlowe describes the behavior of the studio boss's dogs:

> The big one, Maisie, came over and stood beside him. The middle-sized one paused to ruin another begonia and then trotted up beside Maisie. The little one, Jock, lined up in order, then, with a sudden inspiration, lifted a hind leg at the cuff of Oppenheimer's pants.

This adds precisely nothing to the story of *The Little Sister* but is, in itself, an amusing satirical portrait of the studio bosses Ray had encountered.

---

*Procrustes, according to Greek myth, would invite passing guests to sleep in his iron bed and then, at night, he would lop off or stretch a victim's limbs so that they would fit it exactly.

Oppenheimer has no interest in cinema other than what it puts on the balance sheet, and he spends his time raising dogs, letting them urinate all over his office, all over his lot, and all over his leg. The plot might not benefit from this material, but the novel undoubtedly does. Finding space for vignettes like these, though, was hard work, especially as Ray grew more and more tired: "The system works if one is hitting on all twelve, but I've a few leaky sparkplugs now."[55]

The Little Sister centers on Orfamay Quest, a strange woman with a stranger name, who approaches Marlowe because her brother is missing. "I talk too much. Lonely men always talk too much," says Marlowe to his new client at the start of the novel. The trail takes him to Hollywood, and Ray took great pleasure in parodying the characters he had come up against while working there, from Oppenheimer to an agent who claims to be busy all day but, in reality, is being buffed and rubbed by a blonde maid. These were not portraits of specific individuals but of types, based on Ray's own experience and stories he had picked up. He also hinted at the threats facing modern Los Angeles by introducing a gangster, Weepy Moyer, a Brooklyn criminal who may be trying to muscle in on Los Angeles, and who is involved in the killing of Sunny Moe Stein, another gangster. In the real world, Bugsy Siegel was a Brooklyn criminal responsible for making Las Vegas the gambling center it is today. In the mid-1940s, he was murdered in Los Angeles, probably on the orders of other mafia families. He was succeeded by another Jewish criminal and former Siegel associate, Mickey Cohen, who was well known in the city. It seems likely the Jewish names of Ray's characters were meant to hint at these two real-world criminals. Again, he was playing, seeing how closely he could trace real events for fictional effect. In 1949, he wrote a tongue-in-cheek protection clause for the book:

> The people and events in this book are not entirely fictional. Some of the events happened, although not in this precise time or place, and certain of the characters were suggested by real persons, both living and dead.[56]

Originally private, the notice was eventually used by the publisher in their advertising, drawing attention, however comically, to the book's realism. Ray was engaging with contemporary Los Angeles directly, but did so more as a satirist than a realist. This is an important distinction: *The Little Sister* displays a more oblique approach than earlier efforts to contemporize his work, as in *The High Window,* where he retold the events surrounding the Doheny case with almost no embellishment.

One of the most notable characteristics of *The Little Sister* is Marlowe's bitterness. In the period between *The Lady in the Lake* and *The Little Sister,* he has become angrier, aware that he is irrevocably tied to Los Angeles. Around a third of the way through the book, having discovered a dead body and searched it, rather than immediately reporting it to the police, Marlowe delivers the following monologue:

> So I go see Dr. Hambleton, retired (and how) optometrist from El Centro, and meet again the new style in neckwear. And I don't tell the cops. I just frisk the customer's toupee and put on an act. Why? Who am I cutting my throat for this time? A blonde with sexy eyes and too many door keys? A girl from Manhattan, Kansas? I don't know. All I know is that something isn't what it seems and the old tired but always reliable hunch tells me that if the hand is played the way it is dealt the wrong person is going to lose the pot. Is that my business? Do I know? Do I ever know? Let's not go into that. You're not human tonight, Marlowe. Maybe I never was nor ever will be. Maybe I'm ectoplasm with a private licence. Maybe we all get like this in the cold half-lit world where always the wrong things happen and never the right.

This is Marlowe at his most human. Here is no flat figure putting together esoteric clues to solve a puzzle but, rather, a man who acts for reasons he cannot himself divine, through motivations he does not always understand. Marlowe, here, is no more the chivalric knight because, in this passage, he is not behaving honorably, at least by any schoolboy definition. Los Angeles is part of Marlowe's fate and this much he does seem to recognize. Unlike Ray, who always held some affection for the city, Marlowe has come to loathe the place he cannot escape:

> I smelled Los Angeles before I got to it. It smelled stale and old like a living-room that had been closed too long. But the colored light fooled you.

This is not the voice of Raymond Chandler we are hearing; it is the authentic voice of his character, an independent being. Though we are familiar with it, it still retains a shocking quality because it is now so much more than the voice of a mere detective. Ray had his concerns about how complex Marlowe was becoming. In a letter to Hamish Hamilton he wrote:

> I am afraid Mr. Marlowe has developed far more that suspicion that a man of his parts is beginning to look pretty ridiculous as a small-time private detective.[57]

Ray had always planned to write a novel with "a murder in it but [which] is not a mystery."[58] Though *The Little Sister* had not started out as that novel, as he came to write its closing scenes he began to wonder whether a neat conclusion was necessary. With such a richly drawn narrator, was it a conventional detective story at all? James Sandoe, who had an encyclopedic knowledge of crime fiction, had introduced Ray to a wide range of mystery writers and had helped him better understand the genre. It is telling that it is in a letter to Sandoe that Ray began to question the need for a conclusion. He said that *The Little Sister* "breaks practically all the rules there are":

> Does an author feel bound to catch his murderer? Yes, if he is writing a formal mystery. Otherwise the story is an unresolved chord. If he is merely writing a novel of character which uses the mystery form merely for sensational effect, I think not.[59]

Significantly, in another letter written on the same day, this time to Hamish Hamilton, Ray made it clear that the novel lacked "two or three scenes at the end,"[60] which, of course, is the most important part of a conventional mystery novel. He also explains that he had "a very, very tired mind,"[61] and perhaps it was this exhaustion, as much as a desire to innovate, that made him consider the truncated ending. Over the course of the next few weeks, though, he summoned the energy to write the concluding scenes, succumbing, ultimately, to a desire to give his readers, as fans of crime fiction, what they wanted. They are the weakest parts of the novel, written quickly and against a deadline. Ray decided on multiple killers, and they are, of course, both women, as if he was falling back into comfortable territory. Neither are convincing as murderers. For Marlowe, the case is painful and complicated and ends with more death. It came close to the type of book Ray had always imagined he would write but, still, to his mind, stopped short. He underestimated the power of *The Little Sister* as a novel, in and of itself.

Ray sent the manuscript to his new agent in September 1948, and Brandt had sold the serial rights to *Cosmopolitan* by November, *Colliers* and the *New York Post* having turned it down "with enthusiasm."[62] This netted Ray around $10,000, quite a sum, though nothing compared to the sort of money he had been earning only a year before.

Brandt and Ray also made the decision that, for publication as a book, it was time to break away from Knopf, after almost ten years. Relations with them had soured in the mid-1940s, for several reasons. Chief in his list of complaints was how Knopf had handled the sale of the cheap editions. Under their agreement, the publisher could sell rights to reprint cheap editions of his work and earn a large royalty on each sale—more than Ray, in fact. He thought this was unfair and that Knopf had done nothing to earn such a large cut. He had also been disappointed by Knopf's unwillingness to prosecute James Hadley Chase for plagiarism. Brandt, working with his colleague Bernice Baumgarten, approached Houghton Mifflin with *The Little Sister*.

Dale Warren, who worked in publicity at Houghton Mifflin, had been a regular recipient of Ray's letters and had picked up on his dissatisfaction with Knopf. In 1947, he suggested internally that Houghton Mifflin approach Ray's agent but, at the time, it was clear that Ray was distancing himself from Sydney Sanders, so there would be questions about who would negotiate any deal. More importantly, Ray was still writing *The Little Sister* and had put it on hold to work on *Playback*. Because he refused to accept advances until after he had completed his novels, there was nothing to show. By late 1948, once Ray was with Brandt, and this new agent had a manuscript in his hands, Houghton Mifflin made an offer of $4,000 for publishing rights. Ray made it clear on more than one occasion that he wanted to be published by the company, but he was also cautious:

> Sure, I think you [Houghton Mifflin] are good publishers. Trouble is to decide whether there is any valid reason to change publishers. I think there ought to be a very heavy one before it is done. So I

thought I would just keep my trap shut about it for the time being and let the wiser mouths speak. I know what my impulse is.[63]

Houghton Mifflin turned on the charm. Senior members of the company took him out to dinner, and he was offered an advance for *The Little Sister*. After considerable deliberation between Houghton Mifflin and Bernice Baumgarten, Ray agreed to move. In exchange, he got a middling advance but, such was Houghton Mifflin's determination to secure their author, he also won better copyright protection and a much higher return for paperback reprints.

The heavily edited serialization of *The Little Sister* appeared in the April 1949 edition of *Cosmopolitan*. Ray was not impressed by the magazine's use of his story and decided never to allow another serialization:

> The abridgement (of LS) in the current *Cosmopolitan* is quite horrible.
> I expected them to leave almost everything out but I did not expect
> them to stick in their own material.[64]

A British edition was published by Hamish Hamilton in July 1949, and it came out in the United States in September. It attracted some excellent reviews, and it was increasingly clear that, in Britain at least, Ray was being treated as a serious novelist. Unfortunately, he was not able to fully bask in the glory, being distracted by issues closer to home.

In late 1948, Cissy had become ill again, and this time seriously. Her doctor sent her for an X-ray and, when the results came in, diagnosed her with fibrosis of the lungs. This is a rare condition that causes the lungs to become inflamed and then scarred, reducing their capacity to exchange oxygen and carbon dioxide in the blood. The couple were devastated by this news. The fact was that Cissy had begun, slowly, to die.

Ray's immediate response was to try to leave La Jolla. He thought that Cissy's illness would be tempered by hotter, drier air, so, in the short term, they visited San Francisco and Carmel. At the same time, he sounded out friends about moving permanently away from La Jolla. Throughout the 1930s and early 1940s, Ray and Cissy had moved between Los Angeles and Big Bear Lake, which seemed to have helped Cissy's lungs. He wrote to James Sandoe, who lived in Boulder, Colorado:

Please tell me something about Boulder, when you have the time. Climate, how cold, how hot. Elevation, population, what kind of trees, etc. Would it be possible to rent a furnished house there in the spring, etc. I'm getting fed up with Southern California. I'd like to go away somewhere where I haven't been before, put this place on the market, sell it, and then build somewhere fresh, if and when I find a place worthwhile. I love mountain climates, except in winter.[65]

Cissy was less keen to move away from La Jolla. She wanted to get a cabin in the mountains that they could drive to from time to time. One option was Lake Arrowhead, but Ray thought it too full of Hollywood types and, anyway, without the Hollywood money coming in, it would be out of their price range. The flurry of letters about moving suggest Ray's anxiety: he was beginning to realize that Cissy, who had guided him and stood at his side during tough times, would not be around for ever. He began to consider a trip to England, too, because he wanted badly to show his wife the country he loved.

Ray was deeply out of touch with Britain. In a letter to Hamish Hamilton, he made this clear:

What clothes do I need of a special kind? Do I need a dinner jacket etc? I was thinking of having the food parcel man send me some food parcels.[66]

Ray was not quite sure which version of England prevailed. Was it the one he was in love with, where a gentleman needed to dress for dinner? Or was it still beaten down under the cost of wartime rationing? "Much as I have read," he wrote, "it is still a little hard for us to get a firm picture of what living is like in England."

In early 1949, Ray's letters began to make clear that Cissy was beginning to struggle. Theirs was a traditional marriage and she had always been in charge of the cooking and the cleaning. Since moving to La Jolla, she had made more and more use of servants and, as she began to tire, began to rely on the help entirely:

The house is too much for her, and even if it were not too much for her in a physical sense, taking care of it, going to market, cooking and cleaning up, would prevent her from doing anything else.[67]

Ray wanted Cissy to be able to rest and enjoy her leisure time—they were, after all, Californian now, and leisure mattered on the West Coast—but her ailments and looking after the house piled on the stress. Then there was also a persistent worry about money.

It was this, when combined with a desire to visit England, that caused Ray to consider going back yet again on his promises to forget the movie business. Money was a complicated subject for him and even during his hardest struggles he hated to let on that he was struggling. He had kept some of his Hollywood money—enough to live on if necessary, having learned the lessons of hardship in the 1930s—but not enough to support their preferred lifestyle, with secretary, gardener, and cook. Reluctantly, Ray considered the idea of a new screenplay, discussing ideas with John Houseman. He hoped that a new film might offer the chance to go to Britain for a time. In the end it came to naught. Though Ray's films had drawn industry respect he, personally, had been less successful. In 1948, he wrote "Oscar Night in Hollywood" for the *Atlantic*, which questioned the value of the Academy Awards ("As for the personal prestige that goes with winning an Oscar, it may with luck last long enough for your agent to get your contract rewritten and your price jacked up another notch. But over the years and in the hearts of men of goodwill? I hardly think so").[68] Once again he had cast the Hollywood establishment in a less than positive light. Though it did not provoke the same reactions as "Writers in Hollywood," it did not endear him to the industry.

In the end the pressure of the last few months was so great that Ray started to fall ill, too. In the late summer of 1949, the skin along his fingers began to split open. X-rays were required, but the diagnosis was an allergy that meant he was not to touch printed or carbon paper. He had to read with gloves on, "like a fading beauty on the stage."[69] Ray was starting to feel old, and Cissy had certainly become so. On the occasion of Hamish Hamilton's birthday he wrote this:

Too bad you are such an old, old man of 50, or not quite. . . . I have sympathy for you. It is a bad age. A man of 50 is not young, not old, not even middle-aged. His wind is gone and his dignity has not yet arrived. To the young he is already old and stodgy. To the really old he is fat and pompous and greedy. He is a mere convenience to bankers and tax collectors. Why not shoot yourself and be done with it? Think of the horrors that lie ahead. You might even get to be a whiskered bone like Shaw, a voluble cicada, an antediluvian scene-stealer.[70]

Ray, at sixty-one, began to reflect on life. The 1940s had been his most successful decade. He had published four novels, embarked on a new career as a screenwriter, with some considerable success, and his work was increasingly recognized by both readers and critics. His name, in its own right, was suddenly a saleable commodity, as was that of Philip Marlowe, who was taking on a life of his own.

The Adventures of Philip Marlowe had first been broadcast on radio in 1947, and the series was revived in 1948, eventually running for two years. Typically, Ray was never happy with it, though he was paid royalties for the use of the character without having to input: "I have nothing to do with it except to complain to my agent about this and that."[71] Early in 1949, he was approached by a publishing company who wanted to pay him $1,200 a year to use his name on a new publication to be called *Raymond Chandler's Mystery Magazine*. Again, he would have no say in the product or editorial policy, but would have received an income in exchange for his endorsement. He turned it down thinking, in part, it would be dishonest to deceive readers into believing he had written or edited the publication: "They are not even faintly aware that the offer is an insult."[72]

Despite these successes, Ray did not feel satisfied. He considered *Farewell, My Lovely* his best book, not bettered by any that followed, and his films had never achieved the level of artistry he aspired to. He had, at times, increased his drinking to dangerous levels, and he had put his marriage at risk. Above all, he had failed to write the sort of novel of which he had long dreamed, and was ever more tied to Marlowe.

When, in 1949, Houghton Mifflin agreed to publish a collected edition of Ray's stories—he had to fight them to produce only a single volume—it was clear how far his star had climbed. A few years before, Hamish Hamilton had refused to publish the very same stories, thinking that they would damage Ray's reputation, and Knopf had turned them down when Joseph Shaw offered them in 1943. Now, though, *The Little Sister* was selling well and Chandler was a name that resonated. Ray set about tidying the stories up and took the process seriously enough, rewriting the first person narratives as Marlowe stories, banishing less memorable characters like Mallory, removing dated elements, such as references to Nazis in "No Crime in the Mountains," and trying to minimize the amount of material readers would recognize from its reuse in his novels. He also removed "The Bronze Door" from the selection, hoping that it could be part of a future collection of "longish short stories" which would all concern "murder in some sense" and be "in the nature of a spoof on some type of murder mystery."[73]

It is interesting to note here how this plan had been modified since its inception. It was first mooted in 1939 in his notebook, but then there was no mention of murder or mystery. Ten years later, Ray found himself as a man with a reputation to live up to and an audience that expected his work to have something to do with death. It seems forgetting about mystery fiction as he had originally planned was now impossible.

For now though he had to focus on the pulp stories, and the process of review was a dreary but necessary one. The fact that it would bring in income was still a concern, but it sapped the fun from his work. In November he was down about the whole thing:

> I am now trying to remove the Nazi element from a story called No Crime in the Mountains, and also the bits of description I swiped for a book. I don't know why I bother. I guess I have an affection for the story because I have or had an affection for Big Bear Lake country which I knew very well indeed about ten years ago. I think we'll leave out The Bronze Door and Pearls are a Nuisance and bung in all the rest, regardless of faults. Every time I want to throw a story out there is something about it that they howl about.[74]

The following month, though, he was more enthused, giving Dale Warren a rundown of the exact order the stories should appear including, interestingly enough, "Pearls Are a Nuisance." There was also the question of an introduction. Ray decided to use his essay "The Simple Art of Murder," though he worried what his old friend Charles Morton would have to say.

It was an interesting way to sum up his career thus far. Here he was preparing the stories that had launched him in the first place, and they were about to be published after an extraordinarily creative decade. There is little doubt that the 1940s were a successful period for Raymond Chandler, but whether or not it was a happy one for him or for Cissy is open to question. Looking back, it is clear that Ray was in conflict and that he saw his original ambitions were now almost impossible to achieve. La Jolla was not working out either. He and Cissy were ill, Ray having added a case of the shingles to the litany of illnesses the couple suffered. Desperate to escape, they decided, finally, that they would put their house on the market and spent Christmas 1949 dreaming of visiting England.

CHAPTER THIRTEEN

"SUBDUED MAGIC"

Cissy and Ray had wanted to visit London since they first married. With Cissy's health worsening, they were aware that their chances were running out. In January 1950, the couple began to sketch the outline of a trip: they would be in London for four months and stay in a luxurious hotel; they would visit Ray's friends and tour the city; and then, once they tired of London, they would visit Scotland and, possibly, Paris. It was to be the trip of a lifetime, but Ray was apprehensive. Cissy's illness would limit their movements and he, too, had suffered a series of ailments, including his bitterly ironic allergy to paper. The English climate was a concern, too—Britain seemed a cold and chilly outpost to the Chandlers, who were used to the warm sun and dry air of Southern California. Ray continued to write to friends for advice about this and many other issues:

> And what about food? After all you can't very well consume food parcels in hotels. Laundry? Soap? Can one buy shirts and socks and so on freely?[1]

It is clear from his letters that he worked himself up into a state about the trip, nervously chewing over ideas and asking the same questions again and again. He seems to have become so agitated that it affected his health; his fingers started to split again and a recurrent bout of the shingles returned. He began to doubt whether he would be healthy enough for the journey:

I really hope we are really coming to England next May, but I'm a bit scared. I've had a lot of trouble and I don't want to export a semi-invalid to you.[2]

In letters to friends, he blamed his problems on allergies and, in part, this may have been true, but the worry of the trip to England was a major contributing factor. By March, the trip had been canceled: England would have to wait.

It is probably this period of extreme tension that caused Ray and Cissy to reconsider their plan to move from La Jolla. Though consummate movers, it would have put too much strain on the frail couple. Perhaps as a way of distracting himself from his and Cissy's poor health, Ray focused on work. By April he was working on an idea that would become *The Long Goodbye*. He was hard-nosed about the research, writing to his lawyer, Leroy Wright, to check on details that would work their way into the finished manuscript. He asked Wright to find out about a private eye's privileges and duties and whether his fingerprints would be kept on record anywhere. He was trying to find out how a detective in trouble with the law might be able to survive:

> How is a complaint made against him (a) by a private citizen, (b) by a police authority? What is the procedure in hearing such a complaint (assuming the matter to be short of a criminal charge)? On what grounds may his license be canceled? If it is for a specific period (what is the fee?) is it automatically renewed, or must he requalify?[3]

The information that Wright dug out was woven throughout the final novel but, in particular, it was essential to the first scenes in which Marlowe finds himself committing a criminal act for his friend Terry Lennox. When the police catch up with Marlowe, they try to pressure him into revealing what happened to Lennox and he ends up in a cell, resisting all the threats to his career and livelihood. This is a subtle but important shift in Ray's approach. In his first works of fiction, research was kept to a minimum, his work being based more on his understanding and appreciation of people and situations. Too much detail, he believed, would distract from the effect he was trying to achieve. Now, he was much more confident in his character and in the quality of his own writing. *The Little Sister* had benefited from Ray's intimate knowledge of Hollywood, a world he knew far better than the Los Angeles underworld, and he had also become increasingly interested in the actuality of crime, studying real-life murders and murderers. His character, Marlowe, would benefit from a grounding in real detail:

> The private detective of fiction is, of course, pure imagination. He does not and could not exist. He is the personification of an attitude, the exaggeration of a possibility. But that is no reason why he should not know the rules under which he operates.[4]

By July 1950, Ray had completed the first chapter of the new novel and Hamish Hamilton had already offered to publish but, as usual, Ray was soon telling friends that it might be the only chapter he was going to write. It is not clear why he so quickly cooled on the new book but it seems likely that around this time he had a call from his new agent, Ray Stark, to say that Alfred Hitchcock was interested in working with him on a new movie. Stark was associated with Brandt & Brandt and managed the film rights of Brandt's clients, but he also represented screenwriters and, at some point, started working with Chandler. It is not clear why this came about, or why Ray left Swanson:[5] it may be that it was part of the deal with Brandt or that, after *Playback*, Ray hoped that working with someone with a new perspective might bring better projects. Whatever the case, Stark had sent him several books to consider adapting, the majority of which had been returned without comment. But a Hitchcock project was different. The director's reputation was on the rise and, after a successful decade in Hollywood, he was about to enter his richest years as a filmmaker. Ray had met him in the 1940s and liked him, and the long discussion they had about film technique had influenced Chandler's own writing, so he was intrigued by the chance to work with Hitchcock on *Strangers on a Train*.

Hitchcock had stumbled across Patricia Highsmith's novel and immediately saw how it could be translated to the cinema. He quietly bought the rights (he supposedly kept his name out of all negotiations so that the price would stay low) and commissioned Whitfield Cook, a novelist, to help him write a treatment. It was in this early treatment that the shape of the movie was sketched out. Guy was now to be a tennis player with political ambitions, while Bruno was to be more effete than in the novel, with strong hints to his being a closeted homosexual. It was also decided that Guy would not become a murderer, as he does in the novel, but only appear to go along with Bruno's scheme, setting up a dramatic ending.

Ray, who was always susceptible to flattery, was pleased to be approached by a director with cachet. What he probably did not realize was that he was not Hitchcock's first choice, or his second, or even his third. Hitchcock was determined to have a big-name writer attached to the film and a treatment circulated around Hollywood for months: John Steinbeck was mentioned but turned it down. So did Dashiell Hammett. In an interview, Hitchcock said that eight writers had passed on the adaptation and no one had thought it any good. Then someone suggested Raymond Chandler, probably because he was seen by some to be the next best thing to Hammett, even after more than a decade of independent success in fiction and in Hollywood. Chandler thought it "a silly enough story" but agreed to take on the task:

> Why am I doing it? Partly because I thought I might like Hitch, which I do, and partly because one gets tired of saying no, and some-day I might want to say yes and not get asked.[6]

The contract was generous, paying Ray $2,500 per week, plus $50 for secretarial expenses,[7] for a guaranteed period of five weeks. It also allowed Ray to work from home, still something of a rarity in Hollywood. Hitchcock was even willing to accommodate his refusal to drive to the studio in Burbank: script meetings were to be held in La Jolla. Ray started work on July 10, 1950, and shortly after Hitchcock made the first of several visits to the Chandler house, taking a seat on the davenport and sipping his tea. Cissy made herself scarce while the two men settled down to discuss their movie.

It soon became clear that they had very different working methods. Whereas Ray liked to be direct and to the point, Hitchcock was happy to let conversations ramble, seeing their script meetings as social opportunities as much as work. At first, Ray was tolerant, but it did not take long for him to see that there were problems with their differing approaches. Ray was precise and had always tried to have as much control over a picture as possible. On the back of the success of *Double Indemnity*, he had secured a greater amount of influence over *The Blue Dahlia* and *Playback* than many writers ever dreamed of, and had grown used to it. He not only felt he deserved such power but also believed it made him a better screenwriter. No doubt he felt that Hitchcock wanted him to work on the film because of his high profile and expertise, and expected authority over the screenplay, but Hitchcock was not that sort of director.

Since coming to America, Hitchcock had been able to wrestle control of the moviemaking process from his producers. When working with David O. Selznick, who liked to restrict his directors so that they made the movie he wanted, Hitchcock would consciously film and edit in a way that Selznick would find hard to interfere with. By 1950, he was in a position to direct with real freedom. From the very outset, he had a particular plan for *Strangers on a Train* and was not looking for a writer to conceptualize the movie—he just wanted someone to fill in the gaps and provide dialogue.

Almost right away, though, there was confusion. In part this was caused by a letter from Finlay McDermid, one of the Warner Bros. front office staff. He wrote to explain the concerns of the Motion Picture Production Code (MPPC) office, presided over at that time by Joseph Breen, that checked the moral content of movies:

> As set up at present, Guy and all of our sympathetic characters are the ones who are pressing for a divorce. If, instead, Miriam had wanted the divorce and Guy had made some attempts to hold the marriage together but had then accepted the situation, the Breen Office would find this phase of the plot more acceptable. Guy, returning to see Miriam, would find that she had changed her mind again and he would still have the same reactions. The Breen Office is also concerned about two other elements, the rather bald way in which the treatment shows Bruno's home life as a fairly literal oedipal situation and the equally bald manner in which Ann, Barbara and other sympathetic characters disclose the point that there is latent murder in everyone . . .
>
> I pass these things on to you with the assurance that you can cope with such problems. STRANGERS ON A TRAIN will, I know, be a much more impelling, convincing drama after it receives its transfusion of Chandler dialogue and characterization.[8]

Ray, who had run up against the MPPC working on *Double Indemnity*, took this to mean that the story required real changes, but Hitchcock did not agree. The trouble was, though, that the director's manner of dealing with this disagreement was to be obtuse, pointing out problems or adding small suggestions, rather than tackling the big issues directly. This left Chandler puzzled by quite what he wanted, and he described the experience as being akin to that "of a fighter who can't get set because he is continually being kept off balance by short jabs."[9] He sent the first treatment to Hitchcock on August 2. Two weeks later, he submitted the second part, completing the work he was initially contracted to do. But between submitting the first and the second parts he had heard nothing from the director and this confused Ray even further. He referred to it in one letter, to his agent, as "Chinese Torture."[10]

Still, shortly after receiving the second part of the treatment, Hitchcock took Ray to lunch at his club in Los Angeles to talk it through. There were two results from this. First, Ray was instructed to write the screenplay, though even this was characteristically vague: "I gather, in a rough sort of way, that he would like me to go on and write a screen play in master scenes—not a shooting script."[11] Secondly, Ray contracted a bout of food poisoning that left him unable to work for several days. Against the advice of Stark, and to the confusion of studio executives, he refused payment for the period he was ill, also canceling a scheduled meeting with Hitchcock in La Jolla. Once back on his feet, Ray invited the director to a script conference, but his illness and his general dissatisfaction with the job put him on edge and the meeting was tense.

There are competing accounts of what happened when they met, but in none does Ray come out well. One of Hitchcock's biographers[12] reported that the director and his assistant had made their way to La Jolla, where they found Ray in a combative mood. They sat down to tea and Ray launched into a long monologue about all the things he thought were wrong with the project. As this was reaching its climax, Hitchcock stood up and, without saying a word, walked out of the door, his surprised assistant hurrying after him. Ray, equally astonished, did not know what to do and, walking to the door, shouted insults at the director. Among other things, he called him a "fat bastard." In another version of the same story, Ray saw Hitchcock getting out of his car and delivered the same insult in what he thought was a quiet voice but which was, in fact, perfectly audible. Whatever the details, from then on, Hitchcock had decided that he did not want to work with Ray. Chandler, used to the director's confusing and contradictory behavior, seems to have chalked this up to eccentricity and continued to write the script, unaware that Hitchcock wanted nothing more to do with him. For his part, Hitchcock could not yet fire Ray without the studio thinking there was a problem, so he left Chandler to continue, ignorant of any problems.

Further difficulties seem to have arisen in mid-September when, despite his decision to ignore Chandler, Hitchcock decided he needed the script urgently. His assistant, Barbara Keon, passed this message on and Ray, though angry at the news, worked hard to complete it in time, continuing through the weekend. On Monday, September 26, he submitted his final draft. The following day he received a night letter from his agent, Ray Stark, letting him know he had been taken off salary as of Monday evening. Chandler was furious. This, as he saw it, was against the spirit of their agreement. In his mind, he had acted honorably throughout, delivering the final draft on time, refusing pay for a few days when he was ill, and working overtime so he could stick to deadlines. The studio, on the other hand, had lied to him, telling him there was no deadline only to spring on him that there was, in fact, a very important one. His letters suggest that it had still not occurred to him that Hitchcock was so angry.

All in all, it was an exhausting experience, and one that Ray regretted bitterly. In the final movie we see the fundamental difference between the two men. Hitchcock was interested in building cinematic tension and in creating a thrilling experience for his audience. Chandler, in contrast, was much more interested in character and motivation. In this he was probably closer to the spirit of Patricia Highsmith's original novel, and he regularly tried to get Hitchcock to return to the source material. In the script he submitted, Ray appended several notes that showed he had gone to great lengths to figure out the motives of Guy Haines and Bruno Antony. One reads:

> The question is which is the better trigger [to set Bruno thinking he should kill Haines's wife]—the phone call to Guy after the scene with Bruno's father—or the quarrel with the father after the phone call to tell Bruno that Miriam acted true to form and double-crossed Guy on the divorce?[13]

Hitchcock was not interested in this sort of minute detail: he simply wanted Bruno to kill Miriam and did not care too much why. Ray was aware of this, writing in one letter "he is always ready to sacrifice dramatic logic (insofar as it exists) for the sake of a camera effect or a mood effect,"[14] but seems to have continued anyway. This difference, though, was striking, and it should have been clear to all involved that Hitchcock and Chandler were not best suited to working together.

There were other causes of conflict, though. On paper, Ray and Hitchcock had a lot in common. Both had been educated in London, but had left for America to find their greatest successes; they were both exiles in Los Angeles, part of the city and yet outsiders at the same time. Nonetheless, they were fundamentally different on many levels, not least their attitudes to sex.

The introduction of Bruno's homoerotic fascination with Guy may have caused problems for Ray. Cook had purposefully suggested this subtly in his treatment, introducing signals that some of the audience would immediately recognize. He speaks French, for example, and is quite clearly a mother's boy and a dandy[15] and these are all meant to suggest a latent homosexuality. Ray, whose own books contain both sexually ambiguous characters and homoeroticism, was far from comfortable dealing with sexuality. In his letters he expresses some decidedly old-fashioned and offensive comments about homosexuals and there is little doubt that this addition by Cook and Hitchcock would have made him feel ill at ease. It was probably one of several aspects of the story that Ray wanted to talk Hitchcock out of but, evidently, could not. He did not appreciate that this element would help bring the movie longevity.

There may also have been a peculiarly English preoccupation with class and status at the heart of Ray's relationship with Hitchcock. Professionally, Ray felt like he was the director's equal and yet, at the same time, his attitude sometimes suggests a sense of social superiority. Hitchcock was the son of a greengrocer and grew up as a member of the English lower middle classes. Moreover, he had been brought up as a Catholic. Ray's public-school Englishness, and the deep suspicion of Catholicism bred into him as a child, might have led him to expect Hitchcock to defer to him. If so, he had gravely misjudged his own place in the Hollywood hierarchy.

Hitchcock went on to recruit a new screenwriter, Czenzi Ormonde, and is said to have made a great show of holding his nose as he held Ray's draft in his forefinger and thumb before dropping the pages into the trash.[16] This is probably an exaggeration because Ormonde's final script contains several scenes present in Ray's original, including the famous opening shots that track the feet of Bruno and Guy through the station until they meet. However, she did strip a lot of Chandler's work away too, making the film leaner and a lot closer to Hitchcock's vision. Ray may have been able to live with the changes eventually but what particularly upset him was that Ormonde was also a client of Ray Stark's. He was appalled: "It's bad enough to be stabbed in the back without having your agent supply the knife."[17]

Out of courtesy, Ray was sent a copy of the final screenplay, and was not impressed. He wrote to Hitchcock to clarify exactly what he thought was wrong with the film:

> I could understand your finding fault with my script in this or that way, thinking that such and such a scene was too long or such and such a mechanism was too awkward. I could understand you changing your mind about the thing that you specifically wanted, because some of the changes might have been imposed on you from without. What I cannot understand is your permitting a script which after all had some life and vitality to be reduced to such a flabby mass of clichés, a group of faceless characters, and the kind of dialogue every screen writer is taught not to write—the kind that says everything twice and leaves nothing to be implied by the actor or the camera.[18]

The letter itself is at once strange and revealing. Despite having not spoken to each other since September, Ray was under the impression that he and Hitchcock were still friends. Though he is angry in the letter, he is also cordial, addressing the letter to Hitch rather than Alfred or Mr. Hitchcock and, before launching into his diatribe, he tries to frame it as friendly advice: "I feel I should, just for the record, pass you a few comments on what is termed the final script." It is as though Ray has missed all of the not-so-subtle signals that their relationship had ended. He was convinced he had been brought in because of his skill at adapting the work of others when, in fact, the majority of the work had been done by Hitchcock and Cook in their treatment. Though he knew the position of the writer in Hollywood, he seems to have assumed he was somehow above and beyond all that. In the end, it was this misunderstanding that was at the core of a difficult and unproductive relationship.

Eventually Ray did work out where it went wrong:

> The fallacy of this operation was my being involved at all, because it is obvious to me now, and must have been obvious to many people long since, that a Hitchcock picture has to be all Hitchcock. . . . It [the screenplay] had too much Ray in it and not enough Hitchcock.[19]

At first, Ray considered having his name removed from the film's credits, but relented. Even though very little of his contribution made it into the finished movie, his name is nonetheless prominently displayed, giving Hitchcock all he had ever really wanted from Chandler all along.

It is understandable that the novel Ray had been working on at the beginning of the year had been largely forgotten but, with yet another bruising encounter with the film industry over, he could now get back to his own fiction.

Since working in Hollywood, he had come to rely on the services of a secretary. He was used to dictating letters and screenplays to be typed and reviewed. At first, he had been nervous about employing someone, worrying that it would seem too grand for a La Jolla writer, but eventually found that he could not cope without support. He took over two of the three bedrooms in the La Jolla house. Ray himself worked at the end of the hallway in a room he liked to call his study, though he also slept there, in a single bed next to his wooden desk, on which sat one of his typewriters. He turned the room next to Cissy's bedroom into a small office for the secretary, if she could find space amid his files and papers.

In 1950, he hired Juanita Messick. She may not have been his first secretary but she was one of his favorites. A middle-aged mother, she lived in La Jolla and, once she became familiar with Chandler, quickly became used to the rhythm of his day. The morning was taken up with work on the novel, after which they would break for lunch and join Cissy. These lunches were full of talk of books.[20] Whereas Ray was a voracious reader, tackling everything from detective fiction to history, Cissy was slower and more careful and, though these lunches were hardly intellectual debates, Messick often found them compelling. After lunch, it was back to work, often administrative— Ray was very organized about business matters, keeping files in order to track the progress of various deals and royalty payments. One file, called the "Tickler File," tracked payments from publishers, so that he was in a position to chase them as soon as they were late. Once work was over, Ray and Messick would join Cissy for tea, after which Ray would stand solemnly and collect a decanter of sherry, pouring small glasses for his wife and his secretary, but refusing to touch the stuff himself. Messick, who did not know of Ray's past difficulties with alcohol, assumed that he was teetotal. Had Ray stopped drinking? Probably not, as, in the past, he had always preferred to reduce his consumption to manageable levels, rather than becoming totally abstinent.

Ray was an eccentric employer, as demonstrated by a series of guidelines called "Advice to a Secretary":

> Assert your personal rights at all time. You are a human being. You will not feel well. You will be tired and want to lie down. Say so. Do it. You will get nervous; you will want to go out for a while. Say so, and do it. If you get to work late, don't apologize; just give a simple explanation. You may have had a flat tire. You may have overslept. You may have been drunk. We are both just people.[21]

There is nothing unusual in giving guidance to employees but, in this case, Ray dictated it rather than writing it out himself or talking to his secretary directly. It would have been quite a shock for a new employee to receive notes in this format and maybe that was part of the point. Ray was evidently aware that this was unconventional and followed it up with a parody, "Advice to an Employer":

> Never be at a loss for a word. If you are, just look natural and the disagreeable aura will suffice. It is improper for an employer to answer the phone. Always let the help do it: especially if she has gone to the terlet. In this case just yell: "Miss Whoosis, is that THE PHONE?" *Always* mess up the files. This makes sure the secretary can be blamed if *you* have lost something.[22]

This humorous self-deprecation might have been more appealing had it not also been dictated. With Messick, he tried to be more direct, though this clearly made him a little uncomfortable. He knew that he was going to be relying on her more as Cissy's health worsened and made this clear from the outset, though tentatively:

> There is another thing you are probably aware of, although I am a little reluctant to mention it. And that is that my wife is not able to do what she did only a few years ago. . . . I know that secretly she feels a bit depressed that she can't do it now, and I wouldn't even talk to her about it. . . . But the fact is, she can't. . . . So I suggest to you that if the thought occurs to you, "Well . . . I could do that for Mrs. Chandler, if she wants me to" . . . that you'd say so right off, and that you ask my wife if she wouldn't like to you to do so and so. But never hint to her that you don't think she's able to do it.[23]

At the same time, he expected Messick to keep him out of trouble:

> And if you see me starting to do something which you know is going to end in my getting mad at somebody, why come right out and say, "You'd better leave me to do that . . ." or something to that effect. You can be even blunter.[24]

What she made of this is not recorded but it is clear that she quickly became an essential part of the Chandler household, performing services as well as joining the couple for lunch and dinner.

The arrival of Juanita Messick in 1950 was one of the bright parts of a difficult year but, by December, the problems that had arisen had largely been dealt with. On December 14, one last difficulty arose: Taki, the Chandlers' beloved cat, had to be put to sleep. Though Taki was a tempestuous and contrarian creature who hated visitors, hissing viciously at them, the Chandlers adored him and were devastated when his illness reached an incurable stage. To the aging, childless couple, Taki had become more than just a pet. For twenty years, he had accompanied them as they moved around Los Angeles and Southern California, and his absence was keenly felt:

I didn't send any [Christmas cards] this year. We were a bit broken up over the death of our black Persian cat, aged almost twenty years. When I say a bit broken up I am being conventional. For us it was a tragedy.[25]

One of the consequences of Ray's painful involvement with Hitchcock was that it led him to fire Ray Stark. Ray was furious that his agent had provided the writer who replaced him and, as usual, saw what might have seemed to others a mere irritation as an unprincipled act of betrayal. He needed someone to represent the rights to his film work and any adaptations and so signed up with H. N. Swanson once again, but this time saying: "I am not interested in doing a movie job in the near future, nor in fact ever, unless I am sure of the man I do it for."[26] This was not the first time Ray had declared himself out of the movie business, but perhaps he recognized that his behavior with Hitchcock had damaged his reputation:

> Furthermore, it is quite unlikely that anybody would be interested in having me do a movie job. Furthermore, I would only work for someone who could give me something in return besides a sharp pain at the back of the skull.[27]

Though he then tried to settle in to finishing the new novel, there was something else to distract him. Back in 1943, he had noted down a loose idea for a fantastical story to be called "Professor Bingo's Snuff." It was to be a "variation on the old invisibility idea"[28] featuring one Caspar Milquetoast, a timid, downtrodden man who is always walking in on his wife and her boyfriend canoodling. One day, he finds the strange but beguiling Professor Bingo standing at the door proffering a business card and offering something special. Bingo then snorts a pinch of snuff and promptly disappears in front of Milquetoast's eyes only to reappear some way down the street. Intrigued, Milquetoast finds his way to Bingo's office and tries to get his hands on the snuff:

> Various idiotic complications from here on, possibly ending in affair with police trying to arrest Bingo while he is in his office invisible, occasionally opening the door to kick a policeman in the stomach.[29]

That the note is dated March 6, 1943, suggests that the idea had come to Ray during his work on *Double Indemnity*. The inspiration for fantastical stories, though, had been sown earlier and was part of his original plan to escape crime writing, drawn up in 1939. That it took him eight years to return to the idea says a lot about his way of writing fiction. Just like his Philip Marlowe novels, "Professor Bingo's Snuff" required distillation and, in early 1951, he found himself with both the passion and desire to work on the story.

It is in the differences between the story as published and the earlier plan that Ray's growth as a writer becomes clear. What had begun life in 1943 as a comic take on a fantastical idea, to be written as something of a farce, was, by 1951, more measured and mischievous. It is a more mature work altogether. The plot is similar—a strange professor appears in the life of a timid and put-upon husband, now called Joe Pettigrew, whose wife is making love to the lodger—but has been reformed into something of a commentary on crime fiction. In the finished story, Bingo passes a small amount of the snuff to Pettigrew as a sample who, on inhaling the stuff, becomes invisible and finds himself in a position to create the perfect murder. Invisible, Pettigrew watches his wife's lover come into the room in which he is waiting and then kills him out of sheer hatred, only to discover that his victim had himself just murdered Pettigrew's wife. Ray turns the plot that follows into a something of a game, weaving together two distinctly different ideas. On the one hand, the story plays with the idea of the locked room mystery: being invisible gives Pettigrew the upper hand but only for so long because, in the end, the cops solve the murder of the lover anyway, despite being wrong about how it was done. It turns on its head Sherlock Holmes's maxim that "when you have eliminated the impossible, whatever remains, however improbable, must be the truth," as Sergeant Rehder, one of the two investigating detectives, points out:

> You know better than that, Lieutenant. If it's a homicide, the guy had to get out of the room. There's no such thing as a locked room murder. Never has been.[30]

It is important that Rehder is the older but more junior detective: he has seen everything and does not need his "leetle grey cells" to solve the crime, even if he cannot work out every detail.

At the same time, Ray included a parable-like element to the story which helped both emphasize the fantasy of the story and augment its theme. Rather like "The Pardoner's Tale,"* Pettigrew finds that taking the snuff gets him into deep trouble when, having killed Porter Green, he goes to find more at the address given by the Professor. This address turns out to be that of the Hollywood police station. The implication here is that the wish to murder is as dangerous as the act. Merely considering the murder would bring Pettigrew to the same destination. Pettigrew does not need to think twice about his killing, jumping at the idea right away, and it is important, too, that he did not kill out of revenge or any other noble cause but simply because he hates Green. This is the worst transgression and attracts the Professor to Pettigrew in the first place, and the result will always be the same: the death of Pettigrew. Ray explained how these two elements of the story came together in a letter to James Sandoe:

> I started out to do a burlesque on the locked room mystery and somewhere along the line I lost interest in the burlesque and became preoccupied with the thought that a miracle is always a trap.[31]

This letter pulls the story in line with the rest of Ray's output. His fiction explores the difference between the image of Los Angeles and its reality. In books like *The Little Sister*, characters are drawn to Los Angeles by its miraculous abundance and soon trapped in its unsatisfying thrall, just as Pettigrew is trapped by his own miracle.

"Professor Bingo's Snuff" is one of Ray's best stories. He controls the narrative precisely throughout and it is quite different from his much earlier crime work. It is closest to "The Bronze Door," with which it shares a similarly

---

*Three men vow to kill death after a drinking session. They go out to find him, and, on asking an old man where they might find death, they are told that they need to look for an old oak nearby. There they find a pile of gold coins and quickly forget about their vow. The men draw straws to decide who will go and collect bread and wine, and while one is sent off, the other two remain and plot to kill him and keep his share of the money. When the first man returns with the bread and wine, the other two attack him and kill him and celebrate by eating and drinking. Unfortunately for them, the bread and wine have been laced with poison and they die. The three men did indeed find death.

fantastical theme. He did, however, come up against an obstacle that helps to explain why the story had started out as pure burlesque but evolved into something else:

> . . . good fantastic stories are extremely rare, and they are rare for a rather obvious reason, that in them it is almost impossible to turn the corner. Once you have exposed the situation, you have nowhere to go.[32]

Ray understood how to create an effect, and how to write about the supernatural in his own naturalistic style, but, having invoked the fantastic, found that he did not really know what to do with it. "Professor Bingo's Snuff" was his second tale of the uncanny and was also to be his last. Despite having wanted to write stories of that type since 1939, he could not make them work to his satisfaction, and so the idea was relegated to a drawer somewhere, never to be resuscitated.

While he worked on the story, he was also pushing on with his novel. By February, he had made only piecemeal progress and, during that month, found himself in a situation that was guaranteed to vex a man of his character—a visit from the writer J. B. Priestley, a prolific English author perhaps best known today for his play *An Inspector Calls*.

In 1951, Priestley's wife, Jane, had become all too aware that things were not right in their relationship, though she did not know he was having an affair with another writer, Jacquetta Hawkes. Priestley, perhaps wanting to escape an unhappy home, left Britain and headed west, stopping in Guadalajara, Mexico, from where he cabled Ray and asked if he could visit. Hamish Hamilton was good friends with both Priestley and Ray and had suggested that the two men meet. Ray, never the most welcoming of men, nonetheless took it upon himself to collect Priestley from Tijuana. He got into his Oldsmobile and drove down to the border, perhaps noting on the way that he could use the trip as research for his new novel. Shortly after climbing into the car, Priestley, smiling politely, told Ray that he liked his work but he should try to write something without a murder in it. Ray was quietly furious and the drive home was a long and unpleasant one.

Ray took Priestley first to a hotel and then home, where he discovered that the northern English writer was a constant talker. With Cissy sick and bedridden, Priestley's incessant chatter began to grate. Ray seems to have kept quiet throughout, much to Priestley's frustration. The following evening Ray took his guest to the house of a nearby friend, where he could be feted by what Ray called "a reasonable selection of what passes for intelligent humanity in our city."[33]

Ray seems to have been able to keep a lid on his frustration. He found Priestley a "likable, genial guy"[34] despite his patronizing view of crime fiction, or so he told Hamilton. Priestley certainly enjoyed his visit. Ray was, however, relieved when his guest departed:

> I am still a little dizzy from the descent on me of the English novelist, playwright, etc., J. B. Priestley. He cost me a good deal of time and a good deal of money, and I'm not quite sure what I got out of it if anything except the satisfaction of having been as polite as possible to a friend of my English publisher.[35]

This, though, was the price of success. Ray was loved by many in Britain and it is little wonder that some visitors were keen to meet him. He was a private person, lacking the charm and patience to be a good host; he was also overprotective of Cissy. As a result, visitors were never really made to feel welcome, and intruding into the Chandlers' world could prove to be very disorienting.

Ray, relieved at Priestley's departure, started to focus more on the novel, settling into regular writing sessions with the support of Juanita Messick. Cissy, however, continued to decline and, in September, things took a turn for the worse. She began to get much more tired than usual and the tradition of afternoon tea was abandoned because it interfered with Cissy's nap. Soon, she was spending most of the day in her room. She occupied herself by reading, occasionally even picking up the mystery stories that Ray's friends had lent him, though Cissy was never really a fan. She read slowly as "circumstances compelled"[36] and it must have been heartbreaking for Ray to watch. It also changed the rhythm of his day completely. With Cissy out of action and without a housemaid (the Chandlers went through a lot of housemaids, always complaining that they were useless, though one wonders if the housemaids ever got sick of their employers), Ray had to take on domestic duties. He would rise at eight in the morning and make two breakfasts which, by ten, had to be finished and cleared away. He would then go to his study to try and get some work done—"That's not very much but it's probably as much as I'm good for the way things are,"[37] he wrote to Messick. In the afternoons, he would visit the shops and the market to get groceries, which was less of a problem because he did not like to work in the afternoon. Then there was dinner. Ray was a competent cook but it took time to prepare the evening meal—time that otherwise could be spent writing.

After dinner, Cissy retired to bed leaving him to tidy up the kitchen. The house became quiet, but Ray's mind did not:

> I've got to face the fact that Cissy hasn't got any stamina . . . she's never going to get back to where she once was. And I dare say she knows it, although we never talk about it.[38]

This understanding weighed heavily on him. There was an unspoken agreement that they would deny the absolute reality of Cissy's death. It put Ray in a horrible situation: he was broken up but he could not talk about how he felt with the woman he loved most, and in whom he would have confided any other worry.

As summer became autumn, he did start to open up to his closest friends. Interestingly, one of the main recipients of Ray's miserable dispatches was Hamish Hamilton. Though in one letter Ray would say "I look on you as a dear friend, Jamie,"[39] it is worth remembering that the two men had never actually met. Ray nonetheless felt able to open up with Hamilton in a way he could with no one else:

> Cissy has a constant cough which can only be kept down by drugs and the drugs destroy her vitality. It is not TB nor is anything cancerous, but I am afraid it is chronic and may get worse instead of better. She has no strength and being of a buoyant disposition and a hard fighter she fights herself to the point of exhaustion. I dread, and I am sure she does, although we try not talk about it, a slow decline into invalidism.[40]

We see once again the reluctance to discuss Cissy's inexorable decline. Ray admitted to feeling "the icy touch of despair."[41] The world he knew was changing and this made him consider his own situation. In the same letter to Hamilton he reveals his uncertainty about his achievements:

> In every generation there are incomplete writers, people who never seem to get much of themselves down on paper, men whose accomplishment seems always rather incidental. Often, but not always, they have begun too late and have an overdeveloped critical sense. . . . I guess maybe I belong in there. I have enough material success to see through it, and not enough sense of destiny to feel that what I do matters a great deal.

Ray had worried over his own work before but never with such a sense of failure. He was starting to think that he had missed out on something, though quite what, he was not sure. The remarks above throw into new light a letter that expressed similar thoughts about F. Scott Fitzgerald:

> I think he just missed being a great writer, and the reason is pretty obvious. If the poor guy was already an alcoholic in his college days, it's a marvel that he did as well as he did. He had one of the rarest qualities in all literature, and it's a great shame that the word for it has been thoroughly debased by the cosmetic racketeers, so that one is almost to use it to describe a real distinction. Nevertheless, the word is charm—charm as Keats would have used it. Who has it today? It's not a matter of pretty writing or clear style. It's a kind of subdued magic, controlled and exquisite, the sort of thing you get from good string quartets. Yes, where would you find it today?[42]

This was, of course, really about Raymond Chandler. He was concerned as early as 1950 that he had missed out on being a great writer and, in 1951, conscious of his and Cissy's mortality, he returned to the subject again with a new sense of despair.

As an antidote to this frustration, he started to look for a way to raise Cissy's spirits. In September he took her to stay at a "dude ranch" called Alisal in Santa Barbara. For all its cowboy trappings, it was really a countryside hotel, where visitors could enjoy the benefits of the great outdoors. Just as they had once moved between the arid climate of Los Angeles and the cooler, damper air of the mountains, the Chandlers hoped that a different, drier air in Santa Barbara would alleviate Cissy's persistent cough and give them the chance to relax. At least that was the theory. In practice, they were too irascible to enjoy it. They found the whole experience tedious and disdained the company of wealthy Californians living out their Wild West fantasies:

> . . . the lady guests appear for breakfast in levis riveted with copper, for lunch in jodhpurs with gaudy shirts and scarfs and in the evening either in cocktail gowns or in more jodhpurs and more gaudy shirts and scarfs. The ideal scarf seems to be very narrow, not much wider than as boot lace, and run through a ring in front and then hangs down one side of the shirt. I didn't ask why: I didn't get to know anyone well enough.[43]

Once again, Ray seemed determined to stay the outsider.

On their return from Santa Barbara, he went out and found them a new cat in an attempt to cheer up Cissy. It was a small grey Siamese thing, only a few weeks old when it arrived at 6005 Camino de la Costa, and, like most kittens, was wild. It ran around the house freely, chewing furniture, scratching the davenport and the piano legs as it tried to make itself at home. Though it showed the Chandlers a lot of affection, this wildness proved too much for the now elderly couple and Ray, with a heavy heart, had to return the cat to the breeders. Having given one kitten back he decided to buy another, this time a black Persian so much like Taki that the Chandlers gave him the same name. Ray was trying to re-create the atmosphere of 1932, a time when the world was still open before him and Cissy was able to hold his hand as they made their way through it. This nostalgia was a reaction to her illness and, though it was born of sadness, he also found it stimulating and was able to channel some of his frustration into his work.

His new novel had started ambitiously and he had not intended it to be centered on Philip Marlowe. In fact, in a sharp contrast to his past work, it would be written in the third person. This, he thought, was his last chance to write the great work he had dreamed of. In May, Ray wrote to Hamish Hamilton:

> The trouble with my book is that I wrote about half of it in the third person before I realized that I have absolutely no interest in the leading

character. He was merely a name; so I'm afraid I'm going to have to start all over and hand the assignment to Mr. Marlowe, as a result of which I'm going to lose a number of good scenes because they took place away from the leading character. It begins to look as though I were tied to this fellow for life. I simply can't function without him.[44]

Yet again, Ray had come up against the same brick wall, but this time, instead of ditching the entire draft, as he had done in the past, he rewrote the book from Marlowe's perspective. By October, he had completed a first draft of the novel that would take the working title of *Summer in Idle Valley*. It was by no means finished but at least he had something to show for 1951. He wrote to his agent, Carl Brandt, to explain:

I am having a hard time with the book [LG] Have enough paper written to make it complete, but must do it all over again. I just didn't know where I was going and when I got there I saw that I come to the wrong place. That's the hell of being the kind of writer who cannot plan anything, but has to make it up as he goes along and then try to make sense out of it.[45]

As usual, Ray had sat down and written without fully understanding the plot and now had to remove the fat from his text to find the story. The continuing evolution of the book allowed him to channel his anguish at Cissy's illness and his own sense of loss into the novel. *Summer in Idle Valley* was written in a completely different frame of mind from anything he had attempted before and it shows in the final text. He seems to have been much more careful about the construction of this novel, writing it in private, without the involvement of Juanita Messick, who would usually type up a second copy of his work as a back up. He excluded others from the process by saying "The old zest is gone,"[46] implying that the book was too poor to share. Hamilton and other respondents must have been familiar with this sort of comment from Ray by now and did not realize that, on this occasion, he was keeping the book close to his chest because he was more than usually nervous about what he was writing. He knew this latest novel was going to be different—*really* different. Unlike his early efforts, which had promised to be different but had eventually found themselves trapped by the needs of the hardboiled genre, this would be a novel of human relationships rather than a mystery story, despite Marlowe's presence.

In early 1952, Ray was pushing himself to finish the book. Only with the complete manuscript in front of him would he really know if it was any good:

> Somewhere along the line I shall either wake up with a horrible gray feeling, which is the subconscious telling you that you have shot a blank, or else a comparatively warm glow, which is the same subconscious telling you that you have at least achieved passing marks.[47]

He made progress rapidly despite his worries about Cissy and, by early May, had completed the second draft of the book, which he was now calling by its more familiar title, *The Long Goodbye*. On finishing the draft, he decided to send it immediately to Carl Brandt and Bernice Baumgarten at the Brandt & Brandt agency. Ray had grown increasingly close to both agents and had come to rely on their advice. He was even considering moving all his literary affairs to the agency so that they would sell directly to his British publisher, Hamish Hamilton, rather than using a London based subagent. Ray was so keen to get the manuscript to New York that he admitted to having not read it himself, and he made it clear to both Brandt and Baumgarten that he wanted their "comments and objections and so on."[48] He was nervous and excited to be sharing, finally, a work which was so much more personal than any previous effort:

> I wrote this as I wanted to because I can do that now. I didn't care whether the mystery was fairly obvious, but I cared about the people, about this strange corrupt world we live in, and how any man who tried to be honest looks in the end either sentimental or plain foolish.[49]

His excitement proved to be short-lived. Carl Brandt sat down with the manuscript and read through it in a single sitting. Though he enjoyed it, he had some reservations, which he shared with Baumgarten. She agreed with Brandt's concerns and, on May 22, 1952, wrote to Ray with her thoughts:

> Carl and I were immediately struck by the change in pace in THE LONG GOODBYE. The advantages are obvious, an opportunity for real characterization—exploration of character and the psychological

reasons for the actions of your characters—and some of your best writing.

Both of us read it with complete attention. Carl at a single sitting.

Our only real concern was the change in Marlowe himself. His hardness was his great virtue and here he seems to have become almost Christlike. You put with great understanding his necessarily friendless state, and the great value he sets on having made a friend who wants nothing of him, but still we don't recognize the Marlowe we thought we knew. I can understand his being deeply moved by an unaccustomed friendship but I can't believe in him as a sentimental-ist. We feel that Marlowe would suspect his own softness all the way through and deride it and himself constantly.[50]

The letter goes on to question some minor elements in the plot, asking why Terry is impotent and whether there were too many beautiful women in the story. These questions, though, were small things; the major issue was the change in Marlowe. Despite this, Baumgarten thought that the manuscript should be passed on to Dale Warren for comment. Though she had spotted what she considered a weakness, clearly she did not feel that it was a disastrous one.

Bernice Baumgarten must have sent this letter believing that she had responded to Ray's request for frank comments in good faith. She could not have anticipated the fury it would provoke. Ray wrote that receiving the letter was like being "slapped in the face."[51] He was quite simply devastated to receive these criticisms, even though he had asked for them. Immediately he cabled Brandt & Brandt, requesting them to stop their copying of the manuscript and, in a letter a few days later, blamed his own impatience to be rid of the book for sending it in too early. At first, he seemed to think their points may have had some validity:

I knew the character of Marlowe had changed, and I thought it had to because the hardboiled stuff was too much of a pose after all this time.[52]

But he also admitted to a little skepticism: "there is also the possibility—faint as it is, I admit—that you could be a little wrong."[53] Around this time, he also wrote to Hamish Hamilton to explain why he would not be sending a new manuscript:

I am withdrawing the script of my book for revision . . . This happens as the result of criticisms made by Bernice and concurred with by Carl Brandt. Some of these comments, if correct, are devastating, and if incorrect are intolerable. Surely they are more likely to be the former than the latter. The character of Marlowe has become "Christlike" and sentimental, and he should be deriding his own emotions all through the book, or words to that effect.[54]

Again, Ray seems to accept the criticisms from Brandt & Brandt and yet questions them at the same time. This was possibly because, in his frustration and disappointment, he had not actually sat down to reread the manuscript since writing the last word and dispatching it to New York. He finally did so in early June and this cheered him up enormously. He wrote to Hamish Hamilton:

Feeling quite chipper, in fact. I am rather disgusted because I made it clear that the script I sent East [ie, *The Long Goodbye*] was no more than a corrected first draft. . . . Most of the points Bernice criticized in detail would have been changed automatically on revision and a great many that she did not criticize. A couple of her remarks I thought just plain silly. I could not quite swallow her calling Marlowe Christlike, and saying that in his old hardboiled days he would have derided his sentimentality (as of now, presumably). I don't think it's true.[55]

Ray was clear that he felt Brandt and Baumgarten were to blame. Brandt, according to Ray, was nothing more than "a front man whose standard is the POST serial"[56] and, though he could not identify anything concrete to use against Bernice, he wrote enigmatically of her that "there has been a good deal of undercurrent there, for various reasons."[57]

This experience prompted Ray to decide to cut the agency out of any future deals. Clearly, his frustration and disappointment were turning to contempt. He did this often, and it caused him to remain aloof and distanced from people who might have become friends. Rather than listening to their critique, he outwardly accepted it, internalized it, and let it gnaw away at him until it had turned to bitter resentment. He chose not to fire Brandt at this stage, but insisted that they had missed the point of the shift in Marlowe's character:

As to the character of Marlowe, I may be quite wrong but I was trying to write the book the way I wanted to write it and not the way somebody else thinks I ought to write it. The irony of a writer's career—I suppose most writers are confronted with it in some form—is that he may write a couple of books which pass with little notice at the time of their publication, and then as time goes by they slowly build up a reputation and in the end are used as yardsticks by which to measure his later work, sometimes by the very people who were quite unable to discern any merit in the early performance at the time.[58]

Ray felt the Brandt & Brandt agency had utterly the wrong idea about the sort of writer he was and he would not forgive them for this misunderstanding. This entrenchment reveals something essential about Ray: it was a difficult position to hold and it resulted in real isolation, but he simply could not deal with criticism and, much worse, could not understand why people he thought of as friends could not empathize with what he was trying to do. Correspondence, his preferred mode of communication, is not always an effective way of revealing the man behind it or his ambitions, and the business associates he thought of as friends did not always see the relationship in the same light. Paul Brooks, an editor at Houghton Mifflin, unknowingly let Ray down by not responding to a letter:

My letter to him did not demand an answer, nor did it receive one, although at the time a few words of hope and confidence would have fallen very gently into my soul.[59]

Though there may be a hint of irony in the tone, there is also an unmistakable truth too. As a result of this tendency to invest so much in unrequited friendships, he found himself, like his hero, almost entirely alone.

Ray decided that he needed some time away from his book. Though he understood it was flawed, he also knew that what he had written was good. He wanted some space to reconsider it properly and decided to take up an idea he and Cissy had flirted with for years: they were, at last, going to make the long-planned trip to London.

It was not easy. In the age before regular commercial flights across the Atlantic, Ray and Cissy had to travel by sea. They booked themselves aboard a Swedish ship, the *Guayana*,[60] that would take them from Los Angeles to Britain via the Panama canal. The *Guayana* was both a passenger vessel and a cargo ship so the voyage involved lots of short stops at various Caribbean ports. It made for a painfully long journey. They could not even be sure when they would arrive in London, only that it would take roughly three weeks, and that they would arrive sometime around August 20. As a result of their ignorance, despite taking ten suitcases, the Chandlers did not pack any clothes suitable for the balmy Caribbean ports. Instead, they traveled through the Bahamas in the tweeds and thick sweaters they knew they would need in England and resorted to hiding in the belly of the ship because it had air conditioning. That aside, the journey was relatively pleasant. Ray spent most of it reading or sleeping.

Among the many questions about London Ray had asked his correspondent, a frequent topic was hotels and, after much agonizing, he settled on the Connaught hotel in Mayfair, close to Grosvenor Square. He wanted a suite with a sofa bed in the living area so that he and Cissy could sleep separately as they did at home, but this proved to be too expensive, so they probably shared a room for the first time in many years. Cissy coughed badly and constantly and Ray, who was no great sleeper, would have struggled to get much rest.

Though it was a top-ranked hotel, popular with transatlantic visitors, Ray was not impressed with the Connaught. The room was costly and offered less comfort than he would have wished, and the staff caused constant irritation. On one of their first ventures out of the hotel, they tried to take a taxi, but the doorman refused to let the driver park on the curb. As a consequence, Cissy tripped and fell into the car, bruising her leg so severely that it should have been bandaged immediately. Not realizing the seriousness of the injury, Ray and Cissy took off into London and Cissy limped throughout the rest of the trip.

From the start, Ray's mood was dark. What should have been the trip of a lifetime was marred by small but constant problems. London was very different from Los Angeles and Ray was shocked when, on being invited to dinner by Hamish Hamilton, it was suggested he wear a dinner jacket. The Chandlers had not expected this sort of formality and, even though Hamilton was more than happy to make it a more relaxed affair, Ray now started to worry about letting his hosts down with his Southern Californian informality. This was a bigger concern for him than for many visitors because, in his letters, he had made it clear that though he was American, he was still a public schoolboy at heart and proud of his knowledge of proper etiquette. To be caught short like this did not, in his mind at least, reflect well. In addition, it may have been an uncomfortable reminder of what it was like to be a young boy who did not fit in at Dulwich. To try and make up for this, he took Cissy shopping on Bond Street looking for something elegant for her to wear but, despite hours of walking around—in itself a challenge—they failed to find a suitable outfit. Nothing was right or good enough and, an hour before dinner was to start, Ray had to call Hamilton to say they were not going to be able to make it. Obviously disappointed that his guest of honor was pulling out at the last minute, Hamilton suggested that he come alone, but Ray was appalled that anyone would think he could leave Cissy by herself. In the end, the dinner did go ahead but, for Hamilton, was a peculiar first encounter with the man he felt he had come to know so well on paper.

Ray was particularly keen to show his friends that he was the sort of confident, witty former public schoolboy he believed himself to be. On the one hand, he was attracted to the formality of English life and yet, on the other, he wanted to make fun of it. To be self-deprecating about privilege was, he thought, the only possible reaction for an intelligent man. In truth, he was once again an outsider. The Chandlers attended a dinner party thrown by Leonard Russell, the editor of *GO Magazine* and the man who had published "Professor Bingo's Snuff" in Britain, and his wife, Dilys Powell, a film critic for the *Sunday Times*. Ray took great pleasure in explaining to Cissy the English tradition of ladies leaving the men after dinner and, when the time came, Dilys Powell sat trying to catch Cissy's eye, assuming that she would be familiar with the practice. Cissy refused to notice. Ray, understanding what was happening, clapped his hands to get her attention, stood up and cried: "Cissy, look at this!" As the women left the room, Powell reported:

> "An old English custom," he [Ray] added as we shambled out. He was delighted with himself.[61]

At the same time as navigating the pitfalls of refined etiquette, Ray also insisted on being taken to visit the warehousemen at Hamish Hamilton, with whom he would play darts. He did not want to give the impression of being

the typical snooty author but, rather, wished to present himself as a man of
the people. It may have been a pretence but it was the kind of gesture that Ray
believed men in his position should make.

The person Ray enjoyed meeting the most was Roger Machell, Hamish
Hamilton's deputy, and, in a letter to his old friend William Townend, he
describes him in some detail:

> . . . I think we liked best Roger Machell, a director of Jamie Ham-
> ilton, a cheerful, rather pudgey light-hearted character, with a droll
> sense of humor and the sort of offhand good manners which you
> rarely find except in a genuine aristocrat. . . . He is a great grand-
> nephew of Queen Victoria . . . and his mother . . . lives in St. James
> Palace. He was badly wounded in the war and made a joke of it.
> He seemed to think it was characteristic that he should have been
> wounded while telephoning London from a French pub. . . . He has
> the sort of humorous, self-deprecating manner which by sheer magic
> of personality is never overdone . . .[62]

These qualities, of course, were precisely those that Ray wished others to
see in him. That he was of very different stock to Machell did not matter to
Ray and it is telling that he chose to write this letter to a fellow Old Alleynian, who would perhaps best have understood his fascination with the upper
classes and their manners.

Throughout the trip to London, Ray was deeply protective of Cissy. Dilys
Powell thought that he was particularly defensive at their dinner party, largely
because of Cissy's awkwardness. By this time Cissy was increasingly frail and,
even had she not bruised her leg, would have found London exhausting. Powell associated her with "a pale, almost extinct canary color"[63] and she wondered if Cissy used her age to keep her husband's attention:

> . . . I thought I detected in her something propitiatory—propitiatory
> for her age, her physical frailty, the gradual extinction of her energy.

If so, it worked. Ray was wrapped up in his wife and refused to leave her
alone for any length of time. In this, we see him at his most human. However
desperate he might have been to impress his new acquaintances, he needed

most of all to be with his wife, and the importance of protecting her always won out.

Ray was surprised to discover how well respected he was in England. He wrote to Paul Brooks: "In England I am an author. In the USA just a mystery writer. Can't tell you why."[64] Although Marlowe is a deeply American hero, to European readers, he also became representative of their own struggles with America. It is important to understand how complicated British attitudes to America were in the 1950s. It was widely felt that, without America, Britain would have fallen to the Nazi onslaught; it was also clear that America had taken the position of global preeminence Britain had enjoyed before the war, and that Britain now was a poor cousin. Moreover, British manufacturing was recovering only slowly, while US goods were flooding in, along with cultural imports. This, combined with the presence of American soldiers during the war, contributed to a real sense of British culture being swamped. British readers looked for a hero and some found Philip Marlowe. Though an American, he stood up to America's worst criminals, the rich. He may have been beaten and downtrodden by the wealthy and powerful but he never gave up and never let his moral code be corrupted. Marlowe was a man who stood up for the little people against the powerful: people like Harry Jones and Merle Davis. That this moral code was peculiarly British may not have registered with many readers at first but they nonetheless found in Philip Marlowe an example of resistance to unrestrained capitalism and American manners. It is little wonder that Philip Marlowe was one of the inspirations for James Bond, a hero who would stand up for British interests and restore a sense of pride to British readers.

Much as he craved respect as a writer, the attention, far from delighting him, made Ray grumpy and uncomfortable. He was not happy in his hotel and could not relax in the company of others. During one interview with a journalist he said straight out: "You know, I don't like this kind of thing, do you?"[65] Most of his friends seem to have noted that he scowled a lot during conversation. In part this was because he was a shy man by nature and genuinely ill at ease with the attention. To combat this, Ray drank and, worried that it would be a problem to get alcohol in Britain because of rationing, prepared for his visit by dispatching a case of Scotch and gin to the Connaught. In the lead-up to his visit, there is little mention of him drinking at all but, in

London, he seems to have enjoyed a bit more than at home, perhaps as is to be expected of a man on holiday. Most of his engagements in London seem to have included drinking, and Dilys Powell says that he enjoyed the "alcoholic" nature of her party. However, it appears he never went too far or embarrassed himself—at least no more than anyone else around him, in a culture where heavy drinking was normalized. Alcohol had long ago become a constant in Ray's life, but, during this period at least, it was not a debilitating problem.

After nearly two months in London, it was time to head home. Ray and Cissy boarded the *Mauretania* in October and headed back to America. They chose to head to New York rather than take the longer journey back to Los Angeles, but neither enjoyed it. Ray called the *Mauretania* a "damned floating hotel,"[66] perhaps because it reminded them of their rotten experience at the Connaught. The customs officials managed to lose one of the Chandlers' ten pieces of luggage on arrival and, after a wait of an hour and half that left Ray madder than ever, it was produced without a word of apology. This set the tone for the next few days in New York. Ray hated it and Cissy hated it even more. If London had been a challenge, then New York was more so, and Ray was particularly annoyed by its "hard-boiled, dirty"[67] taxi drivers. Dale Warren made the journey from Boston to meet Ray and found himself enjoying occasionally stilted lunches with the writer. Carl Brandt, who was based in New York, was not invited; Ray did not even tell him he was in town. It was only because Warren mentioned in passing that the Chandlers were in New York that Brandt found out about their visit, but by that time it was already too late—they were making their way back to California by train.

Ultimately, the trip had proven how frail Ray and Cissy had become, and quite how unused they were to strange company. One of Ray's first letters to Hamish Hamilton after his return to America was full of apologies for various slights he had inflicted on his publisher. Ray must have realized that his behavior had been far from exemplary. He claimed that Cissy had enjoyed the trip and that was true, to a certain extent, but it had also been costly, and her health had suffered yet another blow.

On arriving back in La Jolla, he started to make some changes. First, he decided to fire Brandt & Brandt. This was a decision he had, by and large, come to earlier in the year, but he found that the more he thought about their comments on the first draft of *The Long Goodbye*, the more angry he became. He canceled their contract in a single-line telegram. Carl Brandt must have been expecting something of this kind. He knew Ray was a difficult man and he had recognized that the letter sent by Bernice Baumgarten was an error. Still, it must have been disappointing to lose a client of Ray's stature. Ray had made his thoughts about agents plain in an article called "Ten Per Cent of Your Life," written for the February 1952 edition of the *Atlantic*. He knew an agent was valuable in some respects—the world of publishing was far too complicated without a native guide—but, when all was said and done, "The agent creates nothing, he manufactures nothing, he distributes nothing."[68] This fact made him suspicious of agents in general. In addition, as "commission men," they were forced to go for the biggest deals, which were not necessarily the best for their authors and, in any case, the accumulation of money in any industry, but particularly in Hollywood, led to some form of corruption. These suspicions, articulated with some verve and feeling, reveal quite how cautious he was when it came to agents and it is little wonder that he chose instead to work directly with Hamish Hamilton in the UK and Houghton Mifflin in the US, excluding a book agent altogether. Swanson would manage everything aside from book rights and Hamish Hamilton would look after Commonwealth rights. Ray was now in charge of his own affairs.

His second major decision was to ignore a lot of Baumgarten's suggestions. Instead, he sat down and started to rewrite the book, scene by scene, finding new ways to say what he wanted to express. By the middle of 1953, he had finished and was in a position to send the first part of the book to both Dale Warren and Hamish Hamilton. Both responded with huge excitement and could not wait to get the next part. They knew, like Ray, that this was something special.

To understand what Ray was trying to do with *The Long Goodbye*, it is worth considering the tone of the book. It is not a thriller or a murder mystery and, even though some of his earlier novels resisted such categorization, they could be absorbed into the genre more easily than *The Long Goodbye*. The novel tells two stories. First, it describes Marlowe's meeting Terry Lennox, a Canadian who had formerly been a soldier in the British Army, and their brief friendship. This seems to come to an abrupt end when Lennox's wife,

Sylvia, is murdered and he appears on Marlowe's doorstep begging for a lift to Mexico. Marlowe agrees to help but on returning to Los Angeles finds himself arrested for getting in the way of a police investigation into the murder. A few days later, Marlowe learns that Lennox has killed himself. The second story focuses on the writer Roger Wade, a successful but alcoholic novelist, with a beautiful wife, Eileen. She is desperate for Marlowe's help because Wade has a habit of disappearing. Over the course of the novel, it transpires that the two stories are intertwined and, even though Marlowe resists involvement, he finds himself pulled into the strange world of Idle Valley, where both the Lennoxes and Wades live.

It is important to note that, unlike previous novels, the central murder in the story, that of Sylvia Lennox, happens offstage. Though Marlowe hears about it, he does not discover the body, nor does he start to investigate it. It is only after he finds that Roger Wade is somehow involved that he starts to look at the connections. In earlier novels, Marlowe's role was that of investigator—an outsider probing the lives of others. In *The Long Goodbye*, he is a player in the mystery itself, with his own emotional stake.

This is a major shift on Ray's part. In classic detective fiction, the detective himself is left unaffected by the events he witnesses. Though Ray never adhered to this convention—in *The Big Sleep*, for example, Marlowe emerges from the story having had an epiphany of a sort not previously found in crime fiction—he is not only affected in *The Long Goodbye*, but is the very focus of the story. His meeting with Terry Lennox upsets the rhythm of Marlowe's life and introduces him to a new way of seeing the world. Marlowe briefly connects with someone in a way he had been unable to in the past and, when Lennox leaves, Marlowe is bereft. However, it is with Lennox's reappearance at the very end of the novel that we see how Marlowe has changed: he has the total realization that not only is he alone in the world, but that the connection he had thought he had found was a fallacy. What hope he had for companionship, or rather, true friendship, is extinguished in the last pages of *The Long Goodbye*. In Marlowe's eyes, Terry seemed to share his vision of the world:

> You had nice ways and nice qualities, but there was something wrong.
> You had standards and you lived up to them, but they were personal.
> They had no relation to any kind of ethics or scruples.

These words could have been spoken about Marlowe and this shared, strange morality brought the two men together. But Lennox's departure and his subsequent belief that Marlowe was a man who could be paid off, despite the death that his actions had led to, meant that this was not a friendship that Marlowe could stand. For him, the friendship was between "two other fellows"[69] and he had already said goodbye to *that* Terry, the man he knew and liked:

> I won't say good-bye. I said it to you when it meant something. I said it when it was sad and lonely and final.

And so Marlowe is left alone, with regrets, fully cognizant that his choices have landed him there. The penultimate paragraph of the book sums this up:

> I watched the door close. I listened to his steps going away down the imitation marble corridor. After a while they got faint, then they got silent. I kept on listening anyway. What for? Did I want him to stop suddenly and turn and come back and talk me out of the way I felt? Well, he didn't. That was the last I ever saw of him.

Part of Marlowe *does* want Lennox to turn back because he is so lonely but, in the end, his moral conscience wins out. He knows that he is on his own and he recognizes that his own choices have brought him here, and he is content that he has done the right thing.

Marlowe's conscience and action had never before been exposed or examined in this way. Ray knew that he had to tread carefully, which is why Bernice Baumgarten's comment that Marlowe was "Christlike" stung so hard. But to an extent, though he would not use that exact term, Ray wanted Marlowe to be like this. He wanted him to feel driven to an inevitable conclusion against his own instinct; he wanted him to be betrayed and to understand why. Marlowe was a knight with a code of honor that was unshakable, even in the most testing times. Ray recognized that he had put him in a situation that might be hard to understand for many of his readers, if treated in the usual way, and so took on the challenge to reveal Marlowe's own motivations and ways of thinking. The honorable martyr was, of course, also the sort of man Ray imagined himself to be.

But Marlowe was only part of the engine powering *The Long Goodbye*. The characters of Lennox and Roger Wade were an essential part of Ray's undertaking. They were examined with the same careful fascination as had been General Sternwood, Elizabeth Murdoch, and Orfamy Quest in earlier novels, but here there was something more. Both Wade and Lennox grew out of different sides of Ray's own personality, too. Lennox, like Ray, is a former Canadian soldier who has fought for Britain, albeit in a different war; Wade is an alcoholic who writes very well when drunk, just as Ray had in the past. It is always risky to draw too close a parallel between a writer and his characters but it seems undeniable that Ray chose to give his major characters such obviously similar qualities to his own because he was consciously trying to explore something in his own nature. This is what gives the book such fierce energy. Ray, particularly in his examination of Roger Wade, was trying to come to terms with his own life.

One of his first questions to Houghton Mifflin was about the title. He had favored *Summer in Idle Valley* largely because taking up his other option, *The Long Goodbye*, would mean that five out of six of his novels would make use of the definite article, which he would have preferred to avoid. But wiser minds held sway: *The Long Goodbye* it was.

Hamish Hamilton wanted to get the book out quickly and it was published in Britain in the autumn of 1953, with Houghton Mifflin releasing the American edition early in 1954. The contract between Ray and Hamish Hamilton offered an advance of just £250 but the actual amount of money Ray received was higher because it also included the royalties accrued from preorders. Still, this was not much of an income, especially when compared to the much higher fees Ray had earned from his film work. By the summer of 1953, he knew that he would not be able to live off his royalties alone. Over the preceding three years he had made several cutbacks in his own life, including stopping sending food parcels to friends in Britain. He was starting to explore other options, pushing for television and radio adaptations, and hoping for a decent serial sale for *The Long Goodbye*, despite his earlier dissatisfaction with the serialization of *The Little Sister*. As these became increasingly unlikely, he felt he had to take drastic action and, in August, decided he could no longer continue to employ Juanita Messick. Characteristically, he attempted to sidestep the awkwardness by breaking the news to her in a letter.

The Long Goodbye sold well in England and was well reviewed. The *New Statesman* said, "the rhythm of his prose is superb, and the intensity of feeling he packs into his pages makes every other thriller-writer look utterly silly and superficial."[70] Good reviews, however, did not pay the bills. On top of money worries, there was also his continual concern about Cissy, who had been in and out of the hospital with intestinal problems since getting back from London. Ray himself was also rapidly losing weight. His doctor told him that he was malnourished and needed to rest and eat. He does not seem to have taken that advice and, by the summer of 1953, was complaining constantly about tiredness and had lost so much weight that he had to add two new holes to his belt. Was this the result of anxiety? In part, surely yes, but, back in 1945, while trying to finish *The Blue Dahlia* and fueling himself with alcohol, he had been forced to take vitamin shots because he was not eating. Ray was also drinking heavily again.

1953 and 1954 should have been good years. The publication of *The Long Goodbye* and its reception should have been cause for Ray and Cissy to celebrate, but illness made that impossible. Ray was getting increasingly frustrated in La Jolla. He thought the doctors there were no good and were not helping Cissy to get any better. Whenever he had to get an X-ray, he went up to Los Angeles. Cissy could not always get out of bed. On other days, Ray would take her for a drive but would have to return quickly when she started feeling unwell. So, early in 1954, they put the house on the market and seriously started to consider moving to the south of France. Just as with his trip to London, Ray sent out a slew of letters asking for information about the area.

In September 1954, Ray broke his toe because he had gout. One of the causes of gout is increased consumption of alcohol. Perhaps Ray was fighting with drink what he must have known to be true: that Cissy was fast approaching death right before his eyes, and there was nothing he could do.

Her condition took a marked turn for the worse in the autumn of 1954. By now she was only getting up for part of the day and to have dinner with Ray. Their afternoon teas had been quietly forgotten. She was suffering from fibrosis of the lungs and, in October, a new doctor suggested that she try cortisone, with which he had had some success. Ray hoped that it would let her get out of bed at least. Cissy did not react well to the drug and began to get confused. Her memory was badly affected and Ray had to measure out the drugs to keep her from taking them over and over again. When it became clear that the cortisone was having no effect, the doctor prescribed another drug, ACTH, which had to be injected. This did not work either and, by the end of the month, she was in the hospital with pneumonia. The toll of the drugs was considerable and they left Cissy puzzled; she could not understand why she was in the hospital and begged to be taken home. When Ray and the doctors finally relented and took her home, she seemed to rally, but, the following day, was demanding to be taken back to the hospital. The doctors then tried more drugs, this time Rauwolfia, which Ray was told would induce "a condition of euphoria."[71] The doctor hoped that it would make her compliant enough to agree to move to a sanatorium, but it did not seem to have much impact and Cissy asked to be taken home once more.

Ray was exhausted and had to rely on Cissy's sister, Lavinia, and then a team of nurses to get through the long days. Cissy could not stop coughing and she could not even go to the bathroom on her own. Very early on the morning of December 7, Cissy appeared in Ray's bedroom. She had somehow evaded the nurses and stood there looking pale and ghostlike. Ray wrote later that this was the point when he truly accepted that she was dying. The following day he took her into the hospital for the last time. She was now in an oxygen tent but would reach out from under it to hold her husband's hand. At one point she asked him "Is this the way you wanted it?"[72]

On the morning of December 12, Ray was at home when he got a call from the hospital telling him Cissy was very bad. Thankfully, Lavinia and her son were staying with him and drove Ray to the hospital, "breaking all the traffic regulations."[73] When they got there, Cissy was in bed:

> they had taken the oxygen tent away and she was lying with her eyes half open. I think she was already dead. Another doctor had his stethoscope over her heart and was listening. After a while he stepped back and nodded. I closed her eyes and kissed her and went away.[74]

In that moment, Ray's life came to an abrupt and shuddering halt. Cissy was dead and Ray, who had loved her indescribably, was now truly alone.

CHAPTER FOURTEEN

"SIT WITH ME WHILE I DREAM"

As Cissy's life faded out to nothing, Ray's own existence began to flicker in and out of focus. Cissy's death undid Ray—it left him in pieces, and he would never be able to put himself back together again.

In the immediate aftermath, he was supported by Cissy's sister, Lavinia, and his nephew. They helped him arrange the funeral and started to tidy up the loose ends left by Cissy's death. After a few days, they had to head back to Los Angeles, leaving Ray alone. He took some comfort from the swell of condolences that arrived in a great flood, writing to one correspondent:

> She was the beat of my heart for thirty years. She was the music heard faintly on the edge of sound.[1]

Usually parsimonious, he allowed himself a transatlantic phone call to speak to Hamish Hamilton, and wrote to him separately a tender letter that the publisher would later share with friends:

> . . . she was the light of my life, my whole ambition. Anything else I did was just the fire for her to warm her hands at. That is all there is to say.[2]

But letters offered only so much comfort; he needed more. Ray spent the days and weeks after Cissy died more or less on his own and took to sleeping in her room—that is, when he could summon up the will to sleep. At other times, he sat listening to her favorite piano music in the living room, drinking, hoping that its ghostly memory would help bring sleep or, at the very least, numb his pain. But one drink was not enough and so, before long, he was hitting the bottle harder than ever. On February 8, Ray celebrated his wedding anniversary in the same manner as always, filling the house with red roses and drinking champagne. The more he drank, the more morose he became.

On several occasions, he called friends claiming he intended to kill himself. Even Roger Machell in London received a call. On February 22, things came to a head. Ray telephoned a friend, a captain in the La Jolla police department, and told him this time he was going to do it. Juanita Messick, who was helping him during this difficult period, had arrived earlier and overheard the conversation. She managed to calm Ray down, sat him in front of the TV and slipped out to make coffee. In her absence, he snuck away. Just as Messick realized that Ray was not where she had left him, a young policeman, who had been dispatched to the house by the police captain, arrived at the door. Together, Messick and the policeman searched the house, but Ray was nowhere to be seen. Then they heard a shot. It had come from the bathroom. The policeman approached the room cautiously and found Ray sitting in the bath, wrapped in a shower curtain, trying to push the barrel of the gun into his mouth. The first shot had missed and a second had failed to fire. The policeman arrived just in time to stop him from trying again.

Ray woke up in the county hospital with a hazy memory of what had happened. His attempted suicide was most likely another cry for help, having failed to elicit the necessary response from friends by other means. He was lucky that the gun was old and the ammunition damaged. A day or so later, his young friend Neil Morgan, a journalist on the *San Diego Tribune*, visited Ray in the hospital and found him in a desperate state. Ray begged Morgan to help get him out. Morgan acquiesced but, as a condition of his discharge, Ray was to be taken to a sanatorium in Chula Vista, close to the Mexican border, to recover his health and to dry out. Once there, he was shut away in a locked ward and pumped full of drugs. They threatened him with electroshock therapy and insulin shock treatment. He found himself in a scene from one of his own books and, after six days, he left. Had he stayed, he might have been given enough help to keep him on a steady path of sobriety, or perhaps the extreme treatments would have caused even more damage. Either way, his suicide attempt landed him in the hospital for the first time but did not get him the help he needed.

During his convalescence, Ray had made one decision: the house in La Jolla would forever be haunted by the ghost of Cissy and so he needed to move out. He checked into a small motel and put the house on the market. With this done, he made plans to travel back to England. London, he hoped, would distract him from Cissy's death. Somehow, despite the frequent misery and frustrations of his last trip, he had fixed it in his mind as a brief period of happiness which he wanted to relive. London had always held a strange fascination for Ray, despite it being a place of painful memories. In part this was because he felt his talent was better recognized there. But, equally, London— and perhaps England itself—reflected Ray's self-image in a sharper form than California had ever done. Either way, he felt comfortable there; at the very least, it would get him away from Southern California.

Meanwhile, Ray's health was deteriorating because of his ever heavier drinking. Before he could go anywhere, he had to visit a doctor to cure his chronic sinus problems. The best was in New York and so, in April, instead of booking on a Swedish cargo ship for his trip to Britain, as originally planned, Ray got a ticket for the *Mauretania*, which would sail from New York. He took a train east to meet the doctor and, a few days later, set sail across the Atlantic. Around this time, he also started to work on his fiction again, sketching out scenes and planning dialogue in an effort to keep his mind busy. He arrived in London in April 1955 and checked into the Connaught hotel, the place of which he had written so disparagingly only a few years earlier.

In London, he found, at last, friends who were prepared to offer him real support. Hamish Hamilton invited him to lunch right away. Although the Hamiltons knew of his attempted suicide, they were not prepared for the morose man that turned up at their doorstep. One guest, Natasha Spender, wife of the poet Stephen Spender, remarked that Ray looked like he had an "aura of despair."[3] She considered him amiable but elderly; awkward but polite. Once Yvonne Hamilton had explained his story, though, Natasha decided to invite him to dinner the following week. Ray accepted her invitation, on the condition that there wouldn't be "any literary heavyweights around."[4]

This was the beginning of a vital relationship for Ray. Natasha Spender would be a rock for him over the next eighteen months. She was at the heart of literary London in the mid-1950s, having married Stephen Spender during the war. Despite his being gay, the couple had started a family and settled in a large house in St. John's Wood in North West London, to the west of Regent's Park. Natasha herself had endured a complicated childhood. Her mother was the celebrated stage actress Rachel (Ray) Litvin, and her father was the equally well-known music critic Edwin Evans. Evans had a wife elsewhere, so, despite a passionate love affair, the couple were not married and Natasha was born out of wedlock. She did not discover who her father was until she reached the age of eleven; she nevertheless inherited his talent for music, along with her mother's wilfulness. When Stephen Spender took her to meet his former housekeepers, two sisters known collectively as Berthella, one sister remarked "she's illegitimate, and don't care who knows it."[5] This strong will must have reminded Ray of Cissy. His wife had been fierce at times, a quality he respected and adored. Like Cissy, Natasha also played the piano, and had performed in concert at the Royal Albert Hall and on BBC radio shortly before Ray arrived in London. Natasha was also extremely beautiful.

Ray turned up to this first dinner at the Spenders' house on Loudon Road not knowing what to expect. He was probably a bit drunk—possibly a lot drunk, in fact—but was warmly welcomed. In an effort to keep his mind off Cissy, the guests at dinner were happy to praise Ray's work. All of them were younger members of the Spender circle without literary connections, according to Natasha, though Sonia Orwell seems to have been among the guests. The next day, he reported back to Hamish Hamilton:

> The whole thing last night was rather weird. Natasha Spender is a charming and devoted hostess and served up a magnificent meal and everybody got tight. They poured it on me a little too thick, I imagine. A Sonia somebody . . . said that I was the darling of British intellectuals and all the poets raved about me and that Edith Sitwell sat up in bed (probably looked like Henry IVth, Part 2) and read my stuff with passion. . . . The funny part of it was that they seemed quite

sincere. I tried to explain to them that I was just a beat-up pulp writer and that in the USA I ranked slightly above a mulatto.

Well anyhow it was a lot of fun.[6]

Spender's recollection was slightly different. She remembered that Ray was self-deprecating and that the evening was generally a jolly one, but she and her guests were also aware of his "great brooding silences and the shadow of his desperation [that] had hung in the air."[7] Though everyone drank that night, Ray drank the most, and Natasha and her friends were alarmed by his behavior, taking pity on the widower. They recognized that he was in pieces and that drinking was his crutch. Cissy was not discussed at dinner, but Natasha was aware that Ray had been harboring the darkest of thoughts. Once he had staggered out and said his goodbyes, she started planning ways she could help him. A few days later, together with a cohort of female friends, she had established a babysitting service for Ray. The members of the "shuttle service," as they termed themselves, thought that he was less likely to try and kill himself if he had an engagement with a lady to look forward to. Ray, they hoped, was too much of a gentleman to let a woman down.[8]

Ray's diary suddenly filled up with a whirlwind of lunches and dinners and teas, but these, though welcome, also tended to involve drinking. Then there were the nights, which were late and long. Ray still could not sleep and would drink and write, or drink and listen to records, through the early hours of the morning. His one constant thought was Cissy. Drink and grief were a toxic combination and Natasha and her friends would sometimes find themselves woken by a phone call in the wee hours only to hear silence on the other end. It was obvious that these calls were from Ray. He would sit there quietly, breathing heavily into the mouthpiece for long stretches of time before launching into a monologue about death. Whichever of the shuttle service had received the call would remind Ray that he had an important date for lunch or breakfast and thereby cheer him up:

> Sometimes "Hang on till breakfast-time" was the only way to deal with those early morning calls if all else failed, and then one or other of us would go have breakfast with him.[9]

Ray was certainly a mess but, as with his previous suicide attempts, there is always a question of the seriousness of his intent. They tended to come about during periods of heavy drinking, as when he had threatened suicide shortly before being fired by Dabney. Was he really suicidal or just reaching out for a connection with somebody? For years Cissy had been there for him. Now, without her, he was confused. Cissy had bought into his view of himself and played along, and now he needed someone else to do the same—a kindly gaze under which to play the gallant, the gentleman, the intellectual. These new friends allowed him to be the protector that he had always pictured himself to be. He chose to forget that they might be helping him and instead, in this situation, would pay for dinner, thank them with gifts, sometimes flowers, at other times expensive jewelry that would have to be quietly returned the next day.

Ray seems to have misjudged some of his new friends' intentions. This was his first experience of female friendship after Cissy and he did not know how to categorize the attention of these women. In his own mind, he was courting them. At the very least, he allowed himself to believe that their attention was because he was a charming, self-deprecating man, rather than driven by pity. In the end, he was sure, they were bound to fall for him and they would end up in bed together. The trouble was, no one in his support group was aware that he might think of them romantically, at first. According to Natasha Spender, most members of the shuttle service assumed he was a gay man locked firmly in the closet. Little did they realize they were playing a part in an elaborate courtship. Sex became an irritating thread that Ray could not help but pull at. He would talk about sex at lunch, regaling his guests with intricate tales of seduction. In one tale, a wealthy blonde divorcée caught Ray's eye and, without his saying very much at all, ended up back in his bedroom to drink Scotch. Ray could make these tales entertaining and vivid and, in this liberal circle of friends, such things were not frowned upon. He wrote several of these stories down, including "A Routine to Shock the Neighbors: Faster, Slower, Neither," which describes, in dialogue only, the difficulties a man has keeping his partner quiet during sex. It is not erotic and only the frank handling of the subject matter makes it in any way pornographic. It is lighthearted, and its mixture of joking obfuscation over the act of love—the rhythm of sex is continually referred to in musical terms—and its parody of English speech suggests that it was intended to tease an audience in an adult way:

> "Oh much better darling. I'm afraid—oh, couldn't you please—an occasional pause rather spices the—"
>
> "Conversation, I expect you were about to say. I gather that you mean presto ma non agitato?"
>
> "Exactly, darling, and you are so understanding. And darling, and—oh—oh—darling!"
>
> "Yes, darling?"
>
> "Oh—darling—darling—darling—please don't speak!"
>
> "Not a word."
>
> "Oh, darling, darling, DARLING!—please don't speak."
>
> "I'm not. You're doing all the talking."

According to Natasha Spender, these fantasies began to increase in number and frequency. They may have started out sexual in nature but became something more. One that she recalled involved a doctor whom Ray could not stand. He was always outdoing Ray with women, but Ray had a habit of besting the man in verbal exchanges and, no matter what the doctor threw at him, he could conjure up a barbed reply to leave him slack jawed. This particular story contains more than a hint of Philip Marlowe and it suggests that one of the motivations behind these elaborate fictions was Ray's desperation to appear like his hero. When he could not outdo his enemies, or could not find someone to kick against, he made up stories to make the same point.

A desire to believe in his own heroic nature also led Ray to exaggerate the situation of some members of the shuttle service and their need for his assistance. One woman was to be alone in her apartment in Eaton Square while her flatmate traveled and Ray was appalled that she should be left unattended, unsupported. He worried about the terrible things that might afflict a lone woman and did not care that she had a close circle of friends, or that she was living in one of London's safest districts. To him, she was as vulnerable to abuse as Merle Davis in *The High Window*. One of his most frequently repeated stories was of rescuing a distressed woman in the street because there was "no one else around to do it."[10] In his drunken state, he was turning his day-to-day world into that of his fiction, placing himself in the role of Marlowe.

The ladies of the shuttle service were not the only women in Ray's life. During his hospitalization earlier in the year, Louise Loughner had written to him. A fan who had read about his attempted suicide in a local paper, she quickly became an important correspondent and in Ray's letters to her from London, he described the city:

> There are many things in London that might amaze you. . . . The breathtaking beauty of the English squares flaming with tulips three and even four feet tall. The flowering pear trees, the blazing green of the leaves, the infinite charm and courtesy of the people, the taxis that turn in the middle of a block, the traffic control system that makes any American city ridiculous, the absolute storm of Rolls-Royces outside any smart hotel at lunch time . . . the absolute indifference of these people to any kind of physical danger . . .[11]

Here, London offers a complete contrast to Los Angeles. California is stale and dry, London verdant and energetic, with people who, though wealthy enough to afford Rolls-Royces, are noble enough not to be corrupted by money. Their indifference to physical danger is presumably a reference to the Blitz, and a quality Ray would often romanticize in his letters. The city here is as much a fantasy as his stories.

By May 1955, Ray had left the Connaught. He claimed he was thrown out for seducing women but, if he was evicted, it is more likely that his drunkenness was the cause. He moved to a second-floor apartment in Eaton Square, placing him at the heart of a circle of friends including Helga Greene, a literary agent to whom he had been introduced. The apartment was luxurious and could be accessed via an elevator that dropped guests off directly in the lobby. The living room was decorated with "some horrible pictures of fruit"[12] so he preferred to eat in the kitchen.

To keep his mind busy, it was arranged that Ray would contribute a long article to the *Spectator* magazine. He was to write three thousand words of "hard cold brutal language"[13] to describe the execution of Erskine Childers, the novelist and Irish revolutionary who had been sentenced to death in Ireland.

Though he would not make any money out of the project, he described the commission as a "dream,"[14] probably because it meant that the literary London crowd had accepted him as a writer. Several of his friends were contributors to the magazine and, in allowing him to write three thousand words, rather than the standard fourteen hundred, Ray felt the *Spectator*'s editors were showing their eagerness to include him among the ranks of their writers. The article fell through. Ray found plenty of people to blame—Erskine Childers's wife, for example, who would not let him access her husband's papers—but, like so many of his projects, a bright and hopeful start had quickly fizzled out.

Shortly after, and much to everyone's surprise, Ray announced that he was going to get sober. In part, this was prompted by his increasingly strong feelings for Natasha Spender. Around this time, he mentioned in a letter that "his one and only"[15] was going to Italy, and it is quite likely that this refers to Natasha. She liked to travel to Italy, spending holidays on Lake Garda in the north. According to her own account of the period, she was certainly the focus of his most romantic actions. Once, during a particularly bad bout of drinking, Natasha and a friend had conspired to keep secret from Ray that she was due to give a concert in Bournemouth. After the concert, Spender and the conductor were invited to a dinner with the mayor and local council in a vast and rather empty hotel dining room. Halfway through the meal, a door at one end of the room swung open with a bang and through it staggered Raymond Chandler with a white face and white scarf, in full evening dress. Though astonished by this arrival, the guests invited Ray to join them, and he proceeded to get drunk. By the end of the evening, the conductor had to half-carry Ray to a waiting Rolls-Royce, which was filled with carnations and bottles of champagne in buckets of ice. Since this was similar to the way he had celebrated anniversaries with Cissy, it must have been meant as a romantic gesture. Not quite knowing what to say, Natasha and the conductor squeezed themselves into the back of the car with Ray and they drove off into the night towards London. The party stopped briefly somewhere in the New Forest to drink the champagne—they were joined by the driver, perhaps to help reduce Ray's own consumption—after which, Ray promptly passed out. Spender noted that, as they approached London, Ray woke up and whispered soberly: "I know what you are all doing for me, and I thank you, but the truth is I really *want* to die."[16] Was this a moment of clarity for Ray? Natasha Spender wrote it off as an attempt to get her attention.

But if Ray's sudden sobriety was prompted by his love for Natasha Spender, the Spender family resolutely refused to notice. As he sobered up, the shuttle service pitched in, nursing him through the darkest hours. To help with his recovery, Ray was invited to join Stephen and Natasha on a break at Lake Garda. Natasha did not say much about the trip in her account other than that Ray remained sober throughout. To keep him so, they took him sightseeing in Venice and Verona, but Ray complained that he preferred to sit in the Cafe Dante and drink coffee rather than look at the buildings. He was not much of a holiday guest. Still, it seems to have worked, and he returned to London sober and was able to reflect on his drinking. His letters reveal some other reasons for his desire to stop drinking, as in this description of his addiction, written in London in September 1955, which reveals a wretched man:

> I start off with a drink of white wine and end up drinking two bottles of Scotch a day. Then I stop eating. After four or five days of that I am ill. I have to quit and the withdrawal symptoms are simply awful. I shake so that I can't hold a glass of water. I can't stand up or walk without help. One day I vomited eighteen times. I wasn't sick at all, but something kept dropping down at the back of my throat from inflamed sinuses and every time that happened I gagged my life out. For three days I could drink nothing but sips of ice water.[17]

Worst of all was that being a drunk reminded him of his father's fate: "My father was an alcoholic and I have lived all my life with the fear of becoming one."[18] The shadow of Maurice Chandler was dark and Ray had never escaped it. The persona of a noble hero that he presented was in some part created as a defence against his father's influence. As a child, he had watched Maurice beat his mother and been unable to help. In London in the 1950s, as he became more and more dependent on alcohol, rather than become a violent drunk himself, he invented situations, as might a child, in which he could save other unhappy women.

In October, a sober Ray needed to head home. He had outstayed his visa and he risked having to pay tax in the UK if he stayed any longer and so, on the sixth, he set off for New York on the *Queen Elizabeth*. "The voyage was hell,"[19] he wrote to his British lawyer, Michael Gilbert. Sobriety made him grumpy and shy so he endured the crossing sitting alone in a corner, observing the rest of the passengers. It was quite a contrast to the young man who had boarded the SS *Merion* in 1912, full of hope and ambition about America. On arriving in New York, he went to stay with friends who lived outside the city and hoped to visit Colorado to see his longtime correspondent James Sandoe, though unfortunately, that trip fell through. Instead, Ray headed back to La Jolla in early November, putting himself up at the Hotel Del Charro ("the price of my room [is] slightly above what I paid at the Connaught, but an infinitely better room"[20]), where he pined for England and the constant attention of the shuttle service.

To remind him of London, Ray smoked Craven A cigarettes ("no match for Benson and Hedges"[21]) and wrote to his London friends:

> Am I comfortable? No. Am I happy? No. Am I weak, depressed, no good, and of no social value to the community? Yes.[22]

Five days later, he could take it no more and booked himself a ticket back to London. This time, to make sure he got there faster, he flew from Los Angeles to Denmark, and from there to Britain. Loneliness was only part of his desire to return: he was also worried about Natasha and felt that her husband was letting her down. Stephen Spender seemed a strange figure to Ray. Natasha had probably told him of his homosexual past, though Ray may also have read about it in Spender's frank memoir *World Within World*, which Hamish Hamilton sent him. At various times, Ray professed admiration for Stephen but, at others, claimed to hate the man for what he had done to Natasha. When he learned that she was to undergo an operation on December 12, one year on from the day Cissy had died, he began to worry that she too would be taken away from him. Under this strain, he started to drink again. His brief period of sobriety was over.

This time, Ray booked a room at the Ritz rather than the Connaught, and there the effects of this new bout of drinking became evident. Natasha was shocked to see him in a worse state than when they had first met and, again, was determined to help him. Ray passed off her willingness to save him as part of her personality:

She said once that if she were sitting in a restaurant, say, and looked across at some person at another table and realized, as she would being a little psychic about such things, that that person was in a state of absolute despair, she would have to do something about it.[23]

He worked himself into a state about Natasha and, perhaps confusing her with Cissy, insisted that she should be taken somewhere hot and dry in preparation for her operation. Though the surgical procedure was regarded by the Spender family as routine, they acquiesced to his wish, more to help Ray than Natasha. She also hoped that a trip to Tangiers would help bring his drinking under control again, but she was wrong. Once they arrived, Ray's eagerness to help turned inward and he became increasingly difficult to deal with, locking himself away in his room, refusing to appear at meals, and, of course, drinking. She wrote:

> He spoke almost incessantly of Cissy, but his previous moods of lyricism and resignation had given way to far more complex emotions concerning his whole past life, and he would be submerged in retrospective anger and active despair.[24]

It was an unproductive trip and it left Ray in a terrible state, but the Spenders continued to support him. When Natasha went into the hospital for her operation, Stephen kept Ray calm. It should have been the other way around, though Stephen was not really worried. Then, sometime after December 12, Ray collapsed at the Ritz in the middle of the night. He woke up in the London Clinic in Marylebone under the care of a doctor who made him take a two-week drying-out cure. This helped in a small way, giving him a new burst of energy, but did not heal his pain, and his first act on being discharged was to pour himself a very large Scotch.

The doctor looking after Ray was a friend of the Spenders and was sensitive to his new charge's problems. Natasha later claimed that the doctor diagnosed Ray with tertiary malaria to spare his embarrassment, but Ray offered a different account. In a letter written a few months later, Ray claimed that the lack of alcohol paralysed his right leg and the doctor blamed only that on the malaria. Chandler refused to accept this and sent the doctor back to try again. He said that, after two days in an X-ray room, the doctor returned with a new diagnosis of diaphragmatic hernia, but Ray refused to accept this, too, and so fired the doctor. His frustration probably came about because, even if his drinking was not being pinned as the direct cause of his problems, he would still be expected to stop. He claimed that another doctor offered up a much better solution:

> The last one gave me about seventeen kinds of pills, and said he thought it was all psychosomatic. There is such a thing, I had a positive experience of it while my wife was dying. He said I was probably drinking too much for the happiness of my liver, but that my history showed that every time I stopped drinking, which I can do quite easily, I lapsed into melancolia [sic], which was far more dangerous.[25]

Ray had already admitted to another friend that he had trouble stopping drinking but, at this point at least, he seems to have forgotten that and embraced the new doctor's explanation because it meant he could keep drinking with a clear conscience. Perhaps this was pure invention on his part—he would not be the first alcoholic to create a fiction to justify his habit—or maybe he really did find a doctor who recognized that it was too late for Ray to be cured, and that the only way to give him any semblance of life was to let him keep drinking.

By now, Ray's bank balance was under pressure, and it was unrealistic to keep living at the Ritz. Natasha found him an apartment at Carlton Hill, close to her own home in St. John's Wood. It was neither comfortable nor stylish, but it came with a housekeeper, Auntie, who, when she was not scared by Ray's drunken hallucinations, kept the place spick-and-span. It also meant that if he was too drunk to look after himself, he could visit the Spenders and stay on their couch. It was Stephen who would sit up late with Ray, listening to his ramblings, rather than Natasha, something which, had he been conscious, might have disappointed him. Why did the Spenders spend so much time on him? In a letter written to Louise Loughner in 1956, Ray claimed that his moving close to the Spenders was part of an elaborate scheme to allow him to conduct a socially acceptable affair with Natasha:

> In rescuing me she probably got in a lot deeper than she intended and you know what happened. But there was never at any time any

question of my being anywhere but on the fringe of her life. There was never any question of divorce because as she said it would be "over my children's dead bodies." And even if there had been, it would have done no good, because I would not have taken on the children. She wanted me to become a part of the Spender family, for the sake of appearances and to avoid gossip, and to live around the corner so that she could drop in on me when she had a chance.[26]

In this letter, Ray goes on to say that their relationship was a sexual one:

Since her operation last December, she hasn't even given me herself. It seemed somehow to affect her sex feelings, which is probably all to the good.[27]

Natasha Spender always denied that she had an affair with Ray. She was asked several times by people who knew her, which, if nothing else, suggests that their relationship did raise questions. She did not see his letter to Louise Loughner before she died in 2010, but her account of their relationship always presents Ray as a fantasist, whose drinking made him believe in his own heroic self. He was certainly drunk for large periods of 1955, and there are other reports of his habit of fictionalizing parts of his life, but, at the same time, there is also evidence that his mind stayed sharp. Michael Gilbert, Ray's lawyer in London, trod carefully around the issue of his drinking in the essay "Autumn in London" (collected in *The World of Raymond Chandler*), but one thing he made very clear was that Ray was well liked. Gilbert described him as "a very human and likable person"[28] and he wrote that:

[In London] There were people whom he [Ray] liked being with, and who liked being with him.[29]

This, enigmatic though it is, suggests that Ray might not have been the awkward, pitiable drunk Natasha Spender described. His letters, written at this time, are varied. The handwritten ones can be a mess but the typed letters are as clear and crisp as ever, though Ray did claim to be able to type perfectly under the influence of alcohol. Could it be, then, that Natasha's essay, "His Own Long Goodbye," masked her true feelings for him and that they did indeed conduct an affair? Ray certainly wanted at least one woman, Louise Loughner, to believe that he could have seduced Natasha.

Whatever the answer, if the Spenders had hoped that being close to them would curb Ray's drinking, they were quickly disappointed. He was drinking as heavily as before and the occasional moments of sobriety that had punctuated his last visit were distant memories.

He continued in this routine through the early part of 1956 until, in March, his nationality suddenly became a problem. Though he had been born an American, he had become a British citizen in 1907 so that he could join the Civil Service. In 1948, the Southern District Court of California ruled that this was invalid, and Ray considered himself an American citizen. He applied for British residency sometime in late 1955 or at the beginning of 1956 but, in March 1956, the British Home Office wrote back to tell him that the government regarded him as a national despite what the court in America had ruled:

> If I applied for a British passport it would be given me, but then our Government would rule that by making this application I was voluntarily expatriating myself, and would refuse me an American passport.[30]

It was a sticky situation to be in. Though he had made it clear that he wanted to remain in London, he did not wish to do so at the expense of his US citizenship. If he gave that up, he would only be able to return home as a tourist, and may have had to convert all his assets into sterling. He remained in England for a few more months but, by May 1956, had long outstayed his visa. In the end, he was forced to return to America, flying to New York via Iceland on May 11.

The flight was delayed by storms and, on arrival, Ray had to deal with the "studied insolence" of American customs officers. All in all, it was a difficult experience but, once through to the other side, he was met by Jessica Tyndale, a friend he had made on an earlier boat to London, who drove him to the Grosvenor Hotel on Fifth Avenue, where he stayed for the next few days. He was not planning on remaining in New York for long. His romantic focus seems to have shifted by this point from Natasha to Louise Loughner.

Loughner, unfortunately, remains an enigma. There are no known photographs and scarcely any details of her life or character on record, other than what can be gleaned from her correspondence with Ray. She had come into his life shortly after Cissy's death and soon became a regular correspondent. She provided a sounding board for Ray to discuss his relationship with Natasha, whether this was a genuine exercise in confession or mere fantasy. His immediate plan was to fly to San Francisco, where Loughner lived, on June 2, and he issued this warning before he set off:

> . . . provide yourself with a bottle of Scotch, although I'll probably have one on me. . . . This is a ten hour flight and I shall arrive in a very dilapidated condition, screaming for a drink.[31]

But these plans were put on hold when Ray was hospitalized again. He visited Ralph Barrow (an old friend dating back to the 1920s when they had both worked in downtown Los Angeles), and his wife in Chatham, but the stay was not a happy one. Ray was not eating at all and, during a visit from Hardwick Mosely, an occasional correspondent who worked in sales at Houghton Mifflin, he fell down the stairs and had to be driven back to New York. By this point, he was really very unwell and, two days after being sent to New York, was taken to a hospital by ambulance, where he endured sixteen hours of blood transfusions. Ray's admissions to the hospital were increasing in frequency and in seriousness. His long slide into debilitating and unrecoverable alcoholism was accelerating.

In the short term, this stay in the hospital seemed to do some good and, in the comfort of the medical care, Ray seemed better and was able to write to Loughner again. Malnourishment was clearly a problem, and the doctors were having to teach him to eat properly:

> Now I am eating three times as much as I normally do, even when I feel well, and the food is not of the quality I am used to either, although for a hospital it is quite fair. They make good soups, but they can't cook simple things like rice or mashed potato. These plus green vegetables are the test of cooking. Still, as I said, I am eating. . . .[32]

Ray was in a very sorry state. Hospitalized and malnourished, unable to stop drinking, his body was in pieces. He headed back to La Jolla and, by the middle of the month, was staying at the Hotel Del Charro, before renting a small apartment at 6926 Neptune Place. In La Jolla, he had more friends than in New York, though still very few, and people like Neil Morgan were willing and able to help out. It also brought him closer to Loughner. Ray was well enough to cook for himself, and his letters to Loughner make much of this. Perhaps he was trying to reassure her that he was a healthy man:

> Last night I cooked two lamb chops, boiled and then fried the last boiling potato, and ate a lot of raw celery. Pretty good, huh? During the afternoon I had a bowl of cream of chicken soup, and sometime during the day I had an egg, two bananas and several slices of bread and butter—and I mean butter. My inside plumbing is back to normal after quite a struggle. I think that is what was making me feverish. Slept around 8 hours last night, got up at six a.m. I guess I woke up because I had had enough. I got up at the same time yesterday, but with less sleep.[33]

This reassurance was essential because Ray was thinking of asking her to marry him.

Ray decided to fly to San Francisco to meet her. For a month, he lived in the Clift Hotel in the city, and courted Loughner assiduously. This was a theatrical affair on his part. He explained it to Michael Gilbert in early 1957:

> The technique is absolute, although rather demeaning. You make a booking in advance and say what sort of table you want. You arrive, and your car is taken away by an attendant in uniform. You enter and are greeted by the maître d'hotel (they have half a dozen captains) and you say: "Good evening, I believe I had a reservation but possibly you could manage to give me that table I rather wanted." At the same time you slip a folded five dollar bill into his hand. No, in this part of the country very few people do that. They demand, they do not politely ask. As a result of this approach (and five bucks) you get the best table in the house, and the captains won't even let the waiters wait on you, or pour the wine.[34]

His date was not allowed to open her own napkin; Ray would hold her chair until she was seated and help her remove her coat or wrap. At other times, he claimed to have arranged for his guest's menus to be handwritten. "An English lady doesn't realize what a rare thing it is in an American for this sort of thing to happen," he concluded and no doubt Louise Loughner was bowled over by this old-fashioned courtesy. When he raised the subject of marriage—it is not clear if he actually proposed to her or if they just discussed it—she was keen to share her life with him, despite his drinking. Ray started the process of changing his will in favor of Loughner and wrote to his friends to say that he planned to marry.

Ray seems to have been drawn to Loughner because he imagined her to be, like Natasha and Cissy, deeply unhappy. Louise Loughner had been married to a man named Sam but the marriage had disintegrated at some point in the early 1950s. She was struggling to survive in San Francisco and was beset by money troubles. Ray worried about what she would do as she got older. It was a familiar theme: he had stumbled upon a woman in need and he felt it was his duty to help her and, tellingly, the quality he admired most in Louise Loughner was her "courage."

In the end, though, the plans for marriage came to nothing. The downfall of their relationship was that Ray could not resist telling her about his love for other women, pouring his heart out to her, talking endlessly about Natasha Spender and Cissy. He would be able to provide for her in the short and long terms, he told her, but she had to accept one thing:

> . . . you must face the fact that I had and have a great love for another woman. . . . In a sense I shall always be in love with her. What has happened between us has cast a pall of tragedy over the rest of my life, because on my part it was a great and deep love and yet a very bitter one. . . . Have I discouraged you? God, I hope not, but it had to be said. No secrets between us at any time. I love you very much [underlined in pen]. I loved my wife very much. I loved Natasha very much. I hope you can understand that these loves do not diminish you; they, if anything, make me more tender and more understanding.[35]

Even if his love for Natasha was unrequited, this is an odd thing to tell a woman with whom you have recently discussed marriage. Ray clearly hoped that being open and honest about his feelings would strengthen their relationship. Shortly after this letter was written, the engagement was broken and Louise Loughner slowly faded from Ray's life. It sits in the archive at the University of California, Los Angeles, and is the last in the Loughner collection; it has been torn in two.

In a further bout of depression spurred on by drinking, Ray checked himself into a hospital in Pasadena. The Las Encinas Sanitarium had a good reputation for dealing with patients with addictions and the classicist in Ray would have appreciated the Latin inscription above the entrance: "Non est vivere sed valere vita" (not just to live but to enjoy living). The staff used psychiatric methods to help their patients deal with their problems, something that Ray had managed to avoid so far. Indeed, psychiatrists generally received short shrift from him and, in 1951, he had written: "I regard psychiatry as fifty per cent bunk, thirty per cent fraud, ten per cent parrot talk, and the remaining ten per cent just a fancy lingo for the common sense we have had for hundreds and perhaps thousands of years."[36] But this time he was prepared to try something different and submitted himself to their treatment. At first he was kept drugged, probably to help him through alcohol withdrawal symptoms and, once he had come through the worst of it, was given a series of tests, including the Rorschach inkblots, wood block, and thematic apperception. Ray was honest about his problems and the result:

> Finally the head guy said: "You think you are depressed, but you are quite wrong. You are a fully integrated personality and I wouldn't dream of trying to interfere with it by psychoanalysis or anything of that sort. All that's the matter with you is loneliness. You simply cannot and must not live alone. If you do you will inevitably drink, and that will make you sick. I don't care if you live with one woman or twenty, as long as you live with someone. That in my opinion is absolute."[37]

When he had been discharged from the hospital in New York, he had claimed that a new calm had overcome him and implied there was hope. A few months later, in California, again, he suggested that there was a solution to his problems as if to reassure his correspondents that his drinking was curable. This was not so. Ray returned to La Jolla and drank just as before. Though the doctor's reasoning that he drank because he was lonely was probably accurate, his friends in La Jolla did not prove as dedicated to him as those in London, and he felt isolated, as his letters from this period make clear: "La Jolla is no place in which to live. . . . There is no one to talk to."[38] He was faced with long, empty evenings, often visiting restaurants on his own when there was no one to go with: "If there is anything in life I hate it is going out to dinner alone. I could cook it, but that would be worse. Four days a week I have someone to go with, but the other three are hell."[39]

There was good news on the horizon in the familiar form of Natasha Spender. She had come to America on a concert tour and, in December 1956, agreed to meet Ray in Arizona for a short break. She had spoken to him by telephone and thought that he sounded well; she must have been buoyed by the reports of good health he was sending. On arriving at Phoenix airport, she found that he was as bad as ever. He had driven to the airport and his nerves were rattled from spending so long behind the wheel; he was also very drunk. He brought Natasha to his car, which he proceeded to drive straight into a post. Once he hit the main roads, he weaved and swerved through the traffic so much that she seriously considered throwing herself from the vehicle.

The next few days were hard. They stayed at the San Marcos Hotel and Bungalows where once again Natasha encouraged him to dry out, but unlike his most recent experience in Pasadena, he did so without the benefit of drugs. The process was horrible, but it worked. Just as she had in Italy and in Tangiers, Natasha took Ray on a short tour to keep him busy, taking in Arizona and Nevada and ending up in Palm Springs. Ray wrote that "Arizona never had such a going over."[40] Natasha began to feel that, despite superficial appearances, he had improved since she last saw him and detected what she called a new "forward-looking realism"[41] in him. She believed that he had become much more self-reliant. This, though, was a proud pose on Ray's part. Had she seen him in La Jolla, desperate, drunk, and alone, she would have known otherwise.

From Palm Springs, Natasha headed to Los Angeles, while Ray went back to La Jolla, where he noted that he had gained ten pounds, and spent most of his time working with his accountant. Ray felt that Natasha had a powerful effect on him and he was eager to spend more time with her. On January 6, 1957, he went up to Los Angeles, where she was staying with Dr. Evelyn Hooker, a psychologist, and her husband, Professor Edward Hooker. Ray seems to have planned to take Natasha away again, back to Palm Springs, but the Hookers were concerned when he arrived. They saw that he was distressed and emotional and they tried to persuade Natasha not to try to look after him, making the point that he needed professional care. Natasha had learned by now that disappointing Ray could lead to his spiraling further out of control, particularly when he was unstable, and so a compromise was reached: they would all spend some time in Los Angeles. Ray agreed, as he would have agreed to pretty much anything that would enable him to spend more time in Natasha's company. He saw in her an opportunity for stability, though it is not clear if he still thought he was in love with her.

The time in Los Angeles was not wasted. Ray was to be included in many of the Hookers' and Natasha's plans. This meant that he was invited to dinner at the writer Christopher Isherwood's home in Santa Monica. Isherwood had gone to school with W. H. Auden and, through him, had become friendly with the Spenders. Auden and Isherwood had left England in 1939 and, while Auden settled in Manhattan, Isherwood had traveled west, to California. He became an American citizen in 1946 and made Santa Monica his home. He had a lot in common with Ray. They had both been educated at British public schools but had turned their backs on England, and Isherwood had also recently been working on screenplays in Hollywood. He was also an admirer of Ray's writing. In an interview, Isherwood's partner, Don Bachardy, said:

> He [Isherwood] anxiously awaited the new Chandler novel. He couldn't get enough. He even reread Chandler and he would never read a book a second time unless he really admired the writer. There was fun in Chandler. Chris liked that.[42]

Ray was charmed by Isherwood and he insisted on taking him, the Hookers, and Natasha for a drive around Los Angeles, pointing out various points of interest, such as the place where Bugsy Siegel, the famous gangster, was shot dead. A few weeks later, he described Isherwood as "the only queer I have felt entirely at ease with."[43]

Despite these distractions, Ray continued drinking. His sobriety seemed to last only as long as Natasha Spender had the energy to fight for it. When she was with him, his eagerness to impress her gave him the strength to stop, or at least reduce his intake. When she was away, he drank out of loneliness. At some point, it was decided that Ray should take Natasha to Palm Springs. His letters suggest that he was still, to some extent, confusing her needs with those of Cissy:

> I've been here since Jan 7th [Palm Springs, Arizona] and may possibly be here until the end of the month, but it doesn't depend on me since I have an English friend [Natasha Spender] staying with me whom I should like to have as much dry air and sunshine as possible before returning to the bloody awful English winter, especially January, February and part of March. I went through it myself last year and it was rugged.[44]

Natasha Spender was not scared of English winters and did not have a lung problem. Ray was simply stuck in a pattern of gallant protectiveness that, for so long, he had enacted with his late wife.

In Palm Springs, as Natasha and Evelyn Hooker lay in the sun by the pool, Ray tried to get their attention by diving from the springboard and asking the women to rate his skills. He wanted to be the focus of everyone's attention because, without Cissy to validate him, he needed approval from elsewhere. When Cissy was alive, he had a reason to be the famous Raymond Chandler. He strove to impress her, and his biggest regret after she died was that he had never been able to write something good enough to dedicate to her. Even when she was ill, she brought him purpose. In Natasha Spender, he either found or imagined a new reason to live. This is also why he preferred London to Los Angeles—in Britain, his literary star burned so much brighter. For Ray, the worst thing was to be ignored. He would get frustrated when, at dinner, his fellow guests would talk about people he did not know:

> *I* think that people are extremely rude when they carry on a very private and intimate conversation (I call it "The Derek-Peter-Nigel Routine") which excludes another guest who may also, and it has happened to me, be the guest of honor.[45]

Without the attention of others, Ray worried that he would fade away and he went to great lengths to gain it, even compromising his much vaunted code of honor. This became clear in one of his most shameful acts of self-absorption. Six days into his visit to Palm Springs, the news arrived quite suddenly that Edward Hooker had died. A good man would have offered Evelyn Hooker his support and comfort; Ray did not. Here was an opportunity for him to show real nobility and self-sacrifice—to live up to years of self-mythologizing—but he failed. He put his own needs first, becoming frantic at the thought that Natasha would abandon him to help her friend. Evelyn, even in her grief, gave way and insisted that Natasha stay with Ray. In the end, it was decided that Natasha would, after all, go to Los Angeles for the funeral but that the following weekend Evelyn Hooker, Christopher Isherwood, and Don Bachardy would return to Palm Springs.

It was during this period, after the funeral, that Don Bachardy filmed Ray diving. The images suggest a perfectly normal holiday, providing no clue as to Ray's fragile health and state of mind. Pictures from the time show Ray as an old man, with a plump white belly protruding above a pair of surprisingly short swimming trunks. His greying hair is thin and his face looks sallow and puffy. Despite this, he looks happy and relaxed posing in front of the camera and there is no hint of the emotional turmoil going on around him.

As her time in California neared an end, Natasha decided to spend the last days alone with her recently bereaved friend. Ray took this decision personally and, in his mind, it "congealed . . . in immutable grievance"[46] according to Natasha Spender. Though they remained in contact, their relationship was never quite as close after this. He could not forgive her for this perceived abandonment, perhaps believing that his own grief entitled him to her support as much as Evelyn Hooker.

Ray headed back to La Jolla alone, but with a new resolve. His doctor had advised him that his drinking was a result of loneliness so he made a concerted effort to make friends. In London, he had found a circle of people who would look after him and, though he recognized that he would not be able to re-create the London shuttle service in Southern California, he hoped that if he could involve himself in the lives of others they might, in turn, take an interest in his. To a certain extent, Ray had always been engaged in the lives of his correspondents. During the war, he had sent food parcels to Hamish Hamilton and his old schoolmaster, H. F. Hose. After his release from the Las Encinas Sanitarium a few months earlier, he had taken up his correspondence with greater determination and focus. In particular, he developed a series of intimate relationships with female pen pals. One such woman was Deirdre Gartrell, a university student from New South Wales, Australia, who had first written to Ray to explain how his novels had helped her during a period of depression. Over time, their letters took an intimate turn, with Gartrell revealing more and more, and Ray responding in kind. He identified his appeal to her quite accurately:

> Surely you realize, that when you write so frankly to me, it is because I am far away and because we may never meet. I rather hope we shall, unless it destroys an illusion. You need the illusion. And it might be that if we did meet, and even if I didn't too much disappoint you, you would never again be able to open your heart to me.[47]

But Ray, too, needed the illusion—needed to feel useful to someone, as in London, where he had worried about and attempted to protect Natasha Spender.

Another woman he wrote to regularly was Helga Greene. She was a literary agent based in London and they had met during his visit there in 1955. Though she had not been part of the shuttle service, she had lived close to Ray's Eaton Square apartment, and visited him occasionally. On his return to America, he wrote to her frequently and they, too, became intimate. Ray would tell her about Cissy—she was a common topic in much of his correspondence—but he would also discuss other private matters. In one letter, he disclosed a teenage crush:

> I remember my first love, but that was a different world. When we met my throat choked up and I could hardly get a word out. To have held her hand would have been ecstasy, to have kissed her would have been unthinkable.[48]

In another, he wrote about his adolescence in more general terms:

> I think I was a strange boy in some ways, because I had an enormous personal pride. I never masturbated, thinking it dirty. (I had plenty of wet dreams however.)[49]

Sometimes, these letters would conclude "All my love, Ray," while others were more ecstatic: "Love, love, love." Greene did not flinch and their relationship quickly deepened. The regularity with which they exchanged missives and the questions Ray seemed to be answering suggest that she wanted to draw this side of him out into the light and he was happy to oblige. Sex was something Ray was used to discussing with his London friends but he always seems to have done so obscurely, writing what he thought were mildly pornographic vignettes, rather than talking openly about his own experiences. He revealed things to Helga he had perhaps told only to Cissy in the past. This gave him purpose, the hope of something more to come. He appointed Helga his agent in mid-1957, perhaps as a declaration of trust, and was soon talking about her as one of his "girl friends," a term he used for the women in his life who allowed him to look after them.

The trouble with these relationships though was that they were remote and so Ray also looked for a connection closer to home. Ray had started to look for a new secretary in January 1957 and placed an advertisement in the local paper, to which Jean Fracasse responded. She was a striking and vivacious blonde with experience in television. An Australian by birth, she had been educated in both Paris and London. She was also going through a vicious divorce.

Jean seems to have shared a lot in common with both Cissy and Natasha. Like them, she was an accomplished pianist but, more importantly in Ray's eyes, she was also a woman in need. He had always told people that he had rescued Cissy from an unhappy marriage and, years later, maintained that the Spender's marriage was a convenient sham. He soon became involved with Jean's family, establishing a relationship that was much more than one of employer and employee. He played with her children and would let them help around the house. Sybil, her daughter, would cut his yellow sheets of paper down to size for him to write on. Ray also helped find Jean a good divorce lawyer and paid her extra when she needed it.

Along with Helga Greene and Deirdre Gartrell, Jean Fracasse and her family gave Ray something to live for. It did not stop him from drinking, but their presence in his life and the feeling that they needed him helped dispel his loneliness. After his difficult and torrid relationship with Natasha

Spender, whether it was an affair or not, this brought a new stability to his life. A stability that he needed very much.

The latter part of 1956 and the beginning of 1957 also saw Ray take up his pen again and, with new focus, he started to work on a project he had abandoned in 1953. As Cissy lay dying, he had toyed with turning his 1947 screenplay *Playback* into a novel, but had grown bored with the project. In 1956, he picked it up again. In part, this was because he thought that writing would please Natasha Spender, and he wrote furiously while they vacationed in Palm Springs. He also recognized the benefits of staying busy, however, and so early 1957 saw a flurry of projects. Along with *Playback*, Ray wanted to write a book about doctors—a work of nonfiction based on his experiences with Cissy. Around the same time, he dusted off an idea he had had nearly twenty years earlier: *An English Summer*. In 1939, he had entertained thoughts that this would be the book that would allow him to leave detective fiction behind. He wrote to Hamish Hamilton to ask if he would be interested in publishing his letters in book form.

At some point, he ceased to be merely "keeping busy" and began to feel under pressure. During this period of frenetic creative activity, Ray was also beset with worries. He was fighting various battles with tax authorities in Britain which, if nothing else, seemed to generate a continuous stream of correspondence. Then there was Jean Fracasse's divorce which had become more and more bitter and with which Ray, ever chivalrous, found himself deeply involved. His solution to overwhelming worry and workload was, as always, to drink. His writing and his enthusiasm for *Playback* waned and, in August, things culminated in an incident—possibly a fall—that resulted in his breaking his wrist and having to return to a sanatorium to rest and recover.

Helga Greene had become increasingly concerned about her client and friend. Ray was discharged from the sanatorium at the end of August into the care of Jean Fracasse. She helped him restrain his drinking and encouraged him to start writing again. Despite these improvements, though, it was clear that he was still troubled. Helga arranged a visit toward the end of the year, flying out in December and staying with Ray in La Jolla before taking him up to Palm Springs for Christmas 1957. In her company he kept working and, on December 28, he wrote to Paul Brooks to say that he had finished the first draft of the novel *Playback*. Helga Greene and Jean Fracasse had, between them, coaxed the book from Ray. As a reflection of his gratitude, he dedicated the book to both.

Playback is generally regarded as the weakest of Ray's novels. It feels somehow incomplete, perhaps because he stitched it together from old material when his mind was not as sharp as it had once been. It was written, as were all his books, scene by scene, and though there was a plot worked out in advance, his method meant that this took a back seat while he created striking individual moments. Though the characters from the screenplay reappear, there are differences in the plot that suggest Ray found it hard to control the story's development.

The book opens when Marlowe is woken at home by a phone call from Clive Umney, "the lawyer," very early in the morning. He is tasked with following a woman who will be passing through Los Angeles station and reporting on her final destination. Following Betty Mayfield leads Marlowe to the town of Esmeralda, a settlement close enough to the coast and to San Diego to give away the fact that it is modeled on La Jolla. There, Marlowe takes a hotel room right next to Betty Mayfield and ends up introducing himself to her, but she flees from him and his offers of help. Later on, though, she reappears and begs for Marlowe's assistance. A man who had been blackmailing her has wound up dead on her balcony, though she does not know how, but, when Marlowe goes to help her, the body has vanished, leaving no hint, other than Betty's memory, as to what happened.

As in the screenplay, Betty has a hidden past—she has been accused of the murder of her husband, a violent drunk who happens to have been the son of a wealthy man on the East Coast. Much to the father's surprise and frustration, she has been acquitted of murder but, to avoid rumor, has left home and changed her name, finding herself in Southern California, hoping to start a new life. Though he does not know it, Marlowe is at first working for her former father-in-law but, when he overhears her being blackmailed, decides to help her instead.

In the screenplay, Ray had Betty accused of the blackmailer's murder and go on the run. An unlikely knight, a police detective called Killaine, believes in her innocence against all the evidence, and is able to help her. But Marlowe was not Killaine, and the introduction of Ray's private eye unbalanced the story. His scenes necessitated a new plot, one that took the story from the original theme—that your past cannot be escaped—but failed to replace it with anything substantial. This is one of *Playback*'s central flaws. Unlike *The Big Sleep*, *Farewell, My Lovely*, or any of the other novels, there seems to be no strong idea at all. In his earlier work, there was anger and frustration directed at corrupt officials and at Los Angeles, a city that encouraged corruption. There is a corrupt character in *Playback* in the form of Henry Kinsolving, Betty's father-in-law, but he is given short shrift by the local police chief, Captain Allesandro:

> Just what would you like me to do? Arrest someone who has been tried and acquitted, just because you are a big shot in Westfield, Carolina?[50]

In the earlier books, this might have been the sort of attitude Marlowe would demonstrate, resisting the power of the rich and humiliating them, but Ray was now moving in a different direction. In this novel, Marlowe is better suited to sex and seduction than being a detective, and this alters the whole tenor of the book. Marlowe wants to stand up for women like Betty Mayfield but he does not let that stop him from sleeping with her.

Indeed sex is much more important to *Playback* than to any other of Ray's novels. Marlowe sleeps with two women, Betty Mayfield and Miss Vermilyea, secretary to Clive Umney, "the lawyer." In *The Long Goodbye*, he slept with Linda Loring, but that was written with relative subtlety. In *Playback,* Ray is anything but:

> I took hold of her and she came into my arms without a word. I picked her up and carried her and somehow found the bedroom. I put her down on the bed. I peeled her skirt up until I could see the white thighs above her long, beautiful nylon-clad legs.

Compare that to the scene from *The Big Sleep*, written twenty years earlier, in which Carmen Sternwood attempts to seduce Marlowe, prompting him to react with fury and disgust. This new Marlowe is much more willing to take advantage of pliable women and to engage with them carnally. Though it is notoriously difficult to align a writer's life with his work, it does seem that a change came over Ray after the death of Cissy, and that leaked into *Playback* and its treatment of sex, and into the character of Marlowe.

Since his first visit to London without Cissy, sex seems to have been on Ray's mind. He would talk about it over drinks and shared his "Routine to Shock the Neighbors" stories. He claimed to have slept with Natasha Spender but also suggested that he had sex with other women, though this was possibly fantasy. To some of his friends, Ray claimed to be sexually naive, while to others, especially younger women, he painted himself as experienced and irresistible. This was definitely a fantasy. Cissy was more than likely his first serious relationship and probably his first sexual partner. Though he had affairs in the 1920s and 1930s, they were rare, and conducted under the influence of heavy drinking. Ray believed in sexual purity and true love for much of his life. Only late in life does he seem to have stopped thinking of sex as repellent and unnerving. Despite his reports to the contrary, it was not easy for a man in his late fifties who drank heavily to have sex in London or La Jolla, but, in *Playback*, he got the opportunity to explore his fantasies in detail.

Perhaps the secret of *Playback* is revealed in its final chapter. Marlowe has returned to Los Angeles, to his lonely bachelor's apartment, where he stares at a "blank wall in a meaningless room in a meaningless house." Typically, Marlowe pours himself a drink of whisky, but does not drink it: "Alcohol was no cure for this. Nothing was any cure but the hard inner heart that asked for nothing from anyone."[51] It seems that our last glance of Marlowe will be of him preparing to be alone forever. And then the phone rings. On the other end is Linda Loring, the woman with whom he had enjoyed a single night at the end of *The Long Goodbye*. For two years, she has remained faithful to him, without his being aware of it, and she asks him to join her in Paris. Marlowe insists on her coming to him in Los Angeles, and she agrees. He has found a partner and, perhaps, a solution:

> I reached for my drink. I looked around the empty room—which was no longer empty. There was a voice in it, and a tall, slim, lovely woman. There was a dark head on the pillow in the bedroom. There was that soft, gentle perfume of a woman who presses herself tight

against you, whose lips are soft and yielding, whose eyes are half blind.[52]

The phone rings again and this time it is Clive Umney, but the conversation is brief and to the point, allowing Marlowe to finish the book with:

I hardly heard it. The air was full of music.[53]

A woman is Marlowe's savior and, interestingly, she is presented in the same terms as Ray often described Cissy—as beautiful music. Was this Ray's epiphany? A moment of understanding where the world became pin sharp, where he saw that love was what was missing? Or was it a signal to someone else, a suggestion to a reader—perhaps Helga Greene or Jean Fracasse—that what he needed was to be loved? The parallels are too close to be pure coincidence. Raymond Chandler was scared to be alone and fantasized, most of all, about love and companionship.

It is little wonder that the novel was received less favorably than its predecessors. *Playback* was published in Britain by Hamish Hamilton in July 1958, and by Houghton Mifflin in America in October the same year. The reviews recognized it as a second-rate novel by a first-rate writer. A few readers might have wondered if it was a farewell but, as it was being made ready for publication, Ray made clear that he still harbored literary ambition. During his time with Helga Greene in Palm Springs, they had planned to write a play. Over dinner they cooked up a plot, the dramatis personae, and even a few lines from the final speech. Ray wanted to put the play on in England ("the best place in the world for it"[54]). He also wanted to write three works of nonfiction in collaboration with Helga, "to establish a professional relationship."[55] He sent the redrafted *English Summer* to Swanson to see if there was anything he could do with it. He planned an exciting year.

It seems his relationship with Jean Fracasse was also developing into something more serious. He had played an active role in her divorce, appearing in court for her, among other things, and he had supported her by giving her work. In February 1958, Ray headed to London, intending to bring Jean and her family over a few weeks later. He was relieved to be back in Britain and was even prepared to pay the steep fine administered on him for his last overstay in 1956. The Fracasses joined him in March and stayed with Helga

Greene in Belgravia for a night before moving to an apartment in Chelsea. Meanwhile, Ray stayed at the Ritz on Piccadilly. He wanted to introduce the family to his friends before they and Ray headed to Jean's native Australia to live for three months. The Fracasses explored London and its sites, eating burgers at a Wimpy Restaurant (they compared favorably with what was available in California) and soaking up the atmosphere. As the time came closer to the family's departure, though, Ray changed his mind. Jean and her children sailed to Australia alone, leaving him in London. It is not clear what prompted him to abandon his plans, but it is possible that his London friends were raising doubts about Jean Fracasse. When a younger woman associates herself with a wealthy older man, suspicions are bound to arise. It is worth remembering, too, that Ray's London friends were incredibly protective of him because they knew how vulnerable he could be when he drank. Or it may have been that he simply did not want to make such a long journey. Whatever the case, he chose to stay in London.

After the Fracasse family left, Ray moved into an apartment in Chelsea, at 8 Swan Walk, opposite the Physic Garden. This was a leafy and expensive part of London, but was cheaper than the Ritz, and close to Helga Greene. Ray and Greene remained close and, after Jean Fracasse had left, he relied on her a lot. Greene had a full-time job running her literary agency and Ray could be less than understanding about her inability to help him whenever he needed it. There were other friends at hand, including Ian Fleming and Michael Gilbert. Ray had also kept in touch with the men who worked at Hamish Hamilton's warehouse and would occasionally join them in a pub for a darts match.

His life was still lonely, though, and when he was lonely, Ray drank. Helga Greene, knowing how successful Natasha Spender had been in her use of travel to distract Ray, planned a trip shortly after the departure of the Fracasses. Before he left the Ritz, she made plans to take Ray to Tangiers but, over lunch with Ian Fleming, it was suggested that they go to Naples instead, where Ray could interview Lucky Luciano, the gangster who had helped reorganize the five Mafia families of America. The *Sunday Times* loved the idea of Ray interviewing a bona fide criminal and offered to cover his expenses, so Ray wrote to Luciano to ask for an interview. The letter is a strange one, perfectly polite but, at points, downright sycophantic:

. . . it is quite possible that you have not been represented to the public of my country as you really are. . . . Some of my questions to you may be brutal, but if you decline to answer them, there will be no record that they have been asked. There will be nothing published by me which you do not say, but of course, I cannot be responsible for editorial comment.[56]

The response arrived quickly. It read: "Don't come on my account. I have nothing to say." By this time, however, the trip had been booked, and so Ray and Helga went anyway. They flew to Rome and then took a train to Naples, checking in to the Hotel Royal. Ray did not give up on interviewing the gangster and was told to leave messages for him at the California Restaurant. After some persistence, Luciano agreed to a meeting.

The article that resulted was stranger than the letter that preceded it. Ray's books were full of contempt and anger for the corrupt men at the heart of Los Angeles. "The System" had fostered a pervading criminality that ruined the lives of ordinary people and his piece on Lucky Luciano might have been expected to probe the nefarious behavior of a violent mobster. Instead, it defended him and attacked the government. Ray argued that Luciano had been framed:

> Every so often we try to salve our consciences by selecting a highly publicized scapegoat in order to create the illusion that our laws are being rigidly enforced. In 1936 Luciano had reached a position of sufficient eminence to be selected. Some such scapegoats are guilty, some half or doubtfully guilty, and some—not many, I hope—are framed.
>
> I believe Luciano was deliberately framed by an ambitious prosecutor. He was outside the law technically speaking but I don't believe the crime with which he was charged: compulsory prostitution, and for which he was convicted, had anything to do with his real activities.

Perhaps this is a reflection of one of Ray's earliest ideas about criminals, articulated in *Farewell, My Lovely* and later novels: that no one is entirely bad? Evil might exist—Carmen Sternwood, surely, is evil with her serpentine qualities—but most criminals have more complicated motivations. That said,

Ray may have also been taken in by Luciano. There are parts of the interview that seem very naive:

> He seemed to me about as much like a tough mobster as I am like the late unlamented Mussolini. He has a soft voice, a patient sad face, and is extremely courteous in every way. This might all be a front, but I don't think I am that easily fooled. A man who has been involved in brutal crimes bears a mark. Luciano seemed to be a lonely man who had been endlessly tormented and yet bore little or no malice. I liked him and had no reason not to. He is probably not perfect, but neither am I.

Ray perhaps put too much faith in his own ability to judge character. Unsurprisingly the *Sunday Times* refused to print the article.

The trip was also full of tension between Helga and Ray. He claimed that she bossed him around (he had no wish to see the sights) and she said the same about him. He was also drinking large quantities of grappa, an Italian brandy. It was tough on Helga and they returned from the trip earlier than anticipated. Soon after, in the first week of May, Ray was back in the hospital. Once again, he was drunk and not eating, and needed to be cared for by professionals. On checking out, he returned to the apartment in Chelsea, where Helga arranged for a male nurse called Don Santry to stay with Ray and look after him. Santry was a patient man, who managed to keep Ray close to sober. Surprisingly, Ray seems to have liked him, probably because he knew that he was essential to his well-being.

That summer in London, Ray tried to be sociable. He joined friends for lunch at the Garrick or the Athenaeum, and went shopping at Harrods during the day. In the evening, he went out to dinner, often to expensive and fashionable places like Restaurant Boulestin, close to Covent Garden, that had a reputation for such exactitude and precision that, even though it was one of the costliest establishments in London, it failed to make a profit. Unfortunately, constant socializing, though it helped fend off loneliness, involved more drinking, and was a drain on his finances.

Lack of money was starting to become a concern. On the advice of his friend Michael Gilbert, he agreed to set up a company, Philip Marlowe Ltd, that was based in the Bahamas and would reduce his tax burden. While this was being arranged, Ray was running out of cash, and with things so tight, was forced to ask Helga Greene to lend him a thousand pounds. In the meantime, his much discussed literary projects had fallen by the wayside. He had wanted to write a cookbook but this was quietly forgotten, as was his adaptation of *English Summer* for the stage. He made some progress with an idea for a new Philip Marlowe novel but, after a flurry of activity, produced just eight pages and a title, *The Poodle Springs Mystery*, before he gave up. The fact that the title contained the word mystery suggests that his heart was never really in it to begin with.

Then, in August, there came a phone call that changed things. Jean Fracasse's husband had suddenly died and she had to return to La Jolla. Ray, ever the gentleman, agreed to meet her there. He turned his back on London and, with Don Santry to support him, headed home to California.

At first, Ray seems to have settled at the Hotel Del Charro, but he was drinking heavily and Don Santry was forced to take him to the hospital. After his release, he rented a small cottage at 824 Prospect Street, one of the main roads in La Jolla and only a few streets from the ocean, which meant he could walk almost everywhere. Don was able to help, but the house was not a happy one and Ray moaned constantly about the food, about the care, about everything. Jean Fracasse visited him regularly. He was furious to learn that her husband had cut her out of his will a few days before he died, leaving her penniless. Though not uncommon, this offended Ray's sense of honor. He stepped in and started paying her, though he thought that she did not have the temperament to be an efficient secretary.[57] To ease her money worries, he deeded her the British and Commonwealth rights to *Playback*.

Ray also missed Helga. He thought of himself now as a European and was out of place in La Jolla. He wrote to her and asked her to visit but she was unable to make the trip. Instead, she sent out a mutual friend, Kay West, who had helped Ray with some secretarial work in London. By this time, Don Santry had left for England. Kay took on the role of Ray's nurse and secretary. Her sudden arrival seems to have upset Jean Fracasse. A few months earlier, she had been named the main benefactor in Ray's will and the arrival of another woman threatened her position. Kay West was shocked at the situation she found in La Jolla and wrote to Helga. She was appalled to hear that Ray had passed over the rights to *Playback* and promptly offered to buy them from Jean for $2,000.

Ray seems to have adored Kay West and the two of them would sit in the small cottage watching TV, playing darts, and talking. As was now conventional when any woman helped him in any meaningful way, he fell in love with her and proposed to her. He changed his will again, making West his benefactor—Jean Fracasse had been right to be wary. It was a difficult time for everyone concerned. The house on Prospect Street was full of tension and the women in Ray's life were resentful of one another. Kay ended up collapsing from the sheer exhaustion of it all and, following a brief hospitalization, headed back to England. Meanwhile, Jean Fracasse hired a male nurse by the name of Leon Johnson to move in with Ray. Johnson was a wiry Midwesterner and the two men got along well enough. A new regime was introduced, under which Ray was again able to work. He had been offered £10,000 by an English paper to write a new Marlowe story and eventually produced a lackluster tale called "The Pencil," which was not published until after his death.

What happened next is not clear. According to Jean Fracasse's daughter, Leon and Jean were able to bring some sort of balance to Ray's life. But Kay West had returned to England with a different story altogether, reporting to Helga Greene that Ray was dirty, angry, and drunk all the time. Helga, who had been ill, flew out to California in February 1959.

Whatever the circumstances of Ray's last months, by the time she arrived he was back in the hospital, vomiting blood and blacking out. She knew that he needed serious support, and when he asked her to marry him, she accepted, perhaps knowing that it might give him something to live for. Ray was ecstatic when she said yes, and they made plans to return to England to live. He said farewell to his friends in La Jolla, including Neil Morgan, to whom he gave his dictionary and collection of pipes, then flew to New York. The city was cold and it was wet when they arrived. They took a room at the Beaux Arts Hotel. Ray had two things to do in the city: first, he had to accept the presidency of the Mystery Writers of America and, secondly, he had to ask Helga's father, H. S. H. Guinness, for his daughter's hand in marriage.

The Mystery Writers of America arranged a reception for Ray but, when the day arrived, he seemed weak and Helga worried that he would not be able to attend. Ray, with Helga's support, summoned the strength to go, but needed a cane to help him walk. He delivered a short speech, but one full of warmth and affection:

> I should thank you from the bottom of my heart for your great kindness in inviting me here. I not only should but I do. But I feel a certain embarrassment before you for two reasons. I now know that the ballot was sent to me, but I never saw it. It was apparently filed before I saw it, possibly in my file headed Don't Bother Me Now, File Later. So when I received a telegram from Catherine Barth telling me I had been elected president against enormous opposition I was stunned.

He concluded:

> I thank you all again for your great kindness to me and I am sure you will be relieved to know that, however much love I may have inside me, I have no more words that need be said.

Though it was a formality, Ray seemed genuinely proud to be recognized by his peers and, though he had railed against the crime writing establishment, was glad to have his achievements validated. After the party, Ray and Helga headed back to their hotel. The weather was still horrid but he was happy.

A few days later came the dinner with Helga's father. Ray was nervous and the dinner was fraught. Henry Seymour Howard Guinness—Sam to his friends—had been educated at Winchester and Oxford and, later, entered the family banking business, where he met the standard expected of a Guinness. He was rich and successful; he was also only a month older than Ray. Ray prepared himself as well as he could, even managing to remain sober, but could not hide his frailty. When he announced his intentions, Guinness said no. Ray thought he had behaved "beautifully" but Guinness was worried that a man of his age was not a suitable match for his daughter. Ray was understandably distraught and blamed other people for setting Guinness against him. The following day, he announced that he could not go back to England with Helga and, instead, made preparations to return to La Jolla. Perhaps he thought that the cold that he had been developing would be easier to get over in California than in England. Perhaps he just wanted to forget himself in drink and knew that Helga would never allow it. Strangely, she agreed, and so Ray went back to the small cottage on Prospect Street, while Helga went home to London.

On March 23, 1959, two weeks after his return from New York, Raymond Chandler was once again hospitalized. The cold he had picked up in New York had developed into pneumonia. The staff of the La Jolla Convalescent Hospital, who knew him well, decided after two days that he needed better facilities. On March 25, he was sent to Scripps Clinic by ambulance. It was to be his last journey. On March 26, 1959, at ten to four in the afternoon, Raymond Chandler died.

Officially, it was the pneumonia that killed him but, in reality, it was so much more. Since Cissy had died, he had been almost constantly drunk, with only occasional periods of sobriety. It was too much for his body to bear.

His death was announced in newspapers in London and New York but, in La Jolla, it was a quiet event. The funeral took place on a bright clear Monday morning at the Mount Hope Cemetery in San Diego. It was attended by seventeen people, one of whom was a representative from the Mystery Writers of America. Helga Greene remained in England. It was a bank holiday there and she could not even send flowers.

Right up to the end, Ray had been thinking about Philip Marlowe. A month before his death he wrote,

> . . . a fellow of Marlowe's type shouldn't get married, because he is a lonely man, a poor man, a dangerous man, and yet a sympathetic man, and somehow none of this goes with marriage. I think he will always have a fairly shabby office, a lonely house, a number of affairs, but no permanent connection. . . . I see him always in a lonely street, in lonely rooms, puzzled but never quite defeated.[58]

Here, in this last letter, was the central difference between Ray and the character he created. Marlowe would have "no permanent connection," but Ray did: with his wife, Cissy. Her death undid his carefully constructed sense of self and left him vulnerable to all manner of hurts, not in the least by fatally weakening his resistance to excessive drinking. Alcohol had cast a long, dark shadow over Ray and, at the end, consumed him almost entirely. But there was more, too. The great undertaking of his life was to write something worthy of his wife, something that might last. He never dedicated a book to her because he thought nothing he produced was good enough. In this, history has judged him to be incorrect. Raymond Chandler wrote some of the finest novels in the English language, capturing a city that had been made brittle by its own greatness, and creating a hero who has captivated generations of readers with his lonely humanity. But for Raymond Chandler, this was not enough. He had failed and this was his life's great sadness. It was one that he expressed in a sonnet the year before he died and, to him at least, it was a bitter epitaph:

> The seasons change, the better things endure,
> Yet what was vibrant, now is dim and slow.
> Oh, that the brilliance were mine to create
> But all the golden thoughts arrive too late.

This then was how Ray saw himself at the end. Thankfully we, his readers, see something better.

AFTERWORD

Raymond Chandler's death in 1959 was not the end of his story. More than seventy years after he published his first novel, his name has become a touchstone for crime writing, representing not just excellent fiction, but also a type of writing that is at once powerful and beautiful. Ray stands alongside Arthur Conan Doyle and Agatha Christie in that his most famous creation has become a household name. But he also stands apart because his writing is about more than murder. His fiction criticizes corruption, indolence, and self-interest in a way that had not been explored in crime fiction before and in doing so he helped shift the perception of what the genre could do.

Readers have found Ray's work engaging for manifold reasons. First and foremost there is the enduring appeal of Philip Marlowe, who easily outgrew the narrow confines of the novels for which he was first fashioned. He is himself an eloquent expression of a word that seems powerfully American: lonesomeness. His urban alienation resonates with readers whether they live in Los Angeles, London, Tokyo, or Paris. In many ways, Philip Marlowe has become the vessel into which the isolation of a million readers has been poured, distilled, and refigured to reflect their own feelings and help them make sense of the world. And this is part of his noble secret.

However, another character looms large in Ray's writing: Los Angeles, and his re-creation of the city has been key to his longevity. This is largely to do with the way in which he renders the detail of its terrain and distills its particular atmosphere. But, to a lesser extent, it is because the subject itself remains so fascinating. Ray understood, before anyone else, that Los Angeles was a fit subject for art. Whether we are happy about it or not, the city has steadily moved to the center of the creative world as both the producer of and the backdrop for many of the key works of modern popular culture, from

Billy Wilder's *Sunset Boulevard* to Ridley Scott's *Blade Runner*. And, as Los Angeles has increased in importance, so too has Raymond Chandler's assessment of it.

Philip Marlowe and his world have proven ripe for reinvention and a steady stream of film, television, and radio adaptations have appeared. Though some of these versions of Marlowe have been forgotten, others have lasted. In 1973, Robert Altman's movie of *The Long Goodbye* was released, written by Leigh Brackett (who also worked on Howard Hawk's *The Big Sleep*) and starring Elliot Gould as Marlowe. In 1975, Robert Mitchum took a turn as the detective in *Farewell, My Lovely* (directed by Dick Richards), reprising the role in 1978 in Michael Winner's version of *The Big Sleep*. Of these movies, it is Robert Altman's that has proved to be the most enduring, but it should be noted that each movie has refashioned Marlowe for a different audience. In Altman's film, Marlowe is relocated to a contemporary Los Angeles, where hippies do naked yoga on their balconies. His take on *The Long Goodbye* appealed to 1970s audiences increasingly anxious about urban alienation and corruption at the highest levels. Michael Winner's interpretation ignored the city altogether and was set in London instead. And other films have used Chandler as a frame. In Shane Black's movie *Kiss Kiss Bang Bang* (2005), Chandler's stories and novels provide the titles for the movie's chapters. Of all the celluloid versions of Marlowe, though, it is a film that did not take Ray's novels as its source but nevertheless expresses a shared vision of Los Angeles that now represents the best of the hardboiled genre: *Chinatown*. This movie, written by Robert Towne, directed by Roman Polanski, and starring Jack Nicholson, explores the connections between water, Los Angeles, and the corruption the city engenders. Had Ray been alive to see it, he might have recognized the world depicted as his own.

But, beyond his writing, Ray himself has fascinated readers. His letters and his life, as well as his novels, have affected them deeply. In particular, his personal correspondence reflects a peculiarly modern man of many facets. The letters are often a vivid mix of attitudes and can be grumpy and articulate, berating yet inspiring, misanthropic but always enlightening. Together with his fiction, they form a flickering image of a life, and of a man, that is as enthralling as it is enduring.

It was not always straightforward though. Immediately after his death, his legacy remained unclear. As in life, Ray's literary heritage was divided between America and Britain. This was both a geographical separation as well as a figurative one. He had already agreed to deposit some of his papers in the Special Collection Department of the Library at the University of California, Los Angeles and the remainder were inherited by Helga Greene and taken to Britain.[1] Meanwhile, critics in the United States were less convinced of his place within the literary canon than their contemporaries in Britain, where Ray was widely regarded as both an artist and a crime writer. As such, the responses to his death were different depending on the location.

Things started to change in 1962 with the publication of *Raymond Chandler Speaking*. The book, edited by Dorothy Gardiner and Katherine Sorely Walker, published Ray's letters for the first time and, for many readers, it offered a first intriguing glimpse of the man who created Philip Marlowe. It was much more than an attempt by a dead author's estate to exploit unpublished material; rather, it sought to fix him in the minds of readers as a writer of real originality and talent:

> Raymond Chandler, who possessed an English classical education, an inquiring and critical mind, an extensive knowledge of languages, and a talent close to genius for the pointed phrase and the *mot juste*, may well have been, as his admirers insist, this century's most brilliant writer of detective fiction; unquestionably he was one of its most prolific and original letter-writers.[2]

How many readers, on first seeing the picture of Ray that graced the front cover of the British edition (published by Hamish Hamilton, of course) imagined that the man with the slicked-back, greying hair, the thick, black-framed glasses, the puffy, almost jowly face, and the flat, thin-lipped nonsmile could have created Philip Marlowe? During his lifetime many of his readers instinctively believed that Chandler was someone far tougher, much younger, and certainly less tweedy than Ray in fact was. As time distanced the fans from the man, this was exaggerated. Had they read the letters they would have encountered a very different version of Raymond Chandler and they would have seen his endless fascination with the craft of writing, his frustration with Hollywood, with publishers, and with agents, and, even, his love of cats.

They would not have seen, however, the less salubrious aspects of Ray's life. In fact, the details of his final years were not published until Frank Mac-Shane wrote the first of three biographies[3] in 1976, revealing for the first time that Ray was an alcoholic and that he had had an unusual, occasionally difficult marriage to Cissy. By this time, Ray's novels had been well thumbed by the academic establishment in both America and Britain but, tellingly, MacShane introduces his biography with a caveat that betrays his own nervousness about excavating the life of a crime writer:

> The first thing I should like to say is that in this book I am treating Raymond Chandler as a novelist and not simply as a detective-story writer.[4]

To some readers, Chandler remained of questionable literary value. But when *The World of Raymond Chandler* was published, a year after MacShane's biography, its contributors included several respected critics (Jacques Barsun was a professor at Columbia; T. J. Binyon taught at Oxford; and Michael Mason taught at University College London), as well as lauded writers of crime fiction (Patricia Highsmith, Michael Gilbert, and Julian Symonds, to name three). In some ways this collection better expressed Ray's literary situation: he was an artist of some considerable skill, who had taken a genre and pushed it beyond bounds no one else had thought breachable. The book itself was a direct response to MacShane's biography and, at its heart, sits Natasha Spender's essay "His Own Long Goodbye." She, in particular, objected to MacShane's treatment not just of Ray but also of herself, and wanted to see a riposte in print. The book's very existence though, along with both *Raymond Chandler Speaking* and MacShane's biography (which was joined shortly afterwards by a detailed anthology of correspondence), stood as a testament to Ray's increasing acceptance in the world of letters. He had, in Britain at least, finally eclipsed Dashiell Hammett as the writer who made crime fiction respectable.

Moreover, his books remained in print. In fact, they multiplied. As his star rose, some of the early pulp stories, which had previously been excluded from anthologies, were republished, along with other, more obscure elements of Ray's literary output, such as his early poetry. The films he had worked on such as *Double Indemnity* and those that had used his work as source material including *The Big Sleep* were appreciated as classics of the genre, and he was increasingly seen as part of the canon of both literature and cinema.

During the 1980s, however, Ray's reputation came under fire. His novels were peeled apart and his attitudes to women, homosexuality, and race rightly interrogated. Above all, what these suspicious new critics laid bare was a writer profoundly conflicted by sex. Ray certainly loved women but he did so in a particular and often troubled way. His attitude to intimacy, in the majority of his fiction at least, is complicated; his revulsion at the physicality of sex is frequently unsettling. And despite his views on homosexuality ("a pansy has no iron in his bones, whatever he looks like"), his novels have been strip-mined for homoerotic content. Indeed, Philip Marlowe's ability to resist easy categorization as either a lover or hater of women, combined with his yearning to connect with other men, has helped contribute to his lasting appeal because he is, in truth, an enigma, whose sexual motivation is unclear and, therefore, it remains both threatening and attractive. It is a brave biographer who seeks too much truth in his subject's fiction but novels are leaky vessels out of which seep the attitudes and poses of their authors. At the very least, his own sexual opacity has helped keep readers of both his fiction and his letters intrigued. In fact, the things that Ray leaves obscured or unstated are as much a part of the thrill of reading his work as the crime, murder, and corruption he reveals. There is something that remains forever mysterious, even in the light.

Billy Wilder once said that of all the people he worked with, he was most often asked about Marilyn Monroe and Raymond Chandler. It is not hard to see why Ray evoked such interest, and this book is a product of the same fascination. As a lover of language he set out to write about the world he knew and, in doing so, he created art. But in his books, in his letters, and in his life Ray, like Philip Marlowe, was conflicted. His troubled childhood, his complicated family relationships, his profound awkwardness about sex and women, and his battle with alcohol all variously frustrated, colored, and fueled his writing. Each of his books is an expression of this tension, but they are, perhaps, best understood in parallel with his letters, because looking at them together we come closest to understanding the man and the writer.

NOTES

A Note on Sources

As he was in life, Raymond Chandler's literary remains are split between two countries: the Bodleian Library at Oxford University and the Charles E. Young Research Library at the University of California, Los Angeles. Many of the most apposite biographical letters have been reproduced in *The Selected Letters of Raymond Chandler,* published by Dell Publishing Inc. in the United States and edited by Frank MacShane, or in the more recent *The Raymond Chandler Papers,* published by Penguin in the UK and edited by Frank MacShane and Tom Hiney. To keep the notes as simple as possible I have not identified any letter's specific location; however should any reader wish to know this information, please write to me at tom .williams25@gmail.com.

When quoting from any of Raymond Chandler's novels, I have quoted from the UK editions published by Penguin (please see the bibliography for the full list). With the stories, I have used the Everyman Library edition of the Collected Stories, published by Alfred A. Knopf in the United States. Passages from the published poetry and essays all come from M. J. Bruccoli's book *Chandler Before Marlowe,* published by the University of South Carolina Press. Some of the later *Atlantic* articles are collected in Robert F. Moss's book *Raymond Chandler: A Literary Reference* (published by Carroll and Graf Publishers in the United States), and I have used this book as a source for "Writers in Hollywood" and "Ten Per Cent of Your Life." "The Simple Art of Murder" can be found in *The Simple Art of Murder,* published by Vintage in America, and "Writers in Hollywood" is reproduced online by the *Atlantic* at http://www.theatlantic.com/magazine/archive /1945/ 11/writers -in-hollywood/6454/

Preface

1. Letter to Dale Warren, January 15, 1950.

Chapter One

1. Faith, N., *The World the Railways Made*, Pimlico, London, 1994.

2. This is according to Chandler's first biographer in MacShane, F., *The Life of Raymond Chandler*, Hamish Hamilton, London, 1986.

3. See Bristow, D. L., *A Dirty, Wicked Town*, Caxton Press, Caldwell, Idaho, 2000, for tales of Omaha.

4. Letter to Charles Morton, January 1, 1945.

5. Ibid.

6. See Stevenson, R. L., *Travels with a Donkey in the Cévennes and the Amateur Emigrant*, Penguin Classics, London, 2011.

7. Ibid.

8. I have located Grace Fitt in Laramie rather than in Plattsmouth, Nebraska, in 1886. Her daughter, Muriel, was born in Wyoming in 1887, and since Maurice and Florence would marry in Laramie that year, it seems reasonable to assume that this is where the Fitts were based.

9. See Plattsmouth census records for 1900 and 1910.

10. MacShane, F., *The Life of Raymond Chandler,* Hamish Hamilton, London, 1986.

11. Larson, E., *The Devil in the White City,* Bantam, London, 2004.

12. Twain, M., *Life on the Mississippi*, Penguin Classics, London, 1985.

13. Miller, D. L., *City of the Century: the Epic of Chicago and the Making of America*, Touchstone, New York, 1997.

14. Florence and Ray returned from Ireland as cabin passengers according to the New York passenger list for the SS *Servia* from October 27, 1890, and it is likely that on their outward journey they also traveled in a cabin. However, no records of their departure from New York or arrival in Queenstown are available.

15. Larson, E., *The Devil in the White City,* Bantam, London, 2004.

16. Letter to Charles Morton, November 20, 1944.

17. Letter to Helga Greene, April 28, 1957.

18. Letter to Charles Morton, November 20, 1944.

19. Letter to Charles Morton, January 1, 1945.

20. Letter to Charles Morton, November 20, 1944.

21. Letter to Helga Greene, April 28, 1957.

22. Author interview with Natasha Spender in September 2006.

23. Decker, J. H., *Men of Steel Rails,* University of Nebraska Press, Lincoln, 1983.

24. Ibid.

25. All figures in this section from Miller, D. L., *City of the Century: the Epic of Chicago and the Making of America*, Touchstone, New York, 1997.

26. Letter to Hamish Hamilton, November 10, 1950.

27. See the Raymond Chandler: Shamus Town website, where Loren Latker has uncovered this new material: http://homepage.mac.com/llatker/index.html

28. This detail comes from Chandler's Canadian Army records, in particular the form "Particulars of Family of an Officer or Man Enlisted in C.E.F."

Chapter Two

1. Letter to Hamish Hamilton, July 15, 1954.
2. Letter to Charles Morton, January 1, 1945.
3. Letter to Hamish Hamilton, July 15, 1954.
4. Ibid.
5. Letter to Charles Morton, January 1, 1945.
6. Ibid.
7. Letter to Hamish Hamilton, December 11, 1950.
8. Frank MacShane interviewed Sir Alwyne Ogden for MacShane, F., *The Life of Raymond Chandler*, Hamish Hamilton, London, 1986.
9. Letter to Wesley Hartley, December 3, 1957.
10. Ibid.
11. Letter to Hamish Hamilton, November 10, 1950.
12. Letter to Hamish Hamilton, December 20, 1949.
13. See Parker, P., *The Old Lie: The Great War and the Public School Ethos,* Hambledon Continuum, London, 1987.
14. Letter to Helga Greene, April 28, 1957.

Chapter Three

1. Maugham, S., *Of Human Bondage,* originally published in 1915. This edition published by Vintage, London, 2005.
2. Letter to Helga Greene, July 13, 1956.
3. See McCrum, R., *Wodehouse: A Life*, Penguin Viking, 2004.
4. Letter to Dale Warren, January 4, 1951.
5. Letter to Roger Machell, March 24, 1954.
6. Ibid.
7. Letter to Hamish Hamilton, December 11, 1950.
8. Ibid.
9. Ibid.
10. Letter to Helga Greene, July 13, 1956.
11. Ibid.
12. Ibid.
13. Letter to Dale Warren, January 15, 1950.
14. Ibid.
15. Letter to Wesley Hartley, December 3, 1957.
16. Ibid.
17. Letter to Dale Warren, January 15, 1950.
18. Letter to Hamish Hamilton, December 11, 1950.
19. Ibid.

20. Chandler's unsympathetic characterization of mothers does not extend to fathers, toward whom, despite his own experiences, Marlowe tends to offer some begrudging respect.

21. Interview given to the *Daily Express*, April 25, 1955.

22. Letter to Hamish Hamilton, April 22, 1949.

23. All the poetry can be found in *Chandler Before Marlowe*, M. J. Bruccoli (ed.), University of South Carolina Press, Columbia, 1973.

24. From "Introduction" in *Poets of Our Day,* N. G. Royde-Smith (ed.), Methuen, London, 1908.

25. It was Stephen's poem "The Port" that incensed his uncle with its reference to "pale lilly boys [who] flaunt their bright lips, / Such pretty cups for money."

26. Letter to A. G. Gardiner, quoted in Harris, W., *J. A. Spender*, Cassell and Company, London, 1946.

27. Letter to Hamish Hamilton, December 11, 1950.

28. *The Oxford Companion to English Literature*, M. Drabble (ed.), Oxford University Press, Oxford, 2006.

29. Letter to Hamish Hamilton, December 11, 1950.

30. "Realism and Fairyland" from *Chandler Before Marlowe*, J. Bruccoli, (ed.), University of South Carolina Press, Columbia, 1973.

31. "The Genteel Artist," ibid.

32. Ibid.

33. Quoted by MacShane, F., from "Autobiographical Statement" in *The Life of Raymond Chandler,* Hamish Hamilton, London, 1973.

34. Letter to Hamish Hamilton, December 11, 1950.

35. Ibid.

Chapter Four

1. Letter to Charles Morton, January 15, 1945.

2. From the Chandler archive at Dulwich College.

3. Letter to Hamish Hamilton, November 10, 1950.

4. Quoted by MacShane, F., from "Autobiographical Statement" in *The Life of Raymond Chandler,* Hamish Hamilton, London, 1973.

5. McWilliams, C., *Southern California: An Island On the Land*, Gibbs Smith Publisher, Layton, Utah, 1973.

6. Ibid.

7. Ibid.

8. The story inspired Roman Polanski's *Chinatown*, one of the great movies about Los Angeles.

9. From "To-Morrow," Chandler Archives, the Bodleian Library, Oxford.

10. McKenzie, F. A., *Through the Hindenburg Line*, Hodder and Stoughton, London, 1918.

11. From "Trench Raid," Chandler Archives, the Bodleian Library, Oxford.

12. Ibid.

13. Letter to Deirdre Gartrell, March 2, 1957.

14. Letter to James Sandoe, February 25, 1948.

15. MacShane, F., *The Life of Raymond Chandler*, Hamish Hamilton, London, 1986.

16. Letter to Deirdre Gartrell, March 2, 1957.

17. Letter to Louise Loughner, undated, but probably May 1955.

18. Albert Ball, quoted by Levine, J. in *Fighter Heroes of WWI*, Collins, London, 2009.

Chapter Five

1. The 1870 census of Perry Lake lists Eugene and Maria Hurlbert but makes no mention of a child. The census the following year does, so she must have been born some time between July 1870 and June 1871.

2. Quoted in Osofsky, G., *Harlem, The Making of a Ghetto: Negro New York, 1890–1930*, Harper and Row, New York, 1971.

3. Dunlap, D. W., *From Abyssinian to Zion: A Guide to Manhattan's Houses of Worship*, Columbia University Press, New York, 2004.

4. Freeman, J., in *The Long Embrace*, Vintage, New York, 2008.

5. The records in which Julian appears give conflicting birth dates.

6. See the *Washington Post*, January 23, 1908.

7. See McGroarty, J. S., *Los Angeles from the Mountains to the Sea*, The American Historical Society, Chicago and New York, 1921.

8. Ray kept all of Cissy's divorce papers, and they are currently archived at the Bodleian Library, Oxford.

9. All poetry quoted here comes from the Chandler Papers in the Bodleian Library, Oxford, unless otherwise stated.

10. See Freeman, J., *The Long Embrace,* Vintage, New York, 2008.

11. Houseman, J., "Lost Fortnight: A Memoir," *The World of Raymond Chandler*, M. Gross (ed.), Weidenfeld & Nicolson, London, 1977.

12. Tygiel, J., *The Great Los Angeles Oil Swindle*, University of California Press, London, 1994.

13. This information comes from my correspondence with Warren and Alma Lloyd's grandson, Randall.

14. This is referred to by MacShane, F. in *The Life of Raymond Chandler*, Hamish Hamilton, London, 1986, and Chandler discusses it himself in a letter to Helga Greene, May 5, 1957.

15. Letter to Helga Greene, May 5, 1957.

16. Letter to Edgar Carter, June 3, 1957.

17. Quoted by Freeman, J., in *The Long Embrace*, Vintage, New York, 2008.

18. Fitzgerald, F. Scott, "Early Success" in *F. Scott Fitzgerald on Authorship*, M. J. Bruccoli and J. Baughmas (eds.), University of South Carolina, Columbia, 1996.

19. The journalist was Matt Weinstock, quoted in Rayner, R., *A Bright and Guilty Place*, Constable, London, 2010.

20. Quoted in R. Rayner, *A Bright and Guilty Place*, Constable, London, 2010.

21. Letter to William Lever, October 12, 1934.

22. McWilliams, C., *Southern California: an Island on the Land*, Gibbs Smith Publisher, Layton, Utah, 1973.

23. Rayner, R., *A Bright and Guilty Place*, Constable, London, 2010.

24. The Doheneys were investigated as part of the Tea Pot Dome scandal in the 1920s and were beset by rumors of bribery and political fixing.

25. The events surrounding the death of Doheney and Plunkett are explored in vivid detail in Rayner, R., *A Bright and Guilty Place*, Constable, London, 2010.

26. White, L., *Me, Detective*, Harcourt, Brace, and Company Inc., New York, 1936.

27. Letter to Helga Greene, May 5, 1957.

28. Ibid.

29. Ibid.

30. Ibid.

31. Ibid.

32. Ibid.

33. Letter to James Sandoe, December 6, 1948.

34. Letter to James Sandoe, November 18, 1948.

35. Letter to William Lever, January 6, 1934.

36. Quoted by MacShane, F., in *The Life of Raymond Chandler*, Hamish Hamilton, London, 1986.

37. See the Raymond Chandler: Shamus Town website, where Loren Latker has uncovered this new material: http://homepage.mac.com/llatker/index.html.

38. See Rayner, R., *A Bright and Guilty Place*, Constable, London, 2010.

39. MacShane, F., *The Life of Raymond Chandler*, Hamish Hamilton, London, 1986.

40. Letter to William Lever, August 12, 1933.

41. Ibid.

42. Ibid.

Chapter Six

1. Both Frank MacShane and Tom Hiney write that Ray headed to Seattle alone, but I have found no evidence of this. According to a letter written on August 12, 1933, to his friend William Lever, Ray and Cissy headed north together: "We went touring around the Northwest where I made several ineffectual efforts to do what I had always wanted to do—write."

2. Letter to James Howard, March 26, 1957.

3. Letter to William Lever, August 12, 1933.

4. Letter to James Howard, March 26, 1957.

5. Letter to William Lever, August 12, 1933.

6. Ibid.

7. *The Notebooks of Raymond Chandler*, F. MacShane (ed.), Weidenfeld & Nicolson, London, 1976.

8. Ibid.

9. Letter to William Lever, August 12, 1933.

10. Letter to Erle Stanley Gardner, May 5, 1939.

11. As argued by Frederick Jackson Turner in his seminal essay "The Significance of the Frontier in American History," first delivered as a lecture to the American Historical Association in 1893.

12. First published in *Black Mask*, June 15, 1923, under the pseudonym Peter Collinson.

13. Letter to the editor, *Black Mask*, June 15, 1923, *Dashiel Hammett, Selected Letters*, R. Layman with J. M. Rivett (eds.), Counter Point, Washington, DC, 2001.

14. Letter from Dashiell Hammett to Phil Cody, editor of *Black Mask*, August 1924, ibid.

15. Gruber, F., *The Pulp Jungle*, Sherbourne Press, Los Angeles, 1967.

16. Taken from J. T. Shaw's draft introduction to *The Black Mask Omnibus*, held at UCLA as part of the Chandler archive.

17. Ibid.

18. Letter from Dashiell Hammett to Blanche Knopf, March 20, 1928.

19. "The Simple Art of Murder" in *The Simple Art of Murder,* Vintage, New York, 1988.

20. Letter to George Harmon Coxe, April 9, 1939.

21. Letter to Charles Morton, October 28, 1947.

22. As pointed out by MacShane, F., *The Life of Raymond Chandler*, Hamish Hamilton, London, 1986.

23. Letter to Hamish Hamilton, November 10, 1950.

24. Letter to Dale Warren, January 7, 1945.

25. Letter to William Lever, August 12, 1933.

26. MacShane, F., *The Life of Raymond Chandler,* Hamish Hamilton, London, 1986.

27. Letter to William Lever, August 12, 1933.

28. Letter to Fredrick Lewis Allen, May 7, 1948.

29. Letter to Alfred Knopf, January 12, 1946.

30. Letter to William Lever, October 12, 1934.

31. Ibid.

32. Letter to William Lever, August 12, 1933.

33. Ibid.

34. Letter to William Lever, January 6, 1934.

35. Letter to William Lever, August 12, 1933.

36. Letter to William Lever, January 6, 1934.

Chapter Seven

1. Letter to William Lever, October 12, 1934.

2. Letter to William Lever, August 12, 1933.

3. Ibid.

4. Ibid.

5. MacShane, F., *The Life of Raymond Chandler*, Hamish Hamilton, London, 1986.

6. See Rayner, R., *A Bright and Guilty Place*, Constable, London, 2010.

7. Ray later republished this story in *The Simple Art of Murder* and renamed the detective Johnny Dalmas. I am quoting from the Library of America edition, which is based on the first book publication (*Finger Man and Other Stories,* Avon 1957) and reproduces Ray's original text.

8. Letter to William Lever, October 12, 1934.

9. Ibid.

10. Ibid.

11. Starr, K., *Endangered Dreams: The Great Depression in California*, OUP, Oxford, 1996.

12. Ibid.

13. Letter to William Lever, January 10, 1936.

14. Ibid.

15. Letter to William Lever, January 6, 1934.

16. "For Cissy," dated October 29, 1935.

17. Ibid.

18. Letter to William Lever, January 10, 1936.

19. Letter to William Lever, October 12, 1933.

20. Gruber, F., *The Pulp Jungle*, Sherbourne Press, Los Angeles, 1967.

21. Letter to William Lever, May 31, 1938.

Chapter Eight

1. Letter to William Lever, May 31, 1938.

2. Ibid.

3. Letter to William Lever, January 10, 1936.

4. Letter to William Lever, May 31, 1938.

5. Ibid.

6. Ibid.

7. Lucy, Calista (ed.), "A College Boy: Raymond Chandler and Dulwich College 1900 to 1905," Dulwich College (private printing), London, 2009.

8. Letter to W. J. Smith, March 19, 1958.

9. Letter to W. J. Smith, October 1, 1958.

10. Letter to Bernice Baumgarten, March 11, 1949.

11. Letter to Paul Brooks, July 19, 1949.

12. Letter to Frederick Lewis Allen, May 7, 1948. See also Chapter 5.

13. Letter to James Sandoe, August 18, 1945.

Chapter Nine

1. From the *New York Herald Tribune*, February 5, 1939, appearing in *Raymond Chandler: a Literary Reference,* R. F. Moss (ed.), Carroll & Graf Publishers, New York, 2002.

2. Letter to Alfred Knopf, February 19, 1939.

3. Letter to William Koshland, November 2, 1938.

4. From *The New Republic*, March 15, 1939, appearing in *Raymond Chandler: a Literary Reference,* R. F. Moss (ed.), Carroll & Graf Publishers, New York, 2002.

5. Letter to Alfred Knopf, February 19, 1939.

6. Ibid.

7. *The Notebooks of Raymond Chandler*, F. MacShane (ed.) Weidenfeld & Nicolson, London, 1977.

8. *The Thin Man* is thought to have sold around twenty thousand copies in the first three weeks alone according to Hiney, T., *Raymond Chandler: A Biography*, Vintage, London, 1998.

9. Letter to Leroy Wright, July 6, 1951.

10. Ibid.

11. Letter to Blanche Knopf, August 23, 1939.

12. Ibid

13. Letter to George Harmon Coxe, October 17, 1939.

14. Letter to George Harmon Coxe, April 9, 1939.

15. Ibid.

16. Letter to George Harmon Coxe, December 19, 1939.

17. Ibid.

18. Letter to Blanche Knopf, January 17, 1940.

19. Letter to George Harmon Coxe, December 19, 1939.

20. Letter to George Harmon Coxe, June 27, 1940.

21. Ibid.

22. Ibid.

23. Letter to Dale Warren, September 15, 1949.

24. *The Notebooks of Raymond Chandler*, F. MacShane (ed.), Weidenfeld & Nicolson, London, 1977.

25. This element of my reading of the book was prompted by Robert Moss's review of Tom Hiney's *Raymond Chandler: A Biography* which can be found at http://home .comcast.net/~mossrobert/html/criticism/hineyrev.htm

26. See October 6 edition of the *New York Times* in *Raymond Chandler: A Literary Reference*, R. F. Moss (ed.), Carroll & Graf Publishers, New York, 2002.

27. See wikipedia: http://en.wikipedia.org/wiki/Anthony_Cornero

28. See http://www.laalmanac.com/history/hi06ee.htm

29. Letter to Charles Morton, October 12, 1944.

30. Ibid.

31. Undated letter to Carl Brandt, sometime in February 1949.

32. Quoted by Parker, P., in *The Old Lie*, Hambledon Continuum, London, 1987.

33. "A Reader's List" in *The New Republic*, October 7, 1940 in *Raymond Chandler: A Literary Reference*, R. F. Moss (ed.), Carroll & Graf Publishers, New York, 2002.

34. Letter to Blanche Knopf, October 9, 1940.

35. Letter to George Harmon Coxe, June 27, 1940.

36. Ibid.

37. Letter to George Harmon Coxe, November 5, 1940.

38. Letter to George Harmon Coxe, June 27, 1940.

39. Letter to Blanche Knopf, September 16, 1939.

40. Letter to Erle Stanley Gardner, February 1, 1941.

41. Ibid.

42. Letter to George Harmon Coxe, June 27, 1940.

43. Letter to Blanche Knopf, March 15, 1942.

44. Chaplin, C., *My Autobiography*, Penguin, London, 2003.

45. Letter to George Harmon Coxe, June 27, 1940.

46. Starr, K., *Embattled Dreams,* Oxford University Press, Oxford, 2002.

47. Letter to Blanche Knopf, October 22, 1942.

48. Ibid.

49. Letter to Blanche Knopf, March 15, 1942.

50. Letter to Blanche Knopf, October 22, 1942.

51. Ibid.

52. See letter to Leroy Wright, July 6, 1951.

53. Letter to Alfred A. Knopf, February 8, 1943.

54. Ibid.

55. Figures from Hiney, T., *Raymond Chandler: A Biography,* Vintage, London, 1998.

Chapter Ten

1. Quoted by Norman, M., in *What Happens Next,* Aurum, London, 2008.

2. Ibid.

3. http://en.wikipedia.org/wiki/Billy_Wilder#Austria_and_Germany

4. Schickel, R., *Double Indemnity*, British Film Institute, London, 1992.

5. Swanson, H., *Sprinkled with Ruby Dust,* quoted in *Raymond Chandler: A Literary Reference*, R. F. Moss (ed.), Carroll & Graf Publishers, New York, 2002.

6. Ibid.

7. "On the Fourth Floor of Paramount" in *Raymond Chandler: A Literary Reference,* R. F. Moss (ed.), Carroll & Graf Publishers, New York, 2002.

8. Norman, M., *What Happens Next*, Aurum Press, London, 2008.

9. Interview with Ivan Moffatt "On the Fourth Floor of Paramount," *Raymond Chandler: A Literary Reference,* R. F. Moss (ed.), Carroll & Graf Publishers, New York, 2002.

10. Norman, M., *What Happens Next*, Aurum, London 2008.

11. Zolotow, M., in "Through the Shot Glass Darkly" quoted by Hiney, T. in *Raymond Chandler: A Biography*, Vintage, London, 1998.

12. Letter to William Lever, January 6, 1934.

13. Sutherland, J., *Last Drink to LA,* Short Books, London, 2001.

14. Letter to Blanche Knopf, October 22, 1942.

15. *The Notebooks of Raymond Chandler*, F. MacShane (ed.), Weidenfeld & Nicolson, London, 1977.

16. Letter to James Sandoe, May 23, 1949.

17. Ibid.

18. Thompson, D., *The Whole Equation: A History of Hollywood*, Abacus, London, 2004.

19. Ibid.

20. Wilder, B., and Chandler, R., *Double Indemnity*, University of California Press, London, 2000.

21. Ibid.

22. Ibid.

23. In the final print of *Double Indemnity,* Phyllis adds, "When I couldn't take that second shot."

24. Wilder, B., and Chandler, R., *Double Indemnity*, University of California Press, London, 2000.

25. Ibid.

26. Letter to Alfred A. Knopf, November 13, 1943.

27. Letter to James M. Cain, March 20, 1944.

28. Schickel, R., *Double Indemnity*, British Film Institute, London, 1992.

29. "On the Fourth Floor of Paramount" in *Raymond Chandler: A Literary Reference*, R. F. Moss (ed.), Carroll & Graf Publishers, New York, 2002.

30. Schickel, R., *Double Indemnity,* British Film Institute, London, 1992.

31. Hiney, T., *Raymond Chandler: A Biography,* Vintage, London, 1998.

32. Letter to Hamish Hamilton, November 10, 1950.

33. Letter to Alfred Knopf, November 13, 1943.

34. Ibid.

35. Knopf Reader's Report published in *Raymond Chandler: a Literary Reference*, R. F. Moss (ed.), Carroll & Graf, New York, 2003.

36. Letter to Carl Brandt, November 26, 1948.

37. Quoted by MacShane, F., in *The Life of Raymond Chandler*, Hamish Hamilton, London, 1986.

38. Letter to Carl Brandt, November 26, 1948.

39. Letter to James Sandoe, January 10, 1951.

Chapter Eleven

1. Letter from Bernard Smith to James Sandoe, May 19, 1943.

2. Letter from Orville Prescott to James Sandoe, August 3, 1943.

3. Letter to James Sandoe, January 26, 1944.

4. Ibid.

5. "The Simple Art of Murder," in *The Simple Art of Murder*, Vintage, New York, 1988.

6. Ibid.

7. Ibid.

8. Ibid.

9. Ibid.

10. Ibid.

11. Ibid.

12. Ibid.

13. Ibid.

14. Ibid.

15. Quoted by Parker, P., *The Old Lie,* Hambledon Continuum, London, 1987.

16. Thompson, D., *The Whole Equation*, Abacus, London, 2004.

17. Letter to Charles Morton, March 5, 1945.

18. Letter to James Sandoe, February 10, 1945.

19. John Houseman, "Lost Fortnight" in *The World of Raymond Chandler,* M. Gross (ed.), Weidenfeld & Nicolson, London, 1977.

20. Letter to Charles Morton, March 5, 1945.

21. Letter to Hamish Hamilton, January 9, 1946.

22. Dating the writing of *The Blue Dahlia* is complicated, and previous biographies have suggested it was written earlier in 1945 than I have. However, I have the following passage from Houseman's essay to date Ray's troubles to April 1945: "Joe Sistrom . . . called a couple of meetings in his quarters on the ground floor of the main Paramount office block . . . it was during one of these meetings, early one afternoon, that a man came running down the studio street, stopping at the various windows to shout something we could not hear to the people inside. When he reached us, he shoved his head in and told us that President Roosevelt was dead. Two days later I was sitting in my office when my secretary hurried in to say that Mr. Chandler was outside." Ray, then, went on to tell Houseman about his encounter with the studio executive. Since FDR died on April 12, the events described by Houseman must have occurred in the days afterwards.

23. Ibid.

24. Ibid.

25. Ibid.

26. Ibid.

27. He said as much to Houseman according to the latter. "Lost Fortnight" in *The World of Raymond Chandler,* M. Gross (ed.), Weidenfeld & Nicolson, 1977.

28. Letter to Hamish Hamilton, May 30, 1946.

29. Letter to Carl Brandt, January 23, 1949.

30. Letter to Carl Brandt, April 3, 1949.

31. Quoted by Freeman, Judith in *The Long Embrace*, Vintage, New York, 2008.

32. Ibid.

33. Parini, J., *One Matchless Time,* HarperCollins, London, 2004.

34. Letter to Carl Brandt, November 26, 1948.

35. Ibid.

36. Ibid.

37. Ibid.

38. Letter to Charles Morton, October 13, 1945.

39. Letter to James Sandoe, August 18, 1945.

40. Letter to Charles Morton, October 13, 1945.

41. Ibid.

42. Letter to Edward Weeks, June 10, 1957.

43. Letter to Charles Morton, October 13, 1945.

44. Letter to Alex Barris, April 16, 1949.

45. Gruber, F., *The Pulp Jungle*, Sherbourne Press, Los Angeles, 1967.

46. Letter to Erle Gardner, November 9, 1945.

47. Letter to Charles Morton, October 13, 1945.

48. Letter to James Sandoe, November 9, 1945.

49. On March 5, Ray wrote to Charles W. Morton, editor of the *Atlantic*, to say "I'm still hoping to do that article for you, sometime in April."

50. "Writers in Hollywood." This is reproduced at http://www.theatlantic.com /magazine/archive/1945/11/writers-in-hollywood/6454

51. Ibid.

52. Ibid.

53. Ibid.

54. Ibid.

55. Ibid.

56. Letter to Charles Morton, December 12, 1945.

57. Ibid.

58. Ibid.

59. Letter to Charles Morton, December 12, 1945.

60. Thompson, D., *The Big Sleep*, The British Film Institute, London, 2000.

61. Letter to Charles Morton, October 12, 1944.

62. Sutherland, J., *Where Was Rebecca Shot?*, Phoenix, London, 1999.

63. Letter to Hamish Hamilton, May 30, 1946.

64. Ibid.

65. Ibid.

Chapter Twelve

1. Letter to Alfred Knopf, January 12, 1946.

2. Letter to Hamish Hamilton, January 6, 1946.

3. Letter to Alfred Knopf, January 12, 1946.

4. Ibid.

5. Ibid.

6. Letter to Blanche Knopf, March 27, 1946.

7. Letter to Erle Stanley Gardner, April 4, 1946.

8. Letter to James Sandoe, January 13, 1949.

9. Letter to H. N. Swanson, August 4, 1946.

10. Letter to Alfred Knopf, January 12, 1946.

11. Ibid.

12. Ibid.

13. Letter to Hamish Hamilton, January 9, 1946.

14. Undated letter to Hamish Hamilton but probably written in January 1946.

15. Letter to Blanche Knopf, March 27, 1946.

16. Letter to H. N. Swanson, August 4, 1946.

17. Ibid.

18. Letter to George Coxe, December 19, 1939.

19. Letter to Erle Stanley Gardner, September 24, 1946.

20. Letter to Hamish Hamilton, October 6, 1946.

21. Letter to Dale Warren, October 2, 1946.

22. Letter to Mrs. Robert Hogan, March 8, 1947.

23. Letter to Erle Stanley Gardner, May 15, 1947.

24. Letter to Charles Morton, January 1, 1948.

25. Letter to Joseph T. Shaw, November 9, 1946.

26. Letter to Erle Stanley Gardner, January 29, 1946.

27. Letter to John Hersey, March 29, 1948.

28. Letter to James Sandoe, March 8, 1947.

29. Letter to H. N. Swanson, August 16, 1947.

30. Letter to Blanche Knopf, June 7, 1947.

31. Letter from H. N. Swanson to Chandler, June 23, 1947.

32. Letter to Erle Stanley Gardner, July 1, 1947.

33. Letter from H. N. Swanson to Chandler, August 11, 1947.

34. Letter to H. N. Swanson, August 16, 1947.

35. Letter to Hamish Hamilton, October 27, 1947.

36. Norman, M., *What Happens Next*, Aurum Press, London, 2008.

37. MacShane, F., *The Life of Raymond Chandler*, Hamish Hamilton, London, 1986.

38. Chandler, R., *Raymond Chandler's Unknown Thriller: The Screenplay of Playback*, Harrap Limited, London, 1985.

39. Unfortunately Ray gives no further details of this early meeting with Hitchcock. The two would later work on *Strangers on a Train*.

40. Letter to James Sandoe, October 2, 1947.

41. Ibid.

42. Chandler, R., *Raymond Chandler's Unknown Thriller: The Screenplay of Playback*, Harrap Limited, London, 1985.

43. Ibid.

44. Letter to John Hersey, March 29, 1948.

45. Letter to Charles Morton, July 28, 1948.

46. Letter to Carl Brandt, November 12, 1948.

47. Letter to Charles Morton, July 28, 1948.

48. Letter to Alex Barris, March 18, 1949.

49. Chandler also worked briefly with S. S. Tyler, but their relationship was short-lived.

50. Letter to Carl Brandt, May 11, 1948.

51. I have based this calculation on a transcript of a Brandt & Brandt memo unearthed by Robert F. Moss. The total number, based on some rounded figures, comes to 2,256,001 copies.

52. Letter to Carl Brandt, May 11, 1948.

53. Ibid.

54. Ibid.

55. Letter to James Sandoe, March 3, 1949.

56. Letter to Mrs. Holton, March 26, 1949.

57. Letter to Hamish Hamilton, July 11, 1948.

58. Letter to Carl Brandt, May 11, 1948.

59. Letter to James Sandoe, August 9, 1948.

60. Letter to Hamish Hamilton, August 9, 1948.

61. Ibid.

62. Letter to James Sandoe, November 18, 1948.

63. Letter to Dale Warren, August 18, 1948.

64. Letter to Hamish Hamilton, May 3, 1949.

65. Letter to James Sandoe, October 24, 1948.

66. Letter to Hamish Hamilton, January 24, 1949.

67. Ibid.

68. "Oscar Night in Hollywood" in *Raymond Chandler: A Literary Reference*, R. F. Moss (ed.), Carroll & Graf, New York, 2003.

69. Letter to Bernice Baumgarten, October 15, 1949.

70. Letter to Hamish Hamilton, December 4, 1949.

71. Letter to James Sandoe, May 14, 1949.

72. Letter to Hamish Hamilton, May 13, 1949.

73. Letter to Bernice Baumgarten, November 8, 1949.

74. Letter to James Sandoe, November 19, 1949.

Chapter Thirteen

1. Letter to Hamish Hamilton, January 11, 1950.

2. Letter to Hamish Hamilton, January 18, 1950.

3. Letter to Leroy Wright, April 12, 1950.

4. Ibid.

5. In fact it is possible that he did not entirely sever ties with Swanson; certainly they remained friends and would work together again.

6. Letter to Hamish Hamilton, September 4, 1950.

7. Memorandum Re: Warners Bros. Controversy, part of the Chandler Papers at the Bodleian Library, Oxford.

8. Letter from Finlay McDermid to Raymond Chandler, July 7, 1950.

9. Letter to Ray Stark, August 17, 1950.

10. Letter from Ray Stark to Chandler, August 15, 1950. Stark is quoting Chandler when he discusses "Chinese water torture."

11. Letter to Ray Stark, August 17, 1950.

12. McGilligan, P., *Alfred Hitchcock: A Life in Darkness and Light,* HarperCollins, London, 2003.

13. From Chandler's original typescript of the screenplay, part of the Chandler Papers at the Bodleian Library, Oxford.

14. Letter to Ray Stark, August 17, 1950.

15. McGilligan, P., *Alfred Hitchcock: A Life in Darkness and Light,* HarperCollins, London, 2003.

16. Ibid.

17. Letter to Carl Brandt, December 11, 1950.

18. Letter to Alfred Hitchcock, December 6, 1950.

19. Letter to Carl Brandt, December 11, 1950.

20. MacShane, F., *The Life of Raymond Chandler*, Hamish Hamilton, London, 1986.

21. Advice to a Secretary, part of the Chandler Papers at the Bodleian Library, Oxford.

22. Advice to an Employer, part of the Chandler Papers at the Bodleian Library, Oxford.

23. Letter to Juanita Messick, undated from 1950.

24. Ibid.

25. Letter to James Sandoe, January 10, 1951.

26. Letter to H. N. Swanson, January 4, 1951.

27. Ibid.

28. From "The Notebooks of Raymond Chandler," part of the Chandler Papers at the Bodleian Library, Oxford.

29. Ibid.

30. Chandler, R., "Professor Bingo's Snuff" in *Collected Stories*, Alfred A. Knopf, New York, 2002.

31. Letter to James Sandoe, October 31, 1951.

32. Ibid.

33. Ibid.

34. Letter to Hamish Hamilton, February 14, 1951.

35. Letter to James Sandoe, February 20, 1951.

36. Letter to James Sandoe, September 15, 1951.

37. Undated note to Juanita Messick, probably 1951.

38. Ibid.

39. Letter to Hamish Hamilton, October 5, 1951.

40. Ibid.

41. Ibid.

42. Letter to Dale Warren, November 13, 1950.

43. Letter to Hamish Hamilton, September 19, 1951.

44. Letter to Hamish Hamilton, July 24, 1951.

45. Letter to Carl Brandt, October 27, 1951.

46. Letter to Hamish Hamilton, October 5, 1951.

47. Letter to Bernice Baumgarten, January 7, 1951.

48. Letter to Bernice Baumgarten, May 14, 1952.

49. Ibid.

50. Letter from Bernice Baumgarten to Raymond Chandler, May 22, 1952.

51. This comes from an undated letter to Hamish Hamilton written in either late May or early July. It is currently held at UCLA.

52. Letter to Bernice Baumgarten, May 27, 1952.

53. Ibid.

54. Undated letter to Hamish Hamilton that was written in either late May or early June 1951.

55. Letter to Hamish Hamilton, June 10, 1952.

56. Ibid.

57. Ibid.
58. Letter to Carl Brandt, June 11, 1952.
59. Letter to Dale Warren, August 11, 1952.
60. Letter to Roger Machell, August 11, 1952.
61. "Ray and Cissy" by Dilys Powell in *The World of Raymond Chandler*, M. Gross (ed.), Weidenfeld & Nicolson, London, 1977.
62. Letter to William Townend, November 11, 1952.
63. "Ray and Cissy" by Dilys Powell in *The World of Raymond Chandler*, M. Gross (ed.), Weidenfeld & Nicolson, London, 1977.
64. Letter to Paul Brooks, September 28, 1952.
65. "The unconventional Mr. Chandler comes to Town," *The Times,* September 21, 1952, in *Raymond Chandler: A Literary Reference*, R. F. Moss (ed.), Carroll & Graf, New York, 2003.
66. Letter to Hamish Hamilton, November 5, 1952.
67. Ibid.
68. "Ten Percent of Your Life" in the *Atlantic*, February 1952.
69. Chandler, R., *The Long Goodbye*, Penguin, London, 1953.
70. "Detection and Thrillers," *The New Statesman and Nation* 48 (January 1954) quoted in *Raymond Chandler: A Literary Reference*, R. F. Moss (ed.), Carroll & Graf, New York, 2003.
71. Letter to Hamish Hamilton, January 5, 1955.
72. Ibid.
73. Ibid.
74. Ibid.

Chapter Fourteen

1. Letter to Leonard Russell, December 29, 1954.
2. Letter to Hamish Hamilton, January 5, 1955.
3. Spender, N., "His Own Long Goodbye," in *The World of Raymond Chandler*, M. Gross (ed.), Weidenfeld & Nicolson, London, 1977.
4. Ibid.
5. Sutherland, J., *Stephen Spender: The Authorized Biography*, Penguin Viking, London, 2004.
6. Letter to Hamish Hamilton, April 27, 1955.
7. Spender, N., "His Own Long Goodbye," in *The World of Raymond Chandler*, M. Gross, (ed.) Weidenfeld & Nicolson, London, 1977.
8. Ibid.
9. Ibid.
10. Ibid.
11. Letter to Louise Loughner, May 21, 1955.
12. Letter to Louise Loughner, date unclear, possibly May 28, 1955.
13. Letter to Louise Loughner, June 15, 1955.
14. Ibid.
15. Ibid.

16. Spender, N., "His Own Long Goodbye," in *The World of Raymond Chandler,* M. Gross (ed.), Weidenfeld & Nicolson, London, 1977.

17. Letter to Jessica Tyndale, September 17, 1955.

18. Ibid.

19. Letter to Michael Gilbert, October 14, 1955.

20. Letter to Helga Greene, November 13, 1955.

21. Ibid.

22. Ibid.

23. Letter to Louise Loughner, undated but sometime in mid-1956.

24. Spender, N., "His Own Long Goodbye," in *The World of Raymond Chandler*, M. Gross (ed.), Weidenfeld & Nicolson, London, 1977.

25. Letter to Louise Loughner, May 16, 1956.

26. Undated letter to Louise Loughner, probably mid-1956.

27. Ibid.

28. Gilbert, M., "Autumn in London," *The World of Raymond Chandler*, M. Gross (ed.), Weidenfeld & Nicolson, London, 1977.

29. Ibid.

30. Letter to Michael Gilbert, quoted by Gilbert, M., "Autumn in London," *The World of Raymond Chandler,* M. Gross (ed.), Weidenfeld & Nicolson, London, 1977.

31. Letter to Louise Loughner, May 16, 1956.

32. Letter to Louise Loughner, June 5, 1956.

33. Undated letter to Louise Loughner, sometime in mid-1956.

34. Gilbert, M., "Autumn in London," *The World of Raymond Chandler*, M. Gross (ed.), Weidenfeld & Nicolson, London, 1977.

35. Undated letter to Louise Loughner, sometime in mid-1956.

36. Letter to Paul McClung, December 11, 1951.

37. Letter to Jessica Tyndale, August 20, 1956.

38. Letter to Michael Gilbert, September 6, 1956.

39. Letter to William Gault, September 7, 1956.

40. Letter to Hardwick Moseley, January 5, 1957.

41. Spender, N., "His Own Long Goodbye" in *The World of Raymond Chandler,* M. Gross (ed.), Weidenfeld & Nicolson, London, 1977.

42. Interview by Freeman, J., *The Long Embrace*, Viking, New York, 2008.

43. Letter to Jessica Tyndale, January 18, 1957.

44. Letter to Will Smith, January 16, 1957.

45. Letter to Jessica Tyndale, January 18, 1957.

46. "His Own Long Goodbye" collected in *The World of Raymond Chandler*, M. Gross (ed.), Weidenfeld & Nicolson, London, 1977.

47. Letter to Deirdre Gartrell, March 20, 1957.

48. Letter to Helga Greene, April 16, 1957.

49. Letter to Helga Greene, April 28, 1957.

50. Chandler, R., *Playback*, Penguin, London, 1958.

51. Ibid.

52. Ibid.

53. Ibid.
54. Letter to Jean Fracasse, December 25, 1957.
55. Ibid.
56. Letter to Lucky Luciano, March 21, 1958.
57. Letter to Hardwick Moseley, undated, probably October 1958.
58. Letter to Maurice Guinness, February 21, 1959.

Afterword

1. They were later deposited in the Bodleian Library at Oxford University.

2. Gardiner, D., "Foreword" in *Raymond Chandler Speaking*, Dorothy Gardiner and Katherine Sorely Walkers (eds.), University of California Press, London, 1997.

3. These full-length books are *The Life of Raymond Chandler* by Frank MacShane, first published in Britain by Hamish Hamilton in 1976; *Raymond Chandler: A Biography*, by Tom Hiney, published in Britain by Chatto & Windus in 1997; and *The Long Embrace: Raymond Chandler and the Woman He Loved*, by Judith Freeman, published in the US by Vintage in 2008. The book that you are holding is the fourth.

4. MacShane, F., *The Life of Raymond Chandler*, Hamish Hamilton, London, 1986.

SELECT BIBLIOGRAPHY

Principal Works of Raymond Chandler

NOVELS

The Big Sleep, Penguin, London, 1970. First published by Hamish Hamilton in 1939.

Farewell, My Lovely, Penguin, London, 1949. First published by Hamish Hamilton in 1940.

The High Window, Penguin, London, 1951. First published by Hamish Hamilton in 1943.

The Lady in the Lake, Penguin, London, 1952. First published by Hamish Hamilton in 1944.

The Little Sister, Penguin, London, 1955. First published by Hamish Hamilton in 1949.

The Long Goodbye, Penguin, London, 1959. First published by Hamish Hamilton in 1953.

Playback, Penguin, London, 1961. First published by Hamish Hamilton in 1958.

The Simple Art of Murder, Vintage, New York, 1988.

STORIES

All stories quoted are taken from *Collected Stories*, Everyman Library Edition, Alfred A. Knopf, New York, 2002.

The stories "Killer in the Rain," "The Curtain," "The Lady in the Lake," and "No Crime in the Mountains" are published in the UK in volume form in *Killer in the Rain*, Penguin, London, 1966. First published by Hamish Hamilton in 1964.

The stories "Trouble Is My Business" and "Finger Man" are published in the UK in volume form in *Trouble Is My Business*, Penguin, London, 1950.

FILMS

Double Indemnity, Dir. Billy Wilder. Perf. Fred MacMurray, Barbara Stanwyck. Paramount, 1944. DVD.

The Blue Dahlia, Dir. George Marshall. Perf. Alan Ladd, Veronica Lake. Paramount, 1946. DVD.

Strangers on a Train. Dir. Alfred Hitchcock. Perf. Farley Granger, Robert Walker. Warner Bros., 1951, DVD.

PUBLISHED SCREENPLAYS

Chandler, R., *Raymond Chandler's Unknown Thriller: The Screenplay of* Playback, Harrap Limited, London, 1985.

Chandler, R., and Wilder, B., *Double Indemnity*, University of California Press Ltd, London, 2000.

POEMS

Bruccoli, M. J. (ed), *Chandler Before Marlowe*, The University of South Carolina Press, Columbia, 1973.

LETTERS

Gardiner, D. and Walker, K. S., (eds.), *Raymond Chandler Speaking*, University of California Press Ltd, London, 1997.

Hiney, T. and MacShane, F. (eds.), *The Raymond Chandler Papers*, Penguin, London, 2001.

MacShane, F. (ed.), *The Selected Letters of Raymond Chandler*, Dell Publishing Inc., New York, 1981.

Moss, R. F. (ed.), *Raymond Chandler: A Literary Reference*, Carroll and Graf, New York, 2003

NOTEBOOKS

MacShane, F. (ed.), *The Notebooks of Raymond Chandler*, Weidenfeld & Nicolson, London, 1977.

Biographies

Freedman, J., *The Long Embrace: Raymond Chandler and the Woman He Loved*, Vintage, New York, 2008.

Gross, M. (ed.), *The World of Raymond Chandler*, Weidenfeld & Nicolson, London, 1977.

Hiney, T., *Raymond Chandler: A Biography*, Vintage, London, 1998.

MacShane, F., *The Life of Raymond Chandler*, Hamish Hamilton, London, 1986.

Other Sources

Ackroyd, P., *London: A Biography*, Chatto and Windus, London, 2000.

Bristow, D. L., *A Dirty, Wicked Town,* Caxton Press, Caldwell, Idaho, 2000.

Chaplin, C., *My Autobiography*, Penguin, London, 2003.

Davis, M., *City of Quartz: Excavating the Future in Los Angeles*, Verso, London, 1990.

Decker, J. H., *Men of Steel Rails,* University of Nebraska Press, Lincoln, 1983.

Fitzgerald, F. Scott, "Early Success" in *F. Scott Fitzgerald on Authorship*, M. J. Bruccoli and J. Baughmas (eds.), University of South Carolina, Columbia, 1996.

Gruber, F., *The Pulp Jungle*, Sherbourne Press, Los Angeles, 1967.

Harris, W., *J. A. Spender*, Cassell and Company, London, 1946.

Hattersley, R., *The Edwardians*, Abacus, London, 2004.

Kanfer, S., *Tough Without a Gun,* Faber, London, 2011.

Kynaston, D., *Austerity Britain: 1945–51*, Bloomsbury, London, 2007.

———. *Family Britain: 1951–57,* Bloomsbury, London, 2009.

Larson, E., *The Devil in the White City,* Bantam, London, 2004.

Layman, R. with Rivett, J. M. (eds.), *Dashiell Hammett, Selected Letters*, Counter Point, Washington D.C., 2001.

Levine, J. in *Fighter Heroes of WWI,* Collins, London, 2009.

Maugham, S., *Of Human Bondage,* originally published in 1915. This edition published by Vintage, London, 2005.

McCann, S., *Gumshoe America*, Duke University Press, Durham and London, 2000.

McCrum, R., *Wodehouse: A Life*, Penguin Viking, London, 2004.

McGilligan, P., *Alfred Hitchcock: A Life in Darkness and Light*, HarperCollins, London, 2004.

McKenzie, F. A., *Through the Hindenburg Line*, Hodder and Stoughton, London, 1918.

McWilliams, C., *Southern California: An Island on the Land*, Gibbs Smith Publisher Layton, Utah, 1973.

Miller, D. L., *City of the Century: The Epic of Chicago and the Making of America*, Touchstone, New York, 1997.

Nelson, C., "Growing Up: Childhood" in *A Companion to Victorian Literature and Culture*, H. F. Tucker (ed.), Blackwell Publishers Ltd, Oxford, 2002.

Norman, M., *What Happens Next*, Aurum, London, 2008.

Parini, J., *One Matchless Time*, HarperCollins, London, 2004.

Parker, P., *The Old Lie: The Great War and the Public School Ethos*, Hambledon Continuum, London, 1987.

Rayner, R., *A Bright and Guilty Place*, Constable, London, 2010.

Schickel, R., *Double Indemnity*, British Film Institute, London, 1992.

Starr, K., *Inventing the Dream: California Through the Progressive Era*, OUP, Oxford, 1985.

———. *Material Dreams: Southern California Through the 1920s*, OUP, Oxford, 1990.

———. *Endangered Dreams: The Great Depression in California*. OUP, Oxford, 1996.

———. *The Dream Endures: California Enters the 1940s*, OUP, Oxford, 1997.

———. *Embattled Dreams: California in War and Peace 1940–1950*, OUP, Oxford, 2002.

———. *Golden Dreams: California in an Age of Abundance 1950–1963*, OUP, Oxford, 2009.

Stevenson, R. L., *Travels with a Donkey in the Cévennes and the Amateur Emigrant*, Penguin Classics, London, 2011.

Sutherland, J., *Last Drink to L.A.*, Short Books, London, 2001.

———. *Stephen Spender: the Authorized Biography*, Penguin Viking, London, 2004.

———. *Where Was Rebecca Shot?*, Phoenix, London, 1999.

Thompson, D., *The Whole Equation: A History of Hollywood*, Abacus, London, 2004.

———. *The Big Sleep*, The British Film Institute, London, 2000.

Tygiel, J., *The Great Los Angeles Oil Swindle*, University of California Press, London, 1994.

Vanden Bossche, C. R., "Moving Out: Adolescence" in *A Companion to Victorian Literature and Culture*, H. F. Tucker (ed.), Blackwell Publishers Ltd, Oxford, 2002.

White, L., *Me, Detective*, Harcourt, Brace, and Company Inc., New York, 1936.

Wilson, A. N., *After the Victorians*, Arrow, London, 2006.

INDEX

Italicized page references indicate photographs in insert. All works are by Raymond Chandler unless otherwise attributed.